TRANSBORDER LIVES

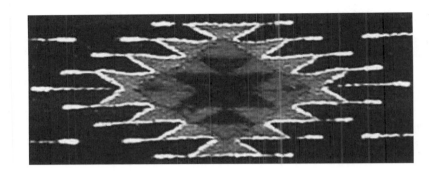

TRANSBORDER LIVES

Indigenous Oaxacans in

Mexico, California, and Oregon

Lynn Stephen

DUKE UNIVERSITY PRESS *Durham and London* 2007

© 2007 Duke University Press
All rights reserved
Printed in the United States of America
on acid-free paper ∞
Designed by C. H. Westmoreland
Typeset in Adobe Minion with
Adobe Jenson display
by Keystone Typesetting, Inc.
Library of Congress Cataloging-in-
Publication Data appear on the last
printed page of this book.

CONTENTS

ILLUSTRATIONS AND TABLES

In July 1997, I drove with Alejandro de Avila from Oaxaca City to the Mixtec Baja town of San Miguel Cuevas. The drive is long, and the road is filled with curves. Alejandro's jeep plowed up and down the hills slowly but safely. Cuevas, as it is known, is perched on a bluff. Parked below the main part of town were more than a dozen pickup trucks. Almost all had license plates from the United States, and more than half a dozen were from the state of Oregon. I was going to visit Santiago Ventura, who now resides in Woodburn, Oregon, and works as an advocate for indigenous Mexican migrants with the Oregon Law Center; he has started a pan-ethnic Oaxacan indigenous migrant organization, Organización de Comunidades Indígenas Migrantes Oaxaqueños (OCIMO) (discussed in chapter 8). At the time we were visiting Santiago in Cuevas, he was home to carry out a *cargo* in his community as Secretario del Consejo de Vigilancia del Comisariado de Bienes Comunales (Secretary of the Board of the Communal Lands Commission) (see chapter 2),[1] and was working out a new set of laws to regulate communal land in his community.

The cargo spanned a period of three years, which for many men in positions like this was a very long time. Part of the work Santiago and others did was to reduce the time that cargos had to be served as a part of the Communal Lands Commission in his community from three years to two years. Almost all of the men who were on the Communal Lands Commission had returned home from Mexico City or various parts of the United States to serve out their cargo. Part of what they accomplished was to help adjust the local system of governance to meet the reality of San Miguel Cuevas as a transborder community where many resided outside of Oaxaca for significant periods of time. Another accomplishment of the Communal Lands Commission during the term Santiago served was to resolve a pending lawsuit involving a local land conflict that no one else had been able to achieve agreement on. Prior to this, Santiago had been at the center of a historic court case that has had a lasting impact nationally on the right of immigrants to a certified translator in their own language in U.S. courts.

In 1986, Santiago was falsely accused and convicted of murdering a fellow farmworker in Oregon. During his trial he had difficulty understanding and communicating with the interpreter selected by the court, who spoke Spanish and English. Santiago's native language is Mixteco. He understood very little Spanish, as did many of the witnesses in his case, who also spoke Mixteco. Santiago and the other Mixteco witnesses were often confused by the questions posed to them in Spanish by the court-appointed interpreter. The jury found him guilty, and he was sentenced to life in prison.

Four years after his conviction and imprisonment, a reinvestigation of the case established that another person was the killer. In addition, linguistic and cultural barriers were strongly implicated in the wrongful conviction. The conviction was overturned, and Santiago was released from prison. He later received a degree in social work from Portland State University. The case received national attention and resulted in major changes as courts and judges across the United States began to examine and improve the use of interpreters in the courts. In 1993, the Oregon Legislative Assembly passed Senate Bill 229, instructing the Office of the State Court Administrator to establish a certification program to ensure a minimum level of competence and quality of interpreters who work in the courts (Rhodes 1999: 1). Oregon's state court system has since developed a robust certification program, and has certified interpreters in Spanish, Russian, Vietnamese, Akateco, Kanjobal, Q'uiche, and Mam (Maya languages spoken by Guatemalan indigenous farmworkers) as well as indigenous languages of Mexico, including Mixteco Alto (a variety of communities), Mixteco Bajo (a variety of communities), Nahuatl, Poqochi, P'urepecha, Triqui (Copala and Itunyonso), and Zapoteco (Ocotlán de Morelos) (see chapter 8). Now, more than half of the states in the United States belong to a consortium that trains legal interpreters in a broad range of languages. Santiago's case was fundamental in bringing about these changes.

Reflecting back on his experience, Santiago commented, "I think my case had an impact in the sense that before a criminal court wasn't required to have certified interpreters. At least now, an interpreter working in Spanish has to be certified in order to work in the court. Unfortunately, in order to have this law, a tragedy like my case had to take place."

In 1997, he returned to San Miguel Cuevas in order to continue his pathbreaking legal work. His accomplishments included the forging of a new set of local laws to regulate his community's use of the land base and protect it from privatization. During our visit to Cuevas, Santiago and his wife treated Alejandro and me with great hospitality. We talked for a long time about indigenous rights in Mexico and the United States, the Zapatista movement in Chiapas (which I was researching and writing about at the time), and life in Oregon, where I was thinking of moving with my family. Santiago told me about a farmworkers' union there called Pineros y Campesinos Unidos del Noroeste (Northwest Treeplanters and Farmworkers United, PCUN) that I had heard about from other West Coast friends. He told me that many PCUN members were from Oaxaca and that many were Mixtec.

Later that summer, in August 1997, Ellen Herman, my partner, and I drove from Tietor, Washington, where we had family, to Eugene, Oregon. On the way, we stopped by the PCUN office in Woodburn, Oregon. It was literally our first stop in what was to become our new home state. I spoke with the PCUN secretary-treasurer, Larry Kleinman, and gave copies of some of my books and publications to people on the staff, saying I would look forward to being in touch with them and perhaps working on a project together. We then went on to Eugene to look at schools, housing, and public parks.

In September 1998, my family and I moved to Eugene, and Ellen and I began work as professors at the University of Oregon. Soon after moving, I made a trip up to Woodburn to visit PCUN again. The PCUN staff, having looked at my materials, decided to work collaboratively with me and a group of students, primarily members of Movimiento Estudiantil Chicano de Aztlán (MECHA). The project they proposed was not the one I had presented to them, which had focused on gender relations within Mexican immigrant farmworker households. Instead, they proposed that we do a general history of the union and of farmworker organizing in the state. The project involved interviewing PCUN staff and members and people who had worked with the organization and also organizing their archives. The primary product of this research turned out to be a history of the organization that proved useful to PCUN in educating staff and in organizing and perhaps was also helpful in fundraising. In addition, we produced a bilingual time line of the organization's history that was mounted in the Union Hall; a copy of it is kept in the union's library.

About ten of the organizers and union participants we interviewed for the history were Mixteco, several from San Agustín Atenango, in the southern Mexican state of Oaxaca. After we completed this project, I carried out a second collaborative research effort with PCUN and a group of graduate and undergraduate students. Called "The Life of the Strawberry," it documented gender, labor, and racial/ethnic relations in the movement of Oregon strawberries and other produce from the fields of the Willamette Valley to food processors, frozen food warehouses, food distributors, and food service corporations and then to their final destination in University of Oregon restaurants and dorm cafeterias. We interviewed more than twenty workers, again including quite a number of indigenous Mexican migrants who worked in the fields and processing plants. Students presented the results of their research in papers and in a bilingual theatrical piece profiling workers' stories; the enactment was presented to the PCUN membership, to university and junior high classes, and at conferences. We also created a webpage, which can be found at http://waynemorsecenter.uoregon.edu/berry.

While working on these two projects I met a number of Mixtec migrants in the state of Oregon and became further connected to the community of San Agustín Atenango. Most of these people were working in the fields and the canneries of Oregon and had lived previously in California, Baja California, and Sinaloa.[2] In 2003 and 2004 I worked with a former PCUN organizer from San Agustín Atenango and interviewed members of the San Agustín transborder public works committee who were based in the Salem, Oregon, area. In association with ten other committees spread out across the United States, they were pulling together an impressive cross-border organizing and fundraising effort to expand their public cemetery in Oaxaca. In August 2004, I visited San Agustín Atenango and saw the progress of the transborder public works committee firsthand. I brought with me letters and photographs from people in Oregon and also their contributions to the local fiesta, which takes place at the end of August. During this visit I got to know the extended families of many people with whom I had become acquainted in Oregon as well as families who had been living elsewhere in the United States and had returned to Atenango for a variety of reasons. Most of the men serving in posts in the municipal government had returned from the United States with their families to do so. I also met women who were raising children in Atenango while their husbands were in the States. During this trip I conducted more than eighteen in-depth interviews and began to investigate the history of the community. I also visited the Juxtlahuaca office of what was the Indigenous Oaxacan Binational Front

(FIOB, Frente Indígena Oaxaqueño Binacional), which became the Front of Indigenous Binational Organizations in March 2005. I discussed a variety of issues with staff during that visit.

I returned in August 2005 to meet again with members of FIOB in Juxtlahuaca, attended part of a regional women's council meeting, and visited FIOB women's income-generating projects in several communities focused on raising chickens and mushrooms for sale in conjunction with communal credit associations. I also returned to San Agustín Atenango.

I continued work from the previous year, but this trip was deeply marked by an unfolding tragedy. On July 16, 2005, seven people left Atenango on a bus to go to the border town of Sonoyta, Arizona, where they expected to cross over to the United States. Sonoyta is located across the border from Lukeville, Arizona, and crossings take migrants into the most desolate areas of the western Arizona desert that incorporate the Tohono O'odham Indian Reservation and Organ Pipe National Monument. In July, the temperature often goes well above 110 degrees Fahrenheit. The group of seven that left San Agustín Atenango consisted of five men between the ages of twenty-six and forty-nine and two boys ages fifteen and sixteen. By August 16, a month after they had left, there was no word from any of them. In conjunction with local officials, their families created and circulated flyers with their photographs, called and faxed family members in California, Oregon, Arizona, and elsewhere, and began to phone and fax Mexican consulates in Arizona and elsewhere. The offices of the FIOB in Juxtlahuaca, Tijuana, Los Angeles, and Fresno were alerted, and NGOs and government organizations such as the Oaxacan Institute for Attention to the Migrant (Instituto Oaxaqueño de Atención al Migrante) were notified of details of the seven *desaparecidos*. The mothers of the two boys, Pablo, age sixteen, and Ubaldo, age fifteen, were unable to eat or sleep and made their way endlessly around San Agustín, Juxtlahuaca, and elsewhere seeking help in locating their children.

In early September, two men from San Agustín Atenango who have legal residency in the United States set out to retrace the steps of the desaparecidos, going to Sonoyta and crossing the border. It was not the first time such a search party had been put together in San Agustín. In 2002, a couple with young children disappeared while trying to cross the border and was never found. In discussing the missing seven in 2005, people recalled the eerie tale of this couple and hoped for a different outcome. During my trip in August 2005 I continued some of my previous fieldwork focused on collecting oral histories and work and migration histories, reviewing the community archives, and exploring the gendered impact of migration, but the disappearance of the seven people came to dominate my work. Producing flyers, e-mailing, and faxing as well as talking with family members about what could be done occupied a central part of my time there and continues to haunt me daily. I returned to San Agustín Atenango in August 2006. More than a year after their disappearance, there was still no word on the seven disappeared. Their whereabouts remain unknown. Most people assume they are dead; some continue to hope they are alive. They remain suspended, between life and death in the collective memory of San Agustín Atenango.

The frame for this and many similar tragedies—as many as thirty-five hundred people are believed to have died crossing the U.S.–Mexico border since 1995 (Berenstein 2005)—is U.S. border policy, which since 2001 has formed part of a larger discourse and policy centered on homeland security that is supposed to keep out terrorists and keep American citizens safe. Beginning with the administration of President Bill Clinton in 1995, U.S. border protection policy has pushed migrants out of such classic crossing areas as San Diego/Tijuana and Ciudad Juarez/El Paso and into more and more desolate areas such as the inhospitable western Arizona desert (see chapter 4). The result has been an increasing number of fatalities due to exposure to extreme heat and cold, unprecedented inflation in the cost of crossing (averaging from two thousand to three thousand dollars in 2005), and the replacement of locally run border-crossing operations with operations in which the smuggling of people is integrated with gun and drug smuggling on routes often controlled by drug cartels. Because most migrants coming over the border now need a guide to help them cross, business is booming. In addition to the physical risks of walking long distances in the desert, as the smuggling of people has gotten more profitable, it has become more dangerous. Robbery, rape, and kidnappings of groups of border crossers by competing *coyotes* (border-crossing guides and smugglers) or by Mexican police or others are further risks migrants assume in attempting to reach the United States. While the U.S. Border Patrol has focused on border defense during the past ten years, increasingly officers are spending their time rescuing people along the border. Those they encounter are men, women, and children, even babies attempting to enter the States to work and to be united with their families.

The term used by people from San Agustín Atenango to describe those who set out to cross the border and are never heard from again is *desaparecidos*. This is the same term used to describe those who were forcibly abducted by paramilitaries, police forces, and official military units in Argentina, Brazil, Chile, El Salvador, Guatemala, Mexico, and elsewhere in the 1970s and 1980s, never to be seen again. The consequences for the relatives of the disappeared are that they have no knowledge of what became of their loved ones, of where they are, of whether they are dead or alive, and of how they may have suffered. They can only imagine, hope, and pray they are alive while grappling with the horror of how they might have suffered and died. This is what family members of the seven desaparecidos from San Agustín Atenango were feeling in Oaxaca, Baja California, California, Oregon, Arizona, Illinois, and other states where they live. Their network of help, love, worry, and prayer is transborder, as is the rest of their lives.

As I show in this book, the experiences of Mixtec and Zapotec migrants both within Mexico and in the Unites States are often quite different. Beginning in the summer of 2001, I returned to Teotitlán del Valle, a Zapotec community where I had conducted my doctoral research from 1983 to 1986 to document changes in community life related to globalization and migration. Part of this research focused on the emergence of more than a dozen weaving cooperatives beginning in the mid-1980s that have come to be a significant economic and political force in the community, particularly for women. Much of this research is documented in an updated and rewritten edition of *Zapotec Women: Gender, Class, and Ethnicity in Globalized Oaxaca* (Duke University Press, 2005). A second piece of the research, however, involved talking in-depth with people in the community about their personal experiences of migration in the United States and focusing on how continued migration had changed the community and also affected those who never left.[3]

The migration networks of Teotitecos differ from those of the people of San Agustín Atenango. After working as *braceros* (referring to *brazos*, arms or helping hands) in the Midwest and the western United States, Teotitecos concentrated their border crossings and bases of support in the Tijuana, San Diego, and Los Angeles corridor. By the 1980s, Teotitecos had set up craft stores and stalls in the markets of Tijuana and Ensenada, and many families set down roots in the Santa Ana and Oxnard areas of southern California. While people from San Agustín Atenango first went to the United States with labor contractors who worked in Baja California, Teotitecos tended to cross through independent connections, and a thick network of border-crossing knowledge and resources sprang up in the Tijuana area. Those who were the first in their family to cross the border often had very difficult experiences, while those who came later were able to travel through known networks.

In discussions in Teotitlán from 2001 through 2005 as well as with Teotitecos in the United States, I found people interested in sharing their border-crossing stories as well as their thoughts about living and working in the United States. Many were eager to discuss U.S. foreign policy and events that affected their experience here, such as how the impact of September 11 decreased the amount of work available in the hotel, restaurant, and tourist sectors in southern California. Here, the increasing dangers of crossing the border were present as well. In 2003, a group of twelve people from Teotitlán crossed the border at Ciudad Juárez to enter the United States. Their coyote abandoned them right over the border, and a group of men assaulted the migrants, robbed them of all their money, and beat some of them severely. They crossed back into Mexico and managed to secure rides all the way west to Tijuana, where they had relatives who received them. Many believe that the coyote received payment from the group who robbed them for revealing where they were. Since that time, people have counseled each other not to cross in Texas and Arizona. In August 2005, Marcelina Ramírez, whose husband was among those beaten up and robbed in 2003, commented to me, "He did make it across later through Tijuana, but he hasn't been home for two years and says he will wait two more years. It is too dangerous to go back and forth. I really miss him. It is sad. We are here with the children, with a lot of work, and always feeling his absence. . . . Now my son wants to go, but I am so afraid of what can happen. We are looking for a way for him to go that isn't so dangerous, but it's hard to find. Now it costs more than twenty-five hundred dollars to cross on the line. That is the only way to try. People here no longer want to go over in the desert. . . . they don't want to die."[4]

The migration testimonies and experiences of migrants and non-migrants from Teotitlán have added an important dimension to my understanding and framing of that community's histories. Like Mixtec friends and acquaintances from San Agustín Atenango who live close to me in Oregon, some of my friends from Teotitlán have also settled near my home. In September 2005, I became the baptismal godmother of the daughter of my first godchild from Teotitlán. The little girl, Cynthia, was born in Portland, Oregon, and is a U.S. citizen. Her parents were born in Teotitlán del Valle and have been living in Oregon for the past two years. They were nineteen and twenty years old when they came to the United States.

My family attended Cynthia's baptism and shared in a day of eating, talking, feasting, and celebrating with her family. While it seems so simple to *convivir* (share) in the delightful event of the baptism of a child and to blend several cultural traditions into something that is optimistically transborder and may represent new possibilities for Americanness, these moments coexist with the ongoing anguish of the family members of the seven desaparecidos from San Agustín Atenango.

ACKNOWLEDGMENTS

This book has been a transforming experience in both my personal life and my research. While it bridges the move that my family made from Boston to Eugene, it also marks the beginning of my strategy of engaging in multisited research in order to understand the meanings of transborder lives. As discussed in the preface and epilogue, several of the projects that fed into this book emerged out of collaborative processes that involved transborder Oaxacan communities based in Oregon, Oregon's farmworker union Pineros y Campesinos Unidos, and my ongoing relationship with friends, *compadres*, and *ahijados* from Teotitlán del Valle who are now here in Oregon as well as in California and many other locations.

My twenty-two-year history of doing research in Oaxaca is a part of this project. Old friends who continue to be key to my life in Oaxaca include Margarita Dalton, Paola Sesia, and Julia Barco. Juanita Ramírez is a dear friend who helps to make life possible in Oaxaca on a daily basis. She and her son Gus are a part of our family.

In Teotitlán del Valle, I would like to express my gratitude to my longtime friends and compadres Paco González and Petra Vicente and to my other compadres Andrés Gutiérrez and Margarita Alavez, who opened their homes and hearts to me and my family as always. Efraín Gutiérrez Alavez and Aurora Lazo González have become good friends, and I thank them for their contribution to my new research in Teotitlán. I would particularly like to thank a group of women active in the cooperatives for their enthusiasm and support. They include Aurora Bazan López, Aurora Contreras, Reina González Martínez, Isabel Hernández, Pastora Gutiérrez Reyes, Josefina Jiménez, Guadalupe Ruiz Soza, Fransisca Ruiz García, and Violeta Vásquez Gutiérrez. Arnulfo Mendoza and Mary Jane Gagnier were particularly generous with their time. I also thank the many people who took the time to share their stories with me in Teotitlán del Valle and in California or Oregon who remain anonymous in order to protect their identities.

In San Agustín Atenango, I want to thank former Presidente Municipal Mateo Sánchez and the rest of the local authorities for their support of my research. I would also like to thank Dagoberto Gómez Morales, Juana Cruz Ramírez, and Paulina Ramírez Pérez for opening up their homes to me when I visit. Lorenzo Justiano Solano López has been a valuable translator, collaborator, and fellow historian during my visits to San Agustín Atenango. Presidente Municipal Elías Díaz Solano and other municipal authorities and staff who began their term in 2005 were also very helpful, and I thank them for their support. In addition, I want to thank the many people from San Agustín who took time to speak with me in Oregon and in Oaxaca who will remain anonymous to protect their identities. Leonides de Avila has been a steadfast friend and supporter of my research with the transborder community of San Agustín Atenango. I thank him for opening many doors for me in San Agustín and among those in the community living in Oregon.

Moving to Oregon in 1998 truly marked a new beginning for me in many ways. There, I was able to begin the process of doing research where I lived that profoundly connected with my past work in Mexico. In 1999, I began an ongoing collaborative relationship with the staff, leadership, and members of Oregon's farmworker union PCUN. I particularly want to acknowledge the support and encouragement of PCUN President Ramón Ramírez, PCUN Secretary Treasurer Larry Kleinman, and former PCUN organizers Erik Nicholson, Jan Lanier, Susan Dopkins, and Leonides Avila. For their support of a project focused on the history of the farmworker movement and PCUN in Oregon and a later project titled "The Life of the Strawberry," I would like to thank Demetria Avila, Cristina Bautista, Javier Ceja, Sara Luz Cuesta Hernández, Lucía Zuriaga, Fransisca López, Marion Malcolm, Macedonio Mejía, Efraín Peña, and Guadalupe Quinn. Two very special groups of University of Oregon graduate and undergraduate students, including María de la Torre, Mayra Gómez, Gabriel Guzmán, Rachel Hansen, Tami Hill, Rosa Itzel López, Sarah Jacobson, Marcy Miranda Janes, Julie Meyers, Jill Nicola, Kristina, Jamie Shephard, and Kristina Tiedje, were wonderful researchers and collaborators in these two projects.

In the fall of 2003, I collaborated on a project titled "Towards a New Pluralism: Strategies for Rural Communities Impacted by Immigration," funded by the U.S. Department of Agriculture, dispersed through Aguirre International. The project was led by Ed Kissam. Interacting with fellow researchers Ed Kissam and Anna García was a rare pleasure. I continue to enjoy exchanges with them and learned a great deal from working with them in Woodburn, Oregon. I also want to thank the group of outstanding students who worked with us in Woodburn, including Rachel Hansen, Tami Hill, Jessica Lowen, Gabriela Romero, and Edwin Vega. Their hard work and persistence in carrying out a large household survey made for a successful project. Julie Samples, Valentín Sánchez, and Santiago Ventura have provided me with invaluable assistance, advice, and education in this project.

In Eugene, my friends and colleagues Terry O'Nell, Margaret Hallock, and Sandi Morgen were very supportive of my research and writing efforts over the years. I gratefully acknowledge two project grants from the Wayne Morse Center for Law and Politics at the University of Oregon that were crucial to getting the research in this book started and funding students to work with me. Additional grants that supported the research reflected in this book include a research grant from the Center for the Study of Women in Society at the University of Oregon and a Summer Research Award for Faculty from the University of Oregon. A sabbatical leave granted during the 2004–05 academic year and funds from my award as a Distinguished Professor of Arts and Sciences at the University of Oregon have also supported the research and writing that went into this book.

I had the pleasure of drafting this book while a fellow at the Radcliffe Institute for Advanced Studies at Harvard University during the 2004–05 academic year. I wish to thank Drew Faust, Judy Vichniac, Sophia Heller, Tony Ruffo, and Melissa Synnott for making the Institute such a wonderful place to be during my sabbatical. Each and every one of my "fellow" fellows provided unique gifts that year. I would especially like to thank Kim DaCosta, Kathy Davis, Julia Glass, Wendy Jacob, Evelyn Fox Keller, John Kelley, Linda Hamilton Krieger, Sue Lanser, Claire Messud, Steven Nelson, Mica Pollock, Karen Rosenblatt, Martha Selby, Ann Sternegal, and Michael Woolrich for friendship, good ideas and writing tips, music, and fun—all of which made for a terrific year. Conversations with Robert Hunt and Peggy Levitt were fun and provided me with very useful insights while writing. While living in Boston in 2004 and 2005 I enjoyed the friendship and support of Kate Dobroth, Jennie Purnell, Petri Flint, Jeffrey Rubin, Kate Raisz, and Lynn Tibbets It was a joy to live near my brother Bruce Stephen and to see my nephews Ben, Jordan, and Daniel on a regular basis–particularly at Ana's Taqueria.

During the fall of 2005 and the winter of 2006 I was able to make revisions and finish the manuscript with the support of National Endowment for the Humanities grant No. FA-50220–04. During this time I received excellent suggestions for revisions to the manuscript from two anonymous reviewers for Duke University Press and from Jonathan Fox, Julie Samples, Valentín Sánchez, and Santiago Ventura. I sent chapter 5 to the journal *Cultural Anthropology* and received three very thoughtful reviews with very good ideas. One of these suggested that the piece would make an excellent book chapter, which it now is. Jacob Bartuff worked tirelessly to produce the excellent maps for this book, and I thank him for his persistence and high quality maps. Jonny Fox's intellectual and personal friendship was an important contribution to this book, as was the work of Michael Kearney and Gaspar Rivera.

I wish to express a special thanks to my editor at Duke University Press, Valerie Millholland. It was originally through a long conversation that she helped me to see how this book could take shape. I have enjoyed our evolving friendship as well as our mutual passion for Mexico and look forward to more projects with her.

As I put the last words of acknowledgment on paper, I must end with my family. Alejandro de Avila, the father of my children, has provided invaluable emotional and intellectual support to this project, but also as a member of my family. My partner, Ellen Herman, is the other half of me, and our walk through life together is a unique gift. Our sons, Gabriel and José Angel, have grown up a great deal while I worked on this project, and they are woven into its core.

CHAPTER 1

Approaches to Transborder Lives

San Agustín Atenango:
Three Generations on the Move

San Agustín Atenango straddles a paved road that runs between Hua-juapan de León and Santiago Juxtlahuaca in the Mixteca Baja region of Oaxaca—*paved* being a relative term in some stretches that sport pot-holes wide enough to lose a pig in. During the past several years enter-prising migrant workers from the region have used their U.S. earnings to set up an efficient system of regional transportation between Oaxaca City, the state capital, and this region. Several privately owned regional transport companies equipped with fleets of new Ford and Toyota vans shuttle passengers between terminals in downtown Oaxaca to regional destinations. To travel to San Agustín, you purchase a ticket in Oaxaca and get into the van with ten to twelve people bound for the Mixteca. The group often includes students who may be returning home from studying in Oaxaca, men and women carrying large bundles of things they have bought or are selling, families, and others. Leaving Oaxaca, the van cruises along the new *autopista*, or superhighway, to Mexico City, zooming past trucks, and eventually enters dry countryside. One hour out of Oaxaca, outside of Asunción Nochixtlán, it moves off of the autopista and onto regional two-lane roads. Two and a half hours after leaving Oaxaca, the van pauses for about fifteen minutes to pick up passengers in Huajuapan de León and then heads down a winding two-lane highway for Juxtlahuaca. The ride to San Agustín takes about four to four and a half hours—depending on the potholes and the weather. The van stops right at the edge of town and then bolts down the road to its next stop.

Passengers get down from the van and proceed first downhill and then

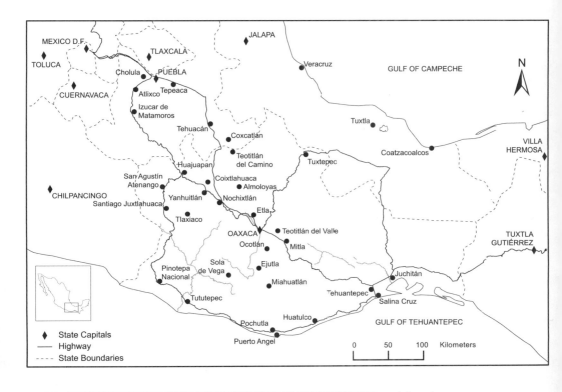

(above) MAP 1.

The state of Oaxaca

MAP 2.

San Agustín Atenango
and surrounding area

uphill, walking down one of the two newly paved roads that run from the highway into the center of town. On the ten-minute walk into the town center, one passes many two-story houses in various state of completion. Some are occupied and equipped with satellite dishes perched on top. More than half are empty, being watched by neighbors or relatives in the absence of their owners, who are invariably somewhere in *el Norte*, the largest clusters of *paisanos* residing in Santa María, Madera, Los Angeles, and Vista, California; Flagstaff and Grand Canyon, Arizona; Las Vegas, Nevada; Salem, Keizer, Woodburn, and Portland, Oregon; and Chicago, Illinois.

In the center of town most of the buildings and businesses show signs of recent investment: new awnings on small stores advertising the name of the store and type of merchandise, vehicles parked on the street, new dining and living room sets prominently visible through open front doors and windows, newly imported appliances for sale. Several privately owned public address systems blare out current bargains to be found in local businesses or calls to help find lost cattle, turkeys, or pigs. Sometimes the speaker systems berate someone for "finding" a lost animal that is not theirs and failing to return it. The local food market has few stalls and little business beyond that done by taco stands. Most people make their purchases in the ever-expanding sectors of small stores found on almost every block. The commercial sector is growing through private investment in family-run stores financed by a steady stream of remittances. Finding a clientele, however, is not always an easy task, as the town is often half empty.

The upper parts of the community are crossed by roads that lead out of town and up into the surrounding mountains and peaks, each with a Mixtec name and very specific history and significance. In the upper reaches of the community there are smaller houses, some with cane-walled kitchens attached to them and others with concrete rooms and roofs connected to older adobe structures. Many of the cane-walled kitchens used to be the primary house structure. There are fewer satellite dishes here, and no vehicles are parked in front of these homes because the only way to get here is on footpaths that wind upward.

At the end of one of these footpaths, high above town and affording a sweeping view, I find Pedro Martínez Morales and Ermelinda Reyes Ramírez, his wife, sitting on their front step weaving hats out of palm fronds. The light is fading, but they are content to sit on the front step and weave. As I approach them, accompanied by their granddaughter

(above) 1. New, unoccupied home in San Agustín Atenango.

2. Older homes on outskirts of San Agustín Atenango.

Laura, they complain about how hot their new concrete house is. "We never sit inside," says Ermelinda in Mixtec to Laura. "It's like an oven. We prefer to be out here." Laura explains to me that her grandmother didn't want to give up her old house, so the cane-walled house still stands, as does the kitchen. We begin to talk about who has come and gone from San Agustín over the past sixty years. Born in 1907, Pedro is one of the oldest men in the community, and his perspective is a sobering one. He begins to talk of going to Orizaba and Cordoba, Veracruz, to cut sugarcane. Back and forth he went, taking his children.

Below I have reproduced parts of conversations I had with Pedro and Ermelinda, Petrona, his daughter, and Laura, his granddaughter. All three generations in this family and in most others in the community have had lives that involve working for long periods of time each year in another part of Mexico or the United States or both and returning periodically to San Agustín to get married, build homes, tend to fields, help sick loved ones, bury the dead, celebrate the fiesta of the town's patron saint, and run the local government and services. Pedro's and Ermelinda's extended family is composed of several dozen people, including their children and grandchildren. What I hope to show by counterposing these three interrelated stories is the utter normality of people living and working for significant periods of time in places other than their homes, places ranging from Orizaba and Cordoba, Veracruz, to Culiacán, Sinaloa, to Ensenada, Baja California, to San Diego, Oxnard, Watsonville, and Chicago. Within this one extended family, there is shared knowledge and experience about these places, even if everyone has not been to every place. Most important, the ability to construct space, time, and social relations in more than one place simultaneously is a part of the daily framing of life in this extended family as well as in others. And it has been for quite some time.

In their almost six decades of collective experience negotiating a wide range of borders, including within the states of Mexico, across the U.S.-Mexican border, and in different regions of the United States, Laura, Petrona, Pedro, and Ermelinda have carried with them cultural and linguistic elements of home in San Agustín and have also incorporated a wide range of other knowledges into their repertoire for defining who they are and what the important values of life are and for deciding how they want to live in the future. They have crossed racial and ethnic boundaries within Mexico that have followed them to the United States. They have crossed class and regional economic boundaries as they have been inserted as workers into different kinds of agricultural production systems and service sector economies at different points in time. They have crossed the boundaries of the nation-state as they move between countries. They have negotiated changes in technologies of travel and communication through time.

For this reason, I characterize their lives and those of others represented in this book as transborder rather than just simply transnational. The borders they cross are ethnic, class, cultural, colonial, and state borders within Mexico as well as at the U.S.-Mexico border and in different regions of the United States. Regional systems of racial and ethnic hierarchies within the United States are different from those in Mexico and can also vary within the United States. Thus the ways that "Mexicans" and "Indians" have been codified in California and Oregon can differ from how they have been historically built into racial and ethnic hierarchies in New York or Florida. While crossing national borders is one kind of crossing undertaken by the subjects of this book, there are many others as well.

PEDRO MARTÍNEZ MORALES AND ERMELINDA REYES RAMÍREZ

PEDRO: I went to Veracruz to cut cane. I already had my kids . . . [about 1949].
I went several times to cut cane. Later I went to Culiacán [Sinaloa] with my daughter to harvest crops. My children have traveled all over.

ERMELINDA: Yes. We have two or three grandchildren in Chicago. We went to Chicago. It is really cold in Chicago. A lot of snow falls there. My daughter-in-law lives there, please say hello to her [I had previously told Ermelinda that I grew up in the Chicago area].

LYNN: Ok. Next time I am there I hope I will see her and be able to pass along your saludos.

ERMELINDA: You know, we stayed there for six months. We didn't like it there. We couldn't get used to the cold and the food there. It is better here.

PETRONA MARTÍNEZ REYES
(Daughter of Pedro and Ermelinda, Age 62)

PETRONA: When I was six years old we went to cut cane in Veracruz [1949]. I got married at the age of fifteen. After that I went to Veracruz again to cut cane with my first daughter. I spent five years in Veracruz between the ages of fifteen and twenty cutting cane, and tying it in bundles. This is what I did. . . . Later we went to another place. I was older when we went to Culiacán. I had three daughters by then. They were working as well. We

(above) 3. Pedro Martínez Morales (age ninety-seven) and Ermelinda Reyes Ramírez (age ninety-two).

4. Elena Martínez Ruis, Petrona Martínez Reyes, and Laura Ruiz Martínez.

built this house herein San Agustín with the money we made in Culiacán [Sinaloa]. Two of my daughters also worked there as well. We spent about four or five years in Culiacán. When the work would finish in Culiacán, then we would go to Ensenada. We came back here to build the house for a while. We started to make the adobe bricks to build it. We would go work there and then come back here for a month.

LYNN: How would you go back and forth? Did you go with someone?

PETRONA: A contractor would come here with a bus. He would take us to work. We didn't have to pay for the bus ride. When we finished working in Culiacán he would bring us back here. I spent about ten or fifteen years doing this. We would work for nine months in Culiacán, and then the other months we would be here making palm hats to sell. If we weren't doing that, then we went to La Paz [Baja California Sur] to pick cotton. We went there for two years and came back. Then from 1994 to 1997 I went to Oxnard, California. My children started to go there little by little as well. I went there with one of my daughters. I also worked in the strawberry harvest and picking vegetables in Watsonville. It was neither good nor bad for me there. The pay was more or less okay. When we worked in Culiacán, we couldn't save anything. I would like to go back to Watsonville. But because my mother and father [Ermelinda and Pedro] are here, I can't leave here. I have to be here for them. My father is sick. If they are going to die, I don't want them to say that I was not here for them. . . . You know, I grew to be old working so much. I moved around so much.

LAURA RUIZ MARTÍNEZ (Age 28)

LAURA: I was born in 1976. When I was six years old my parents and my five sisters all went to Culiacán. We went for six months. When I was twelve years old I remember that we went to Culiacán to harvest tomatoes. We arrived and they put me to work right away. From the time I was twelve until I was seventeen we went every year. When I was seventeen I came here to San Agustín for one year. I was here for a little more than a year when we needed money. I decided I wanted to build a house, so I went north. In 1995 I went to San Diego. My sister Adela was there, and she was the only one who received amnesty. I stayed for a month with her and my other sisters. Then I went to look for work. I found a job through one of my sisters.

It was good work. I worked at the same job for three years. From Monday through Saturday I took care of children. They gave me a room and food. One of the children was six and the other one was three when I started. It worked out well for me. For some of my other friends it didn't go so well. They had a lot of problems with their patrones [employers/bosses]. They wouldn't let my friends ever leave. My employer would leave me alone with the kids. They were in the Air Force. Sometimes I would be there for eight days alone with the kids. On Sunday I would always go and hang out with my sisters. They paid me $150 per week. I worked from six in the morning until ten at night for six days. . . . I came back to the pueblo when my Dad got really sick (in 1998). I haven't been back in the United States since then.

For Laura, Petrona, Pedro, and Ermelinda, living in multiple localities and discontinuous social, economic, and cultural spaces is the norm. What is a challenge for the ethnographer is to try to capture their under-standings and experiences (see Besserer 2002, 2004). They and many others have worked out a social world that exists within a multisited existence. Their community of origin, San Agustín Atenango, does not exist in one geographic place but is now spread out throughout multiple sites in the United States and Mexico. Their hometown is both a real and symbolic site that draws people back repeatedly in many senses, but which is also represented by multilayered forms of social and political organization that may include a federated transborder public works committee in ten U.S. cities as well as in several locations in Mexico, all linked to San Agustín in Oaxaca. We can think of each location of San Agustín as a home and as a locality in its own right with real senses of the local. But these multiple homes of San Agustín are also discontinuous spaces linked through kinship, ritual, cycles of labor, and individual and collectives resources of material and symbolic means.

Border Crossers in Teotitlán del Valle

The marketplace in Teotitlán del Valle is bustling at 9:00 A.M. This is the peak hour for daily shopping. The stalls inside are spilling over with fruits, vegetables, freshly cut meat, dried fish from the Isthmus of Te-huantepec, fresh-cut flowers, and dried chiles spread out on the floor for people to smell and touch. Since the mid-1990s, new parts of the market have developed. An ever-expanding section offering traditional prepared foods such as *atole*, refried beans, and *tamales* also includes several ham-burger stands and small-scale restaurants. The prepared foods section is filled with women of all ages, but a significant sector of the customers are

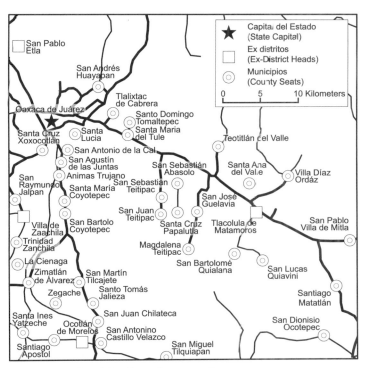

MAP 3. Teotitlán del Valle and surrounding area

younger, married women who no longer rise at four in the morning to grind two kilos of corn for tortillas and atole. Some are return migrants who got accustomed to simply reaching into the refrigerator for breakfast in the United States. Many came from households in which their husbands or other relatives may have been responsible for feeding breakfast to their children while they left the house at 6:00 A.M. to make a 7:00 A.M. housecleaning shift or to go care for someone else's children. As women came back from the United States and no longer wanted to spend six hours per day in food preparation and a demand for prepared food developed, other women who never left and had the economic means also began to purchase more prepared food. Some are using remittances sent home from family members living and working in the United States. Others are using income earned from textile weaving, which is the other major engine of economic activity besides economic remittances from the United States. Teotitlán is integrated with a complex global production, marketing, and distribution system linking the community to large-scale importer-exporters based primarily in the

5. Teotitlán marketplace.

western United States and to consumers in the United States, Europe, and elsewhere (see Stephen 2005b).

The outside walls of the market are painted with graffiti that contain references to Santa Ana and Oxnard, California, where many Teotitecos have settled. Others have established themselves in the border towns of Tijuana, Rosarito, and Ensenada, where they have set up folk art stores or sell textiles and other craft items from Mexico. They are not the first to take Teotitlán's textiles elsewhere.

Some Teotiteco merchants have a long history of regional migration. The Mexican census of 1900 lists eighteen Teotitecos as *viajeros*, merchants who traveled by mule to sell woolen blankets in the valley regions of Etla, Ocotlán, and Miahuatlán, and perhaps as far as Chiapas (Dirección General de Estadística 1906: 44, 45). Interrupted by the Mexican Revolution, which disrupted regional trade, the viajeros resumed selling in Chiapas, the isthmus, and the Sierra Juarez from 1920 until the 1950s (Stephen 1991: 108). Others migrated to Chiapas to work in the cane fields or the coffee plantations. A steady trickle of families from Teotitlán has lived periodically in the southern city of Tapachula, Chiapas, where they worked in the underground economy in the off-season, selling popsicles, popcorn, and other food. At the same time, others went to the United States.

6. Julián Mendoza,
Emiliana Pérez,
Pancho Mendoza
Pérez, and Armando
Mendoza.

The migration of Teotiteco men during the bracero program, which lasted from the 1940s through 1964, established a solid network of Teotitecos in the United States in places like Chicago and the Los Angeles area. Some ex-braceros received legal residency and brought their families. Others who were undocumented but labored in the United States in the 1950s and 1960s were also eventually able to get legal residency. By the late 1970s, extended families were sending second generations to the United States. In the mid-1980s, dozens of people (perhaps more than two hundred by some counts) received legal U.S. residency through the Immigration Reform and Control Act of 1986 (see chapter 3). By the 1990s, many families had third- or fourth-generation migrants who were following community and family networks to the United States.

ARMANDO MENDOZA AND EMILIANA PÉREZ *(Both Age 42)*

Armando Mendoza and his wife, Emiliana Pérez, are sitting in two low chairs surveying their yard and newly expanded house. They have just finished adding two large rooms to their house with money they saved while working in California. The roof was recently put onto the two rooms, an event that was celebrated with a large roof-raising party. In August 2002, when the following discussion took place, the rooms had no floors, windows, or doors.

At forty-two, Armando has a boyish smile that is tempered by the creased lines on his face brought on by many years of laboring in the sun. His wavy black hair is combed back from his face. He smiles broadly as he describes the roof-raising party.

Seated beside him, his wife, Emiliana, looks older than her forty-two years. She has the pinched face and body of someone suffering from diabetes and overwork. She sighs when commenting about how hard they have worked but sits relaxed in her chair with her long, black hair hanging loosely down her back to dry in the sun. In addition to completing the new rooms, they have expanded their small dry goods store at the front of their house, adding space and merchandise. They begin to talk about their time in the United States. They have recently returned after work dried up in the wake of September 11. At the time they were living in Oxnard, California. Armando worked there for a year before Emiliana came with their only child, Pancho.

EMILIANA: I sold flowers in Santa Ana, California. It was hard work.

ARMANDO: Pancho and I worked in a factory packing things. At first this didn't go so well. We went through an employment agency. And it wasn't so good because they don't always give you full-time work and they paid us minimum wage, but the company got more. . . . Getting over the border before that first job wasn't so easy. I had to walk for a week when I tried to cross. I walked in the mountains that are by Tecate. I didn't succeed the first time I tried. I ran into a border patrolman who was pretty nice. He said, "Well, this is my work. Sorry, there is nothing I can do about it," when he picked me up. I was in jail for two hours and he let me go. "You will probably try again tomorrow," he told me when I was leaving. He was from the San Diego office. The second time I paid the *coyote* [guide] eight hundred dollars to go from Tijuana to Santa Ana, California. I made it.

LYNN: How did Emiliana and Pancho cross?

EMILIANA: We came together. We came right over the official borderline. We bought our green card in Tijuana. It cost us each fifteen hundred dollars to cross right there at the border, but we made it through. We paid for it afterwards. Now it is even more expensive. If you want to pass directly over the Tijuana border with a green card it costs twenty-five hundred dollars now, even more. We paid off the coyote a little bit at a time, every two weeks. They didn't cover any interest.

ARMANDO: Later on we were all working okay, but then things changed. We didn't think we would come back so soon. As a matter of fact before September 11 there was a lot of talk about a new amnesty program. We felt very optimistic, like many other people. But after what happened on September 11, this all went down the tubes. All the plans for a new amnesty program went up in smoke. So we said, "Oh well, we are going to have to return."

There was no possibility for amnesty, and the amount of work available in the factory really decreased. Where there had been twenty-five people working at the factory before, there were only twelve. September 11 affected a lot of people we knew. There wasn't any more tourism, and many people working in hotels and restaurants lost their jobs. We decided we had to come back. If it hadn't been for what happened on September 11, we would still be living in Oxnard. But after that, it didn't make sense to stay. We flew back from Los Angeles to Mexico and got back in by showing our electoral voting cards.

LYNN: What did you think about your time in the United States?

EMILIANA: Well, I liked it there. Right now we have no way to really make money here. There, we were all able to work for some time. Here, there is no work for all of us. We rented a room in a house of a friend there and got along okay. Now my husband and son are weaving as pieceworkers for a nearby merchant. He gives them the materials to weave and pays them a small wage. We really have much less money here.

ARMANDO: We have these two bulls. They cost about $6,500 pesos (about US$650) each. We will raise them until they are big and then sell them . . .

EMILIANA: I have some turkeys now that I am going to save up to give as *guelaguetza*[1] exchange for when Pancho gets married. I think that he is going to bring home a wife sometime soon—who knows, but I am getting prepared.

LYNN: Do you think about returning to the United States?

EMILIANO: I think we probably will. I want to go back to earn more money out of necessity, not because I am thrilled to return. I want to go back there so that we can earn more money to finish our house to put in the floor, the windows, to paint it and to build a little house on another piece of land we have near the main road. The other house would be for Pancho for when he gets married. That is how I am thinking.

PANCHO MENDOZA *(Son of Armando and Emiliana, Age 19)*

Pancho stands easily, his large frame filling the doorway of one of the new rooms his family is constructing with dollars sent from California. Brushing his hand over his crew cut, Pancho breaks into an easy grin as he points to a calf he is raising and will sell as a mature bull. Towering above his parents in new cowboy boots, he motions for me to sit down on a chair under the mango tree shading the dirt courtyard. Nineteen years old, Pancho has a slightly chubby but muscular body on a large frame made tough by years of serious basketball playing and physical labor in both Mexico and the United States. We begin talking about the first time he went to the United States. This conversation took place in the summer of 2002:

LYNN: When did you first come to the United States?

PANCHO: In 1999, when I was sixteen years old. . . . I went by Tijuana, by Tecate. From there I went to San Diego and from San Diego to Los Angeles and from there to Oxnard. My father was already there in Oxnard. I went with my Mom.

LYNN: What did it feel like when you arrived in California?

PANCHO: Well, when you come here to California, you think about what people say in Mexico. When you are in Mexico, they tell you, yeah, so and so is there in the United States. They admire you for being here. So when you come here then you begin to know what it looks like in the United States. It is pretty in the United States, but you know there are a lot of different kinds of rules and regulations there that we don't have here.

LYNN: What kinds of rules did you encounter there?

PANCHO: Well, when I was there, because I was in another country, I had a problem because I didn't have any kind of identification. I was a minor when I got there and when I went out I didn't have any kind of i.d . . . like to ride the bus or go on some kind of outing—I had no i.d. This made it difficult for me to get around.

LYNN: Were you afraid because of this?

PANCHO: Well, it made me afraid and uncomfortable because they are always asking you for an i.d.—on the bus if you are a kid, in the bank, to get into a lot of places. They always ask you your name and to see your i.d.

LYNN: What was your first job here?

PANCHO: It was in a nursery. My Dad was already working there.

LYNN: How was the job?

PANCHO: I liked working in the nursery. It's a good job for me. If you are used to working outside in the countryside like I am in Mexico, then it isn't hard to get used to working in the nursery.

LYNN: Were you living with your parents?

PANCHO: I was living together with my parents in a house, in a room in a house in Oxnard.

LYNN: Were there other families there?

PANCHO: Yes. We rented the house together with my cousins. There were two or three families in the house. . . .

LYNN: You mentioned that you were hanging out with other people from Teotitlán. What kinds of activities do people do together?

PANCHO: Well, I was in touch with a lot of people who lived in Moore Park. We used to have a lot of basketball tournaments there that were just for people from Teotitlán. . . . A bunch of teams would get together and decide to play one another and organize what we called lightning basketball tournaments. We would do this every three months or so. That is how I really kept in touch with a lot of people was through playing basketball. I even met new people that way, and we always spoke pure Zapotec in these tournaments and when we would hang out. I would run into everyone that way.

LYNN: What was the name of the team there?

PANCHO: It was called Moore Park. Our team there from Teotitlán was called Moore Park. We would play against other teams from Oxnard, from Santa Ana. All these teams are made up of people from Teotitlán. . . . You know, Moore Park is a small town, it's a small place like Teotitlán. You go out onto the street and you always find another person there from Teotitlán. And everyone is speaking Zapoteco. Wherever you go in Moore Park—to the laundromat, to the store—you will run into someone from Teotitlán because it is a small town.

LYNN: Were there women's and girl's basketball teams as well?

PANCHO: Yes. They played a lot of basketball too. When we had a tournament, first a women's team would play and then a men's team. They would take turns.

LYNN: Let's go back to talking about your work. How long did you work in the nursery?

PANCHO: I lasted about six months there.

LYNN: Why did you change jobs?

PANCHO: I changed because I thought it would be better to work in the factory. They were advertising for workers so I went and applied. They called me up and offered me a job. They offered to pay me a little bit more than I was making in the nursery. In the nursery they were paying the minimum wage, which was $5.75 at the time. In the factory they were paying $6.00 per hour. The work in the factory was very different from the nursery. When I worked at the nursery I was outside all of the time, in the sun. In the factory you work inside. And they also offered me time and a half at the factory—overtime. So I could work more hours. . . . They would pay me $9.00 an hour when I was working overtime. So my check would be growing quickly. I worked at least forty hours and sometimes more.

LYNN: So how did you come back? Did you want to come back? You personally?

PANCHO: By the time we left, I didn't really want to be there any more. . . . I came back on a flight from Los Angeles. When I got to Mexico City, I said, "I am back in my own country. I am finally comfortable. I am at ease." When I got back to my town I could see that it had changed a lot during the time that I wasn't here. My friends were different and it wasn't the same.

LYNN: What had changed?

PANCHO: Well, there was a lot more construction. More of the streets were paved, and people that I knew seemed to have changed. They were still my friends. Some of them spoke to me and some of them didn't pay any attention to me. It's been three years since I came back. . . . I am not sorry that I went. I went with the intention of improving my life here. When you leave your town, your state, your country, you always go with the intention of overcoming your situation, of moving past it, of improving it. You feel really good about being able to come home and build a house. You feel good that you could do it, that you succeeded . . .

. . . I am glad that I went to the United States and that I was able to get to know what it is like there. You know people tell you about it and ask if you have gone. Before you go, you believe everything that people tell you about it. Now I know what it is like. I have been there myself.

Pancho and his parents are part of the most recent wave of migrants from Teotitlán to come to southern California. Armando has come to the United States several times before this, often for extended periods of time of up to four years. Emiliana worked in Mexico City as a domestic worker when she was younger. Armando's father was a bracero worker who was contracted several times to work in the United States. Like the extended family migration story of Laura, Petrona, Pedro, and Ermelinda documented above for San Agustín Atenango, Pancho and his parents are part of a longer migration story that can be traced back through the twentieth century and probably beyond. Migration to other parts of Mexico and to the United States has been a defining part of Teotitlán's twentieth- and twenty-first century history alongside the commercialization of the textile industry (see Stephen 2005). Earlier migrants provided housing and guidance to more recent migrants, and while some have remained in the United States for very long periods of time, others, such as Pancho and his parents, have circulated between the two countries. Coming from a Zapotec-speaking community that only became predominantly bilingual in Spanish and Zapotec in the 1990s, migrants from Teotitlán have always been crossing racial, ethnic, linguistic, and class boundaries between Mexico and into the United States As young people like Pancho accumulate experiences such as living in Oxnard for several years, they also come to incorporate U.S. racial, ethnic, and class hierarchies into their repertoires of discourses and symbolic and real experiences used to construct self-identities.

Experiences of living in the United States also come to affect how people in Teotitlán view their home community in Oaxaca in larger national and international contexts. Events like September 11 that profoundly affected U.S. immigration policy and nationalist discourse loom as large in the lives of Armando, Emiliana, and Pancho as in the lives of U.S. citizens. While hoping to become legal residents in the United States through a potential new amnesty program, Armando, Emiliana, and Pancho returned to Teotitlán when their hopes for legality were dashed with post–September 11 immigration politics and policies and when their sources of work dried up. They made their way back to Teotitlán to begin again as pieceworkers for a local merchant, but changed by their experience in the United States and by the resources they were able to accumulate there. In the fall of 2005, Pancho returned to California to help pay a $15,000 surgery bill his father had incurred.

While their economic remittances are plainly in sight in the form of new construction, the expanded storefront, and two bulls, their social remittances come out only in conversation and in exchanges they have with their relatives, neighbors, *compadres*, and friends. Social remittances in the form of ideas, behaviors, and social capital (skills, knowledge) flow both out of the home community and into it, encouraging people in transborder communities to try on new ideas about politics, culture, and even gender roles (Levitt 2001: 11). The complex connections that exist in the lives of migrants and return migrants such as Armando,

Emiliana, and Pancho suggest that we need to think seriously about the way we conceptualize communities like Teotitlán and San Agustín.

Transborder versus Transnational

For more than two decades anthropologists have been documenting people who were moving from one country to another and who were building transnational links (see Kearney 1988; González 1988; Eades 1987). Such workers have come to be called transnational migrants or transmigrants to distinguish them from immigrants and migrants. Transmigrants are defined by Vince Glick Schiller (2003: 105) as

> those persons, who having migrated from one nation-state to another, live their lives across borders, participating simultaneously in social relations that embed them in more than one nation-state. Activities and identity claims in the political domain are a particular form of transmigrant activity that is best understood as long-distance nationalism (Glick Schiller and Fouron 2001). In some cases individuals maintain hometown ties but avoid a connection with any form of nation-state-building process, although states are increasingly striving to encompass such relationships. (Kearney 2000)

Anthropologists and other social scientists have debated how to conceptualize transmigrant activity, whether as networks, circuits, or interlinked networks in a concept Arturo Escobar calls "meshworks." Unlike networks, which may be focused from one person outward, the idea of meshworks is about understanding interlinked networks and the total effect they can produce as a system. Escobar writes that the characteristics of meshworks include the fact that they are self-organizing and grow in unplanned directions; they are made up of diverse elements; they exist in hybridized forms with other hierarchies and meshworks; they accomplish the articulation of heterogeneous elements without imposing uniformity; and they are determined by the degree of connectivity that enables them to become self-sustaining (2003: 610–11). Escobar states that antiglobalization struggles are best seen as "horizontal, self-organizing meshworks of heterogeneous sites/struggles brought together by diverse interfaces and catalysts, particularly NGOs and pioneering social movements. . . . Meshworks can also be seen as apparatuses for the production of discourses and practices, that is creating discursive fields of action that harbor or capture a number of sites" (2003: 615–16).

In relation to conceptualizing how transmigrants are linked together, Escobar's notion of meshworks may be useful in terms of conceptualizing how people from communities like San Agustín are connected to one another through multiple networks and ties and also how the networks themselves are linked to other networks that in some cases span the United States and Mexico or are particular to each country. As pointed out by Kissam (2005b: 7–8), understanding how interactions between diverse village-based migration networks function is important for explaining how some migrants have "discovered" new destinations after they had arrived in the United States. He also suggests that scaling issues (consideration as to whether larger networks behave like smaller ones) are important in understanding how social and civic life evolves in places where migrants settle. Looking at migrant networks in relation to one another as well as in relation to nonmigrant networks they come into contact with in specific locations allows us to imagine the possible synergy generated by Escobar's model of meshworks.

For example, the community of San Agustín has a transnational public works committee with federated chapters in ten U.S. cities as well as links to the local government in San Agustín. People in the U.S. chapters are linked in turn to other kinds of organizations and networks. In Salem, Oregon, where a local chapter of the public works committee meets, some participants are also members of a farmworkers' union. A few others have been involved in immigrant rights coalitions and events. Through their connections to the farmworkers' union and to immigrant rights groups, they are in turn associated with other kinds of organizations. Others in different cities in the United States participate in churches that have still other kinds of connections. The notion of meshworks can thus help us to visualize the kinds of networks that people from San Agustín are involved in and how they are linked to others. Through these connections, people from San Agustín come into the orbit of a wide range of discourses concerning labor rights, human rights, immigrant rights, different kinds of religious orientations, and much more. These linked networks and the discourses coming from them are also brought back to the physical community of San Agustín through individuals who return to live there for long or short periods of time.

Other scholars have come to prefer the concept of social field as a way to think of transnational migration. Glick Schiller writes, "The concept of a social field enables us to visualize the simultaneity of transmigrant connections across the borders of two or more states. We investigate the ways in which transmigrants become part of the fabric of daily life in more than one state, simultaneously participating in the social, cultural, economic, religious, or political activities of more than one locality" (2003: 107). One useful dimension of this concept for my discussion here is that if we consider a wide range of people with varying kinds of power and power bases who interact within a transnational social field, we can include migrants of varying types and duration, return migrants, and nonmigrants in the same discussion. While the term *transmigrant* suggests a more or less permanent state of being between two or more locations, some people may spend a good part of their lives engaging in this state of being, others may live for longer periods of time in one place or another, and still others may leave their home communities only one time or never. All of the people living within a transnational social field are exposed, in different ways and at different levels, but nonetheless in some shared way to "a set of social expectations, cultural values, and patterns of human interaction shaped by more than one social, economic and political system" (Glick Schiller 2003: 108).

In many ways, the concept of social field works well with Escobar's vision of meshworks. Levitt and Glick Schiller (2004) suggest the concept of social field is a particularly useful way to move beyond the container of the nation-state for social analysis. Like meshworks, the concept of social fields offers a way around the binary divisions, for example, global/local and national/transnational, that have permeated so much of social analysis related to the nation-state. They offer a new way of conceptualizing the lives of people who move across many borders and live multisited lives. They state of local, national, transnational, and global connections:

In one sense, all are local in that near and distant connections permeate the daily lives of individuals lived within a locale. But within this locale, a person may participate in personal networks, or receive ideas and information that connect them to others in a nation-state, across the borders of a nation-state, or globally, without ever having migrated. By conceptualizing transnational social fields as transcending the boundaries of nation-states, we also note that individuals within these fields are, through their everyday activities and relationships influenced by multiple sets of laws and institutions. Their daily rhythms and activities respond not only to more than one state simultaneously but also to social institutions, such as religious groups, that exist within many states and cross their borders. (Levitt and Glick Schiller 2004: 5)

In her study of transmigrant Dominicans in Boston, Massachusetts, Peggy Levitt utilizes the concept of transnational social field, citing the work of Sarah Mahler (1995a, 1995b) on Salvadorans in the United States and others (2001: 8). Her ethnography (*The Transnational Villagers*) shows in a detailed way how migrants, return migrants, and nonmigrants from Miraflores in the Dominican Republic are linked through political parties, religious organizations, and local development projects as well as through kinship. She writes, "The transnational social fields that migration engenders encompass all aspects of social life. Though they generally emerge from economic relations between migrants and non-migrants, social, religious and political connections also constitute these arenas" (2001: 9). Thus actual migration is not required in order to be a member of a transnational social field. Levitt states, "Non-migrants also adapt many of the values and practices of their migrant counterparts, engage in social relationships that span two settings, and participate in organizations that act across borders" (2001: 11).

Others, for example, Federico Besserer (2002, 2004) in his study of the transnational community of San Juan Mixtepec in the southern Mexican state of Oaxaca, have tried to come up with new conceptual models. Besserer has proposed a "transnational topography," which emphasizes transnational communities as multicentric, multidirectional, and with multiple domains."(2002: 173). Using a series of innovative maps, he shows the multidirectionality of not only economic remittances, but also labor flows, educational strategies, and ritual events against a decentered community with dozens of locations spread throughout the United States and Mexico. Certain domains of life are concentrated in certain locations, but not all in one place. For example, Culiacán is an important site for education, while Camalú is a center of work and residence for women (2002: 174). And some domains are concentrated in a small number of places whereas others are extremely scattered. Ultimately, Besserer finds that historically, people from San Juan Mixtepec have participated in simultaneous processes of deterritorialization and reterritorialization and that both are essential parts of the transnational community (2002: 175, 2004). His findings are readily applicable to the communities explored here.

It is certainly important to consider the "national" in the "transnational" part of migrant histories and experience—particularly when it comes to the recognition or lack thereof of basic human and labor rights connected to their positions in relation to the legal frameworks of the nations they are moving between. I want to suggest, however, that we have to look beyond the national in order to understand the complete nature of what people are moving or "transing" between. In the cases of Mixtec migrants like Laura, Petrona, Pedro, and Ermelinda and Zapotec migrants such as Pancho, Armando, and Emiliana, the borders they have crossed and continue to cross are much more than national.

In many communities like San Agustín and Teotitlán, where migration to and from other places has become a norm that spans three, four, and now five generations, the borders people cross are ethnic, cultural, colonial, and state borders within Mexico as well as the U.S.-Mexico border. When Mixtecos and Zapotecos come into the United States, they are crossing a new set of regional borders that are often different from those in Mexico, but may also overlap with those of Mexico (for example, the racial/ethnic hierarchy of Mexico, which lives on in Mexican communities in the United States). These include ethnic, cultural, and regional borders within the United States. For these reasons, it makes more sense to speak of transborder migration in the case I am describing here, rather than simply transnational. The transnational becomes a subset of the transborder experience.

The Contradictions of Border Crossing and Hybridity

Borders have been the topic of much discussion in the social sciences and humanities. There has been a positive side to border-crossing discussions in the work of people like Gloria Anzaldua, who as a *mestiza* wrote of the border as a place of hybridity and of new possibilities (1999). The U.S.-Mexico border zone becomes a metaphor for mobilizing the most creative of Chicana/Azteca/Afro/Spanish roots to encounter a new mestiza. Other discussions of transnational migration have drawn on this discourse of new possibilities with optimistic documentation of new transnational organizations. For example, the Frente Indígena de Organizaciones Binacionales (FIOB), which organizes Oaxacan migrants of different indigenous ethnic groups in Oaxaca City, in the Juxtlahuaca region of Oaxaca, in Tijuana, Baja California Norte, and out of Fresno and Los Angeles, California, is undoubtedly a positive example of cross-border hybridity. The FIOB has demonstrated innovative possibilities for cross-border organizing. It has worked on labor rights, human rights, and indigenous rights issues on both sides of the U.S.-Mexico border where its members are active as well as in both United States and Mexican political campaigns at state and national levels (see Domínguez Santos 2004; Rivera Salgado 1999). As Michael Kearney writes, the ethnography of transnational migration suggests that communities such as San Agustín Atenango and Teotitlán del Valle as well as organizations such as the FIOB are "constituted transnationally and thus challenge the defining power of the nation-states which they transcend . . . members of transnational communities similarly escape the power of the nation-state to inform their sense of collective identity" (1998: 126).

The cultural theorist Néstor García Canclini has grappled with the necessity of framing his discussion of hybrid cultural production on the border within the larger context of a political economy of racism and violence. His words highlight the importance of understanding how new ethnic transborder forms of identity expression such as pan-Mixtec, pan-Zapotec, and panindigenous ethnicity are intimately tied to cross-border labor recruitment practices that leave workers with no rights and little recourse to any labor protections and force them to confront racism and anti-immigrant sentiment; such discrimination has resulted in border enforcement policies that are killing people as they try to enter the United States and anti-immigrant legislation that is eliminating access to basic social services for many immigrant families. He states,

> In the exchanges of traditional symbols with international communications circuits, culture industries, and migrations, questions about identity and the national, the defense of sovereignty, and the unequal appropriation of knowledge and art do not disappear. The conflicts are not erased, as neoconservative postmodernism claims. They are placed in a different register, one that is multifocal and more tolerant, and the autonomy of each culture is rethought—sometimes with smaller fundamentalist risks. Nevertheless, the chauvinist critiques of "those from the center" sometimes engender violent conflicts: acts of aggression against newly arrived migrants and discrimination in school and at work.
>
> The intense crossing and instability of traditions, bases of valorizing opening, may also be—in conditions of labor competition—a source of prejudice and confrontation. Therefore, the analysis of the advantages or inconveniences of deterritorialization should not be reduced to the move-

ments of ideas of cultural codes, as is frequently the case in the bibliography on postmodernity. Their meaning is also constructed in connection with social and economic practices, in struggles for local power, and in the competition to benefit from alliances with external powers. (García Canclini 1995: 240–41)

While acknowledging the importance of organizations like the FIOB and the kinds of creative border hybridity represented in work such as that of Anzaldua and García Canclini (with his words of caution), I want to highlight an additional part of border crossing for indigenous migrants which includes the physical and very real danger of crossing the U.S.-Mexican border and of being labeled illegal in the United States (see Urrea 2004). In addition to the physical dangers of trying to cross the border, migrants live with the ever-present drumbeat of anti-immigrant organizing that not only permeates the border area, but also is prevalent throughout the United States. Anti-immigrant sentiment, which fosters such groups as the Minutemen (described below), is also directly linked to concrete policies like Operation Gatekeeper and other border fortification plans that directly impact the lives of indigenous migrants.

Let's start with the increasing danger of dying in the act of trying to enter the United States. During the fiscal year ending in September 2005, the Border Patrol counted 463 deaths along the two-thousand-mile-long U.S.-Mexico border (Nevins 2006). Immigrant rights advocates place the number much higher. While the Border Patrol reported 177 deaths in Arizona in 2004—now the most popular crossing point into the United States—the medical examiner's office of Arizona put the total at 221 deaths (Almond 2004). In 2005 the number of deaths in Arizona was about half of the national total, or 232 (Rothstein 2006).

In addition, we have to consider the insertion of indigenous migrants into a range of racial and ethnic classification systems and hierarchies in Mexico and in the United States where they are often at the bottom—be it economic, ethnic, racial, social, or political. As documented by Kearney, the experience of racial/ethnic discrimination outside of Oaxaca was a major stimulus for Mixtecos from particular communities and indigenous peoples from other communities to appropriate broader panethnic labels such as Mixteco and Zapoteco and use them as a basis for broader organizing along ethnic lines (Fox and Rivera Salgado 2004a: 12; see also Kearney 1988, 1995a, 1995b, 1998, 2000; Nagengast and Kearney 1989). The use of ethnic labels has also enabled migrant workers to distinguish themselves in local ethnic hierarchies and to differentiate themselves from other Mexicanos, Chicanos, and others. The use of panethnic labels has also provided a way for so-called illegal or alien Mixteco and Zapoteco migrants to construct a new form of identity based on their transborder existence (Kearney 1998: 129). For example, writes Kearney, "Mixtec ethnicity arises as an alternative to nationalist consciousness and as a medium to circumscribe not space, but collective identity precisely in those border areas where nationalist boundaries of territory and identity are most contested and ambiguous" (1998: 129). As I explain in chapter 3, "border areas" are not confined to the geographical areas physically linked to the U.S.-Mexico border, but are also carried on the bodies of migrants, who historically have been read as illegal since the 1930s.

While the borders Mixteco and Zapoteco migrants cross involve positive possibilities such as the creation of transborder panethnic organizations and new organizing possibilities, these same borders are inscribed on migrant bodies and read by those around them in ways that involve explicit racism and discrimination. Such bias affects their experiences and possibilities, as they are labeled illegal, *Oaxaquitos*, *indios estúpidos*, and sometimes as unable to speak because they speak their own language. The experiences of migrants highlighted in this book will certainly validate this perspective. However, hybridity is itself riddled with contradictions for those who live in its manifestations.

The approach I take seeks to recognize both the powers and limits of states in affecting the ways in which transborder communities develop through time and work around and through the political, legal, economic, and cultural apparatuses of states. Thus while specific state-based policies such as the bracero program, implemented by the United States and Mexican government in 1942, and the North American Free Trade Agreement, implemented by the same two states in 1994, have significantly affected directly and indirectly where, when, and how people from San Agustín Atenango and Teotitlán have migrated within Mexico and also to the United States, the power of these policies in the lives of indigenous migrants is also deflected, refracted, and refocused through the changing larger contexts that transborder communities develop and change in. As migrant networks from San Agustín and Teotitlán developed and thickened with time in specific locations within Mexico and later in the United States, these networks and the people and resources attached to them have come to be able to compete with and in many cases outsmart state-controlled legal systems, labor markets, political systems, and border patrolling institutions and technologies. These communities are both beyond and within the control of nation-states.

In his definition of *transnational*, Kearney suggests two senses of the word. The first has to do with forms of organization and identity which are not constrained by national boundaries, such as transnational corporations. The second meaning he proposed for *transnational* is "postnational" (1998: 121). While I believe that communities like Teotitlán and San Agustín can be termed transnational in the first sense in which Kearney defines the word, I find it difficult to describe them as completely postnational, as in beyond the national or completely beyond the reach of the state. They are both within and beyond the reach of the Mexican and U.S. governments. Both communities continue to be tied significantly to the Mexican government through their receipt of funds for municipal development and through women residents' receipt of subsidized milk through a government fortified-milk program and of small stipends to support their families through the Oportunidades Program.[2] Oportunidades is a Mexican conditional cash transfer program in which families receive small subsidies in exchange for having their children regularly attend school and for visiting family health clinics for checkups. The program began in 1997 as Progresa and by 2005 covered about five million families.

Community residents also participate in national elections and have been affected by state development projects like highway construction and other projects. Now that Mexican migrants can vote in Mexican elections from the United States, their links to the state are likely to continue at least at this level. Teotitlán in particular is strongly affected by Mexican trade policy and export regulations in relation to textiles. Once in the United States, some people from Teotitlán and San Agustín continue to communicate with the Mexican government via consular offices. The active outreach programs of Mexican consular offices throughout the United States are certainly an indication of the government's awareness that migrants are beyond their reach, but not an indication that migrants have become completely disconnected.

I agree with Kearney that patterns of transborder migration during the past two decades have more to do with the political-economic and sociocultural ordering of late capitalism than with the construction and defense of the nation-state (1998: 123). States have been reorganizing themselves significantly to meet the needs of late capitalism, particularly in relation to supplies of low-wage labor. As discussed in the next chapter, U.S. immigration policy is focused on controlling the flow of undocumented migrants, not on sealing the border. And over time, U.S. immigration policy itself has been a central factor in the numbers of people who are able to come to the United States without documentation. In San Agustín Atenango and Teotitlán del Valle, transnational labor migration has become a structural feature and is the major engine driving a wide range of transborder processes (Kearney 1998: 125).

The same transborder communities that occupy transnational social fields and are held together by coyotes, human traffic back and forth, electronic money transfers, phone cards, cell phones, and e-mail—all of which facilitate new political and cultural possibilities for a simultaneous belonging in multiple localities—also generate new kinds of racism and discrimination as indigenous migrants come to occupy increasingly visible places both in larger Mexican communities in the United States and outside of these communities. As the number of Mexican migrants becomes dominant in cities like Santa Ana and Oxnard, California, and Woodburn, Oregon, non-Mexicans—usually European Americans—feel they are losing control of geographic space. A defensive Anglo-nationalism took hold in the United States, beginning in the 1990s and reinforced by the post–September 11 fears of terrorism and loss of border control. As noted by Kearney, in areas of California, European Americans have definitively lost control of much geographic space, of boundaries that have been, to use the terminology common in these areas, invaded by foreigners and aliens. But having lost control of geographic space, "they had begun to take fall-back positions to defend social and cultural spaces where the state still has the power to legislate identities and practices" (1998: 126).

Kearney mentions the enforcement of English as the official language in California, Arizona, Colorado, and Florida. State ballot measures have sought to impose other cultural and economic policies as well. In California, anti-immigrant legislation such as Proposition 187 passed by California voters in 1994 (although rejected by nearly four out of five Latino voters) is surely related to the increased visibility of the high influx of migrants from 1990 to the present. If enforced, the law would have denied public education, nonemergency health care, and other social services to undocumented immigrants and their children. The law also required public employees to report to immigration authorities people they suspected of being in the United States without permission.

A federal judge ruled that most portions of Proposition 187 were unconstitutional, and they have not been enforced. In November 2004, voters in Arizona approved Proposition 200, which requires state and local employees to verify the immigration status of people applying for public benefits and to report undocumented immigrants or face possible criminal prosecution. On December 23, 2004, a federal judge lifted an order barring Proposition 200 from becoming law (Carroll and Wingett 2004). Similar measures are likely to be seen in other states as well and are now coupled with anti-immigrant vigilantism, which has been supported even by some public officials.

In March 2004, a retired California accountant named James Gilchrist organized a group of volunteer border patrollers as part of what he called the Minuteman Project, maintaining that he was putting together a volunteer force to defend the country's border from invaders, just as the original minutemen acted to defend U.S. sovereignty from the British.

Assigned to work a twenty-mile-long border area near Naco, Arizona, the volunteers were supposed to man ground observation posts and conduct aerial surveillance from aircraft and a communications center to report illegal aliens crossing into the country. The event "will tune the American people into the shameful fact that 21st century minutemen/women have to help secure U.S. borders because the U.S. government refuses to provide our dutiful Border Patrol with the manpower and funding required to do so," said Gilchrist (Seeper 2005). The Mexican undersecretary for North American Affairs, Gerónimo Gutiérrez, suggested that volunteers from the Minuteman Project and other anti-immigrant protesters on the border could violate the rights of undocumented Mexicans crossing the border. "What there is concern about is that some of these actions that could be taken could be in violation of federal and state laws to the detriment of Mexican citizens," Gutierrez said. "Mexico doesn't want the rights of its citizens transgressed, especially if those actions are in violation of federal and state laws" (Seeper 2005).

According to Grey Deacon, a spokesman for the project, after one month on the Arizona border, the Minutemen claimed they were directly responsible for the apprehension by U.S. Border Patrol agents of 349 people trying to illegally enter the United States during the month (Meeks 2005). The Border Patrol claimed otherwise, dismissing any notion that the Minuteman presence in April was anything other than an occasional nuisance, including setting off more than two hundred false alerts from

7. Minuteman online poster.

motion sensors as they tread too close to the border, according to a Border Patrol spokeswoman, Andrea Zortman (Meeks 2005). The endorsement of the group's efforts by the governor of California, Arnold Schwarzenegger, helped to legitimize its objectives and tactics, however. On April 28, 2005, Schwarzenegger stated on Los Angeles KFI during an interview with the popular radio hosts John and Ken, "They've done a terrific job. And they have cut down the crossing of illegal immigrants by a huge percentage" (Newsmax 2005).

Schwarzenegger's remarks as well as news media coverage of the Minutemen's plans to come to California also rallied significant opposition from Latino and immigrant rights groups. In a summit in May 2005 hosted by the Las Vegas–based Wake Up America Foundation, whose motto is, "It's your country, take it back," the Minutemen and other anti-immigrant groups made plans to organize a national umbrella organization of border defense groups. Outside, some two hundred Latino protesters waved Mexican and American flags and signs protesting the racism of the groups' agendas (Goldman 2005; KVOA 2005).

The Minutemen have contributed to an escalating anti-immigrant sentiment in the United States as visible migration from Mexico has increased. The politics of fear spread by border defense groups such as the Minutemen is leading to new anti-immigrant legislation, to the construction of more physical barriers on the border, and to greater Border Patrol presence. Anti-immigrant sentiments often predominate in non-border states as well.[3] None of this has stopped people from coming to the United States, but it has increasingly resulted in a death-inducing border defense policy and the denial of basic services and rights to immigrant workers who come to the United States in good faith. Too often, the perspectives of those who are the targets of U.S. border defense and immigration policies are invisible.

Structure of This Book

My goal in this book is to weave together the personal histories and narratives of indigenous transborder migrants and the larger structures that affect their lives and to highlight their creative responses in many arenas to a transborder existence. The following chapters are thus organized around the different arenas of transborder lives highlighting the different kinds of borders that people are crossing.

Chapter 2, "Transborder Communities in Political and Historical Context: Views from Oaxaca," briefly describes the histories of San Agustín Atenango and Teotitlán del Valle in relation to migration. The chapter also describes the impact migration has had on local systems of government in each town, often known by anthropologists as civil and religious cargo systems. Such a perspective allows us to see how patterns of migration can profoundly affect local institutions and the expectations for those who have never left, suggesting the presence of transborder political and cultural fields. In addition, the chapter suggests how ideas about governing young women's sexuality seem to be influenced by the standards emerging for young women who migrated to the United States. Despite some changes, young women are still trying to maintain a public reputation as *mujeres decentes* (good women) while participating in serial monogamy.

Chapter 3, "Mexicans in California and Oregon," considers how the national space we refer to as Mexico has grown to include spaces within the territorial boundaries of California and Oregon. The state of California and part of southern Oregon were literally once a physical part of Mexican national territory. During the twentieth century significant numbers of Mexican immigrants have incorporated their political, economic, and cultural connections with Mexico into the fabric of local life in areas such as Los Angeles, Oxnard, and Santa Ana, California, and Salem and Woodburn, Oregon. Different waves of migration have re-created Mexico in these cities and towns. For indigenous migrants who settle in these areas, life often functions as a significant extension of Mexico in both positive and negative ways.

Chapter 4, "Transborder Labor Lives," explores how the structural conditions of U.S. immigration policy, the needs of transnational commercial agriculture and the service sector in Mexico and the United States, and the U.S. consumer market have affected the labor experiences of transborder workers from San Agustín and Teotitlán del Valle. Narratives centered on work in agriculture, childcare, and gardening highlight how Mixtec and Zapotec migrants have accommodated to and struggled against the difficult labor and living conditions they have experienced as low-wage workers. Often the legal, ethnic, and racial borders they are continually crossing are represented in their work experiences in an ongoing way.

Chapter 5, "Surveillance and Invisibility in the Lives of Indigenous Farmworkers in Oregon," focuses on the embodied experiences and memories of indigenous immigrant agricultural workers as objects of simultaneous surveillance and invisibility on the U.S.-Mexico border, in the agricultural fields and labor camps of Oregon, and in processing plants. The chapter emphasizes the importance of the floating nature of the border as the legality of all border crossers is continually contested through the way that they are structurally inserted into the power relations of commercial agricultural and culturally interpreted in Oregon and elsewhere as illegal. This chapter focuses on the legalities of border crossing which indigenous migrants do and how this dimension of their identity and experience interacts with the other kinds of borders they cross.

Chapter 6, "Women's Transborder Lives: Gender Relations In Work and Families," examines how Zapotec and Mixtec patterns of migration to the western United States are gendered. A significant emphasis in this chapter is on how the experience of migration and the kind of work schedule that is demanded of low-wage migrants often rearranges gender relations in Oaxaca and in the United States alike. What happens when farmworkers cook, sew, and clean for one another in labor camps? How do both men and women work full-time in the United States, often at one or more minimum wage jobs on opposite shifts, and share childcare and domestic chores? Transborder mothering is explored in terms of its consequences for women in the United States and in Mexico.

Chapter 7, "Navigating the Borders of Racial and Ethnic Hierarchies," suggests how the racial/ethnic hierarchy inherited from colonial Mexico, which places indigenous peoples at the bottom, is reproduced in heavily Mexican population sites in the United States. The chapter conveys the experiences of racism and discrimination faced by Mixtecos and Zapotecos immigrants as they cross the borders of racial and ethnic hierarchies among other Mexicans in the United States. The chapter also explores their unique position as Hispanic Indians in relation to the other dominant racial and ethnic categories that emerged in the late twentieth century in U.S. cultural and political discourse.

Chapter 8, "Grassroots Organizing in Transborder Lives," uses four case study organizations that Mixtec migrants are participating in to illustrate the ways in which indigenous migrants are engaged in interlinked forms of grassroots organizing that cut across the class, ethnic, and gendered dimensions of transborder migration and settlement. By showing the relationships among these organizations as well as their meaning for those who participate, I hope to illustrate how the concept of interlinked networks or meshworks is useful in understanding the complex web of relationships that is reshaping notions of territory and politics. The case studies are of Oregon's farmworkers' union, PCUN, a women's organization, the San Agustín Transborder Public Works Committee, and OCIMO (Organization of Oaxacan Indigenous Migrant Communities).

Chapter 9, "Transborder Ethnic Identity Construction in Life and on the Net: E-Mail and Web Page Construction and Use," focuses on two primary examples of the use of digital technology by transborder communities and organizations: Web page creation by a community museum and weaver cooperatives in Teotitlán and use of e-mail, faxes, and a website by the FIOB. Both examples show how indigenous immigrants have built a public presence on the Internet and have used it as an organizing tool to exert political pressure in the United States and in Mexico. The two groups have taken a similar approach to how they publicly construct their ethnic identities—simultaneously linking local, regional, national, and transborder or binational dimensions of indigenous identity with a multisited understanding of location.

The conclusions use several theoretical concepts, including the rule of juxtaposition, partial denationalization, and a multilayered model of citizenship, to interpret the key findings of the book. These concepts can be seen as tools for understanding the different dimensions of border crossing emphasized here. An epilogue on collaborative research offers some additional thoughts on the research process that went into the book.

More than anything, the purpose of this book is to document the presence and importance of transborder communities and the individuals who participate in them. By moving beyond the concept of the national as the primary framing device for interpreting the meaning and experience of transborder lives, I hope to push the legal, racial, ethnic, class, gender, colonial, cultural, and regional borders of Zapotec and Mixtec immigrants to center stage. By complicating the context within which transborder communities are understood, we can offer a framework for understanding such communities elsewhere. Transborder communities are a global phenomenon. They have created unique models of governance, communication, education, economic development, and maintenance of language and culture that have important implications for the future. More than 130 million people live outside the countries in which they were born, and they have crossed many borders in the process of getting there. Such communities are a permanent feature of our planet, and we have much to learn from them (Bacon 2005).

CHAPTER 2

Transborder Communities in Political and

Historical Context

VIEWS FROM OAXACA

Transborder Workers and Civil Governance
in San Agustín Atenango

It is late afternoon and Daniel Cruz Pérez is glued to his telephone in a two-room concrete house on one of the main streets of San Agustín Atenango. It is hot and the doors and windows are open. Daniel's face is moist from the heat, and his black hair is plastered to his head beneath a blue baseball cap. Daniel gestures with his left hand while holding the phone in the right. His dark eyes glow with intensity as he tells the person on the other end of the line why it is so important that he consider running for public office. At thirty-five, Daniel is a seasoned transborder worker who has combined periodic migration to the United States with organizing work for the Frente Indígena de Organizaciones Binacionales (FIOB) and for the Partido de la Revolución Democrática (PRD). His first experience of going to work in the States was a rough one, not unlike that of several dozen men from his community. In August 2004 he described his first experience in the United States:

DANIEL: The first year I left was 1987. I went to San Luis Reyes, California.
LYNN: Did you already know people there?
DANIEL: I had a couple of friends who were there already, and we got motivated and went there to work.
LYNN: Was that around the time when it was easier to cross?
DANIEL: Exactly. Back then you could still cross through Tijuana, because of the option that the upper part of the river gives you. I was really hopeful

8. Daniel Cruz Pérez on the outskirts of San Agustín Atenango.

about going to the United States because of the poverty we were in at home. There wasn't any money.

LYNN: Were you by yourself? Were you still single?

DANIEL: No, I already had a family, I was married. I had had my first son. My wife was pregnant with my other son, the one who's in the United States right now. And with the hope of finding a bit of money, I left. I met a boss there named John. We asked him for a job, but there were hardly any at the time. After a while he started giving us a few hours every week, harvesting cherry tomatoes. And after the harvest, we would help pick up the hosing and all the plastic covers. I think they used to pay us about US$5.55 per hour.

LYNN: Was the job per hour or under contract?

DANIEL: Always per hour. But what I wanted to tell you about is that when I was there, I lived like a mountain critter and I couldn't go down to the city.

LYNN: Were you living in the hills?

DANIEL: I was living in underground caves walled with cardboard. We slept there and asked people to give us a couple of mattresses from whoever could spare one. We went to the Catholic Church where they gave us clothing and blankets so that we could sleep underground. We kept all our stuff in there and when we left to work, we covered it all up with tree branches to keep them from finding out where we were. So even though the migra [officials of the Immigration and Naturalization Service] came by, they couldn't find us.

LYNN: What was this place called?

DANIEL: The willow ravine, because there were tons of willow trees by the river.

LYNN: But was this done by many people in the community? Some other people from this town and from others as well have told me the same thing.

DANIEL: Yes, about thirty of us were there, many from this town. The place was dangerous because of all the risk. We were all afraid of the Cholos (derogatory term for Mexican American gangsters as used here) coming to steal from us. In fact, they had actually killed several of us to take our money. And even when we went to the flea market to get shoes or clothing, we still weren't safe because we'd run into the migra. It happened to me once that I was standing at a bus stop, waiting to take the bus. The migra went by, stopped me and asked for my documents. Of course I didn't have any, and I got kicked out to Tijuana. And there we were, in Tijuana again. We really struggled that time around because we had no money with us. But just like that, we went back in. . . . I even learned to cross [the border] by myself. I'd take the trolley, the famous trolley bus. But that was then. Now it is harder. A lot of the guys I was with then, we still know one another.

After his trip in 1987, Daniel returned two times to work in Nevada. Now he is calling places he used to live in the United States.

Daniel is racking up a large international phone bill, as he is placing continuous calls to paisanos from San Agustín in California, Oregon, Nevada, and Illinois to see whether or not they are willing to be candidates on the PRD ticket in the upcoming municipal elections. San Agustín is one of 152 municipalities in Oaxaca where political parties have become deeply involved in local electoral processes. In San Agustín the involvement of political parties in local elections can be traced to 1987, when a conflict between two groups of teachers erupted into violence. One group, the Vanguardistas was associated with the Partido Revolucionario Institucional (PRI). The other group, known as the Democráticos, was affiliated with a group of people who in 1989 became the PRD. The conflict led to a change in how some posts in the local government were filled. As a part of my political education, Daniel felt it was important to tell me this story:

DANIEL: In 1987, we had a mayor who lived in Mexico City for a long time. He grew up there, and his children were born there. And when he came back,

the town elected him as mayor. They thought he was a good person, someone who could really serve his town well. He was very intelligent, and living
in Mexico City he gained a lot of wisdom, a lot of savvy and good preparation. In the end, it was unfortunate that he had all this preparation because
as soon as he came in, he started saying that our teachers here, the people
teaching our children, just weren't doing enough. He said that they didn't
teach well, and that all they ever did was go to rallies and protests. And that
bothered him.

On that occasion, a group of teachers was here to visit during school
vacation. People called them the Vanguardistas. So these teachers got here
and offered the town better work, more time put in, and, according to
them, better teaching. And they managed to sweet talk the mayor. So he
said, "All right. These are the kind of people I need. I need teachers who can
really prepare my people." But the Democrático teachers—the ones who
were already in town—were sent by the federal government. They had more
clout, more of a presence in town. The Vanguardistas, on the other hand,
were only a few, and they didn't have good political connections.

Then the mayor told the Vanguardistas, "Look. When these other fools
come back, we're not giving them anything . . . Instead, we'll give you the
right to educate our children." So in the middle of the school break, these
teachers started registering students and many who agreed with the authorities went ahead and registered their children. But then the Democráticos
returned. Their spots and their jobs had already been taken over . . .

. . . And of course they wouldn't leave. They started inviting parents to the
town square to support them so that they could keep on working. So they
kept on gathering people in the square, and they even had classes there!
After that they started fighting.

LYNN: Who did? The two teachers' groups?

DANIEL: Yes. They started having protest marches. The Democráticos were
saying, "Mr. Mayor, you have to let us work. We won't allow these people to
take our places. We bring with us federal orders saying that you must give us
back the classes that are ours and have been ours for years." They invited
parents in the area to their rally. And the parents were going to join in, too,
but then the teachers told them, "No, ladies and gentlemen, stay out of this:
it's our problem. We can't get the townspeople involved in this." But then,
the municipal president put armed men in the school, to guard the Van-
guardista teachers . . .

. . . When the other group of teachers came back (the Democráticos),
bullets started blazing by, stones were flying from side to side . . . it was a

mess. And the mayor was actually fueling the whole problem. Then this guy about my age comes on the scene. He's in jail now, actually. This person was the mayor's aide. He stormed out, went to his house, took out a 22-calibre rifle, and hid until he saw the mob of teachers marching and yelling and protesting. And this guy just goes nuts and—bam bam bam bam!!! He shoots them all.

LYNN: He shot the Democráticos?

DANIEL: Yeah. And all along his mother was saying, "Here you go, son, here are more bullets."

LYNN: More bullets!

DANIEL: And while they kept marching on he loaded his rifle again and again, shooting up and shooting the ground to scare away the crowd. But instead, his mom tells him, "Just shoot them. Shoot at them, already, so that they all go to hell once and for all.' And when the teachers returned, they felt the gunfire inside the building, so then they started dispersing all over the place. They actually wounded one, and even killed one of them.

After this whole mess happened, people kicked the mayor out of office. The town did. It was a big ruckus; even one fellow who was just walking by was hit by one of the shots coming out of the school. And that was it. For about a month there was a huge quarrel here. But then, the town started coming together and asking, well, why did this happen? The kids didn't have classes for three full years. So the town decided that, before letting something like that continue—or worse, happen again—they would kick out the president. They had a person from Oaxaca come down to take his place. They then appointed a town council, a council of elders, to run the town until the end of the term . . .

LYNN: Was that when elections started working around the political party system?

DANIEL: That's when it turned into a party system. There didn't use to be parties when the Democráticos started. But since under their "democracy" slogan we were all allowed to participate, we tried to make our way into the party, and people from the party intermingled with those in our group. They would say, "We're Democráticos, we invite you to participate with us." And they started handing out government jobs to us, reeling us in. Afterward, we named a municipal party that was elected under the usos y costumbres laws (traditional, customary law), but also had PRI support. But the PRI really had no strength at that time because there were very few members and the Democráticos (our party, which later became the PRD in 1989) had many more. However, because we weren't registered, they didn't take us into account. They downright ignored us. Then, with me as the party's secretary general, we later pushed for and obtained the party registration in 1989.

The entrance of political parties into the local political structures of indigenous communities is not always so violent in Oaxaca. In fact, a majority of local governments are run without the intervention of political parties. Municipal governments (*municipios*) are numerous in the state of Oaxaca. There are 570 municipios in the state, 23 percent of all the municipios in Mexico. The majority of Oaxaca's municipios (418) are governed by their own customary law, referred to as *usos y costumbres*. Such customs often involve a general assembly in which outgoing village officials and the general public propose new candidates. The internal structure of communities can vary, but customary law requires local residents to fill public offices as a part of their responsibilities of participation in their communities (see Stephen 2005c; Kearney and Besserer 2004). In San Agustín Atenango, these local offices are split between those filled by candidates who are elected as part of a party slate (PRD or PRI) and those who are named in a community assembly. Those offices elected through candidates running as part of local party tickets include *presidente municipal*, or mayor, *síndico*, or legal advisor to the mayor, and four *regidores*, or councilmen, for financial reporting, education, health, and public works. Each of these offices has a *suplente*, or alternate. Offices elected through community assemblies that all men and women eighteen and over can participate in include five *principales*, or elders, who form a council of elders who also each have an alternate, eight *comandantes de policias*, or police commanders, four *mayores de vara* (police captains), five *mayores principales*, three *topiles*, or police, and several committees of four to five members each whose jurisdictions include water, communal lands, and security (see Kearney and Besserer 2004 for variations on this system).

In 2004, Daniel was having a particularly hard time getting people to serve in the more demanding offices, such as presidente municipal and *alcalde* (judge). Although all of the offices have paired alternates that in reality function as co-officeholders—often literally called *compañeros*—it is a great hardship for members of Oaxacan communities who now live in other parts of Mexico or in the United States to return for one to three years in order to fill offices. As we will see below in the discussion of Teotitlán, it is a great hardship for those who remain as well. As noted by Kearney and Besserer, for the most part people do return to fulfill their responsibilities, but at significant cost (2004: 453).

Mariano González, a neighbor of Daniel's in San Agustín Atenango who I met in Salem, Oregon, described the hardship he suffered by having to return to be commissioner of communal lands (*comisariado communal*) in the 1980s. Mariano first came to the United States in 1979 from San Agustín and was followed by his wife and six oldest children in 1994. When we first met in 2002, Mariano was eating lunch with his family. His striped, button-down shirt was neatly pressed and hung, untucked, over his khaki trousers. When Mariano finished eating, he picked up his six-month-old grandson and held him in his lap so the boy's mother could eat. A single mother, she lived with her parents. Mariano continued to hold the baby throughout the first thirty minutes of our conversation. He rose to move to the living room, where he sank into a corner of the couch. Fifty-five at the time of our conversation, Mariano had hair that was still black with only a little gray. His face was relaxed and often sported a gentle smile. He was a thoughtful talker who often paused to try out the words in his mind before speaking them. In order to lead up to the difficult situation that was created for him by having to return to San Agustín, he began by telling me about the importance of land and how he came to work in the United States and had to return.

MARIANO: The land we have was obtained for us by our ancestors for everyone. We have *terrenos comunales*, communal lands for all. We can all use these lands if we need gravel or sand from the rivers, firewood, or other products from the trees. No one owns the land or even the trees. We have an agreement that we are all the owners . . . but this land is also not so good for agriculture. There are palm trees also. We cut out short palm trees and use the palm leaves to weave hats. It is something many people do.

My parents wove palm hats. My father also taught me how to work in the fields with a team of oxen. He taught me how to plant corn beginning every year in May and June. On June 24, we ask God to bring rain to the fields.

[At this point in the conversation, Mariano stands up and begins to pantomime how corn is planted. He walks down the middle of the living room with his hand out, illustrating how three seeds—corn and squash and beans—are planted together. At this point I notice that Mariano Junior is wearing a T-shirt that says "Porsche" on it. On the TV a young woman bends provocatively over a man. Mariano Junior is watching intently as I follow the motions of his father demonstrating how to plant seeds. Mariano continues:]

One person walks behind the oxen and they plant three seeds with each step. They have to be planted very precisely. If it is planted too close together, it will not grow well.

LYNN: How is it that you came to the United States?

MARIANO: You know, I didn't really have any choice other than coming to the United States. I barely went to school. I went to primary school for four years. That was all we had in out community at the time—four years. My parents never went to school. I went to school and then went to work in the fields. There was no work for me there as a young man. So in 1978, I went to Ensenada, Mexico. Two of us went up there from my hometown. I went there with a friend. Then later we crossed over the border at Tijuana. It wasn't as hard as it is now. I went up to North Plains, near Hillsboro, Oregon, Sandy, and Moscow [small agricultural towns in Oregon and Idaho]. I was picking strawberries, blackberries, blueberries. They paid us by the box.

LYNN: Where were you living?

MARIANO: I was living on the farms where I worked. They gave us a place to live—more or less. Usually we had bunk beds—one stacked on top of the other. There was a stove. I had to really struggle to cook. I was alone. We used to go to Safeway to buy food and then do the best we could as single men to cook. My wife wasn't with me. She was living with my parents.

I used to send her money and she used it to build a house with a clay tile roof and cement walls. Before that we used to live in a kind of house called a Chinami in Mixteco. This is a house made out of dried organ cactuses for walls and a cane roof. So with the money I sent my wife she built this house. It only has two bedrooms and a living room, but it was something for us.

In 1981 I had to go back to San Agustín because I was named to the cargo of commissioner of communal lands. If you are in the United States and they call you, you have to go home. I was there for more than five years. So I was there in San Agustín in 1986 when everyone in the United States was busy fixing their papers [a reference to the 1986 amnesty law under the Immigration Reform and Control Act—IRCA]. I didn't actually come back to the United States until 1988. I bought some papers that said I had been working in the United States. They sold me these papers on a farm where I used to work near Sandy, Oregon. These papers said that I had been working there during 1985 and 1986. The owner of the farm went to court for doing this. A lot of people wanted the letters he was selling and the court didn't like this. He gave out a lot of letters to people and the court didn't like that . . .

. . . When I came back in 1988, I first picked grapes in Madera, California. Then I went to San Luis Reyes and picked strawberries. Then I went to Santa Maria, California, to work in the strawberries. Then I went up to Madera again to harvest grapes and work in the vineyards. In 1990 I went to Oceanside. There I worked on a big military base in the cafeteria. I prepared their orange juice, their milk, I ran the dish-washing machine, took out the garbage, and put the dishes away.

In 1992 I left to go to Mexico for a few months to see my family who were in San Agustín. I came back in with my green card. In 1994 I brought my family here. They came over with a coyote and I was able to come over with my green card. I wanted them all to come here, especially my kids so they could learn English and go to school here. I wanted to live with my family. But in 1997 when they punched my green card to show it wasn't any good any more, I couldn't return. So none of us have papers.

First I had a green card, but then later they punched it to show that it was no good because the guy who gave the letter to me had these problems with the court. So since that time in 1997, I have not had any papers. Missing out on the amnesty was a real problem for me. It happened because I had to return to San Agustín.

As Mariano indicates, he has been unable to legalize his residency, and his entire family remains undocumented. This is due to the fact that a former employer was prosecuted for selling fake letters to workers validating their presence in the United States during the period that qualified them for legalization under the 1986 IRCA law. Mariano had a legitimate green card for almost a decade, but it was invalidated when the grower who sold the letters was prosecuted. Because he returned to fulfill his cargo during the period when he would have qualified for the amnesty program without having to purchase a letter, he missed out on a chance to have long-term legal residency. This has affected his ability to return to Mexico and makes it very difficult for him to return to fulfill another cargo obligation.

Apart from the civil offices that are filled by candidates elected through the party platform and others elected in community assemblies, there are a series of *mayordomías*, or cult celebrations of local saints and virgins that also have to be filled along with their attendants. Traditionally, San Agustín Atenango had about nine mayordomías every year, each with an accompanying *tendero* (attendant) and a *diputado mayor* (senior delegate). By 2004, only two or three of the mayordomías could be filled. While previously couples would take on one of the attending roles before becoming a mayordomo, now they move right into mayordomías with little or no experience. The same is true of the civil cargo offices discussed above.

While traditionally young men (and now a few women) cycled through civil and religious offices in order of difficulty, accumulating necessary knowledge along the way, this is no longer the case because hundreds of people live outside of San Agustín. Outgoing Presidente Municipal Marcos Sánchez Martínez, age thirty-six, explained how difficult it was to find people who had experience and were willing to make a one- to three-year commitment to fulfilling their cargos. When we spoke in 2004, Marcos was sitting behind his official desk as presidente municipal with his hands folded in front of him. His curly hair cascaded over his ears and over his forehead as he leaned forward and earnestly relayed the problems of trying to put together an experienced government in a population that is often absent:

> Everyone who has the capacity to serve and has lived here for at least three years is expected to fulfill cargo positions. The problem is that a lot of them don't have what is needed. The people who have the most experience and whom people have the most trust in are living in the north. If you look at those of us who are in the municipal government now, we are babies. That is what they told us when we started. Here's my story.
>
> I first went to Ensenada when I was sixteen. I stayed there and worked for five years. Then I came back here for a little bit and then I went to Seattle where I have been for quite a while. Then I got this cargo of presidente municipal. It is a problem because those of us who are living away don't know about the customs here. I never even had one cargo here. I never went up the ladder of cargos. Now no one does this. Before, everyone learned about the cargos and the mayordomías by doing the minor ones first. No more. . . . We have a lot of problems getting young men to serve as topiles or mayors de vara. Look now, we only have a few topiles. We used to have a dozen or more. All the young men are gone.

Marcos ended his term as mayor at the end of 2004 and returned to Seattle. The new mayor is a local teacher, one the few people who was already living in the community who took up a cargo post in 2005.

San Agustín Atenango Histories and Migration

The twin traditions of civil and religious cargos in San Agustín are historically rooted in the political and religious governance structures found in many indigenous communities. Established on its current site sometime during the late 1700s or early 1800s, San Agustín was originally known as San Jacinto. According to local elders, a huge rainstorm filled up all the riverbeds with water, and everyone had to leave after the town flooded.

While younger men such as Marcos make no bones about their lack of knowledge about customs and tradition, San Agustín in not lacking in local historians. During my visit to San Agustín in the summer of 2004, Marcos and others serving out their cargos in the city hall strongly encouraged me to visit Juan Gómez and several other local elders. Marcos sent one of the principales, José Luis García López, with me to translate, as all of the elders I was instructed to visit were monolingual in Mixtec, which I was just beginning to learn. José Luis has white hair which sprouts in tufts from under his broad-brimmed hat. He has bushy white eyebrows and sports a large white mustache and mutton chops which curve upward to match his friendly smile and relaxed manner. José Luis walks quickly for a man sixty-eight years old and is in excellent physical shape from his daily walks to the countryside to tend his corn-fields. I push myself to walk faster as I scamper up the hillside following him to Juan's house, which is perched high up in front of a spring that feeds into a larger river below.

The front door of Juan's house is open, and he is sitting in the fading light weaving a complex tortilla basket of plastic pseudo-palm in several colors with a bird design worked into it. He has thick glasses and wears a thin, orange cotton shirt that is opened several buttons. It is still quite warm, so we all sit by the door to enjoy the rising breeze. Juan has folded himself onto a small stool as he sits facing the setting sun. José Luis sits next to him, often leaning in to catch all of his words. Juan began to tell the story of his community:

> When the riverbed filled up with water in the really big canyon on the other side of the road where the town used to be, they found the image of San Agustín. After that they also found two small saints which are now on either side of the large San Agustín in the church. They went to Huajuapan de León to ask what it was that they found. They say that these people spoke

with the priest there. Then they went all the way to Mexico City. There, they told them that it was San Agustín that they had found. The priest came all the way back here from Mexico City, and they built houses for the saints. These little houses for them were not even made out of tiles. They were made out of nothing but palm. The house they made for the priest was also made out of palm, like all of the houses here. They started building the church way back then—the first date on it is 1810—but they didn't finish the church until I was a kid, about sixteen years old in 1926.

According to Juan's history, the completion of the church was interrupted by the Mexican Revolution. His childhood memories of the revolutionary period were of roving Zapatistas who came to rob his and other neighboring communities several times. In some Oaxacan communities the Zapatistas were popular, but not in San Agustín (see Stephen 2002: 254–63, 280–84). Juan continued:

> Some men came to steal from those people from the town of Santa María Asunción. They stole cows, burros, corn, and everything. People from Santa María came here to inform people about what was going on. They went with some people from here to kill those who had robbed the animals. They were Zapatistas who robbed Santa María. People were Carrancistas, here and in Silacayoapán. Those Zapatistas really got pissed off at those people who killed their fellow Zapatistas. So they came here and they stole more animals, burros, cows, bulls, corn, clothing, money, and even people's shoes. Then they left and went into the mountains. They came back here several more times.

After the Mexican Revolution the people of San Agustín returned to their lives as subsistence farmers. According to local oral history, in the early 1920s a representative from the community went to Oaxaca to seek formal titling for San Agustín's communal lands. It took until 1947 for San Agustín to receive formal resolution of its land because of boundary conflicts with several surrounding communities, including Santa María Tindú and San Vicente de Palmar. According to the presidential resolution to end the border conflicts, the communal land base of San Agustín was originally defined in a bill of sale dated August 24, 1867 (Periódico Oficial 1947: 422). In 1947, this resolution, signed by the Mexican president Miguel Alemán, legally recognized 8,451.10 hectares as the communal land base. The same document puts the local population at 910 people, with a total of 212 *jefes de familia*, or male heads of household.

Two hundred sixty-eight men over the age of sixteen are listed as eligible to receive rights to communal land in San Agustín. Populations from two other small towns encompassed within the limits of the communal lands were also included. San Mateo de Libres (now under the jurisdiction of San Agustín as county head) had a population of 865 people, with 30 male heads of household and 45 men over the age of sixteen eligible for rights to communal land. In addition, the small rancho of San Vicente de Palmar had a population of 57 people with 30 male heads of household and 46 males over sixteen eligible to receive communal land rights (Periódico Oficial 1947: 423). Altogether, 339 men over the age of sixteen were eligible to receive communal land. Only about 10 percent of the communal land was declared to be laborable, or arable, representing about 845 hectares. This worked out to an average of 2.49 hectares of land per eligible male, representing a small holding on land that was not irrigated. People working on these lands primarily planted corn, beans, and wheat "with low yields" (Periócico Oficial 1947: 23).[1] Thus even in the 1940s, when communal land rights were formally recognized, farmers from San Agustín were smallholders whose lands yielded little; sometimes, if the rains were not favorable, they did not yield anything. These kinds of conditions did not encourage men to stay and farm if they could earn cash as wage laborers elsewhere. While decades of land conflicts between San Agustín and its neighbors added to the uncertainty of farming, by 2006 all the conflicts had been resolved except one.

The primary source of cash for people from San Agustín was the weaving of palm products such as petates, or straw mats, but primarily of palm hats; an alternative was to leave the area to work as migrant laborers. Beginning at age eight, much of the community—both male and female—spent their extra hour weaving palm. Juan recalled:

> Before, when I was a child and young man everyone was busy making palm hats. I used to look after the animals and during the day while I was tending to them I would be making a sombrero. Sometimes I would finish two in one day. Those who stayed at home, maybe the women, they could get more done.

Hats were sold by the dozens to merchants in Huajuapan de León. When a family had a large enough load they would make the journey to Huajuapan with a burro, mule, or horse to sell the hats. If they didn't have a burro, they would pay someone to take the load. Juan recalled that if he left at 3 A.M. he would arrive in Huajuapan by 4 p.m with his burro. There, he would tie his burro up and look for someone to buy his hats.

At the same time that many people sold palm goods in Huajuapan, some began to migrate to Pinotepa Nacional in Oaxaca and to Orizaba and Cordoba to harvest coffee and sugarcane. Although Juan has never left San Agustín, he has seamlessly incorporated transborder migration into his local history. His telling of San Agustín's history is crossed with transborder social fields that began when he was a young man:

> When I was a young boy no one left. It was after the revolution that people began to leave. Before that, people were working here. But then people started to leave. A few of them went to harvest sugarcane. There were maybe about twenty or thirty people who started to go to Veracruz. That wasn't so many. But then they started being pulled toward Sinaloa. That is when almost everyone went away. All of the people would go together and it would be very empty here. There were only a few of us who stayed. Even the women didn't stay behind. Only the really old women didn't go. Even the young women went to Sinaloa. I never left. I just stayed here and watched sheep and goats. . . . When the people started going to Culiacán, to Sinaloa, that is when they stopped making the hats. Those who went to work there didn't make hats anymore. But for those of us who stayed it was all we could do. So now there are only a few of us who still know how. Then there were the people who went as contracted laborers to the United States [a reference to the bracero program]. They left too.

The history of migration also marks changes in the religious cargo system. Juan sat up and spoke with animated excitement when recalling the richness of community ritual life before "everyone starting going away." While there was little money to pay for the fiestas associated with the mayordomías, many people collaborated on them, and there was a rich musical and dance tradition that has since dwindled. In addition to migration, the emergence of several evangelical churches in the area has pulled people away from participation in the mayordomías. Juan continued:

> We used to name two mayordomos for every fiesta and two diputados as well. Not like now. And there were a lot of animals that people would sell to raise money. There wasn't any money like people have now. Now people who are not here send money to help with the fiesta. Before there wasn't any way to make money. There wasn't a lot of work, but people did their best. And before, there weren't three or four different kinds of religions and churches around. There were also cofradías.[2] So the mayordomo of the

cofradia was responsible for getting the musicians and the dancers. He had to find all of that. The really big fiestas were that of our patron, San Agustín, then the Divino Redendor and then the Virgen de Guadalupe. The town band would play. But now that doesn't exist any more. It was a way that people had to provide service to the town. They didn't earn any money, not one cent. But if their instruments needed to be repaired, then they gave them to the principales who would take them to Oaxaca to get repaired . . .

. . . We used to have a lot of principales who were part of an elder council. There used to be ten, fifteen, twenty principales. It's not like now where we have a bunch of political parties. All of the principales would go to the assembly. They would decide when it was going to be. And the people would go to the *asamblea* [village assembly].

LYNN: Did women go?

JUAN: No, just men. Women started to go to the asambleas not too long ago. What the women used to do was when there was going to be a fiesta, they would get together to plan that. It's all changed now.

Juan's history ends with sweeping changes in the local political system. Prior to larger scale migration to the United States and to other parts of Mexico, which began in the 1940s and 1950s, the local governance system was strongly influenced by a council of elders, referred to as principales, who provided advice to the officials in the mayor's office. They also advised the mayordomos. Juan also suggests a more public ritual role for women, who, he says, would meet together when a mayordomía was being planned. This structure brought about a decreasing role for the principales and the entrance of political parties in 1987, as outlined above by Daniel. Migration is a core element in Juan's local history, influencing the structuring of local governance and ritual. Behind Juan's historical view of San Agustín Atenango are the parallel histories of larger Mexico and the regions of the United States that drew those "who went away" beginning in the 1940s.

Gender, Migration, and Local Governance
in Teotitlán del Valle

It is high noon in July and the sun is burning hot in Juana López's courtyard off to the side of the two-lane road that winds its way into Teotitlán del Valle from the Pan-American Highway. Two American importers sit with Juana in the shaded overhang to her weaving workshop. She lives there with her mother and her grown son. Her brother, who used to live with them, is married and now resides in Irvine, California, where he is raising four children. Juana has a cousin who has lived in Chicago for twenty years as well. President of one of the longest-standing women's weaving cooperatives in Teotitlán, Juana has become a major broker for women weavers in Teotitlán. Today, she is trying to convince two Texas importers that they should not only purchase her weavings, but also place an order with the cooperative she currently is president of.

From the mid-1980s to the present, women and, later, men organized themselves into cooperatives in an attempt to deal directly with U.S. consumers and importers without having to sell their work through local merchants. By 2005, roughly 10 percent of Teotitlán's population was organized as part of a cooperative, about five hundred people. Cooperatives serve as a source of moral support for members, who sell each other's weavings. Members of cooperatives may also purchase primary materials collectively, take workshops together, and in some cases offer rotating credit to one another (see Stephen 2005a, 2005b). Today, Juana is trying to convince the two Texas women to trust in the cooperative as a group.

Juana's hair is pulled back into a long, thick braid trailing down her broad back. Her face is animated as she shows pictures of the wide range of designs the group can produce—from local geometrics inscribed in the stones in the pyramid uncovered by the colonial church to reproductions of Diego Rivera's paintings. She emphasizes how the women in her cooperative employ natural dyes that their ancestors used before the arrival of the Spanish. Juana's face bears the trace of a smile as she repeatedly emphasizes the quality of the women's work. The two women from Texas, one blond and the other brunette, nod and confer with one another rapidly in English. Juana listens intently to extract some of the English words she knows. The two women decide they need more time. They get up, walk to their car, and drive back toward the Pan-American Highway. Juana waves and retreats to the shade.

Born in 1960, Juana went to Mexico City in 1975, at the age of fifteen, to be a domestic worker. At that time, some women from Teotitlán were migrating to the United States to join relatives, but most who left as young girls or recently married women went to Mexico City as domestic workers. Others went to the border area to help care for children and work in stores that Teotitecos had set up to attract tourists who drove over the U.S.-Mexican border for a day to "see Mexico." Many simply got married at the age of fifteen or sixteen and began to have children shortly thereafter. Juana's story was different:

JUANA: I didn't get married when I was sixteen. I was working. I wanted to weave, but I didn't have a loom. I was sharing with my father, and I always had to wait until he was done. So I went to Mexico City to work so that I could buy my own loom. I went with a friend who was already working there. I asked her to help me find someone who would give me work. I found work in someone's house. I did all of the work in the house. I got up at six in the morning to do all of the chores. I had to bathe the children, get them dressed, get them breakfast and then they went to school. While they were in school I had to clean the house. I had to make the beds and then when the kids came home from school I had to feed them. Their mother didn't do much. She would always go out. She went to "El Club"—a country club. I did this for nine years from 1975 until 1984 in the same house. . . . I used to think that I had found a good job, but now I realize that I didn't. I was working all day long without stopping. When I came back to Teotitlán, I also came back with a child.

LYNN: Was it hard to come back with a child?

JUANA: Yes. It was really difficult because at that time people were really critical. It was hard for my parents to accept me. I don't know if it was good luck or not, but my sister had gotten married and moved to the United States. I think that because there were no more children at home and she was gone that my parents allowed me to move back in with my son. . . . It's very hard. I think it might be a little easier now because people's mentality has changed. But eighteen years ago everyone in this town would realize when there was a single mother. There were so many comments made to me at the time that I didn't even want to leave the house. . . .

LYNN: Is it different now? There are quite a few young women who return with children and young women may be more independent when they live in the United States.

JUANA: I do think it has changed. People aren't going to make those kinds of public comments now. Things have changed a lot, not just when people go to the United States, but here as well. Now, girls who are fifteen or sixteen years old can go to a dance and dance with their boyfriend. You didn't use to be able to do that. Before if a girl were even seen with a boy, people would go to her parents and say, "Your daughter was hanging out with so and so." The parents would get upset and might even beat their daughter.

LYNN: So it has changed. What happened after you returned in 1984 and moved in with your parents?

JUANA: Well, no one expected it, but my father died. My father died really young, and he was extremely fond of my son. He was the first grandchild. It was really hard when he died. It was just me, my son, and my mother. So I started working as a pieceworker for a local merchant. I would finish my tapete [weaving], get paid, and then he would give me more yarn to make another piece. I worked this way for almost eight years. I never liked working that way and thought there should be a better way to get by.

LYNN: When did you start to participate in the cooperative?

JUANA: It was in 1992. One of the members from the original group invited me to participate. They said that they were interested in having me join the group. They told me that they had organized the cooperative to support the women who had the most necessities. I said, well, if there is a group that is ready to support me then I can work with them. I went to a meeting to see how they functioned as a group and to see what the requirements were for joining. I've been with them ever since.

The main reason I joined was so that I didn't have to keep working as a pieceworker for a merchant here. I didn't want to keep selling my work that way. I wanted to find a way to sell my textiles directly. The other reason is that we share a lot together. We have to learn how to work out our differences, but we also share ideas. We teach one another and have really helped one another to learn and improve our situations . . .

. . . I went through a really hard time after my father died. I had to talk to my son and my mother to get them to understand why the cooperative was important as a way to support ourselves. We were in a really bad situation. We didn't even have money for making tortillas to sell. We went to get firewood to sell. We would do anything. We struggled really hard just to survive. My son finally said to me, well if you think that in the cooperative you will have more chances for helping us to get ahead, then I agree.

We went to talk to my mother so that she would understand. She said, "But what about the people who see you going alone to Oaxaca to sell? What are they going to think? They will say her father is dead now so that she just goes anywhere with anyone." This was really hard for me because people really said this about me and the other women. But we put up with it. My mother finally understood and some other people slowly too . . . it is really hard for the married women in the group. But we continued. We are still here.

Juana and other women in her group were among the first women to vote in municipal elections in 2000. While women had traditionally been excluded from Teotitlán's community assemblies, slowly in the late 1980s, some women from the newly formed cooperatives began to be invited to attend community assemblies. A number of the women who were leaders and pioneers in the cooperative movement in Teotitlán were migrants, primarily in Mexico City, and like Juana they labored as domestic workers. Their experiences outside of Teotitlán led many of them to question gender roles within the community. Standards of acceptable behavior for young women appear to be shifting in limited but often contradictory ways, as cited by Juana. Young girls can now go to dances to meet with boys, can talk with boys on the street, and if they become pregnant while unmarried will be able to integrate themselves into community life with less stigmatization than fifteen or twenty years ago—but they still have to watch out for their reputations. As an active member of a cooperative who went to meetings at night and traveled outside of the community unaccompanied, Juana continually had to justify what she was doing to her mother and others as well, assuring them that she was engaging in cooperative business, not sneaking off to an illicit romantic liaison.

In Teotitlán ideas about governing young women's sexuality also seem to be influenced by the standards emerging for young women who migrated to the United States. There, young women seem to try to maintain public images of being *mujeres decentes* (good women) through serial monogamy as they become pregnant without spouses and have common-law marriages or formally marry later after having children. This model resonates with that described by Zavella of a childhood marked by overwhelming silence regarding sexuality (2003: 235–36) and a contradictory context in which "Catholic-based patriarchal ideas and practices in Mexico and the United States create ambiguous notions regarding women's bodies and constrain their views of pleasure" (Zavella 1997; Castañeda and Zavella 2003: 126–27). Thus young women from Teotitlán are often out of the view of their parents while in the United States or other parts of Mexico but continue to be constrained by Catholic-based notions of proper womanhood and the importance of maintaining a good reputation. Other researchers such as Gloria González-López have suggested that as Mexican immigrant women become mothers, they develop a concern about protecting their daughters from sexual oppression. Based on a study of immigrant women from Jalisco and Mexico City living in Los Angeles, González-López found that as mothers, these women "explore ways in which they can safeguard a new generation of women while challenging and/or protecting them from the forms of sexual and gender inequality that they themselves experienced (e.g., ethics of *respeto a la familia* [maintaining family respect through women's reputations—my translation], feelings of guilt after sex)." While some of them promote sexual autonomy and agency through sexual education and impose less restrictive sexual moralities, "the presence of sexism (*machismo*) and mainly protestant religious values regarding virginity permeate some of these mothers' ideas about virginity" (2003: 221). González-López's findings suggest the importance of looking at how the gender and sexuality socialization of second- and third-generation Mexican immigrant women has changed. In transborder communities like Teotitlán and San Agustín Atenango, it seems important to look at both what is happening in home communities as well as in places where migrants have settled, either in other parts of Mexico or in the United States or both.

Zavella has introduced the useful concept of "peripheral vision" as a way to envision how young women in the United States and in Mexico keep track of norms and family expectations in simultaneous locations (2000). As stated by Castañeda and Zavalla (2003: 131), "Whether they reside in Mexico or in the United States, migrants imagine their own situation and family lives in terms of how they compare el otro lado (on the other side of the border)."

Since migration rates for young people increased in the 1990s, some young women have eloped transnationally, often beginning with a taxi ride to Oaxaca. From there, they either flew or took the bus to Tijuana, where they hooked up with known coyotes, with their cross-border journey often arranged by relatives already in the United States. In some cases, young couples may have originally become engaged in an official engagement ceremony but wanted to proceed with a civil marriage before a church wedding. If the parents resist, the couple may go to the United States and proceed to live together there.

Rosa Gómez, who left home at the age of nineteen to follow her boyfriend to California and then Oregon, explained to me in 2004 how she ended up as an unwed mother living with her boyfriend. She has since gotten married in the United States, but primarily for the benefit of her parents. She felt pressure coming from her peripheral vision toward Teotitlán to maintain her reputation as a mujer decente. As stated by

Castañeda and Zavella (2003: 134), "While the virgin–whore cultural discourse has been eroded by a number of social forces, its salience can be seen in the ways in which these women subscribe to notions of silence about sexuality, the importance of virginity prior to marriage, and guarding their reputations as 'mujeres decentes' (good women)." Rosa's discussion reflects all these concerns:

> I didn't think I would get pregnant. Jorge and I were so in love and he kept asking me. So I thought it would be okay just once before he left for the United States. I didn't think anything would happen. Then I found out I was pregnant. I knew my parents would be so upset, so I didn't tell them and I left secretly to join Jorge. . . . We were going to tell our parents, but it was just too hard. Now they know about the baby and its okay, but they still want us to return and get married. We will get married by the law, but they are old-fashioned and don't understand this. It is easier for me to be in the United States now.

As the number of female migrants increases, more and more younger women are entering into common-law marriages that follow a pattern of serial monogamy in the places where they live outside of the community —Tijuana, Rosarita, Los Angeles, Santa Ana, Oxnard, and elsewhere. After some years, a couple may decide to return to Teotitlán and go through the traditional series of ceremonies culminating in a wedding. These women and many young men are no longer under the authority of their parents and can choose their own sexual partners. Even in such situations, however, women are still concerned about their sexual reputations. Cohabitation is considered a legitimate form of sexual expression; having multiple sexual partners is not. Young men are discouraged from having sexual affairs when married, but in contrast to women are often told to experiment before they settle down. These kinds of changes in gender roles and sexuality are related to migration work in combination with shifts happening inside the community such as women's recent participation in the formal political system.

Like San Agustín, Teotitlán's political system is historically rooted in a civil-religious cargo system. Before 1917 in Teotitlán and elsewhere, this system of religious cargos remained outside of state control. Because the religious cargo system was linked closely to the civil cargo system in the first two decades of the twentieth century, ritual authority stemming from men's and women's experience as mayordomos transferred into other kinds of authority as well. Women who were mayordomos continued to exercise political authority, although indirectly. The council of elders regulated who became civil authorities as well as naming mayordomos.

In 1917, the Mexican constitution specified that civil office positions, or what are called civil cargos in municipios, had to be elected by village assemblies, or *asambleas*. Thus the councils of elders, including those in Teotitlán and San Agustín, slowly lost their authority to name local religious and civil authorities. The pre-1917 civil cargo system in Teotitlán had about forty cargos linked to between nineteen and twenty-one mayordomías celebrated in the community's ritual calendar. After the revolution and imposition of the new constitution, the civil cargo system changed considerably, particularly with the addition of a wide range of committees named to support national education and development schemes. Under increased national government scrutiny, by the 1930s the local governance system of Teotitlán del Valle came to resemble that of other Oaxacan municipalities. Political parties never did and still do not participate directly in local elections in Teotitlán, as they do in San Agustín. All local officials are named in community assemblies.

Beginning in 2000, the assemblies were attended by both men and women. The *ayuntamiento*, or governmental branch, includes a presidente municipal, a síndico, three regidores, *jefes de sección* (neighborhood section chiefs—there are five neighborhood sections in Teotitlán), *primer vara* (police commander), mayores de vara, and ten topiles. Except for the topiles all of these offices also have suplentes. There are two paid positions in the ayuntamiento, a secretary and treasurer. In addition, there is a wide range of local committees for the primary school, the secondary school, and the health center and for running water, irrigation, fire fighting, and organization of government holidays. Other committees for public works projects are created on an ad hoc basis. The judicial branch of the government includes two alcaldes and four suplentes (see Stephen 2005b: 244).

By 2004, the number of cargo positions totaled approximately 250. Each independent household in Teotitlán is obligated to provide cargo service every three years or so. Gradually, beginning in the 1980s, women were named to local committees, such as the kindergarten, elementary, and secondary school committees, health committee, and a committee linked to the federal government's Sistema Nacional para el Desarollo Integral de la Familia (DIF/Family Development Agency). By 2004 more women were on these committees and were also participating in significant numbers in the *assembly of comuneros*, the decision-making body of those who hold communal land rights. As women came to serve on some of the local governance committees, their labor was counted for their household's participation in the local governance system. As the number of women's cooperatives and then mixed and men's cooperatives grew in the 1990s (see Stephen 2005a), the cooperatives were also formally recognized as part of the community governance structure, and their members were invited to attend community assemblies.

In the 1940s, male participation in the bracero program drained Teotitlán of approximately two hundred men for several years. After that, dozens continued to work as braceros or returned to the United States as undocumented workers. This period coincides with the slow decline of the mayordomía system, so that by the early 1970s the number of mayordomías celebrated was down to four or five from the original nineteen to twenty-one. By the mid-1980s, only one major mayordomía was being celebrated. With the acceleration in migration to the United States begun in the mid-1980s and spurred on by the granting of residency to dozens of Teotitecos in 1986, mayordomías almost came to a halt. The last remaining mayordomía of the Preciosa Sangre was celebrated once in 1989–90 and again in 1998–99. No mayordomía has been celebrated since 1999.

In addition to the requirement that all households participate in the civil cargo system, all residents—male and female—are required to provide volunteer labor for community projects, known as *tequio*. For men, this often involves physical labor, such as digging ditches for a new drainage system or hauling sand from local riverbeds for construction projects. For women, it may involve food preparation and serving for public events, cleaning, providing ritual drinks, or other more traditional female work. Often people will be asked to perform from three to five days of tequio per year. With up to 20 percent of the community absent at any one time, tequio requirements cannot be met by all. For the past fifteen years, it has become acceptable to pay someone else to perform one's tequio or to simply pay the mayor's office the equivalent of a day's labor so that someone can be hired.

While Teotitlán has not had the same degree of difficulty in finding qualified individuals to serve in civil cargos that San Agustín has, conflicts have emerged over people's assuming cargo offices such as presidente municipal without having the requisite experience and knowledge of local customs. In 1999, when a well-respected local man turned down his election to be presidente municipal because of a land dispute, the community decided to name as mayor someone who had been living in Mexico City for two decades but who was well educated and connected. During his tenure in office there was great dissatisfaction with his style of governance and his ignorance of local custom and tradition. People said "He's not connected to our town. He has a different mentality." Mariano Gonzalez, a sixty-year-old Teotiteco with broad cargo experience explained to me:

> Well they were going to name this guy as presidente (mayor). He had a lot of cargo experience. But he didn't want to. He was mad because he said that the community took away a piece of his land. He didn't want to take on the cargo. But the person we ended up with, he doesn't know anything about how to run the municipio. He doesn't know the customs and he doesn't know how to make the necessary sacrifices. Now he doesn't have the people's respect. He doesn't have authority. Things don't work here like they do in Mexico City.

In September 2001, with the support of a majority of women, a different mayor, Felipe Sánchez, was elected. A long-standing subsistence farmer, he was respected by all and viewed as someone who was extremely well informed about local custom and tradition. Even his ceremonial Zapotec was flawless. He had never left Teotitlán. While most people felt positively about his administration, others stated that he didn't have enough outside experience. His administration included two return migrants who had lived for lengthy periods of time in the United States. It was hoped that as a team they would have sufficient knowledge to govern wisely. By the end of his administration in 2005, many felt that he didn't know enough about how to interface with the national government and had been taken advantage of by two other people in his administration.

During the summer of 2001, a month before he was elected as presidente municipal, Felipe and I talked at length in his home. I had gotten to know him and his family well when I lived in Teotitlán during the mid-1980s. Our conversation was permeated by the influences of migration in the community, even though Felipe had never left. On the day we spoke, he had left at 5:00 A.M. to walk several kilometers out to his cornfields. He had two oxen and at the time was taking them out to plow the weeds under. I was waiting for him with his wife, mother, and five daughters when he returned. Felipe walked quietly into the courtyard with his broad-brimmed hat pulled down low over his face to protect him from the sun as it rose in the sky. His face was moist from sweat, but not flushed. Felipe has glowing dark eyes set deep into his face, which is creased by his lifetime in the sun. He wore a light green cotton button-down shirt open at the neck. His *huaraches,* traditional sandal-like leather footwear with tire-tread sole, were slightly caked with mud. He sat down at the table and began to drink atole, a thirst-quenching corn-based drink. On the table were dishes of beans, tortillas, and the seasonal dried grasshoppers of August. It had been more than ten years since I had had a sustained conversation with Felipe.

FELIPE: You know, I never left here. I never went to Mexico City or to El Norte, to the United States. Every since I was little I took care of goats and cattle. Then I got tired of doing this when I was eleven years old and I started working in the countryside planting corn. I also learned how to weave. When I would come back from the fields in the afternoons, I would weave.

LYNN: We haven't seen each other for awhile. What kinds of changes have you seen since we last talked?

FELIPE: Well, one thing you see now is that some people are really putting a lot of money into their personal parties, like quinceañeras [celebrations held when girls turn fifteen] for young girls, and weddings. They are getting really big. But not us. For the girls' quinceañeras we just had a meal here in the house. . . . Another thing that has changed is that before, after people had been married for about ten years, they would say, "Well, let's sponsor a mayordomía." They decide that it is time to start giving back to the community. Mayordomos are helping to take care of the gods, who in turn take care of us. When we had been married for eleven years we decided to take on the mayordomía of the Virgen of the Soledad. . . . It wasn't as big as the way they have parties for things like weddings now. We only had sixty people. Now if we had to invite everyone from my wife's and my family, all the relatives, it would be two or three hundred people. It would be way too big. Now no one wants to be mayordomos. Before, weddings used to be very small, but now they are big, like in the United States. The last mayordomos were three years ago. Who knows if there will ever be more?

The other thing that has changed is how people are taking on the civil cargos. Before, everyone went up the ladder of cargos. Now, like the current president, he was only a police captain. . . . Things have changed in the local asambleas as well. Now all of the young people speak up even though they have never done any cargos. Before, only those who were experienced expressed an opinion. Now people talk even if they just came back from the

United States. . . . and the political parties like the PAN [Partido de Acción Nacional/National Action Party] and the PRD are trying to get people to affiliate with them. That is why people are starting to fight. I never want the political parties to run our elections. The PRD says that it is going to make gains for workers. The PRI is leaving some people behind. Right now there still is respect shown in the community assemblies, but who knows what will happen in ten years if the political parties get involved. . . .

LYNN: What about the countryside? How is it for farmers?

FELIPE: Well, right know we are really screwed. Now that imported corn from the United States is coming in everywhere, it makes our corn—like the kind I grow—seem really expensive by comparison. It is impossible for people to make a living as a small farmer. Here and in other towns like Tlacocha-guaya, everyone is going to the United States. Here we have the option of weaving textiles, but that is still a hard way to make a living and people still leave . . .

. . . . you know before, the whole town was very closed. No one ever left. Now, everyone is leaving. Almost all the sons and daughters are going to the United States. Some of them go there to save their money. Who can blame them? They are looking for a way to survive.

A month after this conversation, Felipe was elected as presidente municipal of Teotitlán for a term running from 2002 through 2004. He had to stop farming, and his five daughters and wife did their best to support the household. After September 11, tourism decreased significantly in Teotitlán. Felipe built a small house next to the road leading into town in hopes that his five daughters could sell their textiles directly to tourists instead of to local merchants. They had some success in 2000, but in 2001 business fell off. Felipe's wife required major surgery, and his elderly mother also got very sick. His family worked extremely hard during the three years he was in office just to survive. In addition, they often had to prepare extra food and drink for visiting dignitaries. By the time his term was coming to a close in 2004, his daughters were seriously thinking about going to the United States.

Like that of Juan Gómez, Felipe's narrative about changes in Teotitlán's religious and civil cargo system suggests decreased participation in the system. Like San Agustín's, Teotitlán's system of mayordomías began to decline significantly in the period when migration increased. In the 1990s, the importation of subsidized U.S. corn to Mexico made it extremely difficult for small farmers like Felipe to make a living. This encouraged additional people to migrate to the United States. Unlike San Agustín, Teotitlán had a backup source of income to small-scale farming in its textile production. By the late 1980s, however, the export market for Teotiteco weaving had stopped growing. This resulted in increased competition locally and the end of possibilities for the creation of new small businesses built on exporting. As a result, prices paid by local merchants working with exporters in the United States decreased, and weavers were left with lower returns for their labor. The cooperative movement was one of the responses to this situation as explained above by Juana López.

Economic conditions that discouraged small-scale farming, decreased wages paid to pieceworker weavers (which encouraged migration, and prompted the formation of weaving cooperatives) also resulted in the increased participation of women in the formal political system. Although women lost their ritual link to formal politics through the elimination of the council of elders as a governing force in the 1930s and although mayordomías decreased in frequency, changes in gender roles among those living outside of Teotitlán that encouraged greater independence for women outside the home and to some degree condoned women's economic autonomy also affected expectations in Teotitlán. Women with migration experience organized weaving cooperatives to improve their economic situations and to form bases of support for one another. Eventually, these groups were recognized as part of the formal political structure of the community, and on that basis women were encouraged to attend community assemblies.

In Teotitlán, as in San Agustín, migration and shifts in the larger political economies of the United States and Mexico influence what happens in local religious, political, and economic relations in Oaxaca. Thus the social fields of economics, politics, gender, and religion encompass the broader transborder relations between people spread throughout Mexico and the United States. The abbreviated histories in this chapter, told both by people who have migrated and by people who have never left, vividly convey the long-standing links of Oaxaca to the rest of Mexico and the United States. Part of reenvisioning the ways in which transborder communities are remembered historically and experienced today by those who live in them requires us to rethink how we write histories. In order to understand the full historical context of San Agustín and Teotitlán in the twentieth and twenty-first centuries we need to extend our historical discussion to include other major sites where people reside. Envisioning communities such as San Agustín Atenango and

Teotitlán as transborder places must begin with a decentering of the United States and Mexico as separate entities and a refocusing on the region as an integrated whole which forms part of the Americas, traditionally carved up into North America, Central America, South America, and the Caribbean (see Stephen, Zavella, Gutmann, and Matos Rodríguez 2003).

CHAPTER 3

Mexicans in California and Oregon

Any rethinking of the position of states and nationalism in the lives of transborder migrants must reconceptualize how we think about the specific local spaces where Mixtec and Zapotec migrants settle in the United States. We can no longer think of the cultural and historical entity we call Mexico as existing solely below the Rio Grande and the rest of the physical border. In many of the cities and towns of California and Oregon where Mixtecs and Zapotecs from places like San Agustín and Teotitlán have settled there are sizable and sometimes dominant populations of Mexicans from earlier waves of migration or those who have simply always been there—as in the case of California. The numbers of Mexicans are so great in towns like Santa Ana and Oxnard, California, and Woodburn, Oregon, that we could speak of them as extensions of Mexico. In addition, the presence of so many Mexican immigrants has diversified the public space of many communities in terms of restaurants, businesses, schools, and cultural institutions as well as resulting in a wide range of emerging local institutions such as those described in chapter 8.

Waves of migration have re-created Mexico in these cities and towns. For indigenous migrants who settle in these areas, life often functions as a significant extension of their lives in Mexico in both positive and negative ways. In order to fully contextualize the experiences of transborder migrants, we need to look at the ways in which Mexican nationalism and culture are reconstructed within the boundaries of cities and towns in the United States by Mexicans themselves. An additional aspect of this context is the unique ways in which Mexicans have been constructed by non-Mexicans in particular regions of the United States.

In my work on the West Coast of the United States, I have thought long and hard about how to conceptualize the Mexican spaces of Oregon and California. One possibility would be to follow Nick De Genova's suggestion that cities with large populations of immigrants from Latin America be considered as a part of Latin America. He suggests the specific concept of "Mexican Chicago" in relation to the large number of Mexican immigrants there (De Genova 2005). Offered as a corrective to perspectives that see Latin America as being "outside the United States" and assimilation as being the logical and desirable outcome of migration, De Genova suggests that "rather than an outpost or extension of Mexico, therefore, the 'Mexican'-ness of Mexican Chicago signifies a permanent disruption of the space of the United States nation-state and embodies the possibility of something truly new, a radically different social formation" (2005: 190). Earlier, De Genova suggested that "the everyday life practices of migrant workers produce a living space in Chicago that conjoins it irreversibly to Mexico and renders it irretrievable for the U.S. nation-state" (1998: 89–90).

Politically, we need to be aware of how we package our discussion of transnational communities in light of such books as Samuel P. Huntington's *Who Are We? The Challenges to America's National Identity*, published in 2004. Huntington argues that Mexican and other Latin American immigrants are the most immediate and serious challenge to America's traditional identity—defined as Anglo-Protestant—because they fail to assimilate. "As their numbers increase, Mexican-Americans feel increasingly comfortable with their own culture and often contemptuous of American culture" (2004: 254). Huntington opens his book with a description of the American flag at half mast while other flags are raised and then moves directly into a description of a Mexico–U.S. soccer match in Los Angeles in 1998. Images of drunken Mexicans pelting garbage at the American team and at U.S. fans waving American flags prevail. This soccer match is not in Mexico City, Huntington notes, but in Los Angeles. He quotes an upset U.S. fan who feels he should be able to raise the American flag without provoking a response from Mexican soccer fans. This is the image of the future that Huntington implies— loss of American culture and even actual territory to Mexico and Mexicans. They will not assimilate, they will take over (2004: 5).

Many scholars have pointed out that much of the evidence points to the contrary—that within two generations many Mexican immigrants integrate numerous aspects of U.S. popular and consumer culture into their lives as well as learn to speak English (see Alba and Nee 2003; Alba 2004). Mexican immigrants pay taxes and Social Security, are serving in the U.S. military, and hold a wide range of jobs in the U.S. economy. In

2001 there were 109,487 Hispanics—many of Mexican origin—enlisted in the U.S. armed forces, 9.49 percent of the total (Krauze 2004: 32). More than 36,000 service members are noncitizens, making up about 5 percent of active duty service members. About a third come from Mexico and other Spanish-speaking countries (Ritthichai 2003). There are 1.1 million veterans of Hispanic origin (U.S. Census Bureau 2003b). Mexican immigrants are not beyond the reach of the U.S. state. In fact, they are within the reach of both the U.S. and Mexican states but are also creating unique cultural and political spaces that defy a purely national label, either Mexican or American.

One solution is to call spaces such as Santa Ana and Woodburn binational, a term that certainly gets at part of the context and experience of indigenous migrants who participate in such spaces. They mirror certain aspects of Mexico and Mexican nationalism and culture and also profoundly reflect American nationalism and culture. There is another dimension to them, however, which is not completely captured in the perspective of binationalism. Santa Ana and Woodburn are tied to regional specificities and histories, just as Teotitlán del Valle and San Agustín Atenango in Mexico are. Thus we need to think about fleshing out aspects of the translocal as well as the national highlighted by the concepts of transnational and binational. Translocal refers to the movement of place-specific culture, institutions, people, knowledge, and resources within several local sites and across borders—national and otherwise. In the case studies of the multisited communities of San Agustin and Teotitlán, *translocal* refers to the ties people retain to their communities of origin and to new communities they establish as they migrate in search of work. As the journalist David Bacon notes, "Those ties are often so strong, and the movement of people back and forth is so great, that in some sense people belong to a single community" which exists in different locations (Bacon 2003). Alejandra Castañeda provides a useful description of the shifting meaning of the local in transborder communities. She writes, "In the multilocational model the local is revalued as a space in flux, where meanings, cultural forms and practices are produced, transported, and reinscribed through the intensity of migration. The local is not only the place where migrants come from. The local is the space in which they live, which might be connected to various places in different countries" (2006: 12).

My chief concern in this chapter is to capture the relevant context of how Mexicans have been codified historically in the regional cultures of

California and Oregon in the past century and then to briefly sketch the various types of Mexican immigrants who have settled in both states; in relation to this, I want to make note of the complexity within the Mexican population in places like Woodburn and Santa Ana. Finally, in light of this later objective I want to provide some texture to those local spaces we might refer to as Mexican Woodburn and Mexican Santa Ana which transborder Zapotecs and Mixtecs have settled into. Here I focus on Mexicans in Woodburn and the construction of Mexican Woodburn. More broadly, the purpose of this chapter is to incorporate the histories of Mexicans in California and Oregon into the larger histories of transborder communities. In order to understand multisited communities we have to offer multisited histories.[1]

Mexicans in California

The modern State of California has a long of history of literally being Mexican. Claimed by Spain as part of its colony of New Spain from 1767 until 1822, California became part of independent Mexico in 1822. From 1822 until 1846, California functioned as a region of the Mexican nation, and the people who lived there, including indigenous peoples, were given the rights of Mexican citizens. Indigenous peoples who lived in California had lost sizable amounts of territory under the Spanish. A colonization law of 1833 gave the governor of California the power to distribute so-called vacant lands. The law also permitted the secularization of the twenty missions and the vast landholdings that had been established by the Spanish from San Diego to Sonoma along the California coast. Any native peoples who did not claim land as declared Mexican citizens could lose that land, which could then be granted to incoming Spanish settlers. The result was a short-lived system of vast ranches held by Californios (Californians) under Mexican land grants. In 1846, the United States invaded and conquered California. From 1846 until 1849, much of California was under American military rule during the U.S.-Mexican war.

In 1848, California was ceded to the United States by the Treaty of Guadalupe Hidalgo. Californians went from living in Mexico to living in the United States, leading to the saying, "We didn't cross the border, the border crossed us." In 1849, the California Constitution spelled out the legal requirements for voting, a privilege extended to "white males" (Menchaca 1995: 20). Tomás Almaguer suggests that after 1848, a new pattern of racialized relationships existed between U.S. conquerors, the conquered populations in California, and immigrants who settled in the new territory. Mexicans, he argues, were by and large conferred a "white" racial status because of their "Christian ancestry, a romance language, European somatic features, and a formidable ruling elite that contested 'Yankee' depredations" (1994: 4). Mexicans, he suggests, particularly the Californio elite, were viewed as "worthy of at least partial integration and assimilation into the new social order" (1994: 4). Native Americans were not considered U.S. citizens at the time and were not eligible to vote. Unlike Mexicans, "they were categorically deemed nonwhite, politically disenfranchised, and ruthlessly segregated from European Americans" in the new state of California (Almaguer 1994: 5). From 1850 to 1870, a state government campaign was waged to exterminate the "wild Indian tribes" of California, subsidizing private military forays against Indians that resulted in the murder of as many as eight thousand Native Americans (Almaguer 1994: 117–29, 5). According to Martha Menchaca, this left many Mexicans who were viewed as "Indian" subject to the same lack of rights (1995). Later in the twentieth century, racial labeling of Mexicans as Indians was also used as a basis for segregation in public schools as well as in housing.

The discovery of gold in northern California in 1849 brought a huge influx of people to the region, including Anglo-Americans from other parts of the United States and foreign immigrants such as Chileans, Peruvians, Basques, and Mexicans—particularly from Sonora. The Mexican population of Californians prior to the U.S. conquest was 10,000. With the influx of primarily Anglo migrants, the Spanish-speaking population of California was just 15 percent of the total in 1850 and only 4 percent by 1970 (Pitti, Castañeda, and Cortes 2004). The influx of migrants had a devastating result on the Native American population. Estimated at 150,000 in 1845, it decreased to just 16,000 by 1900 ("Key Moments in the Hispanic History of California" 2005). A combination of disease, loss of land and resource base, and forced migration was responsible for the decimation of the indigenous population.

In 1850, California was granted statehood. Soon thereafter, the Land Act of 1851 officially abolished the Mexican land grant system. The Homestead Act of 1862 gave settlers the right to claim land if they lived on it and made improvements. California courts seldom recognized the validity of Mexican land grants, and many people lost their land. The population of the state quadrupled in just a decade, growing from 92,000 in 1850 to 380,000 in 1860 (McWilliams 2000: 11). This burst of population needed to be fed, and as the gold rush died down it became apparent that the larger untapped potential of California lay in its agricultural production. The transcontinental railroad was finished in 1869, and this opened up the possibility of out-of-state shipment of produce. In the space of just a few decades, California land became monopolized by a small number of landowners who held vast tracts of land. Huge railroad grants, the transfer of large Mexican land grants to Anglo capitalists, and land speculation led to the concentration of 8,685,439 acres of land in the hands of just 516 men in 1861 (McWilliams 2000: 20). As white settlers and capitalists claimed more and more land, the Native American population and the Mexican-origin population became the labor force for Anglo-American farmers, mine owners, and cattle ranchers. As described by Menchaca, by the end of the nineteenth century, in many communities an "inter-ethnic subordinate-dominant employment structure evolved . . . in which Anglo-Americans became the owners of the land and Mexicans became the field hands" (1995: 19).

California agriculture made a transition from wheat and cereal crops to fruit and vegetables from the late 1800s into the twentieth century. This transformation was a result of the development of vast irrigation systems in the state that linked agriculture to banking and financial institutions. By 1929, so-called intensive crops represented four-fifths of the total value of California agricultural production (McWilliams 2000: 63). With this shift in production to intensive crops came a need for a reliable rural labor force. The need for a flexible force of farmworkers who were willing to work for low wages and who could be manipulated according to food industry and grower needs also became linked to U.S. immigration policy. The fluctuating need for cheap labor became part and parcel of immigration policy—essentially becoming a labor policy. This coupling of immigration policy to the needs of commercial agriculture continues to this day.

The first group of laborers to predominate in California agriculture was the Chinese. In 1886, Chinese workers were seven-eighths of the agricultural labor force (McWilliams 2000: 67). Carey McWilliams credits the presence of the Chinese in California as the vital factor in making the transition from wheat to fruit acreage possible. The Chinese were a despised minority who were excluded from mining and other labor sectors and viewed by growers as efficient workers who were expert pickers and packers of fruit. Despite the growers' favorable view of the

Chinese as terrific agricultural laborers, anti-Chinese sentiment grew. In 1882, the Chinese Exclusion Act prohibited the immigration of Chinese laborers for ten years. In 1888 the provision extended to all Chinese laborers. The Geary Act of 1892 called for the deportation of any Chinese who were in the United States illegally. Any citizen could file a complaint against a Chinese laborer who was not registered. As a result of the law and public riots against the Chinese, Chinese laborers were driven from the fields and either left the country or moved to the cities.

The development of the sugar beet industry at the turn of the twentieth century in California accounts for how the Japanese came to be the next dominant group in California agriculture, forming the majority of rural workers from 1900 through 1913. Japanese workers were quietly "invited" to California in the late 1800s. According to McWilliams, there were 2,039 Japanese in California in 1890, 24,326 in 1900, and 72,156 in 1910 (2000: 106). By 1909, about 30,000 Japanese were employed as farmworkers (2000: 106). As Japanese workers began to reclaim what had been seen as wasteland to grow rice, berries, and other crops, anti-Japanese sentiment began to grow in the state. The problem with the Japanese for many Californians was that they wanted to own their own farms. The 1907 "Gentlemen's Agreement" with Japan barred the entrance of Japanese workers, and the Alien Land Law of 1913 in California excluded aliens who were ineligible for citizenship (i.e., foreign-born Asians) from landownership and from leasing land for more than three years. The Alien Land Act drove the Japanese out of farming and into the cities. In 1917, a zone that barred Asiatics was created to exclude most Asians from the United States except the Japanese who were needed to harvest sugar beets. The Immigration Act of 1924, which excluded Japanese from entry, pushed the Japanese completely out of California agriculture. From 1907 through 1910 Hindustani workers known as "rag heads" were recruited to work in California fields. They moved rapidly into the landowning class and were subject to some of the same immigration bans as the Japanese. They were also excluded by the Alien Land Act. Armenians, Swiss, Italians, and Portuguese also worked as laborers initially but soon got into landowning as well. The situation of Mexican workers was different.

While some Mexicans and Native Americans continued to work in rural agriculture in some parts of the state in the late 1800s, they did not predominate as the numbers of agricultural workers necessary to support the labor-intensive fruit and vegetable industry increased. From

1910 through 1914, Mexican immigration to California and other western states increased significantly as people fled the Mexican Revolution. Approximately 10 percent of the Mexican population—over a million people—fled to the United States from 1910 to 1920, seeking not only refuge from the war but also economic opportunity (Sánchez 1993: 36).

While movement across the border was not strictly monitored before World War I, the creation of the Border Patrol in 1924 along with passage of quota laws in 1921 and 1924 quickly changed the nature of the U.S.-Mexican border from a porous, weakly defined demarcation to a multi-signified boundary. As Mae Ngai has written, "During the 1920s, immigration policy rearticulated the U.S.-Mexican border as a cultural and racial boundary, as creator of illegal immigration" (2004: 67). Immigration policy was contradictory, classifying from 20 to 30 percent of legal Mexican entrants during the 1920s and 1930s as nonmigrants (often as nonresident aliens intending to stay from six months to a year, usually as seasonally laborers). At the same time, the Immigration Service was apprehending nearly "five times as many suspected illegal aliens in the Mexican border area as it did in the Canadian border area" by the 1930s (Ngai 2004: 70).

From 1917 to 1922, the first temporary worker program (part of the Immigration Act of 1917) allowed temporary workers who would be inadmissible under the act to be contracted seasonally to work in the United States. This was enacted during World War I and extended until 1922. This temporary worker program served as a blueprint for the bracero program begun during World War II. Newspapers and farm journals from 1917 contain references to large groups of Mexicans being brought in to California by truck "to relieve the labor situation" (McWilliams 2000: 124). Although the temporary worker program ended in 1922, the importation of Mexicans to work in California agriculture continued. From 1924 to 1930, it was reported that an average of 58,000 Mexicans were brought into the state to work in the fields each year (McWilliams 2000: 124). According to the 1920 U.S. census, 86,610 Mexicans resided in California (Garcia: 2001: 60). By 1930, the Mexican population of California was estimated at 250,000. Mexicans predominated in the 200,000-person strong agricultural labor force (McWilliams 2000: 124–25). By 1926, 10,000 Mexican pickers worked in southern California citrus groves alone. By 1940 this number had grown to 23,000 Mexican men who labored in orchards, almost 100 percent of the workforce.

About 11,000 Mexican women packed citrus fruit in the south of the state (García 2001: 60).

Mexican labor was viewed as a desirable alternative to other immigrant labor because, in the words of the lobbyist S. Park Frisselle, who reported to the Fruit Growers Convention in 1927, "As you know, the Mexican likes the sunshine against an adobe wall with a few tortillas and in the off time he drifts across the border where he may have these things. . . . If charity spends one dollar on the Mexican in California, the State profits two dollars by having him here. The Mexican can be deported if he becomes a country charge, but the others are here to stay" (McWilliams 2000: 127). While large farms used Mexican labor during the growing season until the early 1930s, during the winter months workers went to nearby cities, where some received public and private assistance aimed at the poor.

It was not only the Immigration and Naturalization Service (INS) that acted to restrict the movement of Mexicans in the United States and to deport them in the 1930s, but also state and local authorities. During the Great Depression, local authorities through the Southwest and Midwest repatriated over 400,000 Mexicans during the early 1930s. Approximately 60 percent were children of American citizens by native birth (Ngai 2004: 72). By the Great Depression the population of Mexicans in the United States was over 1.4 million.

According to McWilliams, who published his book *Factories in the Field: The Story of Migratory Farm Labor in California* in 1935, "The last figures I had on the 'repatriations' indicated that in excess of 75,000 Mexicans had been shipped out of Los Angeles alone . . . but, when the harvest season once again came around, the growers dispatched their 'emissaries' to Mexico and again recruited thousands of Mexicans. Many Mexicans have been 'repatriated' two and three times, going through this same curious cycle of entry, work, and repatriation" (2000: 119). Thus despite the fact that Mexicans were "repatriated" to Mexico, many were then recruited again to work in agricultural labor. In southern California in the citrus-growing regions alone, 18,824 Mexicans and Mexican Americans were sent to Mexico. At the same time, 75,000 to 100,000 Mexican men, women, and children were reported to have made the citrus belt their home between 1930 and 1940 (García 2001: 108).

After the wave of "repatriations" of Mexicans in California, more than 350,000 rural Anglo adults from places like Texas, Arkansas, and Oklahoma migrated en masse to California. By 1937, 80 to 90 percent of farmworkers were Anglo-Americans (Menchaca 1995: 83). An oversupply of farm labor allowed growers to reduce wages by up to half, and many Mexicans were forced to seek employment elsewhere in urban areas. The Anglo domination of California farm labor was short-lived. In 1942, the immigration policy as labor policy trend continued. After the Depression ended and with the beginning of World War II, the demand for Mexican labor emerged again.

In order to bridge the gap between the increasing demand for agricultural workers and their decreasing numbers among the U.S. population, Public Law 45 was created to appropriate the necessary funds to implement an executive agreement with Mexico to import thousands—and eventually millions—of guest workers, or braceros. Although the bracero program was created to alleviate wartime labor shortages, it lasted until 1965. Millions more contracts were issued in the period after the end of World War II (4,746,231) than during the war itself (167,925) (Carrasco 1997; 203, n. 50). The bracero program allowed the importation of Mexican workers for annual harvests with the stipulation that they were to return to Mexico after their work was finished. Braceros were contract workers who were supposed to have certain guarantees met in terms of housing, transportation, wages, recruitment, health care, food, and the number of hours they worked. The contracts—initially negotiated directly between the U.S. and Mexican governments—even stipulated that there should be no discrimination against the braceros. However, compliance officers, including Mexican consular officials, were few and far between. Later contracts were switched to private contractors in the United States. Most growers and the U.S. government ignored the terms of the contracts, but the braceros had no recourse. The bracero program blocked farmworker unionization and has been called legalized slavery by some, including the last director of the program, Lee Williams.

California had the highest number of bracero workers of any state in the United States. According to Matt Garcia, between 1943 and 1947, California drew an average of 54 percent of the total braceros that came to the United States" (2001: 175). The year with the highest level of bracero importation into California was probably 1957, when

> more than 192,000 workers were brought to California, and more than 150,000 other workers to other parts of the nation. By the peak season of September 1960, around 100,000 braceros were at work in California, con-

stituting about 25 percent of the seasonal agricultural labor force. Most worked on the state's largest farms; slightly more than five percent of the farms in the state employed 60 percent of the seasonal workers, including more than 80 percent of the braceros. (Oakland Museum of California 2003)

California growers were one of the main reasons the bracero program lasted as long as it did. During the years of the bracero program, between 1942 and 1964, farm labor wages remained the lowest in the country, compared to similar manual work. In the 1950s, a farmworker could earn an annual income as low as $456, while the average farmworker income was $500 per year (Menchaca 1995: 91, Galarza 1964: 103). Braceros were consistently paid less than Mexican American workers for the same work. For example, in 1958 in the citrus orchards of Cucamonga, the hourly wage for Mexican American workers was between 80 cents and $1, but braceros were often paid between 10 and 15 cents less per hour. "By the end of the season, local workers earned an average weekly gross income of $43.20 compared with $38.40 for braceros" (Garcia 2001: 175). The lower wages paid to braceros were a source of resentment for Mexican American workers, who felt they kept overall wages down.

In 1964, civil rights and labor organizations succeeded in turning public opinion strongly against the bracero program, and it was ended by Congress. What this public discussion did not readily acknowledge was the long-lasting impact that the bracero program had already had on Mexican migration patterns to the United States and the ways in which the bracero program also encouraged what became widespread undocumented migration to the United States. In California, the period of the bracero program resulted in very significant increases in Mexican-origin population that settled in the state. For example, in Santa Paula, California, there were 824 Mexican nationals before 1942. By 1964 there were 3,095 Mexican nationals (U.S. Census Bureau 1942: 01; Menchaca 1995: 93).

In the shadow of the bracero program in the 1950s, a growing flow of undocumented workers (popularly known as "wetbacks") crossed over the border to work in the fields of California. Some estimate that more than 500,000 undocumented people worked on farms in California and other states in the region during this period (Oakland Museum 2003). Some scholars have argued that growers preferred *indocumentados* to bracero workers because they could be paid even less than braceros, could be encouraged to remain for as long as necessary, and, like braceros, could not organize or pursue collective bargaining agreements (García 2001: 186). In 1949 the Border Patrol seized nearly 280,000 illegal immigrants. By 1953, the number had grown to more than 865,000, and the U.S. government felt pressured to do something about the onslaught of immigration (PBS 2000).

The result was Operation Wetback, devised in 1954 under the supervision of a new commissioner of the Immigration and Naturalization Service (INS), Gen. Joseph Swing. In operation from 1954 to 1959, this INS "program" focused on preventing undocumented people from entering the United States and on rounding up and deporting those already here. Between 1954 and 1959, Operation Wetback was responsible for deporting over 3.7 million people of Mexican descent, some of them U.S. citizens (Carrasco 1997: 197; PBS 2000).

Mexican migration decreased during the late 1960s and early 1970s. This period was also the peak of organizing for U.S. farmworkers, particularly in California. After the bracero program ended in 1964, farm wages rose sharply. In 1962 César Chávez and Dolores Huerta founded the National Farm Workers Association (the precursor to the United Farm Workers Association, or UFW) to obtain better wages and working conditions for farm labor. In 1965, the National Farm Workers Association organized a boycott of California grape growers. By 1966, the United Farm Workers Association had won a 40 percent increase for grape pickers, increasing entry-level wages from $1.25 to $1.75 per hour (Martin 2003b: 5). For the first time, farmworker organizing was not eclipsed by wartime arguments that discouraged unionization (see Ganz 2000). Some of those who came under contract for the UFW were ex-braceros. These ex-braceros who worked with the UFW and elsewhere became green card commuters who eventually sent their family members to work in the United States. In 1975, California was the first state to extend many labor laws to include farmworkers. The Agricultural Labor Relations Act (ALRA) granted California farmworkers the right to form or join unions and also confirmed employer and union interference with these rights as unfair labor practices (see Martin 2003a: 93–160).

As the number of agricultural workers under UFW contracts dropped, due to increased wage levels, from 60,000–70,000 per year in the early 1970s to 6,000–7,000 by the mid-1980s, California growers turned to labor contractors who recruited directly in Mexico (Martin 2003b: 5). Employer sanction laws that came into effect in 1986 as part of the Immigration Reform and Control Act (IRCA, discussed below) also encouraged

TABLE 1. Greatest Mexican-Origin Population Changes in Absolute
Numbers in California Counties, 1980–90

AREA	CHANGE IN ABSOLUTE NUMBERS
United States	*4,817,306*
California	*2,481,530*
Los Angeles	876,226
Orange	242,346
San Diego	210,778
San Bernardino	179,345
Riverside	159,812
Santa Clara	77,011
Fresno	76,104
Ventura	57,001
Kern	55,754
Tulare	44,431

Source: Adapted from Turner 1998

growers to increasingly use contractors in order to avoid penalties for
hiring undocumented workers. Labor contractors joined forces with
smugglers, who set up a sophisticated network of smuggling routes,
rates, and information that brought increasing numbers of undocumented Mexicans to California and elsewhere in the United States in the
1970s and 1980s. Significant numbers of indigenous Mexicans from Oaxaca were brought by labor contractors from Baja California to California
beginning in the 1970s and 1980s (see chapter 5).

The significant increase in the number of Mexicans who migrated to
California in the 1980s can be seen in table 1.

The counties of Los Angeles, Orange, San Diego, and San Bernardino
saw significant increases in the number of Mexican-origin residents from
1980 to 1990. A part of this population increase was undocumented.
These undocumented immigrants were often tied to family members or
others from their communities who were legal residents. In 1986, the
number of legal Mexican residents increased significantly.

IRCA, which was supposed to resolve the "illegal alien" problem, did
legalize a great many people but also encouraged the migration of many
more who were connected to those who received legal status. IRCA linked

employer sanctions (fines for employing undocumented workers), guest workers (contract labor like the bracero program), amnesty for undocumented workers already in the United States as of January 1, 1982 (they received temporary resident status), and increased enforcement and militarization of the border. Familiarity with the English language and some knowledge of civics were required to obtain permanent residence. The 1986 IRCA legislation also offered special status to agricultural workers who could prove they had spent at least ninety days during a qualifying period doing agricultural work on specific crops—known as Seasonal Agricultural Workers Program (SAW). On this basis, farmworkers also received temporary residency. IRCA conferred legal status on nearly three million undocumented immigrants. These three million new legal residents became important family and community resources for future migrants. Over one million of these people became legal immigrants by presenting letters from employers saying they had worked on U.S. farms. As described by Philip Martin, since about six million adult men lived in rural Mexico in the mid-1980s, it appears that the SAW program gave about one-sixth of them U.S. immigrant visas (2003b: 6). Many of those who became legal immigrants did not remain in agriculture but settled in U.S. cities and moved into other sectors, such as construction, service, and factory work. Others never were farmworkers. Many brought their family members to the United States. After IRCA, farm labor was increasingly being carried out by undocumented Mexicans. Between 1995 and 2000 almost 90 percent of Mexicans who arrived in California and elsewhere were undocumented (Martin 2003b: 7). That trend continued in the twenty-first century.

While the increase in undocumented workers can be tied in part to people from Mexico following legalized family members to the United States, greatly increased use by employers of labor contractors after 1986 also contributed to the use of undocumented workers. While the reforms in IRCA were supposed to improve farm labor conditions, the result was often the opposite. Undocumented first-time migrants are least likely to question the practices of labor contractors and are also highly dependent on them for off-farm housing, rides to work, false work documents, and food (Martin 2003a: 187) (see discussion in chapter 4).

By 1990, according to the U.S. Census, Latinos made up more then 25 percent of the population of California. By the year 2000, Latinos were 32 percent of California's population, and the Mexican-origin population was about 25 percent of the total population (Inter-University Program

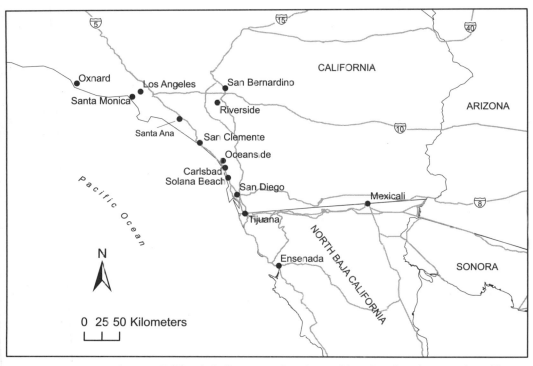

MAP 4. California indigenous migration and immigration sites mentioned in text

for Latino Research 2000). During the 1990s, the number of Mexicans who decided to become citizens also increased significantly. By 1996, 20 percent of all new citizens were of Mexican origin. Seventy percent of new citizens of Mexican origin lived in California (Johnston 2001: 254). By the year 2000, 44 percent of Mexican immigrants in the United States were in California (California-Mexico Health Initiative 2005).

A significant transformation occurred in many California cities and towns between the 1970s and the present. In areas such as Los Angeles, Oxnard, Santa Ana, and San Bernardino, Mexican-origin migrants have become either a majority or a very significant minority. These are the areas of Mexican California where indigenous Mexican immigrants from Teotitlán del Valle have settled. According to the 2000 U.S. Census, 65.9 percent of the population of Santa Ana, California, is of Mexican origin, as is 59.44 of Oxnard, 38.78 percent of San Bernardino, and 29.55 percent of the city of Los Angeles (Population and Demographics Resources 2005a, 2005b, 2005c, 2005d). In Oregon similar processes in the establishment of a Mexican Oregon on a smaller scale are present.

In early Oregon Country, the Mexican border extended to just south of the Medford/Ashland area until 1846, when a treaty signed by England and the United States confirmed U.S. title to what was known as the Territory of Oregon (which also included what are now the states of Washington and Idaho). According to the Oregon Historical Society, "For years, people moved freely along the open border between the Oregon Country and Mexico, trading supplies and cultural influences. Even before the Civil War, Mexican merchants, miners, soldiers, adventurers, sheepherders, and *vaqueros* (cowboys) were in southern Oregon" (Nusz and Ricciardi 2003; Oregon Historical Society 2004).

Some of the earliest Mexican migrants to the state of Oregon were mule packers, miners, and vaqueros who brought their trade from what was greater Mexico to the United States. Mule packers moved supplies from northern California to areas as far north as the Illinois River Valley in Oregon. During the Rogue River War in Oregon in the 1850s, Mexican mule packers supplied the Second Regiment Oregon Mounted Volunteers, who were fighting against native peoples of the southern coastal area (Gamboa 1991). Thousands of coastal native people were forced out of their territories in the 1850s and onto reservations farther north. Many were also killed and died from disease. The population of the Kalapuya, for example, went from 20,000 to perhaps just a few hundred by 1850.

Two decades later, Mexican cowboys migrated to Oregon, coming from California with California cattlemen who settled in remote locations in eastern Oregon. For example, the California cattleman John Devine first came to Oregon in 1869. He brought with him a large crew of Mexican vaqueros to manage large herds that were driven up from California. According to the historian Jeff LaLande, the vaqueros "were Spanish-speaking Californios, Indians of central California who had grown up riding and herding on the Central Valley's Mexican land grants" (2002). Other California ranchers also established themselves in Harney and Malheur counties in eastern Oregon, developing some of the largest cattle spreads in the state. The nation's first transcontinental railroad, completed in 1869, passed across northern Nevada, and the railroad's shipping point at Winnemucca became "the main destination of many southeastern Oregon cattle drives, large and small" (LaLande 2005). Mexicans, along with workers from China, Japan, and the Philippines, built railroads linking the East and West coasts, eventually making mule-pack operations obsolete (Nusz and Ricciardi 2003; Oregon Historical Society 2004).

The historian Erasmo Gamboa (1990) has written the most complete account of Mexican migration to Oregon in the early to mid–twentieth century. Some of the same factors that fueled increased migration to California during the early twentieth century also operated in Oregon. The development of commercial agricultural production in the Northwest, facilitated by the completion of the northern transcontinental railroad and the development of public and private irrigation works, were instrumental in furthering farm production. The fertile Willamette Valley in Oregon and the Puyallup and Skagit valleys in Washington as well as the tablelands of eastern Washington and Oregon were able to produce a rich abundance of specialty crops, including a wide range of fruits, vegetables, nuts, berries, grapes, sugar beets, onions, hops, wheat, and many other crops. All of these crops, however, required an extensive —usually seasonal—labor supply in regions that were often sparsely populated. The need for labor led Oregon growers to recruit Mexican laborers away from the Southwest and from Mexico to work on area farms. By 1910, Oregon ranked seventh among states outside the Southwest with Mexican-born residents (Gamboa 1990: 7).

From 1910 through 1930, Mexicans came to Oregon during and after the upheaval caused by the Mexican Revolution. While fleeing chaos in Mexico, they were also drawn by a demand for labor in the United States. During and after the Mexican Revolution, Mexican laborers entered Oregon, Washington, and Idaho. While the Immigration Act of 1917 established literacy and head tax requirements for Mexicans, within months of its implementation, the U.S. secretary of labor "authorized western sugar beet enterprises to recruit alien labor without enforcement of this restriction" (Gamboa 1990: 9). This waiver, which was prompted by a World War I labor shortage, benefited western growers, who used it to recruit Mexican workers to the Northwest. By 1924, Mexicans were contracted from the southwestern states to work in sugar beets at three dollars per day, and Portland was a significant recruiting ground for Mexican workers (Gamboa 1990: 9). Railroad companies, including several in Oregon, were another prime employer of Mexican workers (Taylor 1931).

Mexican immigration decreased in the 1930s, not only because of a lack of employment in the United States, but also because of the U.S.

policies of deportation and exclusion described above. While the deportations of the depression returned about 20 percent of this population, a vast majority remained, and their labor was still needed. In his discussion of what happened to Mexicans in the Pacific Northwest during the Depression, Gamboa emphasizes the importance of a depressed economy: as crop prices plummeted, farmers cut back on planting and left their orchards unattended. Nevertheless, some crop sectors expanded, such as hops, which expanded significantly after the repeal of Prohibition in Oregon in 1932. Sugar beet cultivation continued to increase in the 1930s as growers received subsidies and restrictions were placed on sugar imports. While a general tide of poor workers flowed into Oregon and the Northwest, there is evidence to suggest that Mexicans were among them, as growers, sugar companies, and others continued to recruit Mexican laborers. Paul Taylor (1937) noted in a government report that Mexican migrants traveled from the Imperial Valley of California to Oregon's Hood River and Willamette valleys (Gamboa 1990: 13). Gamboa has also documented conversations at the office of the Mexican consul in San Antonio, Texas, held from 1939 to 1940 by the Tolan House Select Committee to Investigate the Interstate Migration of Destitute Citizens; the transcripts suggest that migrant laborers from Texas traveled to Oregon and Washington for work as well as to midwestern states (1990: 14). Labor contractors from California also sent workers to Idaho and most likely to other areas in the Northwest as well. Gamboa's documentary work about the continued Mexican presence in Oregon and other parts of the Northwest is an important antidote to the idea that there was no Mexican presence in the region until World War II. He concludes of this era,

> All told, the decade of the Depression did little to alter the migration patterns of Mexican people to the Pacific Northwest. On the surface, it would appear that the general unemployment, the end of Mexican immigration to the United Sates, and the influx of many uprooted Midwesterners to the Northwest were reasons enough why Mexicans would not continue to be recruited to the northwestern states. Yet, paradoxically and in contrast to the 1920s, Mexican migratory workers came in greater numbers. . . . As before, the region's agricultural industry needed workers, Mexicans were sought out because they were available, they could be paid cheap wages, and would accept the laborious jobs that others turned down. . . .
>
> Federal and state relief was not extended to them, and the opportunity to

escape the migratory cycle through the resettlement program was beyond their reach. . . . Paid low wages and excluded from rehabilitation, those Mexicans who became permanent residents in the Northwest and elsewhere had no significant choice but to retreat into the backwaters to the depressed rural communities of the 1930s. (Gamboa 1990: 20–21)

The continued growth of the Mexican population in Oregon was spurred in the 1940s by three related factors: continuing growth in agriculture and a subsequent need for labor, the onset of World War II, and the existence of the bracero program, which was designed to recruit Mexican laborers to replace those who either entered the U.S. armed forces or who left farm labor to work in industry. The demand for food production plus expansion of irrigation and electrification boosted commercial acreage, while the war pulled much of the existing labor force into war production. The demographic shift of workers from rural to urban areas resulted in a labor shortage in Oregon and other parts of the Northwest by 1941. Acute labor shortages during the harvest season of 1941 led Oregon growers to recruit out-of-state strawberry workers (Sasuly 1942). In Marion County, public school teachers organized harvest platoons and enlisted ten thousand students (Reider 1942). In sparsely populated eastern Oregon, labor shortages resulted in the extremely reluctant temporary acceptance of Japanese American farmworkers to harvest sugar beets. After the Amalgamated Sugar Company at Nyssa sold the local Chamber of Commerce on a plan making it responsible for the transportation costs, housing, and safety of Japanese American workers, workers began arriving in 1942 to thin sugar beets and work in other crops (Gamboa 1990: 30). The workers were not welcomed and faced resentment and even physical attacks. They were not accepted as a solution to the labor crisis.

Northwest farmers complained directly to the U.S. government about a lack of labor. While growers wanted the federal government to help them to recruit laborers, most did not want it to impose any conditions on them regarding the circumstances of employment. The U.S. government was bombarded by requests to import workers from Mexico. Commercial agricultural interests made a decision to contract Mexican laborers. In the Northwest, the forthcoming availability of Mexican workers was evident before the ink dried on negotiations between the Mexican and U.S. governments (Gamboa 1990: 41). Sugar beet farmers led the way in the Northwest in contracting Mexican laborers under the Mexican Farm

(above) 9. Mexican braceros weeding a sugar beet field. Oregon Historical Society OregonHi62395.

10. José Valdez, who worked in the Hillsboro pea harvest. June 20, 1943. Oregon Historical Society OrHI 81787.

Labor Program (MFLP), or bracero program, whose Northwest headquarters was in Portland (Gamboa 1990: 41).

The bracero program existed in the state of Oregon from 1942 to 1947
(see Gamboa 1990). Some 15,136 braceros were contracted from Mexico
as farm laborers in Oregon during this time (Gamboa 1995: 41). Additional bracero workers were employed on Oregon railroads in 1943–46.
While the agreements signed by the U.S. and Mexican governments
specified conditions to be met in terms of workers' living conditions,
food, hours worked, transportation, and pay, once braceros were turned
over to farmers, employers had full say and could often do as they
pleased with workers and their contracts. In 1943, two Mexican labor
inspectors in Portland were responsible for all the workers in Utah,
Idaho, Oregon, Washington, and Montana (Gamboa 1990: 53). In Oregon, bracero workers thinned and harvested sugar beets, thinned and
picked apples, thinned and packed pears, and harvested asparagus,
onions, cucumbers, and peas. They were also put to work constructing
fire lanes during fires, and they planted pine seedlings in reforestation
projects for the National Forest Service (Gamboa 1990: 57–59). These
workers were widely praised as being skilled and having excellent perfor-
mance indexes. In fact, the braceros were heavily preferred above Jamai-
cans, itinerant white workers, and others. During the war, most white
farmworkers in Oregon found work outside of agriculture.

Once the war was over, however, returning Anglo workers and their
families began protests against Mexican workers. In 1946, public demonstrations took place in many northwestern communities. Gamboa documents in great detail the very difficult conditions braceros worked under,
including being forced to stay in fields despite freezing temperatures, lack
of health care, lead poisoning from orchard work, job related injuries,
transportation accidents, substandard housing and food, and more
(1990: 65–73). With the support of Mexican government officials, workers
responded with work stoppages and strikes. They resisted as best they
could under conditions in which employers often had absolute control
over all aspects of their lives.

In 1947, PL-45, which had sanctioned the wartime phase of the bracero
program, expired and was superceded by PL-40. The terms of agreement
of PL-40 called for workers' contracts to be negotiated directly between
employer and bracero and for employers to pay for the screening, selec-
tion, and round-trip transportation of workers from Mexico to the
Northwest—previously paid for by the U.S. government. Northwest

growers were shocked at the terms of the agreement and, faced with growing anti-Mexican sentiment and anxiety about the protests mounted by braceros, decided to no longer contract braceros. Thus the program ended in Oregon in 1947, with the advent of PL-40.

Bracero workers were welcome as long as they were obedient and did not question the terms of their labor contracts. The treatment of Mexican bracero laborers between 1942 and 1947 provides us with a clue to future expectations for Mexican farmworkers in Oregon: they should be docile and content with what they are offered; if they try to protest, they will be dismissed. At the end of the bracero program in Oregon in 1947, the labor camps were closed, and all contracted laborers were supposed to return to Mexico. Those who did not could be deported as "illegal aliens"—a practice that increased at the end of World War II and continues to this day (see chapter 4).

Northwest growers led by the larger commercial agricultural interests soon found a new source of labor—Mexican American migratory laborers recruited from California, Texas, and other areas of the Southwest. During the war, new canneries and packing companies were opened in the Northwest in response to increased crop acreage. For example, before the war, Oregon raised twenty-one thousand acres of processing peas and after the war that acreage increased to fifty thousand (Gamboa 1990: 125). Other crop acreage, including that for strawberries, increased as well; Woodburn became known as "the berry capital of the world" in the mid-1950s.

Mexicans in Woodburn, Oregon, and the Building of Mexican Woodburn

By the 1950s, a Mexican American migratory and resident labor force was becoming more commonplace, particularly in the Willamette and Treasure valleys in Oregon. Like California growers, some Oregon farmers recruited undocumented laborers in the 1950s but also continued to recruit laborers from the Southwest. Some of the first Mexican-origin families settled permanently in the Woodburn, Hubbard, and St. Paul area in the 1950s. Many went from states in Mexico like San Luis Potosí, Sonora, Hidalgo, and Nuevo Leon to small towns close to the Texas border such as Progreso and Mission in the 1940s and 1950s. From there they came to form the first population of permanent Mexican families in

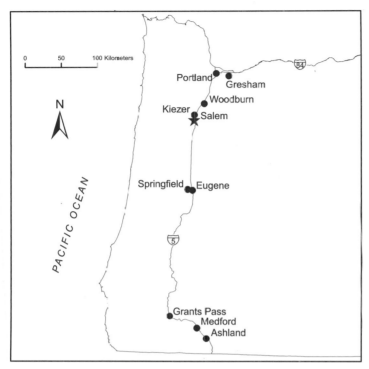

MAP 5. Oregon indigenous migration and immigration sites mentioned in text

Woodburn and the surrounding area in the early 1950s. Many of these families came to the area originally as farmworkers but began to settle and worked in local canneries, on the railroad, and in construction and continued to carry out seasonal harvesting work. As documented by Ed Kissam, while Texas-based migrants began to settle in places like Woodburn at the same time that they did in California, migrants coming directly from Mexico had settled earlier in California. Trips to Oregon from California made places like Woodburn "upstream" destinations for workers who came to work in the berry harvests in June and July before heading to central Washington for the pear and apple harvest (Kissam 2005b). In general, the conditions for farmworkers were abysmal, and in 1950 the average income of farmworkers was reported as being between one and two thousand dollars per year.

The 1950s in Oregon and elsewhere were also marked by Operation Wetback, a program focused on preventing undocumented people from entering the United States and on rounding up and deporting undocumented people already here. The city of Woodburn experienced sweeps through local farms and down I-99 that picked up undocumented workers. A newspaper article in the *Oregonian* on May 15, 1953, ran with the headline, "Agents Sweep Rising Tide of Mexican Illegals South to Border." The paper reported, "Most of Portland's deportees are flown to Los Angeles. The immigration service used to fly them from there to Guadalajara, about 1,500 miles south of this border, just to discourage them from returning so quickly. Now the flood of wetbacks is so great they are being swept back just to the border" (Richards 1953). The culture of immigration raids and the right of INS agents to detain "foreign-looking" workers in any location became entrenched in Woodburn and other areas where Mexican migrants worked and lived.

Mexican families who settled into the Woodburn area in the 1950s and 1960s were often able to eventually purchase small homes, and their children attended local public schools. A few opened local businesses such as small stores or restaurants. Their children and grandchildren now speak English as a first language. Some speak Spanish, but others have left it behind. Some of the Tejano migrants who grew up along the Texas migrants' long-haul crop circuit route (Texas, California, Idaho, and Oregon) and settled in Woodburn have become local civic activists and leaders who bridge different generations of Mexican migrants.

In the 1970s, a second wave of migration came to Oregon from Mexico, including migrant farmworkers from the state of Michoacán and the first indigenous Oaxacans, who were brought up by labor contractors from California (see Stephen 2004). By the 1980s, the labor pool for farmworkers included a significant number of indigenous Mexicans from Oaxaca. IRCA and the accompanying SAW program brought another layer of permanent Mexican residents to the Woodburn area as well as to other places in Oregon. The table below is based on a random sample survey of Mexican-born heads of household carried out in Woodburn in 2003; it suggests the increasing presence of Oaxacan- and Michoacán-based migration networks in the community.[2]

The majority of the agricultural workers granted legal residence through the SAW program were men. In Oregon, 23,736 Mexicans received permanent residency under the program. While this statistic reflects the number who applied and completed the SAW program in Oregon, the figure of between 40,000 and 50,000 may be more realistic because many workers who now reside in Oregon completed the SAW program in California. While it is unclear how many of those legalized

TABLE 2. Leading Mexico-Based Migration Networks in Woodburn, Oregon

STATE AND COMMUNITY OF ORIGIN OF MEXICAN-BORN HOUSEHOLD HEADS	PERCENTAGE OF TOTAL MEXICAN-BORN ($N=67$)
Oaxaca: Sta. María Tindú, Cd. de Oaxaca, San Juan Mixtepec, San Mateo Tunuchi, Ocotlán, Huajuapan, Sta. María Caxtlahuaca, Zaachila	24
Michoacán: Morelia, Quiroga, Jaripo, San Jerónimo, Chupicuaro various smaller ranchos	17
Guanajuato: Pénjamo, León, Silao, Guanajuato, Romita	13
Guerrero: Acapulco, Coyuca, Tecpan de Galeana, Ometepec	6
Mexico, D.F.	6
Morelos: Cuernavaca, Totolapán	5
Jalisco: Rancho la Cañada, ranchos	5
Veracruz: Poza Rica, Coyuca	4
Puebla	3
Nayarit	2
Sinaloa	2
Estado de México	2
San Luis Potosí	2
Zacatecas	2
Tamaulipas	2
Durango	2
Colima	2
Tlaxcala	2

Source: New Pluralism Project—Woodburn Community Case Study, 2003

under the SAW program were Mixtec or from other indigenous groups, in their 1994 survey of Oaxacan village networks in California, Runsten and Kearney found that about "one-half of U.S. migrants from Oaxaca were legalized by IRCA" (1994: viii). There are no similar statistics for Oregon. It might be a reasonable assumption, however, to say that about half of the Mixtec workers (primarily men) who were seasonal workers in Oregon in the mid-1980s received amnesty.

When Latinos or "Hispanics" were first counted in the census in Oregon in 1970, their numbers were small, 32,000, or less than 2 percent of the population. From 1990 to 2000, the Latino population in Oregon more than doubled from 112,707, or 4 percent of the state population, to 275,315, or about 8 percent of the population. In some counties, Latino settlement rates are quite significant. In Jefferson County, 17.7 percent of the residents are Latino, in Marion County, 17.1, in Washington County, 12. 2 percent, and in Yamhill County, 10 percent (U.S. Census 2005). These counties are primarily agricultural. In the agricultural corridor of the Willamette Valley, which includes the towns of Salem, Keizer, Woodburn, Silverton, and Independence, Latino populations—primarily of Mexican origin—now make up very significant percentages of residents. Mixtec migrants settled in significant numbers in these communities, some of whom were identified as "Hispanic American Indians" in the 2000 census (see table 3 and chapter 7).

Woodburn provides a snapshot of how the Mexican-origin population in Oregon increased and, in some places where it concentrated, truly transformed small cities and rural communities. The composition of immigrants in Woodburn is complex, with different waves coming at different times from different parts of Mexico. In addition to Mixtecos, a wide range of people from other parts of Mexico received amnesty in 1986 and 1987 and also began to settle permanently in the Woodburn area. The presence of residents from Michoacán, Jalisco, and Sinaloa became evident through the establishment of businesses identified with these Mexican states. By the mid- to late 1990s, some settlers from Oaxaca had also begun to establish a few local businesses. These included several restaurants, a garage, and a food store dealing in special items like dried grasshoppers and imported *clayudas*—large, handmade corn tortillas that are dried—flown in directly from Oaxaca.

The city of Woodburn is also characterized by the presence of Latino organizations that have offered significant support to Mexican immigrants in the community. The Willamette Valley Immigration Project (wvip), which began in Portland in 1977, moved its offices to Woodburn in 1979. wvip provided important legal service and representation for undocumented workers and others with immigration problems and was the foundation for Oregon's only farmworkers' labor union, Pineros y Campesinos Unidos del Noroeste (pcun, Northwest Treeplanters and

TABLE 3. Cities in Oregon with Significant Latino Populations, 2000

CITY	LATINO POPULATION	TOTAL POPULATION	PERCENTAGE OF TOTAL
Keizer	3,950	32,203	12.26
Independence	1,818	6,035	30.20
Salem	19,973	136,924	14.50
Silverton	857	7,414	11.50
Woodburn	10,064	20,100	50.07

Source: U.S. Census 2000b

Farmworkers United), founded in 1985 in Woodburn (see chapter 8). In the area of health, the Salud de la Familia (Family Health) clinic was established in Woodburn in the 1970s, affording access for farmworkers to medical care and dentistry at greatly reduced rates. Since the 1970s, St. Luke's Catholic Church has offered a wide range of services in Spanish and is now one of the focal points for immigrants in the community.

In 1990, an offshoot of PCUN became the Farmworker Housing Development Corporation (FHDC). The initial low-income rental housing project Nuevo Amanecer was finished in 1994 with fifty units. In 1997, a second development of twelve units, La Esperanza, was completed in downtown Woodburn. In 1999, another forty-three units were completed at Nuevo Amanecer, where in 2003 the Cipriano Ferrell Education Center (Ferrel was a PCUN-cofounder) was opened; it offers space for community meetings, adult education classes, daycare and Head Start programs, and a computer lab. In 2002, the FHDC finished the Villa del Sol housing project, which sold six houses to farmworker families at below-market value (PCUN 2003: 4).

During 1997, local PCUN members, staff, and allied organizations in Woodburn rallied residents to support the naming of one of two new public schools for César Chávez, cofounder of the United Farmworkers (now called United Farmworkers of America) with Dolores Huerta. While the Woodburn school board refused (instead naming the schools Heritage and Valor), the refusal prompted local residents to form the citizen's group Voz Hispana (Hispanic Voice). During the summer of 1997, Voz Hispana rallied more than eighty Latino residents to attend three consecutive school board meetings. Some of the key participants in

TABLE 4. Hispanic or Latino Population and Race in Woodburn,
Oregon, 2000

POPULATION	NUMBER	PERCENTAGE OF TOTAL POPULATION
Total	20,100	100.00
Hispanic or Latino (of any race)	10,064	50.07
Mexican	8,945	44.50
Puerto Rican	26	0.13
Cuban	11	0.05
Other Hispanic or Latino	1,082	5.38

Source: areaConnect 2005

these meetings were fifty farmworker families who reside at the Nuevo Amanecer housing project. In these meetings, Voz Hispana pressured the school board to name the library at Valor Middle School for Chávez, to erect a permanent display about Chávez and his work, to declare his birthday, March 31, as César Chávez Day in all Woodburn schools, and to demand that special schoolwide and classroom activities be organized in celebration of that day. The Woodburn school board accepted all of these proposals. Since that time, special curricula and assemblies have been organized around César Chávez to promote a sense of pride in the farmworker movement as well as educate a broader range of people about the work and beliefs of this national hero. The Woodburn Unified School District has embraced bilingual education and classified 70 percent of its students as "English-language learners" (Kissam 2005c: 87). Voz Hispana continues to take an interest in local politics and has also developed an interest in Latino voting and election participation in Woodburn.

Chemeketa Community College opened a branch in Woodburn and is a key local institution providing access for Mexican immigrants to earn a GED as well as access to English as a second language (ESL) classes, technology, and math training. In 2003, the director of Chemeketa's ESL instruction estimated that the program served about twenty-five hundred students per year (Kissam 2005c: 87). Oregon Legal Aid Services has a special farmworker project in Woodburn, and the Oregon Law Center also has an office in Woodburn that began an indigenous farmworker project in 2002 that provides community education to Oregon's indigenous farmworkers (see chapter 8).

By 2000, Woodburn had a population of 20,100 people, and 50.07 percent of them were Hispanic or Latino, primarily of Mexican origin (44.5 percent of the total town population). This made Woodburn the largest city in Oregon with a Latino majority (see table 4, above).

By 2002, Woodburn's schools were 67 percent Hispanic, 12 percent Russian, and 20 percent Anglo (Bures 2002: 13). The 2003 survey of 128 households in Woodburn carried out as part of the New Pluralism project showed that 25 percent of all persons in households surveyed were English-dominant, 61 percent were Spanish-dominant, 6 percent were Mixtec-dominant, and another 8 percent were other-languages-dominant (with 2 percent speaking Russian) (see table 5).

About one thousand Russian Orthodox Old Believers settled in Woodburn in the 1960s. These Russian immigrants arrived through the intervention of then-Attorney General Robert F. Kennedy in 1963. Many had lived in China, Hong Kong, and Latin American countries, including Brazil, before coming to Oregon (Kramer 2002). While Spanish is the predominant language in the Woodburn Public Schools bilingual programs, Russian bilingual classes are available as well beginning in kindergarten.

As stated above, the community of Mexican migrants in Woodburn is complex and made up of people who have come at different times. Table 6 shows the breakdown of time in the United States for Mexican immigrants to Woodburn in 2003. Mexican migrants have lived in the community for varying amounts of time, some as long as sixty-five years. The data are from a random sample survey carried out in Woodburn.

The ever-increasing presence of Mexicans settling in the community of Woodburn since the 1950s and then by 2000 emerging as the dominant population provides a snapshot of the kinds of transitions that are taking place in many rural communities in the United States. While we can speak of the histories of different types of Mexicans in Woodburn at different times, by 2005 we can also speak of a definite local space as Mexican Woodburn. It is possible to function entirely in Spanish in the community, and the reconfiguration of public space dominated by Mexican-owned businesses and both long-standing and emerging local institutions suggests the appropriateness of a local sense of Mexican Woodburn. What is most interesting about this community is that although there have been some ethnic tensions, by and large the local culture has emerged as embracing multilingualism and multiculturalism and trying to build on the distinctiveness of Mexican Woodburn as a

TABLE 5. Language Profile of Woodburn, Oregon, Heads of Household, Overall Population, and Minors, 2003

LANGUAGE PROFILE	PERCENTAGE OF ALL ALL HEADS OF HOUSEHOLD	PERCENTAGE OF ALL PERSONS IN HOUSEHOLD	PERCENTAGE OF MINORS 0–18 YEARS OF AGE
English-Dominant	33	25	21
Primary Language—English (limited or no other language)	31	19	8
Bilingual—English preferred	2	6	13
Spanish-Dominant	47	61	69
Primary Language—Spanish (limited or no English)	30	37	29
Bilingual—Spanish preferred (Spanish-English)	17	24	40
Mixtec-Dominant	10	6	4
Primary Language—Mixtec (limited or no Spanish)	7	3	<1
Bilingual—Mixtec preferred (Mixtec-Spanish)	1	1	1
Trilingual—Mixtec with Spanish-English	2	2	>2
Other Language Dominant	11	8	6
Bilingual Russian preferred	<2	<2	<2
Trilingual (Other + Russian + English or Other + Spanish + English)	8	5	4
Other (Portuguese, Malay, Triqui) with limited or no English	<1	<1	—

Source: New Pluralism Project—Woodburn Community Case Study, 2003

TABLE 6. Mexican Immigrant Heads of Household's Length of Time in
United States, Woodburn, Oregon, 2003

LENGTH OF TIME IN UNITED STATES	PERCENTAGE OF TOTAL $(N=76)$
Newcomers	21
<3 Years	9
3–5 Years	12
Settlers	79
6–10 Years	25
11–15 Years	19
16–20 Years	10
21–65 Years	25

Source: New Pluralism Project—Woodburn Community Case Study, 2003

source of local pride and business and tourist possibilities. The thickness
of local Latino institutions that provide services and do advocacy work
for Mexican immigrants has also led to developing a presence of Mexican
immigrants that can exist as a precursor to more organized political
participation (see Sassen 2002).

Conclusion

The increasing presence of Mexicans in both California and Oregon and
their historical links to Mexico are important parts of the histories of
transborder communities such as Teotitlán del Valle and San Agustín
Atenango. The arrival of Mixtecs and Zapotecs first as part of the bracero
program and later as workers brought up by labor contractors is part
and parcel of the history of active recruitment of Mexicans as farmworkers beginning in the early part of the twentieth century. As first men
and then women left transborder communities in Oaxaca in increasing
numbers in the later part of the twentieth century for California and
Oregon, their individual lives as well as their communities were changed.
The histories of Mexicans in California and Oregon and in specific sites
such as Woodburn, Oregon, are connected to the histories of places like
San Agustín and Teotitlán through the political, economic, and cultural

connections that have been physically carried in the bodies of people moving back and forth between these places, in the social remittances that the migration experience has brought to the residents of these trans-border communities in all of their sites, and through the transnational social fields of power linked to commercial agriculture, U.S. immigration policy, and the recruitment of workers.

CHAPTER 4

Transborder Labor Lives

HARVESTING, HOUSECLEANING,

GARDENING, AND CHILDCARE

This chapter focuses on the ways in which the U.S. and Mexican economies have become integrated since World War II largely as a result of ongoing economic globalization. Globalization not only has affected the
kinds of work and opportunities available in rural Oaxaca, Mexico, for
people in communities like Teotitlán del Valle and San Agustín Atenango,
but also has resulted in new labor markets for immigrant workers in the
United States, markets that are segmented by gender and race. The chapter begins by linking the specific experiences of two Mixtec migrant
workers, José Luis García López (introduced in chapter 2) and Mariano
Bautista, to a general pattern of Mixtec migration through the twentieth
century that is characterized by continuous involvement with labor contractors who regulate when and where Mixtecos have migrated, even into
the United States. This is contrasted with the experiences of Catalina García and Emiliano Gómez, which are more typical of a different pattern of
migration seen among Valley Zapotec migrants. That pattern involves
more direct movement into the United States and insertion into the service sector, providing somewhat more stable work conditions. The next
section lays out how the integration of commercial agriculture in Mexico
and the United States and the creation of a consumer market for year-
round fresh vegetables and fruits have affected the migration patterns and
experiences of Mixteco workers such as Mariano Bautista. To illuminate
the experience of workers such as Catalina García, the final section discusses the development of a labor market for domestic work in the United
States that targets immigrant women to do caring and cleaning work.

Mixtec and Zapotec Migration Patterns:
Contracted Labor versus Network Migration

The link between the development of certain types of jobs in industry, the service sector, and commercial agriculture and the creation of mobile and flexible migrant labor forces can be seen clearly in the bracero program, launched during World War II. As both a labor and immigration policy, this program was a cornerstone in establishing Mexican migrant labor and residency patterns in the United States beginning in the 1940s. Nevertheless, although Zapotec migrants from towns like Teotitlán del Valle and Mixtec migrants from communities like San Agustín Atenango both participated in the bracero program as contracted laborers, other than this shared experience, the trajectories of their migration and the kinds of work experiences they have had both within Mexico and in the United States are often different. While Zapotec migrants from other communities in the valleys of Oaxaca did work as agricultural workers in Sinaloa and Sonora, as many Mixtec workers did, by the late 1970s and early 1980s they had moved out of agriculture into the service sector, primarily in the Los Angeles area.

Men from the Zapotec community of Teotitlán del Valle were recruited into the bracero program beginning in 1944, when the *presidente municipal* publicized the program. For many in the community, this program was the first opportunity to earn substantial cash income. Braceros recall buying their first pairs of shoes and coming home with tailored pants that were the envy of all. Estimates of the numbers of male migrants to the United States in the late 1940s were about 25 percent of the male population over fifteen, or about two hundred of the eight hundred males in the community (Stephen 1991: 110–11). Approximately 25 percent of the households in Teotitlán continued to send one or more workers to the United States on an annual basis throughout the duration of the bracero program, that is, until 1964. By that time, many had established permanent footholds in a number of areas, including Chicago, Los Angeles, and even New Mexico. Those who stayed in the United States in the 1950s and 1960s were often able to secure legal residence. After the bracero program ended, even more people went as undocumented workers, staying with their established relatives.

Cash earned through the continuous labor of braceros and then undocumented workers in the United States served as an important part of the process that allowed some members of this weaving community to become entrepreneurs and merchants in Oaxaca, on the border in the markets of Tijuana and Rosarita, and in some cases in the United States. Kinship and relationships of *compadrazgo*, or ritual kinship, were quite significant in recruiting young people to work for those who had established themselves on the border with stores in Tijuana. Ensenada, Rosarito, and in a few locations in the United States. Often grandchildren, nieces, nephews, and godchildren went to work for older relatives or their godparents to help out in running a small family business or, in the case of girls, giving a hand with domestic work or childcare.

About twenty-five people from Teotitlán del Valle are believed to have obtained legal U.S. residency after the bracero program, a few moving to Colorado and others to California, primarily to Santa Ana (Lopez and Runsten 2004: 261). These earlier legal residents did not seem to have much influence on migration to the United States from Teotitlán. A steady migrant flow from Teotitlán to the United States did not come into full swing until the mid-1980s. Many of these people began by first going to visit relatives and *paisanos* (fellow community members) established in the Tijuana area and then went up to Santa Ana, where some of the early legal residents had settled. The successful expansion of the weaving industry for tourism and export in the early 1980s (see Stephen 2005b) provided money to fund people's journeys north. Most went on their own to Tijuana, used a local coyote to cross over with few problems, and then landed with relatives or friends in the Santa Ana area, at least initially. Most ended up working in the service industry in the Santa Ana area (López and Runsten 2004: 254).

Emiliano Gómez comes running through the door of his family compound. A small band of sweat is visible under his broad-brimmed hat. His face breaks into a grin as he explains why he is late. A neighbor's refrigerator was broken and he had to go and fix it for them. A small-scale farmer, weaver, and appliance repairman, Emiliano earns money in as many ways as he can in his community of Teotitlán del Valle in the central valleys of Oaxaca (see Stephen 2005b). Once he takes off his hat, Emiliano sits down on a wooden chair next to mine. He is still warm in his white cotton T-shirt and jeans but begins to cool down as we start to talk in the night air.

Emiliano Gómez went to the United States for the first time when he was nineteen years old. Prior to that he had been working at home with his parents as a weaver, producing high-quality textiles for a local mer-

11. Emiliano Gómez in Teotitlán del Valle.

chant who sold them in the United States. Emiliano worked for a total of
four years in the United States, living there on two different occasions.
When he returned to Mexico for good in 1990, he remained in Teotitlán;
he had no desire to go back to the United States. He has a wife and three
children. He also has a house with an interior patio filled with grass,
flowers, and fruit trees, one of the nicest patios in the community—a
reflection of his days as a gardener in the States, a job he found after two
other disagreeable ones. He told me his story during the summers of
2001 and 2002 as part of many other conversations.

After a stay in a California labor camp near Santa Ana, Emiliano
responded to a local radio ad looking for someone to clean houses and
garden in the San Bernardino area. It turned out that the person running
the ad was from Teotitlán del Valle. For three years he lived with her
family in what turned out to be a very mixed experience. Emiliano
described this work experience to me in 2002, beginning with his phone
call in response to the radio ad.

I spoke to the woman on the other end. "What kind of work is it?" I asked
her.

"Well," she said, "I need someone who can clean up the house for me,
who can tend the garden, and do other work around the house."

"Ok," I told the woman. "I can do this work. If you give me this job then I will come right over to your house."

"Well," she said to me, "I need someone who will live here, not someone who will come and go. I want someone who will be here in the house all the time."

"Ok," I responded. "That's fine."

When I got back to the house where I was staying with this guy from Teotitlán, I told him I had gotten a job. I told him the address and asked him if he could take me there. He knew the whole area. The job was in San Bernardino on Arriaga Street. He took me there.

When we got there I saw that the woman whom I had talked to on the phone was from Teotitlán. She was an older woman, about fifty-five years old. Her name was Marina Alavez. I stayed with this señora, and she told me what I had to do. She told me I could stay with them. She had two daughters and a son living with her. The very next day she took me to work to go clean. She and her daughter took me to clean houses. The señora liked how I worked and she told me I could stay.

They bought me shoes and some pants so that I had something to wear. I didn't have anything. She bought me a towel and other things. They gave me a room to live in that was a garage that was closed up, and there were two beds in it. That was where I stayed.

I stayed with them for a long time. I think she was paying me about $120 per month. I had already suffered quite a bit in the United States. I was afraid to leave. I thought that if I left, then I wouldn't be able to find my way back. A lot of people invited me to go to other things.

"Come on," they would say. "Why don't you come and pick strawberries with us? If you do that you can earn $300 per week or every two weeks. In one month you can earn $800 or $600 picking strawberries." But I wasn't sure about that. I felt more secure living with these people. It's true that $120 per month is very little. But I felt secure because I had food and a place to live. I didn't have to pay for anything. At least the $120 was mine to keep. Once I had been there for two months, they paid me $150 per month. After three months they paid me $200 per month, and they paid me that rate for about one year.

During the second year I lived with them, I learned how to drive. They taught me how to drive the vehicles they had. They had one pickup truck, a larger truck, and two small cars. I would take the cars out and fill up the gas tanks. They would tell me. "Today there isn't much work here. Take the cars and fill up the tanks." I had access to everything they had. I could watch TV with them, I ate with them. We made our meals together. They taught me how to cook. They taught me how to make tortillas. They taught me a lot of different things. When I had more confidence, they took me to Disneyland. They also took me to Las Vegas, Los Angeles, and other places. I couldn't go to these places alone because I didn't know how to get there. Once I started to drive, I knew how to get around more. I would go to the store for them.

I was living with them when my brother Jorge came and later my other younger brother, Porfirio. I came back to Teotitlán in 1986. I lived in that house for three years. My brothers stayed there. After I left, they didn't like living there. They didn't like how the señora treated them. Sometimes she would get mad and she would yell at us if she didn't like how we did the work. Sometimes we would get really tired of all the pressure she put on us. She was getting older and she got mad more easily. It seemed like with every day that passed she got more and more mad and difficult. They left because they couldn't put up with her any more.

Emiliano went back to Teotitlán for several months. The first time he told me about his time working in California he skipped smoothly from one job to the next, narrating his return in early 1987. One year later, he invited me back to his house and told me that he had to add something to his story. What he added were two very painful events he had experienced in the United States. He found it difficult to share them with me but felt it was important for me to know. These occurrences were the chief reasons he never wanted to return to the United States. After returning in 1987 and working briefly, he and his brother were badly wounded in a robbery in a park. Having no health insurance attached to their jobs cleaning houses, they became liable for huge hospital and physical therapy bills. The family they had worked for and lived with for years did nothing to help them with their medical costs. Emiliano recounted this period as follows:

EMILIANO: When I came back in 1987, on the second of January, my brother Jorge went out on his bike. He had bought the bike about a month before. On that day he was late and as his older brother, I felt like it was my responsibility to go out and see what was keeping him. When I got to where he was in a park I saw that some guys had taken away his bicycle. I stood in front of them and said that it was his bicycle. They wanted the bicycle. I pulled the bike back from them. When we had recovered the bike from them, one of them pulled out a knife. He wanted to fight with us.

"Come on. Let's go." I told my brother.

There were two of them behind me. They were not going to let us leave. We were going to have to face them. I had only my fists and both of them had knives drawn at that point. I learned a little bit about fighting when I was a kid. I remembered that the first thing I had to do was to disarm them, to get rid of the knives. I disarmed one and there was still one more. When it was clear that we might win because we knew how to knock the knives out of their hands, some other guys who were parked in a car on the other side of the street started firing a gun. I heard the sound of a shot in the air. Then I felt a great pain and heat in my legs. I felt five bullets. Then I heard my brother.

"I can't feel my feet," he cried. He had fallen down. "I can't feel my feet," he screamed.

"Don't move," I said to him. I was on the ground at that point too. "Stay quiet," I said very softly.

We lay there very quiet for some time. When they saw that we didn't move at all, then maybe they thought we were dead. They ran to their car and then they sped off.

I was able to get up and sort of walk. I had bullet wounds, too, but I carried my brother from the park to the house where we were living. By the time we got there, his pants were totally soaked with blood. He couldn't feel his feet at all. He kept saying, 'I can't feel my feet." When we got to the house we called an ambulance and the police. They took us in an ambulance to the county hospital. They wanted to take out all the bullets. They tried to take out the bullets, but some of the bullets were lodged in the bone. They were going to have to operate on both of us.

They put me in a separate room from my brother. I was in the hospital for eight days. My brother stayed for another three. After I had been out of the hospital for about five days, they sent me a list of all the things they had done and all the materials they had used to take care of us in the hospital. My bill was for $20,000 and Jorge's was for another $20,000. I thought, "Where am I going to get $40,000 to pay for both of our bills?" I had never even seen that much money. I couldn't walk without crutches and my brother couldn't walk at all. He was in a wheelchair. When he got out of the hospital I had to do everything for him. I had to bring him his food; I had to take him to the bathroom. I had to take him into the shower. It was a very hard time. He had a big cast on.

LYNN: Did your parents know what happened?

EMILIANO: No. They didn't know at the time. I spent a lot of time trying to figure what to do about the big hospital bills. I had to knock on a lot of doors. I went to the county government to see if they could forgive my debt. This was a huge amount of money for us. We never would have been able to pay for it. They sent me to an office of the government that supports victims of crimes. It was the U.S. government. This office opened an investigation to see if we were at fault or the thieves. If it turned out that it was our fault, then we had to pay. If it turned out to be the thieves' fault, then we didn't have to pay the bill.

Months passed in this investigation. They had to ask us a lot of questions. This was very hard for me. I didn't speak English and every time we met I had to have someone translate for me. Finally after a long time, they ruled that we didn't have to pay this money and that we would be free from this debt. I spent months working and then going to this office. I had to go to court, and my brother needed a lot of physical therapy. I had to take him to physical therapy and to pay for it. This was a total nightmare for us, this time. When I came back here to Teotitlán I was pale and demoralized. I felt terrible.

Shaken, Emiliano returned again to Teotitlán in late 1987 and returned to working in the cornfields and weaving. In 1989, in order to pay for the costs involved in having a formal wedding in Teotitlán, he returned once again to the United States and worked first in a factory and then as a gardener in San Bernardino.

EMILIANO: I went back again in 1989. When I arrived I went to live with my brother Jorge. He wasn't working for that woman anymore. He had his own apartment with my youngest brother and they were both working in a factory. The boss there gave me work, and our check was about $300 or $350 per week. We were paying taxes.

I worked in the factory with my brothers for a little while and then I decided to change jobs. I met some guys who worked as gardeners in what they called "yardas." They worked outside taking care of people's yards. I thought maybe I could make more money doing that work than I made at the factory. They were going to pay me $300 per week in cash. I had a driver's license and I knew how to drive. They put me in charge of a truck and a few workers. I went to work all around the Los Angeles area. We went to Long Beach, Corona, from Corona up to Anaheim, from Anaheim to Santa Ana to Orange and then from Orange I would go to Costa Mesa, Newport, and then I would return to San Bernardino. I worked from six in the morning until six in the evening and sometimes even on Sunday.

LYNN: Did you like this work?

EMILIANO: I liked this work much more because I was traveling around. I had more freedom. I enjoyed it and was able to make money. But then something else happened.

I bought a truck after a while that cost me $3,000. I fixed it up really nice. I fixed up the motor, I bought new tires for it and I fixed up the inside. It was a 1967 Ford pickup. I was using it for my work. I was going to bring it back to Mexico.

In attempting to sell the truck, Emiliano was robbed at gunpoint by two men who stole the truck. It was eventually recovered, but had a great deal of damage done to it. He fixed it up as best he could, sold it, and returned to Teotitlán for good. His concluding remarks focus on why he has no desire to return to the United States:

This was the last time I set foot in the United States. When they stole my truck. I thought to myself, "The United States is not for me." Now you can see why I don't have any desire to return there or to work there. I am fine working here. I can make $200 pesos a day (about US$20), and I am happy. I like my life here. I am living much more peacefully here. Nobody is pressuring me. I don't have to work seven days a week. I am more independent. I have my own house here. I am working as a plumber and working as a weaver. I have a kitchen, beds, water. I have everything I need. We have animals, a bull, some sheep and chickens. This is plenty for me. I don't need more.

Emiliano has been living in Teotitlán since his return. His trajectory of moving from cleaning to factory work to independent gardening is fairly typical. Emiliano has been able to apply some of the skills he learned while in the United States to building up a small business in Teotitlán that offers an alternative source of income to weaving and farming. The difficult times he suffered while working in the United States underline the trying conditions faced by many Zapotec workers.

The case of Teotitlán is somewhat typical of other Zapotec patterns of migration from the central valleys of Oaxaca. Oral histories I conducted in the 1980s in Teotitlán del Valle of some of the communities' oldest male and female residents indicated that a few had migrated to Oaxaca City, Tapachula, Chiapas, and Mexico City to work following the Mexican Revolution in the 1920s and 1930s. In Chiapas men worked either on plantations or selling *paletas*, equivalent to popsicles, on the streets of Tlacolula. In Oaxaca and in Mexico City men were either household

MAP 6. Teotitlán internal migration paths, 1920s to 1990s

servants or worked in construction. Women worked primarily as domestic servants for wealthy families. In his study of migration histories and experiences in twelve Oaxacan, primarily Zapotec communities, Jeffrey Cohen suggests that Oaxacan migration in the early decades of the twentieth century was marked by short-term seasonal moves to places in the region or elsewhere in Mexico (2004: 55; see also Iszavish 1988). Oral histories he collected from other Zapotec communities close to Teotitlán such as Santa Ana del Valle and Díaz Ordaz as well as from other Zapotec communities indicate similar trends (2004: 56–60). Marije Hulshof, drawing on research from several master's theses carried out in three Zapotec communities in the late 1980s, also documents significant internal migration from Zapotec communities to Tapachula. For example, in the 1930s villagers from San Bartolomé Quialana began to migrate seasonally to Tapachula, where they worked harvesting coffee, sugarcane, and, later on, cotton. Before the advent of the Pan-American Highway, men walked in small groups for up to twenty days to reach their destination (1991: 33).

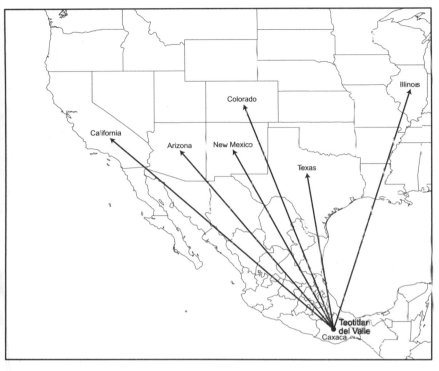

MAP 7.
Teotitlán del Valle migration paths during bracero program, 1944–64

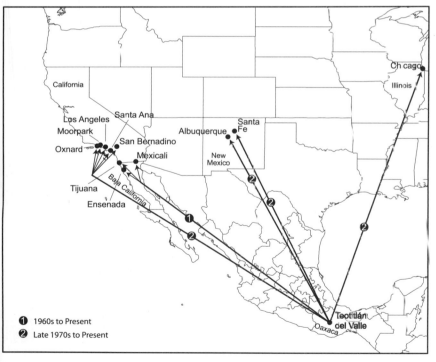

MAP 8. Teotitlán del Valle migration paths to the United States and U.S.-Mexico border

Some men from valley villages such as Santa Ana del Valle, San Lucas Quiavini, Díaz Ordaz, San Miguel del Valle, Teotitlán del Valle, and San Bartolomé Quialana participated in the bracero program (Cohen 2004: 60; López and Runsten 2004: 262; Stephen 2005b: 145; Hulshof 1991: 33). In the mid-1960s, once the bracero program ended, contractors from Sinaloa and Sonora began to recruit seasonal agriculture workers from some Zapotec communities such as San Bartolomé Quialana (Hulshof 1991: 33).

In 1974, some villagers from San Bartolomé went with an acquaintance from Tlacolula to work in the cotton fields in southern California. Their numbers increased and until 1979 about eighty people worked in California agriculture. By 1980, a significant number of people had moved into restaurant work in Santa Monica and into gardening in Stanton and Santa Ana (Hulshof 1991: 35). By 1990, there were about three hundred migrants from San Bartolomé in Santa Monica, one hundred in Santa Ana and Stanton, and ten in Fresno and the state of Washington (1991: 35).

Valley Zapotecs began to migrate in significant number to the United States in the 1970s (López and Runsten 2004: 262). While the path for Teotiteco migration to the United States is closely tied to the development of craft markets on the border and the development of tourism in Tijuana, Ensenada, Rosarito, and then northward to Los Angeles, others from the central valleys began to arrive directly in Los Angeles in the 1960s. Zapotecos from the central valleys depended primarily on social and familial networks to migrate and to gain access to jobs (López and Runsten 2004: 251). In the Tlacolula region, one Zapotec-speaking coyote brought people from a number of neighboring villages to Los Angeles (López and Runsten 2004: 263). Hulshof documents migration from the community of San Pablo Huixtepec (below Zimatlán) to Monterrey, California, during the bracero program, and some stayed there after 1964. In the 1970s people from the neighboring community of Santa Inés accompanied people from San Pablo to the United States and worked in agriculture in Monterey, Fresno, Bakersfield, and as far north as Oregon. By the 1980s, however, migrants from both communities had settled into the restaurant sector of Monterey, Pacific Grove, Carmel, and Seaside (Holshof 1991: 44).

In data that Jeffrey Cohen collected on migration in the late 1990s and early 2000s from twelve Oaxaca communities (including three that were predominantly Zapotec-speaking), a majority of migrants headed for the Unites States settled in southern California, with a majority (54 percent) moving into the Los Angeles area (2004: 78). People from Tlacolula and San Lucas who migrated in the mid- to late 1960s began working in the restaurant sector, often beginning as dishwashers or janitors. In time, some made it into other kitchen positions, such as prepperson, lead cook, kitchen, manager, or chef. They found jobs for other friends and family who arrived in the area as well (López and Runsten 2004: 265). Thus those from towns like Teotitlán del Valle, Tlacolula, and San Lucas who were in the service sector and in restaurant work tended to have year-round, stable positions—albeit at minimum wage. But by the 1990s, some had saved enough money to open small businesses. By 1992, the first Oaxacan restaurant was opened in Santa Monica by four brothers from San Marcos Tlapazola and another man from Tlacolula who pooled their money. By 2003 there were twenty-eight Oaxacan-owned restaurants in Los Angeles. Eighteen of them are owned by valley Zapotecs from the Tlacolula district. One is owned by a family from Teotitlán del Valle (López and Runsten 2004: 267–69). Cohen's data on migrants to the United States from the central Oaxacan valleys indicated that 48 percent were employed in the service sector, including restaurants, hotels, gas stations, and convenience stores. Only 16 percent were employed in agriculture, 14 percent in construction and unskilled labor positions, 13 percent as gardeners for private households and small landscaping firms, and 8 percent as domestic workers (2004: 79). This is consistent with the employment patterns reported by López and Runsten for Zapotec migrants in Los Angeles and by Hulhof as well (1991).

Some Zapotec migrants from Teotitlán who began working at entry-level jobs in supermarkets, drugstores, warehouses, and in factories were sometimes able to stay in the same job and be promoted until they reached managerial positions. Francisco Gutiérrez from Teotitlán, who began work stocking shelves at Long's Drugs in the early 1980s, is now a regional manager for the chain and travels throughout the West, earning a middle-class salary. His wife, Mariana, does some housecleaning but spends more time at home. She can now work less because her husband earns a good salary and has benefits that include health care. Mariana and Fransisco have been legal residents since 1987. Their two children were born in Santa Ana and are U.S. citizens.

The migration of Teotitecos and others like them from the Zapotec communities of the central valleys of Oaxaca has been characterized by stable employment that in some cases led to possibilities for advancement. Felipé López and David Runsten, who made a detailed study of

Zapotec migration and employment in Los Angeles, believe that because the Zapotecs migrated directly through kin and community networks, resisted contract agricultural work in northwest Mexico, were located close to the capital city of Oaxaca, and had entrepreneurial experience through tourism, they were able to successfully integrate themselves into the service sector in the Los Angeles area and prosper in the United States (2004: 274–75). The overall migration experience of Zapotecs from Teotitlán and elsewhere in the central valleys, contrasts significantly with the experience of Mixtecos from communities like San Agustín Atenango, who have remained contracted agricultural laborers, first within Mexico and then in the United States. Some have managed to move out of agricultural labor into the service sector after five to ten years in the United States, but others have not.

While Teotitecos shared the experience of being contracted laborers under the bracero program with men from San Agustín Atenango, after the bracero program was terminated, the similarities in the two migration experiences ends. Mixtec migration has a long history. According to Moisés de la Peña, since the last part of the 1800s, workers from the Mixteca Alta worked as contracted laborers in Valle Nacional in significant numbers when the cultivation of tobacco was formalized and in smaller numbers prior to that time in cotton (1950: 153). At the same time the development of coffee cultivation in Córdoba and Orizana, Veracruz, and sugarcane in the lowlands of Veracruz accelerated migration to that region from the Mixteca Alta.

Labor contractors, or *enganchadores*, have had a major role in the history and specific localities of Mixtec migration since the early twentieth century (López and Runsten 2004: 254). De la Peña writes about how labor contractors who were recruiting Mixtecs made verbal agreements and gave workers an advance so they could leave some money for their families while they traveled and worked (De la Pena 1950: 154; López and Runsten 2004: 255). Migrant workers began their contract in December each year and worked under contract for three to five months per year. After 1910, the number of Mixteco palm weavers doubled in an effort to increase their income (De la Peña 1950: 154). Palm weaving and seasonal migration were the primary means for the poor to try to increase their incomes. Municipalities in the Mixtec Baja region such as Juxtlahuaca and Silacayoapán were averse to migration in the first decades of the twentieth century according to de la Peña, in part because of monolingualism (1950: 155). Those who consistently migrated before the Mexican Revolution

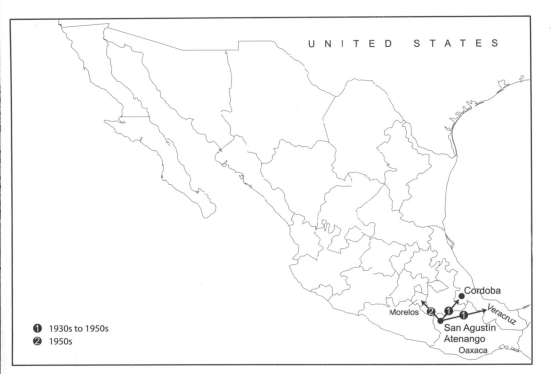

MAP 9. San Agustín Atenango internal migration paths, 1930s to 1950s

mestizaje y lengua

were from Spanish-speaking "mestizoized" communities. Oral histories from San Agustín suggest that migration to the coffee and sugarcane producing regions of Veracruz probably did not begin until the 1930s. When migration did begin, workers combined contract labor in Veracruz with the weaving of palm hats and subsistence farming in corn and beans. According to one source, as early as the 1940s—coterminous with the bracero program—some ranch owners from Baja California Sur sent labor contractors to Sinaloa and Oaxaca to recruit workers: "The recruiters who went to the Mixtec villages of Oaxaca offered good jobs and health and life insurance, and they promised to return workers back home. In some of these cases transportation ended up being only one way; seldom were these workers returned home, and most promises were never kept" (López and Runsten 2004: 255).

The recruitment of men from San Agustín into the bracero program occurred in a context in which many men and some women were already migrating in regular circuits within Mexico. José Luis García López,

12. José Luis García
López relaxing in San
Agustín Atenango.

introduced in chapter 2, was born in 1936. He currently lives with his
wife, daughter, daughter-in-law, and four grandchildren in San Agustín
Atenango. He continues to plant corn and beans and to weave *tenates*
(basket to hold tortillas) and hats out of the short local native palm tree
that is used for palm products produced in the Mixteca region. José Luis
worked as a contracted bracero in the United States in 1961 and again in
1963. Prior to that, he worked in Veracruz harvesting coffee and sugarcane. After being a bracero, he worked as a farm laborer in Sinaloa and
Baja California with his wife and children. He has not returned to the
United States, but his son is living and working in Santa Maria, California, while his wife and two children remain in San Agustin. We spoke in
August of 2004. The conversation began with José Luis alone, but his
daughter Margarita joined in as we switched to talking about farm labor
in Mexico. She was born in 1971.

JOSÉ LUIS: I had an uncle who had a coffee ranch in Presidio, Veracruz. It
belonged to him and his sister. He wasn't from here, he was from a nearby
town they call Natividad. A lot of people from this community went there

to harvest coffee. Señor Pedro, his brother, and his sister. an uncle of mine whose name is Felipe and his daughter—they all went. We would go there for the coffee harvest. When it was over, we would come back here. We also harvested sugarcane there as well. The sugarcane work began in December and continued through May. The coffee harvest began in September and went until November. We would spend June, July, and August here and the rest of the time there. People went there to work every year. Some people also began to plant their own crops there as well. I went to Veracruz every year from 1945 until 1955 until I was nineteen or twenty years old. I went there for nine months a year . . . I remember that I was really young the first time I went there. The first time everyone went out to work they left me. I started to cry, and when they came back they brought me some oranges which calmed me down. I was nine years old.

In 1955, I started going to Morelos to pick tomatoes and corn for four or five months every year. From 1955 until 1960 we went there every year to pick crops. Then the contractors started taking us to Sinaloa.

LYNN: When did you go to the United States?

JOSÉ LUIS: In 1960, I first went to the United States as a bracero. I went there for forty-five days to work in Texas. They gave me a contract to work in the United States. I went with a friend and we worked in the cotton harvest. When the contract was over, we came home. I went again in 1963 to Sacramento. The second time I was there for three months. Look, here are my papers. [He holds out a card that is labeled "Alien Laborer's Identification Card," then another card labeled "Unión de Ex-Braceros"]. This is the one they gave me recently. They are trying to get our money back for us that was taken out of our checks when we were braceros.[1]

As mentioned by José Luis above, a number of families from San Agustín had been migrating for nine months a year to Veracruz to harvest coffee and cut sugarcane during the 1940s and 1950s and probably earlier. Others went to the state of Morelos in the 1950s.

In the early 1960s, at the time José Luis and others were recruited to work in cotton and other harvests in the United States through the bracero program, they were also targeted by Mexican labor contractors and encouraged to work in Sinaloa harvesting tomatoes, chiles, and other crops. Here we can see the overlap of efforts on the part of the U.S. government and Mexican growers to create a reliable migrant Mexican labor force that couldn't unionize or control its conditions of work. Mexican commercial agriculture is developing in the north, and labor

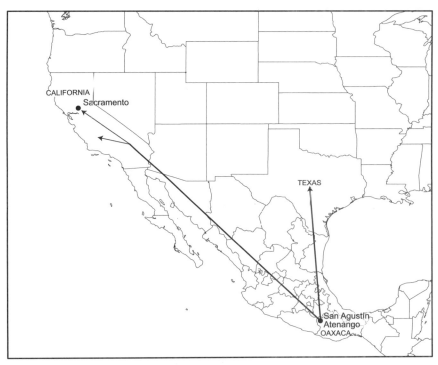

MAP 10. San Agustín Atenango bracero program migration, 1942–64

contractors are establishing themselves in the Mixteca region of Oaxaca in an effort to move workers from Veracruz to Sinaloa and Baja California. These recruiters began operating in Mixtec villages where Spanish was spoken. By the early 1960s they had worked their way into much more remote regions of the Mixteca region such as San Agustín and the district of Juxtlahuaca, towns which were predominantly monolingual in Mixteco at that time. The last period of the bracero program overlaps with the beginning of significant Mixtec movement from Oaxaca northward to northwest Mexico and into the United States

In her study of health and international migration in the Mixteca Baja community of Ixpantepec Nieves, Konane Martínez documents similar patterns of migration. Drawing upon oral histories and the research of Teresa Mora Vásquez (1982), Martínez describes how migration in Nieves in the 1970s included both temporary migration of heads of households and often dependents who migrated seasonally and returned home as well as permanent migration. Mora Vásquez carried out a survey in

Nieves in 1977 that indicated that 10 percent of the community had migrated temporarily and 11 percent had migrated permanently. Between 1960 and 1970, the population of Nieves dropped from 2,608 to 1,528 (a loss of 41 percent of the population) (Martínez 2005: 61). Of those who migrated temporarily (representing about 152 people in relation to the 1970 census figures), almost all (91 percent) were working as *jornaleros*, or day laborers (Mora Vásquez 1982: 22). Among this majority of day laborers, 67 percent went to Sinaloa, 24 percent to the United States, and 8 percent to Mexico City (Vásquez 1982: 22, cited in Martínez 2005: 52).

The anthropologist Federico Besserer's long-term study of migration from the municipio of San Juan Mixtepec to areas throughout Mexico and the United States also provides confirmation of the general patterns found in San Agustín Atenango and among other Mixtec communities. Besserer literally maps the geographical dispersion of Mixtepec as it spread from south to north in Mexico and into the United States and from the west coast to the east coast. Citing people's memories of significant life events, including work patterns from survey respondents in San Juan Mixtepec, he documents two kinds of movements from 1920 to 1940. The first involves Mixtec muleteers, who traveled throughout the state, and the second involves wage workers, who established a separate circuit of statewide movement (2004: 35–37; see also García Arellano 2000). Besserer's respondents recall that from the period of 1940 to 1960 they traveled to locations that included the states of Sonora, where they worked in cotton cultivation and Baja California, where they worked in the tomato fields. Many worked for numerous years in circuits between these two crops. Another group of workers labored in the tomato fields of California during this period as part of the bracero program (2002: 79). From 1960 to 1980, Besserer documents migration to the northwestern states of Mexico and to the United States, up the West Coast to California, Oregon, Washington and east to Idaho, Utah, Arizona, and New Mexico (2004: 40). The maps he put together from these interviews also indicate the presence of some people from Mixtepec in Alabama, Georgia, South Carolina, Virginia, Indiana, Ohio, Pennsylvania, and New York during this period as well (2004: 40, 42). Between 1980 and 2000, the geographical dispersion reflected in his interviews spread within Mexico along the Gulf of Mexico coast and in the United States to many states as far north as those on the Canadian border (2004: 37–41). It is important to keep in mind that Besserer documented not permanent settlement but traveling routes of workers. His larger point in this discussion is to help readers conceptualize the process of the deterritorialization of San Juan Mixtepec, but also to understand the unevenness and fluidity of migration as a process spanning several generations. "It may be more fluid than settled, as is the case of families of Mixtepequenses with children born in Oregon and now living in Virginia mobile homes—underscoring the temporary yet not-localized character of their transgenerational traveling condition" (2002: 82; 2004: 41). Laura Velasco, who has specialized in the study of Mixtec migration to the U.S.-Mexico border region, provides a similar overview of Mixtec migration patterns from the 1940s to the present. She highlights urban and rural migration and the work that Mixtec women have done in the domestic service sectors of cities as well as their participation as agricultural workers (Velasco 2002: 56–59; 1995).

By the 1970s, Mixtec migration was well established and significant in northwest Mexico and had also begun to spill over into the United States, as discussed above (López and Runsten 2004: 255). By the late 1980s and early 1990s, there was a significant population of Mixtecos in Baja California (Zabin et al. 1993). Velasco writes, "Beginning in the 1970s we could speak of a massive arrival of Mixtecos to the northwest border of Mexico . . . according to different sources of information, it is calculated that there are about 200,000 indigenous Oaxacans in California and Baja California, in large part Mixtecos. In general the Mixtecos who are arriving to the border region are from the districts of Huajuapan de León, Silacayoapan, and Juxtlahuaca, located in the heart of the Mixteca Baja" (2002: 59). The number two hundred thousand refers to the 1990s. Yet these numbers fluctuated because many Mixtecos who were residing in Baja California in places like San Quintín were further recruited by agents of farm labor contractors who operated in the United States (López and Runsten 2004: 255). Labor contractors who worked for growers in the Baja region were also reaching further and further into remote regions of the Mixtec region, recruiting not only Mixtecos, but Triquis as well. Many of these workers first went to San Quintín, Camalú, or other Baja regions and from there some headed right away for the United States. José Luis's story reflects this trajectory. His daughter Margarita, who also worked in Sinaloa and Baja California, joined the conversation.

JOSÉ LUIS: When I came back from the United States the first time, I started to go to Sinaloa. First I went by myself and then I started to take my wife and

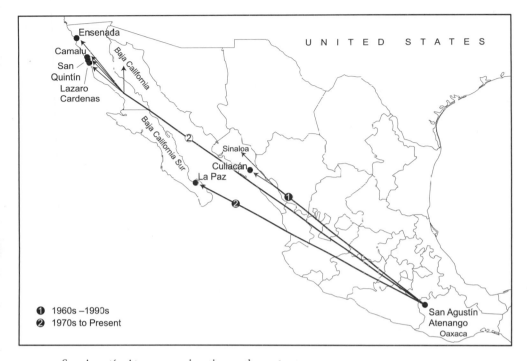

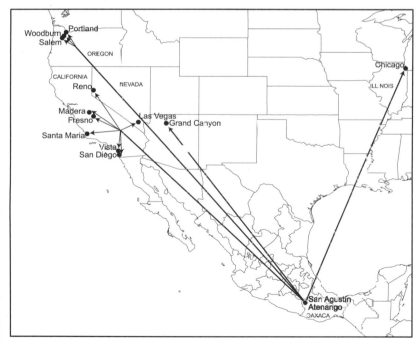

my kids when they were little. They were about two years old. This is how old they were when we went to Camalú in Baja California.

MARGARITA: I was born in 1971. So if I was two, then it was 1973.

JOSÉ LUIS: We went to Camalú, then we went to Rosario and to the place they call Cárdenas. They were already working, my kids. They were already helping me out. They were big enough so that they could help me to work.

LYNN: Did they go to school there?

MARGARITA: No. All we did was work. We studied here, primary school.

LYNN: So the kids would go to work after school?

JOSÉ LUIS: No. What happened was that when they started to go to school, I didn't take them with me any more. They stayed here and went to school.

LYNN: Did they stay with their mother?

JOSÉ LUIS: No. They stayed with my mother, their grandmother. My wife went with me. After that I started to go more to Rosario, to Vizcaino, to La Paz, to the Valle de la Constitución. I went there by myself and wandered all over there working.

LYNN: When did you finish primary school, Margarita?

MARGARITA: I finished in 1984. Then we all went again with my parents to work. They were in Cárdenas.

JOSÉ LUIS: In 1986 we began to plant here and I didn't leave again. One time I went to the United States in 1987. My son wanted to go by himself, but I didn't let him go alone. So I went with him. We went to Madera in 1987. He went that year and then came back here. Then he went back to the United States again. He went back alone and that is when he fixed his papers. He came back here very pleased because he had his green card. I never got one while I was there. Now I am just living here. I don't think about going back.

Mariano Bautista is a forty-eight-year-old Mixtec agricultural worker from the town of San Juan Cahuayaxi. His hair and short mustache are almost white. He wears a blue baseball cap. He has a friendly, open face that reveals a sad smile. He often feels tired from working a shift at a local fruit and vegetable packing plant. He is sitting in the living room of a two-bedroom apartment he shares with his wife, their five children, and two grandchildren. He has another daughter who lives in Madera, California, with her four children. Mariano and his wife receive frequent visitors, who come to them for *limpias*, or cleansings. Mariano has an herb garden that supplies him with necessary herbs for his sideline business of acting as a *curandero*, or healer. Their most sought-after talent is massage, which he and his wife may perform once or twice per day. Mariano also worked in Mexico City and Veracruz before working in Sinaloa and Baja California. From the time he was ten years old, he worked in many different parts of Mexico and then in the United States, always as an agricultural worker. His story takes him through the major commercial agricultural areas of Mexico and the western part of the United States

MARIANO: I was born in San Juan Cahuayaxi, in the municipio of San Juan Mixtepec in the Mixteca Alta. When I was three months old, my father left my mother. He went with another woman. My mother waited five years for him to return, but he never did. She had to marry another man to get by. I went with her and with the other man she married. He had five sons. It was not easy for me to live with them. I couldn't do anything.

I was five years old and still really small. They made me take care of the animals. I was six or seven years old when I went to live with my grandparents because my stepfather beat my mother a lot. He simply rejected me. He didn't accept me as his son so it was better for me to go and live with my grandparents.

LYNN: How was it living with your grandparents?

MARIANO: It went really well for me there. I was only there for about a year or two when my birth father came to get me and took me to a town called Las Minas, which is in the municipality of San Juan Mixtepec. He took me there to take care of his goats. He didn't allow me to go to school. I was there for six months with them and then I decided to leave home. I left when I was about ten years old. I hid in the back of a truck that went to Tlaxiaco.

LYNN: Why Tlaxiaco? What did you do there?

MARIANO: I hid myself in a truck in order to get there. I got off in Tlaxiaco and I first found work taking care of sheep. I just couldn't keep living with my stepmother—the new wife of my father. She hardly gave me anything to eat. She gave bread, milk, and meat to her own children, but she hardly gave me anything. I didn't even have a pair of shoes. I didn't get my own shoes until I was about eleven years old. Only then did I start dressing in a shirt, pants, and shoes. . . . I went back once to my mother's house in Cahuayaxi, but nobody wanted me. No one wanted to take care of me. . . .

. . . There were some people from Mexico who were visiting Tlaxiaco. They had come for the patron saint's fiesta. They gave me a ride to Mexico City. I left Oaxaca. They were workers who took me to Mexico City. When I got there, I was amazed. I loved it and admired it. It was like another world. What I couldn't do was to communicate there. I didn't know how to read or how to write. I could only speak Mixtec.

LYNN: How did you survive there?

MARIANO: Well, no one had any work to give me there at first. There are lots of big markets in Mexico City. What I did was to dedicate myself to cleaning up the fruit markets, carrying around the large baskets of fruit and working as a porter for people moving things for them in the market. I started to sell popsicles and to shine shoes. So I was there shining shoes, selling popsicles, and cleaning for five years. I slept in the street, in the garbage dump of the market and in abandoned houses. When I was sixteen years old, I went to Veracruz.

LYNN: Was there a particular reason why you went to Verzcruz?

MARIANO: I went because I heard that it was really beautiful there. Some people I knew took me there. It is a port and the city is on the sea. I went to work in the port. I gutted and cleaned chickens and fish. I helped to fill up the big baskets with fish.

One time I came back to Cahuayaxi to look for my family. I felt really sad. I didn't have anyone there in Cahuayaxi who I could call family. I was there for a week. After that I went to Culiacán, Sinaloa, with some people from Cahuayaxi who were working in agriculture. . . . When I first arrived in Culiacán I didn't know how to harvest tomatoes. They paid you about sixteen pesos per day for this work. There were some people there working in the tomatoes from Cahuayaxi. There were a lot of people from Oaxaca there as well. They were there from Huajuapan de León, from San Miguel el Grande, other places . . .

. . . There in Culiacán, the tomato season lasted for three months. From there, you went on to harvest cotton in Obregon. When the cotton was over then there was another cotton harvest that happened in Hermosillo. When we finished there, then we would go to La Paz, Baja California. There in La Paz was where we went to pick chiles, tomatoes, beans. This was my route every year.

From 1978 to 1996, Mariano went back and forth over the U.S.-Mexican border between southern California and Baja California. He worked in the United States in order to earn money to purchase land to build a house in San Vicente, Baja California. While he worked in the United States his wife and children stayed in San Vicente. In 1993 a storm destroyed his home in Baja California. After that he went further north to Madera and in 1996 brought his entire family.

I started coming to the United States to work so I could save money to buy some land in San Vicente, Baja California. I spent ten years going back and forth. By 1989, I was able to save a little money and I bought that land. I thought we could plant tomatoes, chiles serranos, watermelon, and corn. I didn't want to come back to the United States. I had built a little house with three rooms, and I really felt like my luck was changing. So I stayed there.

Then in 1993, there was a huge storm and the bridges fell down in San Quintín, in Colonia Guerrero, and in Rosario. There was no transportation and no way to get food in. The Mexican government sent in the army to get us out of there and they put us all into a camp called El Walter next to a hospital. We were given shelter there and food. We lost everything in that storm. I was left with nothing. I lost everything I had built up. That was why I eventually decided to leave Baja and come to the United States again. In 1996 my whole family came to Madera, California. I didn't think that it was good for us to live separated and for my children not to know their father. So we came to Madera where there were other people from San Juan Cahuayaxi.

When workers like José Luis, his daughter Margarita, and Mariano began to migrate on a regular basis to Baja California, some of them also settled there. Mariano was able to save up money from working both in the United States and in Baja, bought land in San Vicente, and built a small house. The first settlers in Baja were documented at the end of the 1950s in Tijuana in the Colonia Obrera. Some who settled in Tijuana came to work on a daily basis in Tijuana. Others who settled later in San Quintín, Lázaro Cárdenas, Camalú, and El Rosario and elsewhere even participated in petitioning the Mexican government for *ejido* land to build houses and to have small plots to farm. Others purchased land privately. In their documentation of migration flows from the community of Asunción Naranjos, Juxtlahuaca, López and Runsten found that migrants came to work in the agricultural area of Del Mar, Oceanside, Vista, and Oxnard in the late 1970s. By 2003 there were about sixty families from Asunción in Oxnard and some families who migrated to Gresham, Oregon (López and Runsten 2004: 258).

Moving from a base in California to Oregon or another state is common. Mariano began coming from Madera, California, to Woodburn, Oregon, where he worked in the fields. Eventually in 2001 he brought most of his family except for his eldest daughter and her children to Woodburn. There he continued in agricultural work, which is primarily seasonal. Mariano's family has had a difficult time in Oregon as he relates below.

MARIANO: My family stayed in Madera while I came to Woodburn, Oregon, so that I could look for work. I worked harvesting strawberries, blueberries and also in the cannery. I came up here first to look for work. Then in 2001 I decided to bring my whole family up here.

LYNN: What was it like when you first moved to Woodburn with your family?

MARIANO: It was very hard when we first came. When we first arrived, we were living on the farm owned by a Russian. Then we were renting an apartment on Young Street with a cousin of mine. But because we didn't have a lease for the apartment, they didn't want to let us stay there and they threw us out. So at that point we started to sleep in the street. We slept in our car parked on the street during the winter. My wife and I slept in the car. We put one of our kids in one house with relatives, another one with another one, and so forth. We used to meet each other in the park during the day to see one another. My wife and I slept in our car in front of the post office. Then a man from Oaxaca told us we could park the car in the parking lot of his garage. We finally found housing here [at a farmworker housing project called Nuevo Amanecer] for about eight months. Now we have to find something else, and my job at the cannery is about to end for this year . . .

. . . There is no work for me during the months of November, December, January, and February. Right now in September, October there is a little bit of work in the grapes, but after that there is nothing. You can only find work here in Woodburn for part of the year. . . . As someone who is an agricultural worker, I have to really struggle to keep my kids dressed, to buy them shoes, to buy their sports clothes.

Mixtec immigration to the West Coast of the United States appears to have increased significantly from 1995 to 2005. One recent estimate put the number of Mixtecos in California at one hundred thousand (Stanley 2005). One of the premier destinations for workers from San Agustín is Santa María, California, in the county of Santa Barbara. There were an estimated two hundred people from San Agustín living there in 2004. There is a local San Agustín Atenango Mixtec community group in Santa María that is affiliated with the FIOB.

According to the reporter Melinda Burns, about eleven thousand Mixtecs live year-round in Santa María, ten times as many as there were in 1995. In addition to San Agustín, they come from seven other Oaxacan communities (Burns 2004a: 10). Most of the adults and increasingly teenagers fifteen years old and older are picking strawberries and other crops, earning between seven thousand and twelve thousand dollars per year (Burns 2004a:10; 2004b). According to officials at the State Center for Assistance to Oaxacan Migrants (Coordinación Estatal de Atención al Migrante Oaxaqueño), the rate of migration from the Mixtec region has doubled since the mid-1990s. In some Mixtec communities in Oaxaca only 10 percent of the population remains (Burns 2004c: 4). In San Agustín, about 60 percent of the population remains, but out-migration has increased significantly in the past ten years. In her study of Ixpantepec Nieves, Martínez found that a majority of adults between the ages of twenty and sixty-four were absent by the year 2000. Between 1988 and 2000, the population of Nieves went from 1,435 to 1,112, a decline of 22.55 percent (2005: 54–55). In Nieves, as in San Agustín Atenango and elsewhere, it has become a normal part of social development to finish secondary school and then to migrate to the United States. This type of norm certainly is suggestive of what Jeffrey Cohen terms "a culture of migration." Cohen elaborates on this term, stating that it signifies not only that migration is pervasive and has a historical presence but also that the decision to migrate is one people make as a part of their everyday experiences; furthermore, he claims, most people view this everyday decision as one path toward economic well-being (2004: 5).

The pattern of migration reflected in the stories of José Luis, Margarita, and Mariano is representative of the overall pattern of Mixtec migration. Mixtec migration has a long history in the twentieth and twenty-first centuries. Workers first left to labor closer to home in Veracruz, Oaxaca, and Morelos. They then went farther afield through the bracero program to the United States. Simultaneous with their recruitment to the United States, Mixtecos were recruited to work in Sinaloa, Sonora, and Baja California as export agriculture expanded in that region. From there, they went again to the United States to work in agriculture. Mixtecos have largely remained in agricultural labor with some moving into other kinds of work such as year-round positions in nurseries or in the service sector. Because they have continuously engaged in seasonal work that pays minimum wage and have been in some of the most exploitative labor contracting circumstances (including in the labor camps described in chapter 5), Mixtecos have had a more difficult time than Zapotecs from places like Teotitlán saving money and having any kind of surplus to invest in entrepreneurial activities. Mixtecos historically have had much higher rates of monolingualism and less education and fewer Spanish-speaking skills than Zapotecs. For more than four decades, Mixtec migrant farmworkers have provided the cheap, mobile labor force needed to support the commercialization of agriculture in Mexico and the United States. When the economic integration of the U.S. and Mexican economies accelerated in the 1970s and Mexico's economy underwent a process of "structural adjustment" in the 1980s, Mixtec workers were part of the invisible glue of poverty and extremely difficult working conditions that held the integration together, as Besserer notes (2002: 288–89).

Mexico's "structural adjustment" and "open economy" had a tremendous impact on agriculture. The new model reduced government support for peasant agriculture in order to encourage peasants to migrate to high-wage regions. Supposedly, salaries would rise in the areas of peasant production as those seeking employment migrated elsewhere, while migrant remittances would also flow back into peasant zones to provide them with productive capital. Meanwhile, the migrant agricultural force would "contribute" to zones of agricultural export production by providing low-cost labor (as it did). The result was massive mobilization of migrant workers from the traditionally peasant regions of the country such as Oaxaca, Guerrero, Puebla, Morelos, Estado de Mexico, and Hidalgo, mostly states with a high proportion of indigenous population. The states receiving both international investment in agriculture and low-cost indigenous labor were Sinaloa, Sonora, and Baja California. Mixtec, Zapotec, Mixe, Triqui, and other ethnic peoples became workers for transnational agricultural producers in their own country. They quickly migrated even farther into the sites of global agricultural production in California, Oregon, Washington, and to many other states in the United States, becoming transnational workers in yet a second sense, namely, as workers who cross national borders.

What Happened in Mexico to Cause So Many People from Oaxaca to Migrate?

As outlined above, Mixtec migration in particular has been tied to the commercialization of Mexican agriculture beginning after World War II. For the past two decades, liberalization of trade barriers between Mexico and United States has made it much easier for U.S. agricultural products to enter Mexico and for more Mexican products to enter the United States. Mixtec migrants from towns like San Agustín Atenango come from agricultural subsistence communities. While many of the residents of San Agustín have access to plots of communal land where many continued to plant corn and beans, beginning in the mid-1980s falling Mexican corn prices, gradual withdrawal of government support, and increased labor recruitment of workers to Baja California and into the United States resulted in at least half of the fields remaining uncultivated. As stated succinctly by Melinda Burns (2004c: 1):

The Mixtecs form part of a de facto border exchange, one in which the U.S. exports cheap corn to Mexico and imports Mexican corn farmers to labor in the fields of California (and elsewhere). Nearly two decades of free trade have deepened the poverty and unemployment in Mexico's countryside, studies show. Mexico's three million peasants were simply outgunned by 75,000 farmers in Iowa who—with the help of ample rain, state-of-the-art technology, and millions of dollars in government subsidies—could produce twice as much corn at half the price.

As early as the 1960s, Mexico's farmers began to leave the countryside. In 1965, the average rural wage was more than a farmer with a small parcel could earn by relying on his or her own labor and that of the immediate family. In the 1970s, wholesale food prices failed to keep pace with the rural cost of living and with the cost of tools and inputs required by subsistence and small-scale farmers. Government support prices for basic grains dropped from 85 percent of their 1960 value in 1977 to 76 percent in 1979 (Fox 1992: 62). From the 1970s until significant reforms in agricultural policy were put in place in the mid-1980s, the primary way small farmers with rain-fed (unirrigated) land were able to continue was through government support prices. The Compañia Nacional de Subsistencia Popular (National Basic Foods Company, or CONASUPO), a major player in government intervention in agriculture, instituted programs for eleven basic crops: barley, beans, copra, maize, cotton, rice, sesame, sorghum, soybeans, sunflower, and wheat. CONASUPO not only provided support prices, but also processed, stored, and distributed these crops as well as regulating trade through direct imports (Taylor et. al. 2005: 87–88). Some policy makers in CONASUPO viewed their job as regulating domestic grain markets through periodic imports. Prior to the crash of the peso, imports appeared cheap in light of the overvalued peso. In 1980, CONASUPO increased support prices for corn by 28 percent, but since inflation was also 28 percent, the price supports simply slowed down the decline of the real value of what producers received for their corn (Fox 1992: 109). By 1981, Mexico's imports of basic foodstuffs were greater than its agricultural exports, but this did not necessarily indicate increasing dependency on imported corn and other grains. The record level of grain imports in 1981 masked the success of record domestic corn production for human consumption, which has continued to be high despite the neoliberal economic model implemented in relation to agricultural policy beginning in the 1980s and culminating with the North American Free Trade Agreement (NAFTA). In 1981, Mexico incurred a very high agricultural balance of payments deficit with imports at US$3.6 billion while exports were at US$1.7 billion. Ironically, that same year domestic grain production reached record levels of 1.95 million tons of domestic maize (Fox 1992: 111).

The mid-1970s in Mexico (as in the rest of the world) mark the beginning of what is now called economic restructuring or economic globalization—shorthand for the deepening of the integration of national economies. U.S. and European markets were stagnant in the mid-1970s, and corporate profits had begun to decline. In order to increase profits, Western transnational corporations began to explore new markets around the world and to search for cheaper costs of labor. Transnational corporation investments overseas, free trade agreements, " 'lean and mean' worker dismissal policies of neoliberalism and the 'runaway-plant' strategy of setting up assembly plants in low-cost labor areas like Mexico" began to predominate (Cockcroft 1998: 248). By 1994, U.S.-based transnational corporations employed 40 percent of their workers in the so-called Third World nations (Cockcroft 1998: 248). The emphasis on economic development in Mexico was on small islands of modernity that were focused on development of the *maquiladora*, or in-bond assembly plant sector of Mexico. Industrial expansion was limited to capital-intensive areas that provided few jobs.

The agricultural policy that accompanied economic restructuring focused on pushing subsistence farmers out of what was seen as unproductive subsistence farming. The policy begun in the 1980s and was formalized in 1992. That year marks the changes made to Article 27 of the Mexican Constitution, which encouraged the privatization of the 50 percent of Mexico's land base held in nonprivate status and increased investment in export production of fruit, produce, and other crops. Prior to 1992, land held in communal, or *ejido* status, could not be privately owned by an individual. Ejidos were created after the Mexican Revolution to satisfy the demands of landless peasants who had seen their communal village land eaten up by large agricultural estates and who had served as laborers on those estates. Ejido land is held in a communal form of land tenure in which members have use rights, usually in the form of an individual plot. The ejido also refers to a specific area of land as well. For many communities their ejido also refers to their territory, as does communal land, or *terrenos communales*—actual land tied to the community. Specific areas of land granted as ejidos or regained as terrenos comunales often, but not always, have long-standing historical meaning. This is particularly true if they were occupied precolonially and then usurped during the colonial period (Stephen 2002: xxvi–xxvii).

In addition to ejidos, a significant part of rural land held in nonprivate or social tenancy lies in *comunidades agrarias*. This land constitutes a significant part of the holdings of indigenous communities and is based on historical claims, usually dating to pre-Columbian or historical times. In many cases these lands are known as *comunales* (communal lands). Both Teotitlán del Valle and San Agustín Atenango have significant communal holdings or comunales. Teotitlán has 6,601 hectares of communal dry land, including forests (Stephen 1991:70). The communal lands of Teotitlán del Valle are documented in colonial maps dating to 1564, 1596, and 1797 which are on display in the community museum. The communal lands of San Agustín Atenango were first purchased in 1867 but were formally constituted by the Mexican government as terrenos comunales only in 1947 (Departamento Agrario 1947). An ongoing dispute with San Mateo Libre and San Vicente del Palmar (beginning in the 1940s) over part of this land was finally resolved in the Agrarian Tribunal of Huajuapan de León in 2000 confirming that San Agustín Atenango has 8,451.10 hectares of communal land. As described in chapter 2, only about 10 percent of this land is usable for farming.

The lowering of trade barriers and tariffs through the 1994 ratification of NAFTA permitted ever-increasing amounts of U.S. corn—primarily yellow corn for animal feed—and other products to enter Mexico to compete with those produced by subsistence farmers. Recent studies evaluating what happened to corn farmers in the 1990s have revealed some interesting trends. Rather than knocking out all corn farmers from production in Mexico, U.S. imports of yellow feed corn in combination with the end of guaranteed prices (initially for basic crops other than corn and beans and then later income support programs for all farmers producing basic crops) resulted in an increase in corn production among middle-size and larger farmers with access to irrigated land. Many of these farmers converted to corn from other crops such as oilseeds.

Smaller-scale subsistence farmers who grew corn and beans primarily for their own subsistence continued to produce at a loss, even with the subsidies provided by post-CONASUPO programs. The real higher costs of producing corn for farmers in subsistence-based communities such as San Agustín became too high for most people to continue farming after CONASUPO subsidiaries and price supports were phased out by the mid-1990s. In San Agustín, many migrants returned for at least part of the year to maintain subsistence crops of corn and beans in local fields. By the mid- to late 1990s, however, this pattern had changed dramatically as migration became less circular and people began to settle in Baja California and in the United States. In Teotitlán del Valle, about 26 percent of the population were full-time subsistence and small-scale farmers in 1980. By 1986, this percentage had decreased to 11 percent as people increasingly took up textile production and migration (Stephen 1991: 72). Understanding what happened in rural Mexico from 1980 onward is a crucial component to understanding the migration and labor stories in this chapter.

In 1982, Mexico experienced a deep economic crisis linked to the slashing of oil prices, expanded international borrowing at high interest rates to develop the petroleum industry and other infrastructure, runaway inflation, and problems of corruption and accountability in the government (Cockcroft 1998: 271). In August 1982, Mexico announced that it could not meet its debt payments, and a two-stage 100 percent devaluation of the peso was completed. When the dust settled, a U.S.-led financial bailout of Mexico totaled ten billion dollars. In exchange for the restructuring of its debt, Mexico had to radically change its economic model, ending import substitution and protectionism and entering a full-tilt program of what is now known as neoliberalism. In exchange for its financial assistance package, Mexico had to reduce the public sector deficit from 18 percent of GDP in 1982 to 3.5 percent in 1985 in an effort to reduce foreign borrowing and restrain inflation (White, Salas, and Gammage 2003: 10).

When translated into agricultural policies, this involved the elimination of producer price supports for five basic crops (copra, cotton, safflower, sunflower, and sesame seeds), and CONASUPO, which had purchased basic grains, provided price supports; further, a network of stores that subsidized basic goods in rural areas was downsized significantly. In 1992, guaranteed prices for wheat, sorghum, soybeans, rice, barley, safflower seed, and sunflower were eliminated. In 1995, CONASUPO eliminated all domestic price supports and became "the buyer of last resort" for producers (White, Salas, and Gammage 2003: 11). By this time, the implications of NAFTA for the agricultural sector had also begun to appear, exacerbating an already difficult situation in which prices for basic crops declined and the prices of things like fertilizers, seeds, and equipment increased.

Under NAFTA, all nontariff barriers to agricultural trade between the United States and Mexico are to disappear. NAFTA also required the Mexican government to reduce price supports for domestic farmers and to reduce import restrictions (White, Salas, and Gammage 2003: 13). In the early 1990s, there were about three million corn producers in Mexico, equivalent to about 40 percent of all rural Mexicans working in agriculture (Woodall et. al 2001: 23). At that time, corn farmers received about $240 per ton of corn from CONASUPO owing to what remained of pre-NAFTA price support policies (Woodall et. Al 2001: 23). Within thirty months of the implementation of NAFTA, Mexico eliminated its corn quotas from the United States and CONASUPO reduced the amount of crops it purchased from farmers. From 1994 through 2002, with the exception of 1997, U.S. corn imports to Mexico have increased, tripling in comparison with levels prior to NAFTA (Fanjul and Fraser 2003: 16). The amount of corn CONASUPO bought "fell from 45 percent of domestic corn in 1994 to 20 percent in 1995. The real price farmers received for corn declined by 26 percent between 1993 and 1995" (White, Salas, and Gammage 2003: 14). By 2001, real corn prices had fallen more than 70 percent, meaning that corn farmers and their families had to live on less than one-third of the income they earned in 1995 (Fanjul and Fraser 2003: 17). While one might think that the availability of cheaper U.S. imported corn in Mexico would mean cheaper prices for consumers, it has not. The price of a kilo of tortillas—the basic foodstuff of poor Mexicans—rose threefold, in real terms, between 1994 and 1999 (Fanjul and Fraser 2003: 18).

While the Mexican government has offered roughly one hundred dollars per hectare to small-scale and subsistence farmers to offset their losses from NAFTA through a program called PROCAMPO (see Stephen 2002: 66–67), this has not been enough. Between 1991 and 2000, the total number of corn producers for household consumption declined by 670,000, and the number of producers cultivating corn for sale declined by 343,000. Thus a little over 1 million corn producers (1,013,000) have stopped producing corn and have had to find another source of income

(White, Salas, and Gammage 2003: 18). While the number of corn producers decreased by about 21 percent among *ejidatarios* and communal farmers, the total amount of land devoted to corn in Mexico remained fairly stable from 1991 to 2000. The explanation for this is not surprising, given the dynamics of increased stratification in many sectors within Mexico under NAFTA. After the revisions to Article 27 in 1992, some farmers began to rent land from others, particularly from ejidatarios and comuneros who had small plots. By switching to corn on irrigated land and collecting about eighty-five to one hundred dollars per hectare through PROCAMPO and other direct payments through a second scheme called the Program of Direct Supports for Marketing and Development of Regional Markets, medium- and large-sized farmers who had a marketable surplus were able to produce corn under favorable conditions. Their access to irrigated land greatly increased their productivity compared to that of rain-fed land. The Direct Supports Subprogram provides producers with a surplus of marketable output with access to a fixed subsidy per ton directly from the Mexican government through the Ministry of Agriculture, Livestock, Rural Development, Fishing, and Nutrition (SAGARPA). In 2002, expenditures in the amount of 37 percent from the Direct Supports Subprogram went to white corn producers in Sinaloa, Sonora, and Baja California (Zahniser and Coyle 2004: 8). Sinaloa produced 42 percent of the corn cultivated on irrigated land in Mexico that year. Marketing supports and rental of ejido lands have facilitated the "emergence of large-scale farms for corn and dried beans" (de Ita Rubio 2003). By 1997, grain yields on irrigated land was 3.4 times greater than on rain-fed land (Taylor et. al 2005: 98). In other words, very small-scale subsistence producers with rain-fed land on ejidos and in comunidades agrarias dropped out of agricultural production, but other farmers, who had more resources to begin with, were able to continue producing white corn for a domestic market at a relative advantage. This may change in 2008, when PROCAMPO is scheduled to phase out and all supports to Mexican corn farmers are supposed to end in accordance with the provisions of NAFTA.

Some of the small-scale corn farmers who dropped out of production may have found work in the commercial agricultural sector in horticulture, industrial food production, and fruit production. Since the implementation of NAFTA, the number of jobs in these sectors has grown by 20 percent, reaching approximately 1,847,680 by the year 2000 (White, Salas, and Gammage 2003: 17). While the number of jobs in these sectors increased somewhat, the wages for agricultural workers fell dramatically between 1991 and 2003, as they did elsewhere in Mexico. Monthly income for agricultural workers in constant 1994 pesos fell from 550 pesos per month in 1991 to 483 pesos in 2003—an average of 2.8 pesos per hour, or about US$2.50 per hour in a forty-hour week. Self-employed farmers had even more dramatic wage losses. In 1991, self-employed farmers earned 1,959 pesos per month, and in 2003, 228 pesos for the same amount of work (as measured in constant 1994 pesos) (White, Salas, and Gammage 2003: 19). This is a devastating loss of income for subsistence farmers under NAFTA. According to these figures, by 2003, subsistence farmers were earning only 11.6 percent of what they did in 1991!

Another way to look at this is in terms of what subsistence farmers could purchase through the sale of one metric ton of corn before and after the economic restructuring of the agricultural sector began in the early 1980s. In 1980, one metric ton of corn could purchase 6.1 baskets of basic goods. A basic basket of goods (*canasta básica*) is defined by the Mexican central bank (Banco de Mexico) as the cost of basic goods and services for the average Mexican based on eighty essential items, including expenditures for food, clothing, health, public transportation, housing and rental estimates, as well as costs associated with primary and secondary education, school supplies, and uniforms. A hearing of the Mexican Senate in December 2000 put the cost of the official canasta básica at approximately 3,300 pesos (US$330/month) (Kada 2004). Thus by 2000, one ton of corn could purchase only 2.4 baskets of basic goods (White, Salas, and Gammage 2003: 24).

The proportion of rural households living in poverty increased from 56 percent in 1992 to 60.7 percent in 2000 (White, Salas, and Gammage 2003: 27). Poverty is defined as that income which fails to meet a basic basket of goods. All of these figures spell out one clear trend: those who had previously earned a living in small-scale or subsistence agriculture or even as agricultural workers in Mexico had to find additional sources of income to survive in the 1990s and beyond. Data from the Mexican National Rural Household survey of 2003 suggest that rural out-migration (both internal and to the United States) rose dramatically during the 1990s. The number of migrants from Mexican villages who relocated to other parts of the country rose 352 percent between 1980 and 2002. The number of migrants from rural Mexico in the United States was 452 percent higher in 2002 than in 1980 (Taylor et al. 2005: 102). Many rural workers and farmers did not find work in Mexico during the 1990s because of insufficient growth in manufacturing employment. Many now work in urban informal services or have migrated to the United States (Taylor et al. 2005: 103).

Even urban manufacturing workers who had jobs had a hard time in the 1990s, including those involved in what until quite recently was the most successful sector in Mexico's engagement with neoliberalism—the maquiladora sector. A maquiladora is a form of production in which raw material, parts, and equipment are imported into Mexico for the purpose of being assembled or transformed in Mexico (as in putting together clothing and electronic goods or engine parts) and subsequently exported to foreign markets, including the United States. In 2004, the government-mandated minimum wage for workers on the border was US$4.20 per day—the same as ten years ago. Many maquiladora workers earn close to this wage. It takes a maquiladora worker in Ciudad Juárez almost an hour to earn enough money to buy a kilo of rice. A gallon of milk, which costs US$3.00, requires five to six hours of labor (Bacon 2004).

Many observers of NAFTA thought that the expanding maquila sector would save Mexico and make up for job losses elsewhere by creating good permanent jobs in assembly plants. By 2001, 1.3 million workers were employed in two thousand border plants (Bacon 2004). This number of jobs was created from the late 1960s to the present. These jobs are tied to the U.S. market that the plants were producing for. At the same time that maquiladoras were producing some new jobs every year, about 1.5 million young Mexicans were entering the workforce every year. While providing a small outlet for Mexicans being shut out of other sectors since 1994, the job growth in maquilas stopped and reversed by 2004.

In 2001, when U.S. consumers stopped buying consumer goods in large quantities, a recession hit and maquiladoras began shedding workers. The Mexican government estimated in 2004 that up to 400,000 jobs disappeared (Bacon 2004). While the Mexican government has blamed the loss entirely on China, Mexico's vulnerability to consumer patterns in the United States is also part of the story. More than 520 factories in Mexico have shut their doors and moved to China since December 2000, including the Japanese television maker Sanyo, which closed six plants in Tijuana, laying off 1,900 workers (Sneider 2003). According to Merrill Lynch analysts, Mexican hourly wages, including benefits and taxes, now average US$2.96. Move to China and you only have to pay 72 cents per hour, wiping out the advantage Mexico has of proximity to the American market (Sneider 2003). Job growth inside of Mexico was anything but certain for the later part of the twentieth century.

What Happened in the United States to Encourage Mixtecos and Zapotecos to Migrate and Settle There?

"Fresh" Produce Markets in the United States and Mexican Workers

At the same time that Mexican agriculture pushed out subsistence and small-scale farmers such as those in San Agustín Atenango and elsewhere, commercial fruit and vegetable production expanded in northern Mexico and became incorporated with that of the United States, providing an alternative labor market for rural Mexicans. This change was driven in part by U.S. consumer demand. On any day of the year you can walk into the produce section of any grocery store and find a wide array of fresh fruits and vegetables: tomatoes, strawberries, melons, cucumbers, lettuce, apples, oranges, and carrots. American consumers can pick up prewashed and precut salad mixes, cut and washed fruit salads, and more. A complete line of "fresh" temperate and tropical fruits and vegetables is available anywhere, anytime. As pointed out by Walter Goldfrank, *fresh* refers to the "pristine appearance of the foodstuff, not [to] its space-time proximity to the consumer" (1994: 268). In fact, the appearance of freshness is made possible by the availability of counterseasonal produce that can be delivered through what are called long-distance cool chains that allow fruits and vegetables picked "weeks or even months in advance to be cooled, stored, and/or shipped with the aid of spoilage-retardant chemicals, handled by workers at multiple job sites" (often in different parts of the globe) to be delivered on demand to supply affluent consumers everywhere (Goldfrank 1994: 268). Efforts to develop new items for produce consumers accelerated in the 1980s. The average supermarket produce department sold 65 items in 1975, and 210 in 1988 (Goldfrank 1994: 271). As American women entered the paid labor force in greater numbers, their demand for domestic services and for easy-to-prepare foods increased. Fresh produce and fruit that requires no preparation beyond washing is viewed as nutritious and healthy.

The availability of such allegedly fresh fruits and vegetables year-round in the United States is also tied to the integration of the U.S. economy with others, often through the neoliberal reorientations that began in the

1970s. By 1998, Mexico dominated the U.S. market for fresh vegetable imports, totaling US$2.1 billion (Cook 2002: 16). Although the number of U.S. farms producing fruits, nuts, and vegetables continued to decline in the 1990s, in key production regions such as California a few large growers became "forward integrated" into the marketing of their own production and the production of other growers—hence their designation as grower-shippers. Grower-shippers control production, packing, and cooling facilities and also arrange for domestic and export sale, transportation, and promotion (Cook 2002: 21). Many grower-shippers are multiregional, multinational, and multicommodity so that they can have a year-round presence in grocery stores. The rapid growth of multi-location firms beginning in the 1980s led to the integration of the Mexico-California-Arizona vegetable industry (Cook 1990). In the early 1980s, San Diego grower-shippers began to work in Baja California, attracted by lower labor, land, and water costs. According to Carol Zabin, U.S. grower-shippers entered into joint ventures or other arrangements to finance and market tomatoes and other crops with about a dozen Mexican growers.

Production technologies have been transplanted intact from southern California to Baja. Patented seeds, plastic mulching, and planting in plastic tents are common practices in both areas, as is drip irrigation. The tasks carried out by field workers—which include transplanting, staking, pruning, and harvesting—are almost identical. Baja growers belong to the same U.S.-based trade organizations as their counterparts north of the border and call upon University of California extension agents when they have a pest problem (Zabin 1997: 341; Cook 1991).

Nevertheless, while there has been greater market access and expansion of Baja California agriculture, the bulk of fresh vegetables produced by California and Arizona firms is still produced in the United States owing to infrastructure, technology, and efficiency advantages (Cook 2002: 21). This has kept a significant number of harvesting jobs in the United States, not only in California and Arizona but in other states as well, such as Oregon.

The use of computerized forecasting for when crops will ripen according to ground conditions, temperature, and other factors has led growers to be able to predict when they will need a certain number of farm laborers. Processors set the schedules for when fruits and vegetables should be harvested and delivered. For growers, this means communicating with labor recruiters about how many workers they will need when. The use of cell phones, e-mail, and faxes can facilitate communication between growers in the United States and labor recruiters in Mexico.

In the 1990s, growing consumer demand for convenience-oriented fresh-cut produce in supermarkets also produced new U.S. jobs in the production of things like bagged salads, broccoli and cauliflower florets, sliced mushrooms, cored pineapples, fresh-cut melons, stir-fry vegetable mixes, packaged baby carrots, carrot and celery sticks, and precut vegetables (Cook 2002: 23). Farmworkers who harvest in the fields are often working second shifts in what is called postharvest handling, and specialty produce or in canneries and frozen food processing plants that are located in close proximity to where fruits and vegetables are harvested in the United States. In many food processing plants, frozen vegetable mixes with such labels as "Oriental vegetables," "Mediterranean vegetables," and "flavor fiesta" may include vegetables from several global locations—but marketed under a regional ethnic label. With the integration of production, processing, and marketing of fruits and vegetables in the United States and Mexico, a new labor market for displaced subsistence and small-scale farmers emerged.

The labor histories of transborder workers such as José Luis and Mariano often revolve around following products such as the tomato or the strawberry from one location to another. Their journeys began at a young age when they started working outside of their natal communities, spreading elsewhere in Mexico, and finally to varied locations in the United States. Such histories often combine various experiences in different places into one articulated chain of following products from one place to another without necessarily reflecting directly on the larger structural conditions that produce repeated experiences of low-wage work in both Mexico and the United States. The kind of knowledge that workers talk about might be thought of as practical knowledge they have accumulated through their own experiences and those of others in their border-crossing lives as they move from one site to another but often continue to engage in similar kinds of labor.

In his analysis of the greater transnational community of San Juan Mixtepec, Besserer describes how what he calls "transmigrant workers" understand the spaces they labor in as they follow transnational commercial agriculture:

Transmigrants' practical understanding of the discontinuous space of post-fordist agriculture revealed important erasures that tended to obscure the fact that greater profit comes to agribusiness from the articulation of agricultural hyperspaces. Transmigrants frequently narrated their lives in terms of having been "in the tomato," forgetting the specifics of where they had been while "just remembering" specific events they experienced. (2002: 300)

It is important to contrast such product-driven memories with structural discussions of how and why, for example, U.S. and Mexican commercial agriculture has merged to form one continuous field of labor relations and production cycles that are geared toward providing the North American market with year-round access to fresh fruits and produce (increasingly organic).

The Domestic Services Market and Mexican Workers

At the same time the U.S. market for ready-to-eat produce was expanding, a demand for other kinds of convenience services emerged. The same woman who wanted to purchase a bagged salad and fresh fruit to feed to her children because she didn't have a lot of time to prepare food was also looking for assistance in cleaning her home and caring for her children. There was a rise in demand for domestic workers in cities such as Los Angeles, where capital concentrates began in the mid-1980s (see Sassen 1991). Global cities like New York, Rome, Paris, Tokyo, Mexico City, and Los Angeles help to integrate global economies and are also reflective of the nations, economies, and cultures they pull together as a kind of global command post (see Sassen 1991). Los Angeles is a dynamic economic center for the Pacific Rim that has a large, diversified economy supported by a huge manufacturing sector as well as the entertainment industry. As Pierrette Hondagneu-Sotelo writes,

The Upshot? Los Angeles is home to many people with highly paid jobs. . . . Many people employed in business and finance, and in the high-tech and entertainment sectors, are high-salaried lawyers, bankers, accountants, marketing specialists, consultants, agents, and entrepreneurs. The way they live their lives, requiring many services and consuming many products, generates other high-end occupations linked to gentrification (creating jobs for real estate agents, therapists, personal trainers, designers, celebrity chefs, etc.), all of which in turn rely on various kinds of daily servicing that low-wage workers provide. For the masses of affluent professionals and corpo-

13. Catalina García (*right*) with her mother.

rate managers in Los Angeles, relying on Latino immigrant workers has almost become a social obligation. (2001: 6–7)

From 1989 to the present, Catalina García has served as a nanny for affluent professionals in the greater Los Angeles area. Born in Teotitlán del Valle in 1946, Catalina worked as a weaver and a mother of five children until she came to the United States. Her husband left her after five years of marriage when her children were quite young. She has spent much of her adult life raising her children with the support of her mother-in-law, who died in 2005. In August 2004, we spoke in Teotitlán del Valle—one of many conversations we have held over the past twenty years. On that occasion Catalina had returned temporarily to Teotitlán to prepare for her youngest child's wedding, which was taking place later that month.

Catalina's hair is pulled together in one long, thick braid that snakes down her back. The braid is now slightly tinged with gray but is mostly black. She has a wide, round face which is open. Her eyes are dark pools of kindness that reflect someone who knows suffering. She has a quick smile and often tilts her head when her smile is relaxed. Her arms are thick and strong, as are her hands. This comes from grinding cornmeal by hand since she was eight years old and decades of hard work cooking, cleaning, and taking care of her own and other people's children. Here she describes twelve years she spent raising the children of an Anglo couple in the Greater Los Angeles area as well as the friendships she developed with other nannies and domestic workers from Latin America.

CATALINA: At first, I was living with my sister and my brother-in-law and I was cleaning houses with my sister Margarita. After that, one of the women we were cleaning for, her name was Rose Hoffman, took me to her house. I went there with my sister Margarita. Rose had a little boy named Carl who was one year and four months old. She liked my work, and sometimes she would leave her little boy with me. She was pregnant with a girl at that time. So she told me that I could take care of him for one or two hours while I was there cleaning. She told me that she liked my work, but I didn't speak English and she spoke very little Spanish.

When she was close to giving birth to her baby, she asked my sister Margarita if I could work with her and take care of her kids. The woman who had been working for her taking care of her son was very old. and she wasn't going to be able to take care of two small children. So she asked me if I could take care of them. This was in 1991 . . . I told her that I couldn't because I couldn't speak any English and they didn't speak Spanish.

LYNN: How much Spanish did she speak?

CATALINA: Very little. So she told me that I could go to school to learn English so I could learn to talk with her and she could teach me what I needed to do. But I didn't want to go to school for a long time because it is very difficult to learn another language. Well, she started to cry and said, "Please, I want someone I can trust."

My sister Margarita had been cleaning her house for some years and she knew her very well. Margarita said to me, "Rose really wants you to work with her."

I said to Margarita, "No. I came to help you. I am not going to look for other work. Besides, I can't work for her because I don't speak English."

. . . The señora called me every day asking me to work for her. She called my sister every day, too. . . . Finally my sister said, "Please, she really wants you to do this. Can you please do this?" So finally, I said, "Yes. I can do it."

. . . So I started working slowly for her, four hours here, then five hours every day. Margarita was living in Santa Ana, and Rose Hoffman lived in another small town nearby. So Margarita my sister took me there everyday to work. It was very hard for me because I didn't understand anything the señora told me. She took me by the hand and taught me everything. I was like a mute person with her. I couldn't speak. It was very hard, and I felt really sad because I couldn't communicate with them.

Her husband would go to work at 5:30 or 6:00 in the morning. Rose wasn't going to work when I started out. But when the child was born, I had been working with her for two months. The few days she went to the hospital when the baby girl was born she didn't use me. She told me that after three days I should come to work.

When the baby was four days old, she came home. She told me then, "Thank you so much for coming to work with us. Now the new baby has arrived and you are going to take care of the children. I will be very kind to you and I will teach you everything about taking care of the new baby." She was only home for a week, and then she went back to work, and I stayed with the kids. I was there all day long. I started taking care of them at six in the morning.

LYNN: Did the baby nurse?

CATALINA: The baby didn't nurse during the day. The señora would pump her milk and then I would put it in a bottle. She would leave enough to fill up three bottles and she told me that I should give it to the baby when she cried. So I gave the milk to the baby. The baby was quite pretty. I had to always change her clothes and then the other child was there also. I was running around like a crazy person because I had two babies. The little boy was really something—*tremendo*. He was always getting into mischief. Sometimes when their grandmother would come, she would bathe the baby and I would bathe the little boy. But most of the time I was taking care of the two of them alone for twelve hours a day.

LYNN: When did you go back to see your sister and your kids?

CATALINA: I went back on the weekends to be with them. During the week I was just there to sleep and then back to work. My two children were going to school in Santa Ana. I was working five days taking care of those kids and resting on Saturday and Sunday.

LYNN: Did you really rest or did you work more?

CATALINA: I was working because I wanted to help out my sister. On Saturdays I would help Margarita wash clothes and I would wash my kids' clothes . . .

. . . I spent two and a half years like this. Then this family moved further away to San Pedro and they took me with them. The señores didn't want to look for another person. Where they moved was about an hour away from Santa Ana where my sister and kids were living. I worked for them for a total of twelve years.

One of the most difficult issues for nannies and domestic workers like Catalina can be an inability to communicate effectively with their employers and their young charges. For Catalina, learning English was important, not only for being able to communicate on the job, but to be able to maneuver better in the United States. Through a network of other domestic workers she met with in the park, Catalina eventually went back to school and learned to read and write—something she had never been able to do in Teotitlán. Her network of friends also helped to sustain her during the week when she was away from her own children, a common situation for live-in nannies.

LYNN: Did it continue to be so hard? You said at first, you were very sad because you couldn't communicate.

CATALINA: Well, everything changed because the señora had a lot of patience. When we moved to San Pedro she would sit down at the table with me at night and she would teach me a little English and I would teach her Spanish. She was very smart. She taught me some English, but I spoke Spanish with the kids. After the little girl was four years old, I was able to speak English. But then she told me she was really happy that I spoke Spanish with the children.

. . . I had this friend Olga who was from El Salvador. She told me I should try to speak English with the kids because then I would learn English. She said that if I wanted to change jobs and couldn't speak English, that I wouldn't be able to find a job. So after that I started to speak more English with them. I don't know what kind of English I spoke, but I did speak with them.

LYNN: How did you get to know Olga?

CATALINA: I got to know her there in San Pedro. She was working close by in another house. She did the same work as I did, taking care of kids. I also got to know others who were doing this work too. I got to know four women from Guatemala, three from El Salvador, and two from Chiapas.

LYNN: What did you talk about?

CATALINA: First we would talk about where we were from, the kind of work we were doing. We also talked about the English school, about learning English and our work. We talked to each other about how we felt about our bosses. Often we would see each other in the park We would all take the kids we were taking care of there and each lunch together. We would take the kids on walks together. They were important friendships.

. . . I also got to know an American woman there as well. Her name is

Marion. She worked in the library and she helped me to study English. She was the *patrona* (employer) of one of my friends, named Graciela from Guatemala. My friend spoke to her patrona about me. She told her that I didn't know how to read or write or really speak English. My friend Graciela told me that I would need to learn all of these things. . . . So when I would take the kids over to play at the house where Graciela worked then her patrona would teach me some English.

LYNN: Is that where you learned to read and write?

CATALINA: Yes. I learned with her. I learned how to read a little bit. And after this my friend Olga told me, "You need to speak with your patrona about going to school." So I spoke with my patrona. I told her, "I want to go to school."

The little boy was already in school and the little girl was still in the house with me. She told me, "When the little girl begins to go to school, then you can go to school too." She told me that I could go to the school for a couple of hours if I had someone to take me there. Because the school was kind of far from the house where I lived and there was no bus line that arrived there. . . . So my friend Marion took me to the school. She picked me up and brought me back home.

The labor of workers like Catalina became vital to significant parts of the population in California in the 1990s and beyond. In 1998, Catalina received legal residency with the assistance of her employer. She now works independently as a nanny, returning home at night.

In 2004, the Mexican filmmaker Sergio Arau and his wife, Yareli Arizmendi, produced a film titled "Un día sin Mexicanos" (A Day Without Mexicans). In the film, all of the Latino immigrants in California disappear one day without leaving a trace. A mysterious cloud envelops Los Angeles, and it is completely cut off from the outside world—the phones don't work, the Internet is interrupted, and the territory of California is completely isolated. Within a short period of time restaurants cease functioning because there are no waiters, cooks, or kitchen staff, no one cleans up anything anywhere (from city garbage to houses), vegetables and fruits rot in the fields, and the public schools also cease to function as many of the pupils, teachers, and staff have disappeared. The invisible workers become temporarily visible as most public and private services and businesses fall apart in California (see Wides 2004).

The visibility of Mexican immigrant service workers in Los Angeles and other global cities began to increase in the 1990s. Hondagneu-Sotelo reports that twice as many gardeners and domestic workers were working in Los Angeles in 1990 as in 1980. These jobs are performed by Mexican, Salvadoran, and Guatemalan immigrants who by 1990 "numbered about 2 million and made up more than half the adults who had immigrated to Los Angeles since 1965" (2001: 7). For women like Catalina, some of the best job opportunities were in housecleaning, childcare, elder care, and other paid domestic work.

The labor force participation of women in the United States rose steadily beginning in the 1960s and leveled off to slightly over 80 percent by 1995 (Fair and Macunovish 1996: 2). By 1990 in the United States, women were 45 percent of the total labor force (Goldin 2002: 1). This statistic included a group that has resisted joining the labor force—married women with small infants. While the numbers of women—particularly married women with children—who are in the paid labor force have increased dramatically in the past three decades in the United States and in other industrialized countries, they still remain responsible for what is known as the reproductive labor of households. Rhacel Salazar Parreñas defines reproductive labor as "the labor needed to sustain the productive labor force. Such work includes household chores; the care of elders, adults, and youth; the socialization of children; and the maintenance of social ties in the family" (2001: 61; see also Glenn 1992). For professional women, the easiest way to maintain their professional positions is by purchasing the services of other women to perform work as day-care providers, after-school baby sitters, and as privately hired domestic workers and nannies. Having high incomes, families that include professionals have the flexibility to buy the services they need. The hiring of Mexican immigrant women such as Catalina as private nannies and domestic workers is a gendered and racial dimension of the integration of global economies.

In her analysis of Filipina domestic workers in Los Angeles and Rome, Salazar Parreñas emphasizes the ways in which the globalization of the market economy has extended the politics of reproductive labor into the international arena. She calls for an understanding of the racial division of reproductive labor in its globalized dimensions as part of the international division of labor (2001: 62). This international transfer of caretaking from one group of women to another involves social, political, racial, and economic relationships between women in the global labor market. Salazar Parreñas elaborates: "This division of labor is a structural relationship of inequality based on class, race, gender, and (nation-based) citizenship. In this division of labor, there is a gradational decline in worth of reproductive labor. As Rothman (1989: 43) poignantly describes, 'When performed by mothers we call this mothering . . . ; when performed by hired hands we call it unskilled.' " Regional race, class, and gender relations contain specific histories of the domestic worker–employer dyad between women.

Mexican immigrant women and Mexican American women have filled the occupation of domestic worker along with Asian, African American, and Native American women in the western part of the United States since the late nineteenth and early twentieth centuries. This stems in part from the area's proximity to Mexico and also from the fact that much of the southwestern United States was part of Mexico until 1848. From the 1880s until World War II, domestic work provided the largest source of non-agricultural employment for women of Mexican descent (Hondagneu-Sotelo 2001: 15). This trend continued well into the 1970s in some regions and into the present in places such as Los Angeles. As Hondagneu-Sotelo points out, by opening up public sector jobs to African American and Mexican American women, "the Civil Rights act made it possible for them to leave domestic service and move into jobs as secretaries, sales clerks and public service employees as well as into low-paid service jobs in convalescent homes, hospitals, cafeterias and hotels" (2001: 16). By the mid-1970s, immigrant Mexican and other immigrant women (primarily Latin American and Asian) began to fill the shoes of Mexican American, Chicana, and African American women who had predominated in domestic labor. In Los Angeles, "the percentage of African American women working as domestics in private households fell from 35 percent to 4 percent from 1970 to 1990, while foreign-born Latinas increased their representation from 9 percent to 68 percent (Hondagneu-Sotelo 2001: 17). During the 1990s and beyond these numbers undoubtedly grew as the number of Latin American immigrants increased significantly not only in Los Angeles, but elsewhere as well. Many undocumented women initially start as live-ins, as Catalina did, before moving on to other kinds of more independent work. Thus the trend in service-based economies that favored immigrant women's providing reproductive labor services emerged in tandem with the adoption of neoliberal economic models around the world. The trends outlined above, which were exacerbated by NAFTA in Mexico—such as lower real wages and decreased supports to consumers for basic consumption goods—combined with increased demand in the United States for domestic labor. For people like Catalina and Emiliano these conditions produced a situation that made it difficult to refuse domestic work in the United States when earning possibilities were fewer and at significantly lower wages in Mexico.

Conclusions

As we have seen in this chapter, the political and economic integration of Mexico and the United States throughout the twentieth century is closely tied to the movement of people within each country and across borders. The work experiences of people like José Luis, Mariano, Catalina, and Emiliano are closely linked to the larger political economy of the United States and Mexico. In their daily life experiences, however, the personal, emotional, and physical experiences of work are what they emphasize in their recollections of migrating and working in Mexico and in the United States. The effort and dignity they bring to their work are stressed as are their relationships with employers, other workers, and other migrants. The challenge for ethnographers is to both conceptualize the larger structural conditions framing migration and work—such as the emergence of consumer markets in the United States for fresh produce and domestic services and the effects of neoliberal economic policy in Mexico—as well as to capture the human relationships and lived and remembered experience of cross-border workers. Thus the geographies we create of cross-border migration and work have to be multidimensional, responding not only to structural conditions but also to embodied memories and experience. As we will see in the next chapter, work experiences and memories are also integrated with the status of actual or presumed "illegality" that many workers have faced when they were undocumented and simultaneously trying to remain invisible while also the objects of surveillance.

CHAPTER 5

Surveillance and Invisibility

in the Lives of Indigenous Farmworkers in Oregon

Americans face a dilemma. While in our post-9/11 culture many are calling for stricter border controls and ever more stringent immigration legislation to prevent the entrance of terrorists to the United States, we have a food economy that is highly dependent on recent immigrant labor—much of it Mexican and much of it undocumented. On February 17, 2005, the *New York Times* reported, "New intelligence information strongly suggests that Al Qaeda has considered infiltrating the United States through the Mexican border, top government officials told Congress" (Jehl 2005). Undocumented workers and others who are read as undocumented in the United States and increasingly as supposed possible terrorists have been living in the world of surveillance and limited personal liberties for quite some time. They live in a contradictory state of trying to maintain invisibility while simultaneously being the object of significant surveillance at different points in their journey and work experiences in the United States.

Scholars such as Alejandro Lugo (2000) and Renato Rosaldo (1997) have questioned overly optimistic readings of the border that leave behind the militarized, policing, segregation, and surveillance aspects of border life for working men and women. While the border is perhaps the most intensive location of surveillance, for undocumented workers and even for those who have papers, being watched continues to be one of the most difficult parts of their work experience because of continued nervousness about being undocumented. In farm labor camps, surveillance of workers extends far beyond the kind of supervision normally found in the fields and food processing factories. Labor contractors often strictly control who can have access to labor camps, the forms of transportation available, access to medical help, and even access to food. But even once workers are in the field, the idea of being watched can be experienced and interpreted not only as supervision, but also as suspicion.

In this chapter, I focus on the experiences and memories of indigenous immigrant and migrant agricultural workers as simultaneous objects of surveillance and invisibility on the U.S.-Mexico border, the agricultural fields and labor camps of Oregon, and in produce processing plants. The aspects of surveillance and invisibility explored here are deeply connected to the concrete conditions shaping the experiences and behavior of the indigenous migrant and immigrant workers described in this book. The individual experiences of the different kinds of surveillance described in this chapter are directly linked to the legal contexts, structure of labor markets, management practices, immigration policies, exigencies of making wages fast, and often saturated labor markets that shape the work lives of indigenous migrants and immigrants in farm labor. Key to understanding these experiences and memories is the flexible and moving nature of the border away from its physical location as the legality of border crossers is continually contested through the way that indigenous workers are structurally inserted into the power relations of commercial agriculture and often culturally interpreted as being illegal. I discuss the construction of illegal aliens through a brief reading of recent U.S. immigration policy, which, along with U.S.-Mexican economic integration, has encouraged and increased undocumented immigration through time. Historical construction of the "Mexican illegal alien" also involves the racialization of this term through casting it as a cultural category with its own inner essence or substance. Racialized readings of Mexican indigenous immigrants and migrants as illegals, undocumented or not, result in surveillance from many people in the United States, from border guards to factory supervisors.

This chapter also details how indigenous migrant and immigrant workers often try to remain invisible in the larger world to avoid detention and deportation by U.S. Customs and Border Protection (formerly the INS, known among migrants as *la migra*). Extended conversations with workers reveal how the border permeates their memories and self-identities regardless of their location or actual immigration status. The contradictions of transborderness are highlighted here in the minds of individual workers as they struggle to reconcile the truth that they have physically crossed the border but are actually living in the United States without permission and need to appear invisible—in other words, appear not to have crossed the border. Appearing not to have crossed the border when in fact one has done so without documentation involves creating alternate identities, securing documents when one has none, and appearing to be legal when one is not. The movement of the border with the person who crossed it and the wearing of the border inside and outside as an undocumented person is another form of moving across borders—in this case in a contradictory framework of simultaneous surveillance and invisibility.

The Construction of Illegal Aliens and the Encouragement of Undocumented Immigration through U.S. Immigration Policy

U.S. immigration policy in relation to Mexico and other countries has served primarily as labor policy—inviting workers in when they are needed and then showing them the door when it became politically expedient to "defend" the border. While U.S. immigration policy has consistently maintained the theater of defending the border from what are called illegal aliens, deeper historical analysis of particular policies directed toward Mexico—for example, the bracero program of 1942–64, the IRCA, and the SAW program of 1986—and a close examination of the accelerated integration of the U.S. and Mexican economies under economic neoliberalism and NAFTA suggest that U.S. immigration policy toward Mexico has in fact encouraged and facilitated increased immigration (see Massey 1997; Martin 2003). In many ways, past U.S. immigration policy is directly responsible for increased levels of undocumented immigrants in the 1980s and 1990s, in Oregon and elsewhere in the country. The most recent piece of major immigration legislation related to significant increases in the number of undocumented people in Oregon and elsewhere is the IRCA and the accompanying SAW program, discussed in chapter 3. Philip Martin notes that as workers who were legalized under SAW were free to search for higher wages and better work outside of the farm labor sector, many wound up in midwestern and southeastern fields and in farm-related meat and poultry processing jobs (2003: 187). Those who went to new locations to secure better jobs became anchors for others from their hometowns, giving rise to what has been called the Latinoization of the rural United States.

IRCA/SAW seems to have particularly encouraged increased numbers of women and children to come to the United States from Mexico. The majority of Mexicans who received permanent residency under the saw program in the Pacific Northwest were men (about 85 percent), a fact that was repeated elsewhere in the country. In an assessment of the impact of the 1986 immigration law Wayne Cornelius states, "The migration of women and children has increased since IRCA's enactment, both to take advantage of the amnesty programs and for family reunification. Some male family heads who secured amnesty for themselves began sending for their wives and children in Mexico, whether or not these dependents could qualify for legalization" (1989: 14–15). One of the clear outcomes of the saw program and the general amnesty program of IRCA was the reuniting of some family units in the United States with differential legal statuses in the same family—most often with men as legal residents, women as undocumented residents, and children who had a mixture of legal statuses, including U.S. citizen, legal resident, and undocumented resident (see Stephen 2001a).

Recent analysis of the 2000 U.S. census as well as microstudies confirm that many immigrant households living under the same roof in the United States are composed of people with different legal statuses. An Urban Institute report (1999) states that "85 percent of immigrant families (i.e., those with at least one noncitizen parent) are mixed-status families" (Fix and Zimmerman 1999). In Woodburn, Oregon, 27 percent of all households are of mixed status, and 8 percent are unauthorized, i.e., all family members are undocumented according to a random sample survey carried out in 2003 as part of the New Pluralism Project discussed in chapter 3.

In Oregon, some male laborers working in the lowest-paid and most labor-intensive part of agricultural production were able to gain legal residency through the 1986 immigration legislation. While some had been working in the state of Oregon for perhaps five years, they had not established long-term networks. When they brought their families in the late 1980s and early 1990s, these families became the basis of more permanent communities and networks. Later in the 1990s, unattached younger females and males also began to migrate, attaching themselves to older relatives such as siblings, aunts, and uncles already in Oregon.

Many male farmworkers who did receive legal residency in the mid-1980s through IRCA or saw and whose family members came to be with them illegally did not immediately petition to legalize their wives and children. Only when the Illegal Immigration Reform and Immigrant Responsibility Act of 1996 (IIRIRA) was passed, triggering a deadline of

January 1998 to apply for legal residency in the United States, did the number of male farmworkers petitioning to legalize family members increase significantly. And many did not make the January 1998 deadline. Thus significant numbers of women and children remained in the United States illegally, residing with husbands, fathers, and other male relatives who do have legal residency. As he left office in late 2000, President Bill Clinton extended a special "sunset provision" that gave another chance to all of those who had missed the January 1998 deadline to apply for legal residency if they already have a family member here. A small window of opportunity was created between December 21, 2000, and April 30, 2001, under the Legal Immigration and Family Equity Act (LIFE). The act allowed a person who qualified for permanent residency but was ineligible to adjust status in the United States because of an immigration status violation to pay a one-thousand-dollar penalty to continue processing in the United States.[1] This made it possible for some undocumented women and children to apply for legal residency. The high cost of the fine, however, inhibited some people from applying. According to the National Agricultural Workers Survey of 1997–98, about half of farmworkers earned less than seventy-five hundred dollars per year. Given this level of income for many farmworkers, the one-thousand-dollar fine plus legal costs for each person processed made the opportunity unavailable to a significant number of people. Some undocumented farmworkers and their family members took advantage of this program, but others did not.

Douglas Massey notes that the wages of undocumented Mexican workers have suffered because of IRCA:[2] "We found that before IRCA migrants without documents earned the same wages as those with them, and that the specific rate of pay was determined by a person's education, duration of U.S. experience and English-language ability. After IRCA, however, undocumented Mexican migrants earned wages 28 percent below those earned by documented migrants with similar characteristics. . . . The post-IRCA wage penalties were especially severe in agriculture and among migrants hired through subcontractors" (1997: 11). One of the reasons that wages for undocumented workers dropped is lack of enforcement of employer sanctions contained in IRCA. As part of the 1986 legislation, employers who knowingly hire, recruit, or refer for a fee undocumented workers can face fines of up to ten thousand dollars and criminal penalties of up to six months in jail.[3] As for the impact of employer sanctions on undocumented workers, Massey states, "the primary effect of IRCA's employer sanctions has not been to reduce undocumented immigration, but to push the employment of Mexican migrants underground, yielding a new black market for immigrant labor" (1997: 11).

The Politics of Fear and Food

Oregon has more than 100,000 farmworkers, 98 percent of whom are Latino, primarily of Mexican origin.[4] Farmworkers and their dependents living in Oregon numbered approximately 174,000 at the turn of the twenty-first century (Larson 2002: 23).[5] The most recent farmworkers, many of whom live permanently in Oregon and should be considered immigrants workers, are indigenous. Others work temporarily in the state and move on to other areas of the United States and Canada as well and should be considered migrant workers. Whether or not a worker is undocumented is not necessarily a predictor of immigrant (settled status) versus migrant (temporary resident and repeated movement within the United States or across the U.S.-Mexican border).

According to the Department of Labor, about 53 percent of farmworkers in the United States are undocumented. In California, estimates are as high as 90 percent (*The Economist* 2005). While no hard figures are available, it is often estimated that from 50 to 80 percent of those who labor in Oregon's fields are undocumented. Within the processing plants and canneries the number of undocumented workers is lower, but still relatively high. Many of the people I interviewed who worked in the canneries and frozen food plants were documented, but many had worked there in the past before receiving documentation and mentioned friends and family members who worked there with purchased documents. A 2002 internal policy of the Social Security Administration of sending letters to some workers informing them that their Social Security numbers do not match their names and are thus invalid has discouraged some; others continue to work with documents they have purchased. I don't believe anyone really knows how many people fall into this category.

The importance of undocumented Mexicans in food production and processing is not an isolated case. By March 2005, the undocumented population of the United States was nearly eleven million. Approximately six million, or 54.5 percent, were from Mexico. About 80 to 85 percent of the migration from Mexico in recent years has been undocumented (Passel 2005: 1). Since the advent of stronger U.S. border enforcement in the mid-1990s and the increasing cost and dangers of crossing over, both legal and undocumented workers are staying longer in the United States. The staying time of undocumented workers has notably increased in the 1990s (see Cornelius 2005: 11; Massey, Durand, and Malone 2002: 128–33; Reyes 2004). In 1992 about 20 percent of Mexico to United States migrants returned home after six months, whereas in 1997 about 15 percent did, and by 2000 only 7 percent did (Cornelius 2005: 11; Reyes, Johnson, and Swearingen 2002: 32–33).

In 2006, it was estimated that there were between 125,000 and 175,000 undocumented Mexican immigrants residing in the state of Oregon (Pew Hispanic Center 2006). However, the actual number of documented and undocumented workers may be much higher. Mexico's consul general in Oregon stated that the uncounted in Oregon—the migrant population and seasonal workers—is closer to 600,000 in the state (Rico 2005b: 1G). These undocumented residents in the United States in combination with those who are here legally make a major economic contribution to their country. During 2004, Mexicans living outside of Mexico sent home US$17 billion in remittances and 18 percent of the adult population in Mexico reported receiving remittances in 2003 (Suro 2003). In 2004, Mexican immigrants in Oregon sent $218 million to Mexico (Rico 2005c: 10G). By 2005, Mexicans living outside the country sent home $20.034 billion (Narita 2006: 2). This contribution to the Mexican economy is second only to international oil sales, which generate the highest level of foreign exchange.

It was no surprise that during a visit to Washington, D.C., as President George W. Bush's first state visitor in early September 2001, President Vicente Fox of Mexico stated, 'The time has come to give migrants and their communities their proper place in the history of our bilateral relations. . . . We must, and we can, reach an agreement on migration before the end of this very year" (Milbank and Sheridan 2001). Prior to September 11, immigration was one of the top priority issues of the Bush administration. Cabinet officials from the Bush administration and others had been discussing different types of arrangements that would allow those working illegally in the United States to gain some form of legal status as part of a revision of immigration policy. Such a plan was seen as necessary to win over Latino voters and to please employers seeking workers.

Then, just days after President Fox left the country stating that there had to be a new immigration policy by the end of the year, the attacks of

9/11 happened. Instead of an opening of U.S. immigration policy that would have the effect of legalizing those who are undocumented and perhaps findings ways to manage migration flows that are part of how an interconnected world functions, the response of many Americans has been to call for an increase in resources devoted to border control and increased enforcement of current immigration laws (Camarota 2001). While the possibilities for a new bracero or contracted agricultural worker program between Mexico and the United States that might permit some path to legalization are still being debated, for millions of undocumented Mexicans and others this means continued invisibility and decreased personal freedom and security.

Cultural Readings of "Illegal Aliens" and the Infinitely Elastic U.S.-Mexican Border

Within the United States, Mexican workers may be documented or undocumented, but the historical construction of Mexicans in the United States as "illegal aliens" through U.S. immigration policies results in many being automatically read as illegal. The legal labeling system that includes the terms *citizen*, *resident alien*, and *illegal alien* is historically wedded in Oregon to a racial hierarchy that first glossed *Mexicans* as *Indians* and denied them the right to own land and vote in the state Constitution of 1853. The second-class status of Mexican workers is reinforced by the racial history of the western United States, which has continually defined people of Mexican descent as racially inferior, biologically suited for agricultural labor, culturally traditional and backward, and in need of supervision and programs of assimilation in order to fit with American society (see Foley 1997; García 2001; Gutiérrez 1995; Menchaca 2001).

In Oregon, use of the label *illegal* for Mexican workers can be traced most recently to changes in the ways that contracted workers were categorized while working under the bracero program from 1943 to 1947 and afterward. Agricultural workers went from being written about as heros when they arrived in the state in 1943 and 1944 in headlines such as "Wheat Saved by Mexicans," "Mexican Harvesters Doing a Great Job in Fields and Orchard"[6] to being called wetbacks and illegals by the late 1940s and early 1950s in the same newspapers. Headlines such as "Agents Sweep Rising Tide of Mexican Illegals South to Border" became typical.[7]

Many of the farmworkers hired under the bracero program continued to be recruited by growers once the program ended, and other growers joined them in the 1950s, 1960s, and 1970s. Throughout the 1980s and into the mid-1990s, the INS continued to conduct raids in agricultural areas of Oregon. In 1981, INS officials rounded up ninety-two "suspected undocumented aliens" in a raid on a Castle and Cooke mushroom farm in Salem (Manzano and Walden 1981a). Workers were reported to have hid on compost beds inside the mushroom farm to escape from INS agents. Temperatures became unbearable in the compost beds along with noxious fumes as the beds were treated with ammonia. One man who was detained, Clemente Porros, commented, "We knew that this was going to happen. . . . We think about it every day" (Manzano and Walden 1981b). Porros, it turns out, was a legal resident.

In an analysis of broader anti-immigrant sentiment in the United States as expressed in the media, Leo Chavez (2001) provides a detailed content analysis of over seventy cover images from popular magazines since 1965. In his analysis, Chavez notes that while the discourse on immigration generally found in the cover images he analyzed includes both alarmist and affirmative imagery, the "magazine covers that reference Mexican immigration . . . have been overwhelmingly alarmist. The magazine covers on Mexican immigration begin with alarmist images and maintain that perspective during the entire thirty-five-year period. Alarm is conveyed through images and text that directly or metaphorically invoke crises, time bombs, loss of control, invasion, danger, floods, and war" (2001: 215–16). One such powerful message and image is a cover from an issue of *U.S. News & World Report* in 1979 showing several presumably Mexican persons on the border being arrested by an INS agent; the title reads, "Illegal Aliens, Invasion Out of Control" (Chavez 2001: 225). Four years later, another cover from the same publication continued the invasion theme.

Such images also contain a racially coded message which equates darker color and the speaking of Spanish with illegality. Images such as those documented by Chavez operate at multiple levels, drawing a circle around all Mexican immigrants as others and aliens and also working to reinforce hierarchies of skin color within the Mexican population. In his multifaceted analysis of "border inspections," Alejandro Lugo reminds us that "the system of color hierarchy . . . has its roots in the Spanish colonial period" (2000: 360). Lugo suggests that the "social taste and preference for light skin and respective inverse for darker skin, continues today . . . though more informally and unofficially (thus unrecognized, not open for discussion), even as we enter the 21st century." Cultural hierarchies of color in working-class border communities that Lugo writes about form part of a wider racial classification system within Mexico, the border region, and within Mexican communities in the United States (see chapter 7) that reinforces U.S.-based cultural readings of anyone who "appears Mexican" as illegal. Indigenous Mexican workers are often darker in skin tone and can fit that wider racial classification of "appearing Mexican."

Anti-immigrant cultural and political forces have pushed back at Mexican immigrants, often rendering them as different from the dominant society because of racial, cultural, and linguistic characteristics that mark them as other (Flores 1997: 256). In the case of Mexican immigrants, what initially was a legal and cultural label (undocumented/illegal Mexican immigrant) became racialized as images of supposed illegal aliens such as those documented by Chavez (2001) flooded the American public. Nicolas De Genova has also focused on the specific process of racialization of undocumented Mexicans in Chicago as contrasted to Puerto Ricans, who are legal citizens (2005). As Nina Glick Schiller has written, when "the concept of culture is used in ways that naturalize and essentialize difference . . . people may speak culture, but continue to think race" (1995: iii, cited in Medina 1997: 762). When ethnic and legal differences come to be seen as absolute and natural, "ethnic identities . . . become racialized: like physical appearance, cultural practices and values may be defined as an inner essence or substance" (Medina 1997: 762). As pointed out by John and Jean Comaroff (1992: 60) and others (Hall 1988: 2), socially constructed categories such as race and ethnicity become perceived as impassible symbolic boundaries that become fixed in nature and take on the appearance of an autonomous force capable of determining the course of social and economic life. Thus Mexican indigenous workers who are continuously read as dark and illegal become subject to treatment that is justified by their appearance. Such treatment includes surveillance because of their presumed or potential illegal/criminal status. A further dimension of being read as illegal is that one can never safely cross the U.S.-Mexican border, either physically, legally, or culturally.

Mexican indigenous workers have a strong sense of continually being read as other and different in Oregon and California by non-Mexicans, who have begun to see Mexican immigrants for the first time as their numbers intensify in certain areas. Part of the feeling of being watched also relates back to a fear of being categorized as illegal. Many workers I talked with never really relax because of the continued presumption by some non-Mexicans that all Mexicans are undocumented and, as such, potential criminals. After 9/11, the fear of being seen as criminal and undesired became even more pointed.

Patricia Cruz is a twenty-year-old Mixtec woman from Tezoatlán de Segura y Luna in western Oaxaca. She first came to the United States in 2000 and landed in Flagstaff, Arizona. There she worked two eight-hour shifts every day cleaning offices for less than minimum wage. She then went to Los Angeles for a few months and then to the Yakima Valley of Washington state, where she worked in the apple orchards. In 2001, she came to Oregon to get a high school degree through a High School Equivalency Program run at the University of Oregon in Eugene. Patricia has long black hair that nearly reaches her waist. It is pulled back by a barrette. She is dressed in a tight tee shirt and jeans with black boots. We sat at the kitchen table in the apartment she shares with her brother and talked about an incident at work that happened right after 9/11. Her dark eyes flashed with anger as she spoke to me in April of 2003, remembering how she felt:

PATRICIA: I did notice something different after September 11. . . . I noticed because it is like the Hispanos, those who are not from this country, and we noted a kind of rejection although it wasn't necessarily directly to us. But people would say, or at least those people who are Americans would say something . . .

LYNN: What did you notice at work? What did you feel?

PATRICIA: . . . When I got to work the same night [of September 11], all that everyone was talking about was that it was immigrants who did this, that if there were no more immigrants in the United States nothing would have changed. They said that it was the fault of the immigrants that there were so many problems in the United States. We know that we didn't do anything to cause these things to happen. I think it is really hard to explain this to people and have them understand. But I am telling you that one person in my work said something directly to us and told us that we shouldn't come here [to the United States] to mess everything up for the rest. . . . I just started to smile. I could have answered her in English, but I said to myself, why should I? She will just think I am a person who knows nothing.

If she could just think about how it is that she and people like her are destroying their own country, their own nationality. I think that a person like her is causing more destruction to her country because while people think like that, there is more hate and racism. This is what causes destruction of a country more than anything. . . . I think she is destroying her country far more with her words and deeds than a Mexicana who just comes here to live or try to survive, trying to earn enough to eat. I think that now this person until this day doesn't like me just because I am Mexican. I just ignore her and do my work. I think that during this time after September 11] there were changes that were really hard for Latinos, for people who are immigrants.

Patricia's words capture the indignation, anger, and hurt experienced by many who have felt even higher levels of suspicion and surveillance in relation to their presence in the United States since September 11, 2001.

For many scholars, the experience of Mexican immigrants who can never "cross" the border requires a reconceptualization of the border itself—not as an actual physical place but as an interconnected cultural/ legal/racial divide that can move through time, space, and place (see Anzaldua 1987; Kearney 1991, 1995a, 1998). Lugo argues that the U.S.-Mexico border is "an incitement to an always unfilled locality and residentiality. Yet it reinforces nation and its privileged subjects. Consequently, it also marks as peripherals those other peoples, as those 'Other Victorians' in Foucault's *History of Sexuality*, who should belong elsewhere, in some other place of residence, on some other side" (2000: 358). Arturo Aldama takes Lugo's definition of the border and adds class and color specifications about those who are able to successfully "cross" and those who never are able to "cross the border" regardless of their actual physical location or legal status. The following are the last two of four proposals he makes about the U.S.-Mexico border:

> 3. Even though the border is selectively open to those whose class positions confirm their tourist and student status, it forces a discourse of inferiorization onto Mexicans and other Latinos, especially those whose class position, ethnicity, and skin color emerges from the campesina/o and urban proletariat groups.
>
> 4. Finally, once crossed, the border is infinitely elastic and can serve as a barrier and zone of violence for Mexicanas/os, Centroamericanas/os, and other Latina/os confronted by racialist and gendered obstacles—material and discursive—anywhere they go in the United States. This means that the émigré/immigrant continually faces crossing the border even if s/he is in Chicago (or any other location in the United States)—a continual shifting from margin to margin (2001: 135).

Surveillance: Worker Views from the Border,
the Fields, and the Plants

In the ethnographic descriptions and conversations with Mexican indigenous workers that follow, the elasticity of the border and the inability of people to believe they have ever safely crossed it are remembered through experiences of surveillance on the border, in the fields, in labor camps, and in the processing plants. The cultural framework through which Mexican indigenous workers are read is partially assimilated into their emotional memories of work itself. The reminder of being other, of being different, and of legal and cultural limbo is a constant presence, even after people have obtained official legal status. For many, repeated attempts to cross the border and, if they are successful, living in the United States without the ability to return home freely are a constraint woven into the daily fabric of their lives.

The Border: A Lifetime Barrier

In everyone's testimonies about migrating to the United States, the narrative about actually crossing the border is an important event. Often crossings are traumatic and repeated, and they remain difficult secrets that migrants carry with them. After Emiliano Gómez (introduced in chapter 4) told me his story, I transcribed it and gave him the transcription to read. He told me then that he had never told this story to his wife but had decided to share it with her once it was written down. His eyes filled with tears as he recounted her loving response to his difficult crossing. "I never told her before. I just carried this with me," he said. "Maybe it is good to share such a difficult story, but it was very hard to remember." Emiliano did not have an easy time in the United States, and he has no pleasant memories of crossing or living there.

EMILIANO: The first time I went to the United States was in 1984 when I was nineteen years old.
LYNN: Why did you want to go to the United States?
EMILIANO: Well, at the time I began to see that we in our family didn't have very many things and that there were not many possibilities for studying here in Teotitlán. . . . I finished primary school in 1978, and there were not any further possibilities then for studying in Teotitlán. There was no secondary school. I started going to a secondary school elsewhere, but I

couldn't continue. I was weaving and working in the countryside in the fields here, but I began to have some doubts. I saw that other young men of my age went to the United States, and they had things like clothing, shoes, pants that people wore during that time and I didn't have access to those things. We didn't have enough economic resources in our family to buy those things. So that is when I thought I would go to the United States

The truth is that I didn't tell my parents that I was going to go to the United States. I had a relative in Mexico City I thought I could stay with. I had a cousin here in Teotitlán who said to me, "Let's go to Mexico City and see if we can find work." So I told my parents I was just going to Mexico City to look for work. When we got to Mexico, I told my cousin that what I really wanted to do was to cross the border, to go to the other side. He said he wanted to go too. I really had very little money, and he didn't have much money either.

So I said, "Well, maybe if we pool our money we will have enough to get to the northern part of Mexico." So we bought tickets . . . on the train. It was the cheapest way to go. There is first class and second class. We went second class. We got on the train from Mexico City to Guadalajara. Once we got to Guadalajara, we took a bus. It was cheaper to get a bus ticket to Tijuana from Guadalajara than from Mexico City.

We were in Tijuana for just a few days, and then we found someone who would help us cross the border. Although we found someone who helped us to get across the border, our luck ran out. The migra caught us and put us in a big holding cell where everyone is sent. My cousin got out at five in the morning, but I didn't get out until ten in the morning. When I got out, I wandered through Tijuana, but I couldn't find my cousin. He had already caught up with some other friends, and I was alone. If I saw someone I knew, I asked if they had seen him. So I went on my own and looked for someone to help me across again. I tried again, but they caught me again. Then I was in Tijuana for about a week.

During that time I ran into some other people who told me they would help me get to Los Angeles. They said they would leave me in Los Angeles if I had a relative there who would pay for me. I didn't know these people. I had just met them.

LYNN: Did you have a relative who could pay for you?

EMILIANO: Well, I had an uncle. I had his telephone number. He was living near Santa Ana in a labor camp called Santiago. So these people I just met helped me across on the condition that my uncle would pay for the trip. They left me in San Isidro and then San Diego. In San Diego they put us on an airplane to Los Angeles. And then they started to divide up the people.

Some of them went north, some south. They took me to Santa Ana so that my uncle would pay the coyote. It was about three hundred dollars for each person they brought over. I had some bad luck because my uncle either didn't have any money or he didn't want to pay. So they took me back to Los Angeles and told me that they were going to take me back to Tijuana if no one paid for me.

On the way back to Los Angeles I figured out that the people who brought me over were not just coyotes. They were also drug traffickers. I saw what they were doing and their businesses. I heard them talking with other people about how they had to bring their cargo back into Mexico and that they were going to bring me back as well. I got scared and started thinking, if I get caught by the police or the migra with these people and with drugs, then I might never get out of jail. I have to escape. I have to get out of here, I thought. So I escaped.

LYNN: Where were you when you escaped?

EMILIANO: I was in a place called El Monte on one side of Los Angeles. I didn't know that it was called that until afterwards when someone told me. They had taken me to a house that was very small. There they locked me into a small room and I was trying to hear what they were saying. They were talking about what they were going to do with me because no one had come to pay for me. Then I heard them talking about how someone was going to come to this house to look for them. I don't know if it was the police or who, but they were talking about how I knew who they all were. They were worried that I would tell someone. When I couldn't hear them in the house anymore, I began to run. I ran and ran until I came to a road and there I asked where the center of the city was. The place where I was held was not in a city. It was in big open fields. At that point I ran into an old man, like a grandfather. He asked me, "What are you doing here?"

"I am lost," I told him. "I am looking for someone to help me get to the center of town." I asked him what the name of the place was.

"It is called El Monte here," he said. "Walk until you reach the railroad line and there are a few restaurants there. Maybe they can help you there."

I followed his advice and ran, fueled by my fear. I was afraid that some bad people who were smugglers were going to look for me and find me. I found two young men in a restaurant and bar. They were Mexicanos. I asked them if they could help me. They told me to wait until they finished eating. They offered me something to eat. I was really hungry. I hadn't eaten for two days. They told me they would bring me to the bus station. Then they told me how to go, which was very confusing.

They said, "First you have to go to Los Angeles. Then you have to go to Santa Ana. Do you know where to go?"

The truth is that I had no idea. It was like a labyrinth in the bus station. They bought a ticket for me to go to Santa Ana. The only way I got there was by constantly asking. And Santa Ana is a big city and I didn't know anyone. I got there at about ten or eleven at night. There was another restaurant at the bus station. I went in and asked a man there if he could give me a ride to the Santiago labor camp. That was the only place I knew to go because I thought some people from Teotitlán were there.

I told him, "Look, I don't have any money, but I have some relatives there and if you give me a ride there, then I can ask them to give you some money to pay for the ride."

"Fine," he said. "Just wait for me for a little while and I will give you a ride.

The problem was that by the time he was ready to go, he was drunk.

"Ok," he said. "Let's go. But first, let's go to my house. I have to get some money in order to fill up my gas tank. Then I will take you to where you want to go . . ."

. . . Then he took the keys to the car and we drove to the gas station. He put in the gas and then he got on the highway. He was flying down that road, just like he was drunk. I thought, "God help me. This is going to kill me." I had been afraid almost nonstop for several days.

We got to the Santiago labor camp at about 12:30 at night, after midnight. There an older guy, a grandfather kind of guy, was the night guard to the gates of the camp where the cars went in.

He said to us, "Hey, what are you doing here so late at night?

"I found a ride here," I said. "Do you know any people from Teotitlán del Valle?" I told him my uncle's name.

"Sure," he answered. "He's here. Come on in. Let's see where we can accommodate you." He motioned me inside of a cabin and tried to find me a bunk bed to sleep in. All of them were occupied except for one that was half broken. It was almost just pure wiring with no mattress. So they put some pieces of cardboard on the wires that hold the mattress and I slept there. It was very hard to sleep. It was February and it was really cold. I was so cold that I couldn't move my fingers. A cold wind was blowing into the room.

I woke up there early in the morning. When I sat up, all of these people from Teotitlán were there. They said, "When did you get here? Who brought you here? How did you get here if yesterday the coyote took you away?"

"I escaped," I told them.

Then the people from my town, Teotitlán, my paisanos, told me, "You can stay here with us."

They brought me some food because I didn't have access to the kitchen since I wasn't paying to stay there. One person brought me a tortilla. Another person brought me some black beans. Another one brought me a piece of fruit. I was really happy to eat. Then someone also brought me some clothes—some pants and a shirt. They even gave me a hat and a towel and shampoo to wash my hair with. "Take these things," they said," so that you can bathe yourself." I changed my clothes because I was really dirty.

LYNN: You didn't have anything with you?

EMILIANO: Nothing. I did have some stuff with me, but I lost it in my journey. I had taken a small suitcase with me. But when I escaped from that house, I didn't want to take anything with me because I knew I had to run. So between all of them in that labor camp, they really helped me out. It was the first time I stopped being afraid in days.

Emiliano's crossing story reveals the motivations prompting many people to come over the border as well as the perils they face. Inspired by the clothes, shoes, and money he saw other young men bringing to Teotitlán after they had migrated to the United States, Emiliano decided to set out with a cousin for the border region. Unable to continue his education because of the family's need for him to work, Emiliano was working in his father's cornfields and weaving for a local merchant before he went to the United States.

What stands out in Emiliano's testimony is the drama of his fear and escape and the difficulties he faced in trying to find his way alone. Once he reached people from his community in the labor camp he felt safer and was able to obtain basic necessities and begin to work. Emiliano's border crossing story is sprinkled with great detail. What was remarkable in talking with him in 2001 and 2002 was just how vivid the story still was. When telling it, his face was etched with the pain of remembering his fear at the time. Not unlike survivors of torture and political violence who share their experiences, a border crosser who tells the story of a difficult border crossing summons up detailed psychological and physical memories—perhaps the best evidence of how deeply engrained such stories are in the psyche of migrants. While the section of Emiliano's narrative cited above focused on the physical crossing of the border, the border itself is remembered and worn by people well beyond their experience of actual border crossing. The experience of Marina Bautista, detailed below, emphasizes the power of the border as a permanent presence in a person's life.

It is a Saturday morning in Woodburn, Oregon, on a wet March day. I am sitting in a small office of PCUN. Marina Bautista is sitting opposite me wrapped in a dark brown wool cardigan to ward off the chill. Marina's shoulder-length black hair is gathered in a ponytail. She sits with her legs crossed and leans against a desk, her dark eyes examining the political posters on the wall. She pauses for a long moment to examine the gaze of César Chávez, whose face is front and center on a UFW poster hung on the wall. Marina's face is taut as she begins describing her childhood. Marina is a twenty-seven-year-old undocumented immigrant from the Mixtec region of Oaxaca who has been in the United States on and off since 1991. Marina has worked in the fields, at NORPAC Foods Inc. (North Pacific Canners and Packers, one of the largest food processing companies in the West and the twelfth largest in the United States), in a nursery, and in a store. While her family migrated without legal constraints within Mexico as farmworkers, once in the United States, her experience changed. She currently lives in Woodburn. After we talk for some time, she hands me a life history essay she wrote in Spanish to gain entrance into a local GED program in Woodburn. This is her essay.

> I was born in Santa María Tindú on the 13 of February of 1974. I am of Mexican nationality, originally from the state of Oaxaca. . . . My family is made up of seven people, my parents and five brothers and sisters, including four women and one man. We are of very humble origin and because of this we moved to the state of Sinaloa in 1975 and after that we moved from one place to another, wherever there was work. My parents were rural workers. We moved around until we got to Baja California and settled in a town called San Quintín. We stayed there, and my parents bought a small piece of land and made a very small house. They stayed there.
>
> I didn't start to go to school in San Quintín until I was nine years old and then I only went for three years because my mother was gravely ill. I had to stop going to school because there wasn't enough money to pay for my uniform, my shoes, and my books, and my father was one of these people who didn't worry about us. My older sister was the only one who was working so we could eat. So there wasn't enough money for us to keep studying. After I left school at age eleven, I started to work in San Quintin

until 1991, when I came to the United States. I got here to the United States at the age of sixteen years, but I didn't go to school out of ignorance and because I thought I had come to earn lots of money to send back to my country. It didn't work out that way.

I didn't find any work except working in the fields, and I returned to Mexico that same year with very little money. In 1992 I tried to come back to the United States again, but I wasn't able to get over the border. It was very hard. In 1993, I tried to get over the border another time and I was able to get by. I came and worked for two years in a nursery, and I went to visit my parents in Mexico. I came back to the United States in 1996, but I haven't been back to Mexico since because I don't have a green card. Even though I really want to return to visit my parents, and sometimes they are sick, I can't leave to visit them because I am afraid I won't get back in. Right now I don't have any stable work either. Right now I am going to classes to try to learn English because you really need it. It is very hard to get work if you don't speak English and don't have permission to be here.

Marina's self-history relates how she and her family moved freely from Santa María Tindú, Oaxaca, Mexico, to San Quintín, Baja California, across state borders, but these borders did not constrain their movements. Their economic status does. Once Marina came to the United States in 1991 with the hope and expectation of earning money to send home, the border and permission to work begin to figure significantly in the construction of her life story. She went back to Mexico in 1991 after earning a little money working in the fields and tried to come back to the United States twice. Successful in her second attempt to cross the border, she stayed in the United States for three years, returned once to Mexico in 1996, and has not been back again despite the fact that her parents have been quite ill. She does not have a green card, the document required to legally pass the border, and will not return to Mexico to visit her parents because of her fear of not being able to get back into the United States. The border separates her from her parents and also from a legitimate status in the United States The border remains a constant geographical, cultural, and legal feature in Marina's life, pursuing her all the way to Woodburn, Oregon, where she is still struggling to "cross."

Alejandro Mendoza, now fifty-two years old, first came to the United States in 1978. He is a pleasant, calm man who appears relaxed in the middle of the chaos of his living room. A grandchild is playing with toys on the floor. Two of his teenage daughters are watching MTV, and a radio is playing *norteño* music in a bedroom off the kitchen. Alejandro's hair is graying, as is his mustache. He has on a blue button-down shirt and khaki pants. He wears a pair of Nike sneakers. Alejandro picks up his grandson from the floor and orders his two daughters to get off the couch. He motions for me to sit down and holds his grandson up in the air to make him laugh. His wife, Angela, comes in to join us. She has a broad face that easily smiles against the tension of her black hair pulled back in a tight ponytail. Angela has on a loose cotton dress that buttons down the front; over the dress she wears an apron. She has been cooking.

Alejandro is from San Agustín Atenango. He left home at age seventeen, first to work in Mexico City, and then he traveled north to Ensenada, Mexico, close to the U.S. border. After working there for several months, he crossed over the border into California. He was robbed of his money and clothes during this first trip. Alejandro received his legal residency in 1988 through the IRCA program. Angela came to the United States in 1988 and received legal residency shortly thereafter as a result of being married to him. Alejandro winced as he recalled his first time in the United States. He lived through extremely difficult conditions simply because he wanted to come and work:

ALEJANDRO: I paid a coyote one hundred dollars there in Tijuana. I landed in Carlsbad and Oceanside. There were other people from my town there as well. Some of them went to San Quintín.

[Alejandro then turned with a sad smile and said,] Then I started to make my house. . . . [He paused and then continued:] But not the kind of house you think. I made my house below the ground. We dug way under, like this [pointing to the height of the table and even higher]. We made it really deep. It was big enough so that fifteen or twenty people could sleep there. We did this because we didn't want anyone to see us. We didn't want to get caught by the migra. We used a green tree branch for the door. We pulled it over the mouth of our house at night. That was how I started out in this country for the first time. A really hard life. We would leave in the morning to work in the fields and then come back at night to our house underground.

Later in our conversation, Alejandro and Angela recalled what they felt like when they were both in the United States and had yet to get their legalization documents:

LYNN (to Angela and Alejandro): What did it feel like when you first arrived?
ALEJANDRO: When I first arrived in 1979 I was really glad. I came here and I

thought I was going to start again. I decided not to smoke or drink. I said, I am in a new place and why should I keep doing the same thing in a new place? So being here made me happy, on the one hand. On the other hand, when I was here without work and I had to pay for food and a place to live, it was really hard. . . . Later in 1988, I didn't have any papers. My boss wrote a letter for me to get amnesty [legal permission to work].

ANGELA: It is really hard for people. They are far away from their families. People never forget the fear they have when they don't have any papers. . . .

ALEJANDRO: It is really important for people to know why I came. I came here with a good purpose in mind. I didn't come to cause problems. I just came to work . . . That's all I came for.

Alejandro spent almost ten years without documentation. Alejandro and Angela have been living together in the United States in Salem for almost fifteen years. They have both worked full-time in a range of agricultural jobs. Angela has harvested strawberries and works in a nursery. Alejandro planted trees for the U.S. Forest Service, harvested strawberries, worked for ten years in a mushroom plant, and now is employed in the same nursery as Angela. Their oldest daughter is about to graduate from high school and hopes to continue her studies in higher education. She is, however, undocumented. She worries about how her legal status may prevent her from being able to study further despite her good grades. For her, the border continues to limit her future visions.

Alejandro's narrative highlights his experience living underground, literally, in an effort not to be seen by the INS. This is an extreme example of the lengths undocumented migrants go to in order to not be seen. It is almost identical to the living conditions described by Daniel Cruz Perez (see chapter 2). In fact, Daniel's and Alejandro's experience of living underground is shared by more than a dozen men I have spoken with from San Agustín and other Mixtec Baja towns who worked in southern California in the late 1970s and 1980s.

Mariano Bautista (introduced in chapter 4) recalled his first trips to the United States in a conversation in the fall of 2003 in Woodburn, Oregon:

In 1977, we went to Ensenada. I came to the United States for the first time in 1978. I was living in Oceanside and San Luis Rey. . . . During this time we were very much afraid of the migra. We lived in the riverbed. We dug ourselves a hole on the riverbank. It was big enough for two of three of us to fit in there. We covered it up with cardboard and green branches so that the migra wouldn't know that there were people living there.

LYNN: This sounds like a very difficult time . . .

MARIANO: Yes, it was. But I had already decided that I was going to stick it out no matter what happened. I had always been alone. Sometimes on Saturdays and Sundays a lot of Cholos would come to assault, rob, and kill people. Every day we lived in fear of the migra. At night we couldn't really sleep for fear of the assailants, the Cholos from Oceanside. Several Mexicanos died there. They would stab them with a knife while they were robbing them. . . . It was a very hard time. We didn't have anywhere to bathe ourselves or to prepare food. We only ate things in cans and nothing else. I spent that whole time fleeing and hiding like a criminal. I will never forget it. Now I have my residency, but I still haven't applied for my children and my wife. My wife doesn't have a birth certificate so we can't apply for her.

The pressure to remain invisible and escape from what was perceived as constant INS surveillance made a big impression on these men, who can recall in great detail their experiences of life underground. In many cases this existence was dangerous, as they were often preyed upon by local thieves who would target them on paydays when they came home with their wages in cash. These memories don't die, and, like Emiliano, Alejandro and Mariano vividly remembered the fear and pain they lived with on a daily basis while living underground and working so hard not to be seen.

Surveillance and Control of Undocumented Farmworkers
by Labor Contractors

Once undocumented workers get over the border and begin their journey and residence in the United States, their experience of being watched continues and may even intensify. If they are contracted laborers who come to work in the fields through interconnected networks of smugglers, contractors, and labor camp managers, they are at the bottom of the wage scale and the most vulnerable to the kind of exploitation historically associated with migrant worker populations (see Rothenberg 2000). In the ever-increasing pressure of a global economy and continued free trade agreements, first-time contracted laborers remain a cheap option for some growers under pressure to underprice imported produce.

Perishable hand-harvested crops such as berries, grapes, cabbage, and pumpkins require human labor to be effectively picked. Increasingly, many of the fruits and vegetables we eat are actually harvested elsewhere and shipped to the United States for consumption. For example, very little broccoli is now grown in Oregon. Instead it is grown in Mexico, shipped to the United States, and worked into frozen vegetable mixes in Oregon food processing plants. Many Oregon farmers fear that this international competition will put U.S. farmers out of business because they cannot compete with the cheap labor of countries like Mexico and China. Therefore, some growers have come to prefer a cheap immigrant workforce in order to be able to keep up with the international price competition of agricultural products. To get what they view as the best quality labor for the best price, some growers will work with labor contractors who hire workers directly in Mexican communities.

As noted by Philip Martin, case studies of post-IRCA and post-SAW labor markets found that few employers were making the changes hoped for by immigration reformers. Instead of raising wages and improving working conditions, there was significant evidence of "farmers hiring workers through contractors and eliminating fringe benefits" (2003: 187). Martin further notes that while labor contractors are able to assemble crews of workers at the times and places that growers need them, "few understood or obeyed the complex laws regulating contractors. . . . The switch to contractors left many workers worse off, since contractors pay less per hour, and workers who had lived on the farm when they were hired directly by the farmer now had to pay for off-farm housing and rides to work, which reduced worker earnings by 30 to 40 percent" (2003: 188).

The likelihood of abuse of farmworkers by labor contractors increases in direct relation to the amount of control contractors have over a farm-worker's daily existence. Contractors may pay farm laborers for fewer hours than they work, loan them money at high interest rates, and require workers to pay for food, rent, tools, and transportation—often charging exorbitant prices. They may also provide other services for undocumented workers, such as providing them with false documents, which also carries a charge. Contractors may pocket wage deductions like Social Security that are supposed to go to state and federal governments. Many labor contractors are from the same ethnic group as laborers and speak the same language. Many contractors are not registered, and although growers are obligated by law to use registered contractors, some do not. As noted by Martin, as long as contractors tend to hire newly arrived and undocumented workers who are not familiar with U.S. workplace rights, workers are unlikely to complain (2003: 188). The complexity of contractor-worker interactions and the ever-increasing number of un-documented workers used by labor contractors make it highly unlikely that labor law violations will be caught.

Working with contractors may be lower-level farm supervisors called *mayordomos*. They assign workers to rows and walk the rows monitoring the workers. They also discourage contact with union organizers and are usually allied with farm contractors. Another group of individuals who work with labor contractors are camp operators called *camperos*. Often close relatives of the labor contractors or of the mayordomos, camperos run the labor camps that contracted laborers live in. They enforce the grower's rules about who can and cannot come into a camp, monitor the comings and goings of workers, and often inspect the cabins workers are renting. In Oregon a bed in a cabin stuffed with bunk beds piled two to three high and up to ten people to a room will cost from two to four dollars per day. Privacy is hard to obtain in the camps because of close monitoring and the density of people living together. There are an esti-mated 10,000 migrant farmworkers living in Oregon's 382 registered labor camps. Others live in unregistered camps.

An additional aspect of the control and monitoring system of con-tracted laborers involves human smugglers called *coyotes*, *polleros*, or *pateros*. These people smuggle undocumented migrants over the U.S. border for a fee—in 2005 fees from southern Mexico to Oregon varied between two thousand dollars and five thousand dollars, depending on the kind of trip desired and the level of documentation provided (see Cornelius 2005: 13). Some coyotes operate only between border cities such as Tijuana and San Diego, staying with migrants just until they have crossed the border. Others will transport migrants from their homes in Mexico directly to job sites in California, Oregon, Texas, or elsewhere. Some work alone, others are part of complex networks involving cross-ing guides, drivers, and houses where workers are hidden until their smuggling fee is paid off. Some coyotes work directly with contractors delivering laborers from within Mexico to work sites in the United States.

Migrant workers who are contracted in their home communities, for example, in the Mixteca region of Oaxaca, have their every movement monitored and controlled from the time they leave their communities until they arrive in labor camps. Once in labor camps, their surveillance continues. Some laborers who are on their first visit to the United States may be monolingual in Mixtec, Triqui, or another one of the indigenous languages of Mexico and be further dependent on contractors who speak their own language. A nonrandom sample (snowball) survey done of Marion County labor camps in the summer of 2003 by the Oregon Law Center counted 231 out of 387 people, or 59 percent, as indigenous. A majority of those indigenous workers surveyed were Mixteco (145). Other indigenous languages recorded in the labor camp surveys included several varieties of Zapotec, Yucatec Maya, Chinanteco, and Mixe. In a separate survey, 200 Triqui-speaking workers were found in one camp and 80 in another (Samples 2003).

Contracted workers may be constantly reminded by their contractor that they did them a favor by bringing them over the border and then finding work for them. Lorenzo Alavez, a forty-five-year-old Mixteco farmworker from San Agustín Atenango who was a labor organizer for PCUN talked with me in 1999 about how contractors worked in his home region of the Mixteca Baja in Oaxaca, Mexico. There, the houses of Mixtec labor contractors are conspicuous because of their large size and the presence of SUVs and TV satellite dishes.

Before and after his stint as a union organizer, Lorenzo worked as an agricultural laborer in Mexico and in the United States. In 2005, he was working in a local fruit and vegetable processing plant as well as in the fields during the summer. Lorenzo has a compact, muscular body that wears the years of physical labor he has endured well. His jet-black hair slightly streaked with gray sticks out of his John Deere cap and matches the thin mustache above his lips. Thoughtful and always watching, Lorenzo is a keen analyst of the contract labor system he has both worked under and attempted to organize around in the labor camps of the Willamette Valley in Oregon. Part of Lorenzo's organizing work has taken him to visit workers in their home communities during the off-season in Mexico, often in the marginalized regions of Oaxaca, Guerrero, and Veracruz.

LORENZO: Well, I will tell you a little bit about how the system actually works because there are more indigenous immigrants coming now . . .

LYNN: Ok. I'd like to hear about it.

LORENZO: Well, the reason why more and more people are coming from the furthest places like Oaxaca, Guerrero, and parts of Veracruz is that the growers are using this kind of tactic to control the workers. . . . The growers have their contractors, and the contractors have connections to the coyotes, the ones who transport the workers.

LYNN: And who are the contractors?

LORENZO: The majority are Mexicans, but they can also be Chicanos. Thus they have their connections with the smugglers. They use these coyotes to bring people here, but the people they are bringing here don't know anything about their rights, and they often can't even speak Spanish. So these contractors bring them here and really control them. . . . We recently spoke with some new immigrants who came from Mexico to a labor camp. And they started to tell us that the coyotes said, "Come with us, there is plenty of work, there is free housing, even washing machines." Well, as you know, there is housing, but it isn't free. At that camp they charge workers four dollars per day. So the coyotes tell this to people in Mexico, and they come here and then the contractors and coyotes control the workers. When they bring people who are more and more marginalized in Mexico, they know less and less what their rights are. In the last years of the 1990s they have begun to bring people here from the most marginalized areas of Oaxaca and Guerrero.

LYNN: Where are the contractors going?

LORENZO: They are going to Copala, Juxtlahuaca. . . . indigenous regions of Oaxaca and elsewhere.

LYNN: So the contractors are going to the corners of Mexico and collaborating with coyotes and others. So the contractors are important?

LORENZO: Well, the growers are the key part of this system because it stems from them. They say, "How can we dominate the workers? How can we do this if all of those people who already came have rebelled against the conditions? Well, we have to bring more new people." And that is what they have been doing all these years. They are trying to bring new people every time who are more and more marginalized so that they [the growers] can maintain their position. . . .

LYNN: Do you think that the workers come to realize some of what goes on with time?

LORENZO: Well, they are seeing part of what goes on, but at the same time, they think that maybe the contractors did them a favor. The contractors tell them that they were doing them a favor by bringing them. The contractors tell this to them like they were doing them a favor charging them fifteen hundred dollars for bringing them and giving them work.

LYNN: How much would it cost me to come from your hometown in Oaxaca now?

LORENZO: It would cost two thousand—twenty-five hundred dollars . . . And since the indigenous person or worker doesn't have the money to pay this up front, there is an agreement between them and the labor contractor that they have to work here, and the contractor takes the money out of their checks. And so the worker has to at least finish the season with the grower in order to be free of this debt . . . to be free of the "favor" that the contractors did for them. . . .

LYNN: Is it possible to come and work for four months and go back to Mexico with nothing?

LORENZO: Yes, exactly with nothing. A lot of workers come with the idea that they will stay for four months, but they end up staying for a year or more in order to cover their expenses and to save a little bit of money to be able to return to Mexico.

For contracted first-time workers who may not even speak Spanish, the experience of dependence and constant surveillance is a common one. They are watched at work, in the labor camps, and constantly reminded about their obligation to the contractor and indirectly to the grower. Because of the difficult conditions many first-time undocumented workers labor under, most are unwilling to return a second time to work with contractors who have overcharged them for their passage, food, and housing. And indeed, after a period of ten to fifteen years working in the fields, many farmworkers move on to something else. This creates a revolving door situation that encourages the continuation of the labor contracting system. There are always new workers needed.

Being Watched in the Fields

Another focus of worker narratives is the experience of being closely monitored in the fields after they arrive in the United States and begin working. Many of the men and women I interviewed were from rural towns in Mexico. Most have experience working in the fields in Mexico. There, they had more independence. If they had the experience of working on their own land, they came and went when they pleased and set their own schedules. In Baja California, commercial agricultural workers are more closely watched but report more flexible conditions of work than in the United States (Zabin and Hughes 1995).

In the work histories of farmworkers in the United States, mayordomos assume a major role in terms of the quality of people's working experience. Mayordomos are an indirect source of surveillance. Although the consequences of supervision by mayordomos are certainly different from being caught by a Border Patrol agent, management practices of squeezing as much work as possible out of farm laborers and encouraging them to make wages quickly make it unlikely that they will complain. In addition, the fact of being an undocumented worker makes it unlikely that such workers will complain about working conditions that violate minimal labor standards for farmworkers. If a worker complains to a mayordomo, the unspoken threat is that the mayordomo can call la migra, which can result in the worker being deported. Until the mid-1990s this actually happened occasionally, making the threat credible. For many, the minimal right to taking breaks while working in the fields is viewed as an important source of respect and dignity, and mayordomos who take the breaks away are despised but get away with it because of workers' fear of possible deportation. In Oregon, workers are supposed to receive ten minutes of paid rest period for every four hours of work, and if their workday is six hours or longer they are supposed to receive thirty minutes for lunch (unpaid). Often, however, breaks are shortened or nonexistent, and lunch is discouraged. Workers are told they have to work overtime if they want to take breaks. Practices in farm labor supervision that discourage these minimal standards can be effective because workers are afraid of the unspoken threat of arrest and deportation.

Mariano Martínez is a fifty-one-year-old Purepecha man from San Gerónimo Purenchécuaro, in the municipality of Quiroga on the shores of Lake Patzcuaro in Michoacán. He has worked in Oregon since 1979, when he crossed the border at Tijuana with several other men from his hometown. Before coming to the United States, Mariano worked planting corn and as a traveling merchant specializing in the sale of fish from Lake Patzcuaro. At the time, he paid four hundred fifty dollars to go from Tijuana directly to Woodburn, Oregon, with coyotes based in Quiroga. People from his town had begun to migrate to Oregon in the mid-1970s, and by the time he arrived there was a well-established network in Woodburn. From 1979 to 1982 he lived with other workers in an apartment building in Hubbard, Oregon. In 1982, INS officers raided the apartment and deported him and others to Mexico. But as Mariano reported, "They turned us loose in Mexico at ten in the morning and by two in the afternoon we were back here again. We spent about a day in Oceanside, California, and then we started to come up here again." Mariano came back to the Woodburn area and worked in a nursery until 1988. Since that time he has worked a variety of jobs in agriculture, in nurseries, and in processing plants. In 1986 he received legal residency under the SAW act aided by the Immigration Service Center affiliated with PCUN.

Mariano has white hair and leathery skin that mark his life as an agricultural worker. His shoulders are slightly stooped as he sits in a chair and shares his work experiences. In our conversation in 1999 about his experiences crossing the border and living and working in the United States, he remembered being denied the basic decency of a break. During our conversation, Mariano spent about twenty minutes dwelling on the topic, emphasizing its importance to him:

MARIANO: Making the minimum wage, that is the best you can do. It's better to work in a market, lining up the shopping carts or cleaning bathrooms, making the minimum wage. But in the fields. they make you work when it is raining, when it is snowing. and they pay you just about anything. Like I said, it is much better to work somewhere like a market. . . . They pay you the same and you are inside. In that kind of work you get a break, you can drink a coffee; eat a piece of banana, a piece of bread, whatever you want. You can sit down and eat. But in the fields? In the mud? What kind of break do you get? Often, none. The grower or mayordomo will tell you, "No break. You will lose a lot of time. Let's go. Get used to it." No, no, no. I worked in a camp like that. They never gave us breaks. They said, "No, its fine. Just work." And the break? "You didn't get a break," they said, "we're going back to work." And if you did get a little break, then they made you work twenty minutes or an extra half an hour at the end of the day. . . . No, they just want you to work . . . and if you complain, well, what if the migra shows up? What then?

While working indoors is often an improvement over the fields, canneries and food processing plants also have systems of supervision. In both settings, surveillance of workers is often linked to boosting productivity rates. Structural conditions that push workers not to speak to anyone isolate them and can produce feelings of alienation. For indigenous Mexican workers, who have almost all had to assimilate a fear of being "seen" during a period when they were undocumented (or continue to be), additional systems of surveillance found at work, such as in processing plants, can reawaken these earlier fears. While state systems of border surveillance and the checking of legalization documents at work sites are different kinds of surveillance systems than those that monitor worker productivity, they are often experienced as being connected.

Workers state that many food processors in the Salem area have become stricter about wanting to see documentation of a worker's legal status before hiring him or her. Many described experiences of going to initial interviews, returning, and then being told there were no jobs. They often concluded that it was because their documentation didn't check out. Thus even applying for a job involves subjecting oneself to scrutiny and the fear of being labeled as illegal. Once offered a job, the surveillance experience for workers which began with the careful scrutiny of documents can feel connected to plant supervision practices.

Being Watched in the Plant

In the processing plant, freshly picked fruits and vegetables are selected, cleaned, cut, and packaged or canned. In most cases, much of the operation is done in huge open rooms with workers arranged along a sequence of conveyor belts where fruits and vegetables are cleaned, sorted, and directed to either a cooking and canning operation or a freezing regime. Workers are organized according to their particular task and in relation to a specific location, usually around a conveyor belt. Each belt has a supervisor in charge of workers in his or her section.

Many farmworkers also work late shifts at the canneries and processing plants to accommodate two jobs: one in the fields and one in the cannery. When adult family members work two jobs, household income can be increased. Women and some men actually work three shifts—the last being at home with their children (see Stephen 2001a). The work in the processing plant is seasonal and usually lasts from July to mid- to late October. In 2000, the plant workers got paid the minimum wage ($6.50 per hour in Oregon in 2000) for eight-hour shifts. However, sometimes when the harvest is slow, workers are sent home early before they have completed eight hours. During an eight- to ten-hour shift, workers get two or three breaks to rest and eat.

Dolores Alavez is a Mixtec woman from San Agustín Atenango who came to Oregon in 1987. She worked for several years at a cannery, where she sorted fruit and vegetables, and she also worked in the fields. Dolores is a short, slight woman who moves quickly around the room. She wears her shoulder-length, jet-black hair swept back in a barrette. Her angular face has finely chiseled features framed by faint lines around her eyes and mouth. She has an intense look on her face as she talks, but when she breaks into laughter her face softens. She is comfortable in blue jeans and a green sweater which keep out the fall chill. She sits up very straight with her shoulders relaxed. Her arms are sinewy and strong. In her discussion, the mayordomo or supervisor is also extremely important in terms of setting the conditions for work. She describes what it was like to work at a conveyor belt sorting vegetables while being closely monitored. She describes the strictness of the floor-supervision style of Anglo mayordomas in contrast to that of the recently hired Mexicanas, who are looser in their supervision of workers in the plant. But while recent supervision on the part of Mexicana overseers inside the packing plant may have loosened, surveillance of workers' legal status by the same overseers has greatly increased. In her narrative the two acts of checking and watching are connected. She moves seamlessly from the topic of supervision on the floor to the checking of documents. For her, both constitute surveillance, even though they are rooted in two very different structures related to her experience as a worker: one relating to U.S. immigration law and the other to management practices to encourage productivity.

These two issues are also linked to the issue of seniority for her. Because the Anglo supervisors didn't check people's documents so closely and reserved their oversight for the shop floor, people could return season after season and receive more hours because of seniority. This was a trade-off for much tighter control on the plant floor. Now, with Mexicanas hired to check people's documents, Dolores feels that they are eliminating seniority and hiring new people so they can pay them less. For her this has translated into fewer hours of work and a loss of seniority.

DOLORES: The beans first come into the plant from outside where they wash them. Then they come onto a big conveyor belt, and this one feeds it into different sorting belts . . . that is where people work. I was there on the sorting belt removing the garbage from beans and other vegetables when they enter. I had to take out mice and all of the stuff that comes in with the beans. The first conveyor belt is where we get rid of all of the dirt that comes in with the beans, and then we pick up the produce and sort it. These beans come in with sticks and thorns, all kinds of things. The first conveyor belt is where all of this comes, and it is the dirtiest place to work. By the time the beans pass onto the second conveyor belt they are not as dirty. After that, they go to a third belt, where it is just leaves and the beans. . . . it's a labyrinth of conveyor belts in there . . .

. . . The first belt is the worst one to work on because no one wants to grab the rabbits, snakes, or mice that come in with the beans. I have worked there because I wanted to. It isn't as boring as the other conveyor belts. In the other ones where the beans are really clean, there is nothing to do and the time goes really slowly. So I prefer to work where it is dirtier so that the time goes more quickly. When it's time for me to work in the beans, I pick this conveyor belt and just plant myself in front of it. Because right now there are only Mexicanas who are the mayordomas (supervisors). They don't know how to work things. They are not well organized. . . .

. . . They didn't have any experience working on the conveyor belts. They didn't know how to stop and start them. They don't know anything about how the water works either. Before, you couldn't move around at all. The supervisors were very strict. You couldn't go work someplace else unless the supervisor told you to. . . . Before, the Anglo supervisors, they used to control things more. You couldn't move without permission. . . .

Now we can work where we want. But now they send you home before you have even finished a day's work. Let's suppose there are beans that were finished at seven or eight at night [only four or five hours into a shift]. They would send a whole group of people home even though the shift is over at eleven. . . . it doesn't matter if you have been working for a year or more or were just hired. They send you home. This is what they are doing now. Before, they used to let people work by seniority. The people who had been working there the longest were allowed to stay, and they sent home the new workers if the work finished before the shift was over. . . . Now they seem to prefer the new workers. They also started to ask for papers in order for people to work there two years ago.

LYNN: Why?

DOLORES: Because they said they didn't want people working there without papers. Now if you go to apply for a job, the Mexicana secretaries there ask you for your Social Security number and your i.d. And then they say, "We are sorry, but we can't accept these papers you are giving us [Social Security cards, driver's licenses]." And they won't give you an application. They say this in front of all the people there so that people are really embarrassed.

LYNN: How do they know which papers are no good?

DOLORES: Well, now two of the secretaries are Mexican. I think they are the ones who called attention to that because they know what false i.d.'s look like. Before that, the Anglos didn't know this. All kinds of people went there to work with all kinds of papers, and they didn't do anything. . . . I think that the Mexicanas who are now working as supervisors are harder on people when they come in to look for work, checking everything. Before they were harder on you while you were working, watching everything.

At the time Dolores described her work to me, in 2000, she had recently received legal residency. Nevertheless, she was still acutely aware of the different types of surveillance practiced on her at work, both in terms of her legality upon applying for a job and varying levels of supervision on the plant floor. For workers like Dolores who spent time being undocumented before receiving legal residency, the initial fright of crossing the border with small children while trying to be invisible and then living and working without papers and trying not to get caught—avoiding forms of state surveillance—become linked with their other experiences of surveillance at work, such as those documented here. While state forms of surveillance packaged as "controlling the border" and, now, "keeping out terrorists" are tied to the physical U.S.-Mexico border, other state forms of this same policy—verifying people's legality in the employment process—can bleed over into forms of monitoring and controlling worker productivity if both are done in a public fashion. If applying for a job involves a public assessment of one's immigration status, such as the process described above by Dolores in a Salem processing plant, then systems of monitoring workers on the open plant floor can logically be seen and experienced as part of the same structure of surveillance.

Conclusion: Surveillance, Invisibility, and the New World of "Security"

This chapter has focused on the experiences of Mexican indigenous immigrant and migrant workers on the U.S.-Mexican border and in the fields, labor camps, and produce processing plants in central Oregon. Being an object of surveillance and observation from the first time they attempted to cross the U.S.-Mexican border to the present, when they go to work in the fields and plants, is a significant part of workers' experiences of work and memories of them. The flip side of their memories of surveillance is the simultaneous burden of trying to remain invisible while they are undocumented. All of the workers whose stories were told here had some period of their residence in the United States when they were undocumented. While I have focused here on several particular contexts of surveillance—the border, the fields, labor camps, and food processing plants—writers such as Alejandro Lugo have written about how the culture of surveillance for Mexican immigrants is generalized to a wide range of contexts, including nightclubs, buses, and elsewhere (Lugo 2000). For those who are undocumented, these additional areas of surveillance often discourage them from being seen in public places.

Being an object of surveillance—by Border Patrol agents on the border, by coyotes and labor contractors while crossing the border, by mayordomos, labor contractors, and growers while working in the fields, and by mayordomos and supervisors in food processing plants—signals power differences tied not only to color, but also to where people are from in Mexico (rural/urban, indigenous or not), how long they have been in the United States, their language abilities, and their position in the relations of work. The hierarchies of color found within Mexico, on the U.S. border, and in Mexican communities throughout the United States intersect with the U.S. cultural process of classifying immigrant workers as aliens by virtue of their color and language, as described above and as further emphasized in chapter 7. This intersection results in a formidable hierarchy of power differences experienced in its most intensified form by recent undocumented indigenous workers who come directly from rural Mexico to labor camps in states like Oregon. For these workers, hierarchies of economic, legal, and cultural power as experienced through the mechanisms of surveillance and the pressures of invisibility involve intimate contact and dependence on other Mexicans. For example, for contracted workers in a labor camp, their daily contact with mayordomos and camp supervisors is a much more vivid part of their remembered experience than more distant contact with non-Mexican growers and others who may come into their world.

Nevertheless, in the personal histories of all indigenous workers I have interviewed, there is also a larger sense of being an object of observation simply by virtue of appearing and sounding different from the dominant society. U.S. agriculture and food processing plants as well as many other sectors continue to depend on Mexican labor to care for, harvest, and process much of the food we eat—some of the cheapest food in the world. Our food security depends in significant measure on the labor of Mexican immigrant workers while our national security policies appear to discourage further immigration and to step up surveillance of those who are already here. In the world of post-9/11, we need to be able to distinguish between potential terrorists and those who come to this country to do the crucial work of producing our food, providing services, and doing other important jobs. The politics of visibility and invisibility, of surveillance and security, have to be made flexible and transparent so that the complex reality of the global economy in the United States can be approached at a human level.

CHAPTER 6

Women's Transborder Lives

GENDER RELATIONS IN WORK AND FAMILIES

Women from Oaxaca have been migrating to other parts of Mexico to work for many decades and to the United States in significant numbers for the past thirty years. As discussed in chapter 4, Zapotec and Mixtec patterns of migration differ. These overall differences are also reflected in the experiences of women. While Zapotec women like Catalina (see chapter 4 and below) have most often migrated to urban areas of the United States and found work in the service sector, most Mixtec women begin working in the fields in the United States and may move later into jobs in canneries and processing plants or into service jobs such as elder care. While jobs in canneries and processing plants may be unionized, often through the International Brotherhood of Teamsters, accessing union benefits usually requires a certain level of seniority, and in some cases workers being paid minimum wage may prefer not to pay what they see as high union dues for small-scale benefits. Many remain in seasonal agricultural work for long periods of time, often combining it with jobs related to food processing.

Most Zapotec women from Teotitlán migrated either to the Tijuana border area or to the greater Los Angeles area along with men or both. Men and women usually went to the same places. In cases such as that of Catalina, women who are single mothers (her husband left her early in her marriage) may migrate initially without their children and then try to bring them later. Their ability to bring their children to live with them depends in part on the changing politics of U.S. immigration policy, as explained below.

Mixtec patterns of migration were different for men and women until the early 1990s. A survey conducted by Carol Zabin and others in the early 1990s in California and Baja California Norte documents the way in which Mixteco migrant families were caught in a labor market segmented by gender in which agro-export employment provided "stable employment, albeit low-wage employment, for some members of the family close to the border (especially women and children) while allowing other members of the family to assume the risks of U.S. immigration"—primarily men (Zabin and Hughes 1995: 395). In a nutshell, families were divided.

The work environment for farm laborers on the West Coast of the United States differs from that in Baja California. Zabin and Hughes found, for example, that 64 percent of Mixtec farmworkers in the United States are paid by piece rates compared to 2 percent in Baja. Work takes place at a much more rapid pace under a piecework scheme (1994: 190). Child labor laws are enforced in the United States, but in Mexico young children form a significant part of the labor force. Because there are often chronic labor shortages in Baja, workers do not lose their jobs if they miss a day or two of work. In California and often in Oregon, where there is a surplus of workers and higher wages, growers operate under stricter standards and demand great efficiency from workers.

Because women remain the primary caregivers to children, employment conditions in Baja are often more conducive to women's dual role as wage earner and caregiver than in the United States. Frequent unemployment on the West Coast in the United States means that growers have their pick of workers: "Lone males provide a flexible workforce for growers because they are mobile, can work long hours when the harvest is ready, and are often willing to travel long distances" (Zabin and Hughes 1994: 191).

Maintaining Families in Mexico When Men Go to the United States

Because the majority of migrants who came from Zapotec and Mixtec communities from the 1970s until the late 1980s were men, a significant number of women who were married to migrant men or who had fathers and brothers who migrated remained in their home communities or in ethnic enclaves within Mexico. In communities such as San Agustín Atenango and Teotitlán del Valle, which had long histories of a strongly gendered division of labor, the absence of significant numbers of men during this period had a major impact. Male absence in households, in community systems of governance, and in the economy strongly affected those who remained behind. It is important to note, however, that "women who stay behind" is not a permanent category. Many women who have remained in communities like Teotitlán and San Agustín at one point in their lives have migrated either to other parts of Mexico or to the United States (or both) at another point in their lives. Such factors as immigration status (documented versus undocumented), stage in the life cycle, number of children, and other factors are all important in structuring the migration experiences of both men and women. Finally, as pointed out by Jennifer Hirsh (2003: 181), "the lives of even those women who have never left Mexico have been profoundly affected by migration."

In Teotitlán del Valle and San Agustín Atenango, women first experienced what it was like to be left behind in the 1940s, when the first men went to the United States with the bracero program. During that time, men were contracted for specific periods of time, often four to six months, and would return home to the community for part of the year. Some men in these communities worked as braceros for up to fifteen years. In cases such as these, entire households adjusted to having the senior male absent for about half of the year. While some men sent home regular remittances or could be counted on to bring their earnings back with them when they returned home, others sent nothing or arrived with little or nothing to share with their families. If men never sent or brought home anything or withheld remittances for long periods of time, women and children had to go to extraordinarily measures in order to earn cash and to carry out subsistence agriculture if that was part of the family economy. In many cases this involved either paying someone to do work that men normally carried out—such as plowing and planting of corn and beans—or women and children doing the work themselves. In almost all cases it also involved women and children engaging in a variety of petty income-earning activities in order to make ends meet.

Natalia Gómez Bautista was born in 1927 in Teotitlán del Valle. She wears her graying hair in two long braids intertwined with green satiny ribbons coiled around her head. A black shawl speckled with white is wrapped around her broad shoulders as she sits on a short stool on her patio. Natalia's round face is etched with lines and bronzed by decades of being outdoors. She walks with a limp now. Her knees are giving out after so many years of grinding corn everyday and carrying heavy loads of firewood in from the countryside. Twice a day Natalia feeds her pigs, chickens, and turkeys, softly clucking to the birds as she approaches with their food. She smiles at the animals, who have been her constant companions. She is reluctant to leave for long because they need to be looked after every day.

We have known each other since 1983, and our conversation in August 2001 revisits many of the things we have talked about in the two decades before. Natalia's experience of being left behind began when she was married and for twelve years her husband went to the United States as a bracero for part of each of those years. She continued to be left behind when all but one of her children permanently migrated to the United States and left her with only one child at home. She has met many of her grandchildren only once or twice and knows them primarily from pictures and occasional telephone calls.

Natalia grew up extremely poor and began working at the age of five. She married her husband, Feliciano, at the age of eighteen. Shortly after they were married, he took her to Mexico City, where they lived for three years. After they returned to Teotitlán in 1950, when Natalia was twenty-three years old, she had her first child. Every two years for the next sixteen years she had another child. After her first child was born, her husband became unhappy and began to beat her when he returned home. She endured decades of domestic violence until he became ill and died in 2000.

In 1952, Feliciano began to go to the United States as a bracero for six or seven months each year. While Natalia remembers this period as a very difficult one, she also remembers it as a time when she felt safe, happy, and content. When her husband was not around, she could relax, despite the economic difficulties she faced.

NATALIA: I wasn't really able to feel happy until he started going to the United States. Some years he would go for six months, sometimes for eight months. Until he started to leave, I couldn't really feel content with my children and my work. I was much happier when he was gone. But he never sent any money. And when he came back he didn't even bring a little bit of money back with him. I don't know how I was able to take care of things. For twelve years he went.

LYNN: What did you do to eat during that period?

NATALIA: We all worked, *ajeno* [see below], doing whatever we could. Working for other people. We would work for anyone who would come to the house and said, "Please, can you come and grind our corn and make torillas for us? Can you sell us a chicken?" We did whatever we could to make a little bit of money that way. My daughter Caterina would also take tortillas we made and go to Oaxaca and sell them. She worked a lot too. And my other older children, Patrocinio and Mariana would weave. They would work really hard and make two *tapetes* per week. He never sent us any money at all, but we survived.

While Natalia's narrative is about a period in her life between 1952 and 1964, her experience bears an uncanny resemblance to the memories that Dolores Alavez from San Agustín Atenango and Fidelia Domínguez from Ixpantepec Nieves have of the difficulties they went through when their husbands left them for long periods of time while working in the United States in the 1970s and 1980s—well after the bracero program terminated in 1964. These women grew up under very stark conditions of poverty, having little to nothing before they were married. Both Dolores and Fidelia became migrant workers themselves as children, going to Sinaloa to work in tomato and other harvests. They did this with their extended families. As adult women, they faced a different kind of experience as they remained in their communities of origin when their husbands went to work in the United States.

Both worked *ajeno*, as did Natalia and her children in the 1950s. *Trabajar ajeno* (to work for strangers or wherever one can) is shorthand for saying that one is extremely poor and willing to work for anyone (*hacer de la gente*). It often implies willingness to work as a domestic servant for short or long periods of time in better-off households in one's community. The phrase connotes a certain level of desperation and the necessity to do whatever it takes to earn a small amount of money through working for others at whatever they need done. The availability of local jobs working for other families has been important in minimally maintaining families while some members are away.

The lack of widespread work at home, however, is also tied to the need to migrate. Ninety-seven-year-old Valentina López, the mother of José Luis García López (introduced in chapters 2 and 4) has her own analysis of the relationship between the lack of local employment and migration after watching her husband and children go first to Veracruz, then to Sinaloa, Baja California Norte, and then to the United States over a period of six decades:

There are no rich people here. We don't have enough people for whom we can wash their dishes, wash their clothes, and take care of their things.

Because we have no rich people here, everyone has to go to *el norte* to build a house. There are only poor people here. For years and years the poor have left here to find work. The poor men go north to find work and there are only women here. This town is very sad because there is no work here. Everyone has to leave to work, and they are dying there in el norte.

Although both Fidelia and Dolores spent significant periods of time in their home communities of Ixpantepec Nieves and San Agustín Atenango while their husbands worked in the United States, both eventually migrated to the States under somewhat different circumstances. Here I share the initial parts of both their stories to demonstrate how the context they grew up in is linked to their memories and understanding of staying behind while men migrate. Neither suffered from the ongoing domestic violence that Natalia endured, so they do not find the safety and emotional relaxation that Natalia remembers during her husband's absences. They both had profound senses of economic and emotional insecurity that was related to the absence of their husbands while they were left in Mexico with very young children.

Fidelia is a slight woman with intense brown eyes. She holds her body tightly, sitting up straight in the chair. Her hands punctuate her story as she talks. Her fingers are slender but strong with a coiled strength within them revealed as she flexes her hands. Occasionally she touches her shoulder-length black hair, which hangs straight down from the crown of her head, tucked behind her ears on the sides. She is bundled in a sweater underneath a winter jacket. It is winter in Oregon, and the room we are talking in is cold. She has on thick socks under her sneakers.

Our conversation took place in 2000 in the library of PCUN. Fidelia has become a major presence in the organization Mujeres Luchadoras Progresistas (Women Fighting for Progress), as we shall see in chapter 8.

FIDELIA: My name is Fidelia Domínguez, and I come from Mexico. I was born in the state of Oaxaca in a small town called Ixpantepec Nieves in 1958. I speak Mixteco. As you will see, I am here because of my history. When I was a small child, I was six years old when my father taught me how to work. Sometimes it is a little painful to tell my story, but I feel like it is important to share it. Later my father sent me to a nearby city to study Spanish just like I am studying English now.

LYNN: Where did you go to learn Spanish?

FIDELIA: Juxtlahuaca. After I learned to speak Spanish there, I came back to my home. I was seven years old, and I started to work from sunup to sundown. I still couldn't speak Spanish very well, just a little bit. I was just working with my family.

LYNN: Can you tell us a little bit about the life with your family? Did you have brothers and sisters? What kind of work did everyone do?

FIDELIA: Well, my father was never home because he was always traveling looking for work so he could support us. He went to Veracruz to work in the harvests. At that time, there were three of us. But little by little more children came and we ended up being nine brothers and sisters. One of them is older than me. We all went to work for other people, what we call working ajeno. We did this because we didn't have any land to work. You work for anyone who needs you. We didn't even really have much of a house. We had a really small little house. We all slept there, and my mother cooked there when she was able to find corn to cook. There was no food there. There was no refrigerator, no stove. We cooked with firewood there. We made all of our tortillas by hand. My mother fed us so that we could grow. We were so poor that we didn't even have clothes. We walked around without any clothes. We didn't have any sandals, what we call *huaraches*, shoes. None. We had nothing.

Later, when I was nine years old, I went to the city of Oaxaca to work. I had an aunt and uncle who lived there. They had a clothing store and I worked there. They were from my town of Ixpantepec. They wanted to give me a chance to study. I stayed there for awhile.

But my mother and father were really poor. So they came to take me with them to work in Sinaloa. When I was eleven years old my parents took me to Culiacán, Sinaloa, to work in the tomato harvest. It was really hard work. They gave us these big buckets to fill up that held eighteen kilos of tomatoes. I could barely lift up the bucket. We all went together to Sinaloa to work— my mother, my father, and my brothers and sisters. After we worked in the tomato harvest we went back to our town, but because there were so many of us and the money didn't last, we always went back with nothing. And we always had to return to work again in the tomatoes.

I started to grow up, and I married the husband I have now. I was *robado* (taken without permission) as they say, or I robbed. I am not sure. That's how we got together.

LYNN: How do you understand *robar*—taken without your permission or did you agree?

FIDELIA: Well, the men say, "You robbed me," and we also say, "Well, you robbed me." So really we robbed each other. We both agreed to it. That is my story. We went to live in the house of the parents of my husband. They had a lot of land, they still do. They had a lot of hectares of land. . . . But the truth is that there isn't enough water to work the land so that we could make some money. There is no place to work there where you can make a little money. You can plant some corn, but that is all you can do with this land. It has no irrigation. Sometimes it produces corn, and sometimes it doesn't. That's why my husband came here to the United Sates in 1974.

LYNN: Did you have any kids when he came to the United States?

FIDELIA: When he came here at first we only had one child. Then a little while later two more were born. One of my children was born in Sonora and the other two were born in Oaxaca. I suffered a lot when he came to the United States. I stayed behind in Ixpantepec.

I was working and looking for ways to support my children. When he went to the United States he earned very little money. He was in California, and he didn't have any papers. He couldn't find any good work. He was in Madera, California.

LYNN: Did you do anything to work the land while he was away?

FIDELIA: Yes. I had to pay someone to go and plant. I went and plowed the field myself with the oxen. One time I took the animals and took them out to plow and plant. They were already full-grown those oxen. I had to take care of them. They require a lot of care. And even though I took care of them, they don't provide for us. I didn't have any money to buy food for them. And the land needs fertilizer to be productive. It was really impossible. I couldn't do it.

Fidelia's childhood, like that of many children from the Mixteca Baja, involved working as a migrant laborer within Mexico. At the age of eleven, she went with her parents to harvest tomatoes in Culiacán, Sinaloa. She continued that pattern after she was married at age fifteen and her first child was born in Sonora, where she and her husband were working.

In 1974, when her husband went to the United States, she remained in Nieves. In 1984, Fidelia decided to come to the States and rejoin her husband. Initially, she left her children behind in the care of her mother-in-law. Once in the United States, she became just one of many women whose families are split between the United States and Mexico.

A second narrative from San Agustín Atenango underscores the difficulties women experienced when left alone with small children. Conversations about living without their husbands, who were working in the United States, bring back sadness and a flash of anger for women such as Dolores Alavez (introduced in chapter 5) as they recall painful periods of their lives.

Dolores's story begins in San Agustín Atenango, Oaxaca, where she grew up and lived as a young married woman. Shortly after she married, her husband migrated to the United States and left her behind. In 1987, she came to Oregon to join her husband. We spoke in November 2000 in her home in Salem. (The interview was conducted by me and a graduate student, Maria de la Torre.)

DOLORES: I was born in San Agustín Atenago in 1960. I grew up there alone because my mother didn't raise me. I didn't really know my mother. She died when I was very young. So I was raised with my brothers and sisters. For most of the time it was me and my younger sister and my grandfather and my father after my older siblings left and got married. . . . My grandfather lived in his own house, and he would come to visit us in the mornings because we would give him breakfast. Then he would return to his own house. What I remember growing up is living with my older brother Lorenzo, a sister I have who lives in Ensenada, and my sister who is younger than me. . . . I have three brothers and four sisters. Almost all of the sisters were already out of the house when I was little.

MARIA: What kind of work did your father and your siblings do when you were young?

DOLORES: As I said, all my older sisters were married. They dedicated themselves to working for their families. They would go out to the fields to plant and would take food out to their husbands. My younger sister was here in the house with me doing the housework. My father was a petty merchant. He would go to buy things in the other towns like chiles, bananas, fruits. He maintained us by selling fruits and vegetables and by what he harvested. . . . He used to go to a nearby town called Juxtlahuaca. He would go there to bring back bananas, chiles, tomatoes that he would then sell here and in surrounding towns.

MARIA: How old were you when you began to work?

DOLORES: I started to work when I was about nine or ten years old. All my older sisters were married, so I had to stay there and make the tortillas for us and the sauces and other food. I was doing this in my father's house. . . . I stayed in San Agustín until I was seventeen years old. Then I went to Sinaloa to work with my brother Lorenzo and another sister. I was nineteen years old when I got married. I came back to San Agustín to get married.

In 1977, at the age of seventeen, Dolores went with her siblings to Sinaloa to work in the tomato harvest. While she did not spend her childhood as a migratory agricultural laborer, as Fidelia did, both women's experiences reflect significant trends in female Mixtec migration in the 1970s and 1980s. The researcher Laura Velasco began studying female Mixtec migration to the U.S.-Mexican border region in the early 1980s. Drawing upon a large survey done in the Mixteca Alta and Mixteca Baja (see Velasco 1986), Velasco found that in 1981 women represented 31.78 percent of Mixtec regional migration. At that time, almost half of the women who migrated were working in domestic services, primarily in Mexico City. Forty-four percent went to Mexico City, 11.6 to Veracruz, 3.04 percent to Morelos, 9.9 percent to Sinaloa, 3 percent to Baja California, and 17 percent to the U.S.-Mexico border region and to the United States (1995: 43–44). Among girls and women who migrated, 38.4 percent had made their first trip between the ages of six and fifteen, and 29 percent between the ages of sixteen and twenty. The rest were over the age of twenty. A majority of Mixtec girls and women surveyed in 1981 were single (66.10 percent) and 29.38 percent were married or in monogamous "free unions" (Velasco 1995: 44). The 1981 study also found that girls and women who went to Veracruz, Morelos, Sinaloa, and Baja California were most likely to be traveling with their husbands or families and working in agriculture. Those who went to Mexico City to engage in domestic work were more likely to be younger and single (1995: 47). Thus the experiences of Fidelia and Dolores were typical of the patterns reflected in the research of Velasco on the migration of Mixtec girls and women who worked in agriculture. Once Dolores got married, she returned to San Agustín Atenango to live:

> . . . After I got married, I continued to live in my community. I was living in my mother-in-law's house. I lived there for seven years until I came to the United States in 1987. I came to the United States after my husband sent for me. But I spent seven years in my community when I was married.
>
> MARIA: So he came to the United States and you remained behind?
> DOLORES: Oh, yes. He came here. We had only been married for two weeks when he came to the United States. He came back after nine or ten months. He was with me for about two weeks and then he went back to the United States again. That is how it was. There was one time when he left me there in the village for four years. He left me without anything. I was left there with lots of debts. Before that he brought me to San Luis Rio Colorado in the state

of Sonora (on the U.S.-Mexico border, about twenty-five miles south of Yuma, Arizona). We were living there and I had one child, my oldest son. Then he brought me back to San Agustín. My daughter was two months old. She was really tiny. That was when he left me for four years in San Agustín. He never came back to see his daughter until 1987. . . . When my first child was born, my son, I was also alone in the community for nine months. My husband didn't come back until my son was nine months old. That was in 1981.

LYNN: What was it like giving birth to your first child in your in-laws house without your husband there?

DOLORES: Well, that is how it happens a lot there. The husbands are never around, only your mother-in-law. But she didn't attend to my son's birth. She took me to a clinic that was only fifteen minutes away by car in the nearby town of Tonalá. That is where they took me. My mother-in-law said she preferred for me to have the baby there since it was my first one. She was scared that something would happen to me. She didn't want me to give birth in the house. There are midwives in San Agustin who come to people's houses to attend to the births, but she didn't want this.

It is very hard in the middle of the night to find someone to take you to the clinic. My labor began in the middle of the night. There were only a few people who had cars at that time. Most of these people were not around because they were taking a tomato harvest into Oaxaca to sell. So there was only one car left in the whole town. The guy who owned the car was drunk, and he drove me. My mother-in-law had to go wake him up from his stupor to get him to take me to the clinic.

LYNN: How was your life after the baby was born?

DOLORES (smiling): Well, I had to keep on doing all of the chores. I was breastfeeding my baby while I was also making tortillas and cooking food. When the baby was asleep I could get something done. But he was really sick when he was little, and I had to struggle to just get him to eat for a long time.

MARIA: Did your mother-in-law help you?

DOLORES: Yes. She did. My sister-in-law helped me too. She was a single mother living there. Between her, me, and my mother-in-law we took care of everything. There were no men there. They were all in the United States. My husband had four little brothers who lived with us, and they were all in school. So we supported them. My father-in-law worked two and a half hours away and wasn't there that often. At that time one of the brothers was in Chicago, and my husband was in San Luis Reyes, California

LYNN: So what was the situation like in 1983, when your husband left you with two children in San Agustín for four years?

DOLORES: Well, it was really difficult for me to be there in the village . . . It was hard because during the first two years my husband sent us money and wrote to us. But during the last two years he really distanced himself from us and we didn't have contact. There I had to wash clothes, iron, and make tortillas to sell in order to have money for food. I had to help out my mother-in-law. She tried to help us out with the food, but because of all of my husband's younger brothers who were still living at home and studying it was hard for her too.

LYNN: Were there other women in similar situations?

DOLORES: There were other women in the town who had this same experience of being left for four years or more.

LYNN: Did you talk to each other about this?

DOLORES: Yes. There were a lot of women in this situation. I was not the only one. There were some women whose husbands never returned. They got involved with another woman in the United States and completely abandoned their wives. There were a lot like this. . . . Their husbands come here to the United States and they get another woman and leave their wives. . . .

Dolores's experience of being left in San Agustín was punctuated not only by economic difficulty, but also by ongoing uncertainly about the stability of her marriage and its future. As she attests, a significant number of women in San Agustín in the 1980s were living in uncertainly. Their husbands had left for the United States and were gone for extended periods of time, sometimes without communicating or sending home any economic support. Since women like Dolores and Fidelia have no personal experience with what life is like for their husbands and others in the United States, their pictures of what goes on in the lives of their men is strongly informed by what people who come back to town tell them and by gossip. Strong undertones to this discourse suggest the likelihood that men who have gone to the United States may have started other families and have other female partners. This is often the ongoing assumption until proven otherwise. The assumption made by many in the community can erase women's ties to their husbands and put them in a new social category as abandoned women. Dolores felt she was in this category until her husband suddenly contacted her after four years and sent her money to come to Oregon.

Changes in the Gendered Division of Labor in the United States: At Home and at Work

While the gendered division of household labor changes for women left behind in Mexico when men spend extended periods of time in the United States, it also affects the experience of the men who are in the United States. While many men who have migrated may have been reluctant to cook, clean, and wash clothing in Mexico, once they come to the United States they inevitably end up doing this work.[1] Initial patterns of Zapotec and Mixtec migration to the United States involved many more men than women, particularly during the 1970s and 1980s. As most men who came to United States arrived without their wives and children, they frequently had to take responsibility for tasks normally done for them by their mothers, sisters, and wives.

First-time male migrants to the United States—particularly those from the Mixtec region—initially began to work in the fields and spent some period of time living in labor camps. There, groups of men often cook together, wash their clothing, and have to work out minimal domestic arrangements. In the labor camps I have visited in Oregon, most have what are termed cabins. These cabins consist of one large room with bunk beds lining the walls, and usually they have an attached kitchen that is shared by the twelve to twenty-four people who live together in the cabin. In some cases there may be lockers or shelves available for clothing. The kitchen usually has a refrigerator, a small stove, and possibly a sink. Bathroom facilities are often separate from the cabin.

Men who live together in the cabin are often from the same region of Mexico and usually include groups of relatives and friends. Two siblings and their three cousins might constitute one such group, for example. Most labor camps have one or two cabins that are for families. A few have spaces for single women. In many cases, however, women who are not attached to men will have to be in a cabin with men they have no relationship with. In such cases, a blanket is often hung from the top of one or two bunk beds to section off part of the cabin for women. A chief complaint of women farmworkers is the lack of housing available to them.

The majority of labor camp populations continue to be made up of men, although there are some exceptions. Some growers have successfully recruited families to come and work for them on a repeated basis. One such farmer in Woodburn, Oregon, recruited a group of about eight

Zapotec families from Coatecas Altas who work for him about four to five months a year and then return to their base in Madera, California, where they work in the grape harvests. These extended families each shared a cabin. Women carried out a majority of the domestic work, although men were doing some chores such as washing their clothes and helping to wash and care for children.

Men who are living alone in labor camps take responsibility for their own domestic chores. Dozens of men I have interviewed stated that they learned to cook while living in labor camps in the United States. Diego Ramírez from Teotitlán commented of his time in labor camps, "Well, you get tired of just eating out of cans so you learn how to cook—rice and beans, chicken, everything." Others learned cooking skills not only in labor camps, but also through work in restaurants. Daniel Cruz Pérez of San Agustín learned how to cook steaks, fried chicken, cornbread, pasta, and other foods through his stint as a short order cook. Men learn how to do other domestic tasks as well. When clothing is ripped in the fields—as it frequently is—men have to get out a needle and thread and repair the holes. When blue jeans are caked in mud from the fields, men wash them, often by hand in camp bathrooms or in buckets. Thus many of the domestic chores that may have been regarded as women's work at home become men's work. For some men, the ability and lack of shame about performing such tasks continues in their work routines back in Mexico or with their wives and children once they come to join them in the United States. Many men who do such work choose not to advertise it and ask their wives to not talk about it.

In her book *A Courtship after Marriage*, Jennifer Hirsch emphasizes the importance of where in the life cycle a woman migrates to the United States and how this may affect her experience, not only overall but also in relation to her husband (2003: 186–87). Women like Dolores and Fidelia who migrated after they had children and were living in Mexico and who continued to have children once they arrived in the United States faced the initial dilemma of whether or not to bring their children with them when they came to join their husbands. Once they had more children in the United States they faced the further dilemma of what to do with these children while they worked.

While it is true, as Hirsch writes, that women's labor in the United States brings them much closer to economic independence than their efforts in Mexico (2003: 200), it is still very difficult for either a single parent or a two-parent household with children to survive economically on just one minimum wage (or less if paid under the table) salary. If dependent children are U.S. citizens, they have a right to Medicaid, food stamps, Women, Infants, and Children (WIC) assistance, and other programs. In many cases I have encountered, however, undocumented women are afraid to try to access the government services their children have a right to as U.S. citizens. In some cases women are reluctant to ask for these services for fear they will be disqualified for U.S. residency in the future. In November 2004, voters in Arizona approved Proposition 200, which requires state and local employees to verify the immigration status of people applying for public benefits and to report undocumented immigrants or face possible criminal prosecution. This kind of anti-immigrant measure discouraged women from applying for benefits for their children who were U.S. citizens. Thus for many women who come to live with their husbands and children in the United States it is considered completely normal that both parents work outside of the home, often on opposite shifts so that domestic chores and childcare can be shared. Two jobs are also necessary to provide basic household expenses and for unexpected medical emergencies.

The Challenges of Obtaining Health Care

For those working in the fields, nurseries, and low-end service sector, jobs are likely to be at minimum wage with no benefits. Lacking health insurance and fearful of accessing services like Medicaid, immigrants find that accidents, major illnesses, and even tooth decay can become a source of significant debt. In 1998 and 1999, the California Endowment commissioned a study on the health of California's agricultural workers. The subjects included 971 people, 36 percent female and 64 percent male. Ninety-six percent of them said they were Mexican, Hispanic, or Latino. Ninety-two percent were foreign born; 8 percent were of indigenous origin. The median reported total annual earnings from all sources is between $7,500 and $9,999 (Villarejo et al. 2000: 6). The results of the survey are stunning. The following highlights from the report provide important context for the two cases discussed below:

—Nearly 70 percent of all people in the sample lacked any form of health insurance, and only 7 percent were covered by any of the various government-funded programs intended to serve low-income persons.
—Just 16.5 percent said that their employer offered health insurance, but

nearly one-third of these same workers did not participate in the insurance plan that was offered, most often because they said they could not afford either the cost of premiums or because they could not afford the copayments for treatment.

—32 percent of male subjects said that they had never been to a doctor or clinic in their lives.

—Half of all male subjects and two-fifths of female subjects said they had never been to a dentist.

—More than one-third of male subjects had at least one decayed tooth. And four out of ten female subjects had at least one broken or missing tooth. (Villarejo et al. 2000: 6–7)

In further analysis of this report, Bonnie Bade (one of the report's authors) suggests that while there are numerous health-care programs that do offer access to health care for California's farmworkers and their families—as is the case in Oregon—general health care coverage does not exist. It is limited to emergency- and pregnancy-related programs, federal health programs such as for tuberculosis, or other immigration status–specific programs (2004: 219). Access is the critical issue, not only in terms of the existence of programs, but also of people's ability to afford even reduced-rate options. In addition, Bade found that in low-income rural agricultural towns in California, where Mixtec families largely reside, farmworkers may have no primary care physician or there may be many fewer physicians serving the population than in more affluent towns (2004: 219; 1994; see Martínez 2005: 203–21, 226–36). Finally, for indigenous migrants, language can also be a key issue in that many are unable to communicate well in Spanish in describing their ailments.

In Oregon, farmworkers have access to some special clinics but, as in California, most are uninsured. The U.S. Health Resources and Services Administration funds fourteen migrant and community health clinics in Oregon, but even access to such special clinics can be difficult (League of Women Voters of Oregon 2000). Using statistics from 2002, the National Center for Farmworker Health estimated that the migrant and seasonal farmworker population in the counties where the migrant clinics provided health services is 116,546. The reported users represent 14.81 percent penetration of this population, indicating that a majority of farmworkers are not being reached through the clinics (National Center for Farmworker Health n.d.). Often people go to emergency rooms or simply do their best to cope with a problem on their own.

A man from Coatecas Altas living with his family in a labor camp in Woodburn told me the following story in 2003.

> A few weeks ago my son burned his feet on some hot broth that was cooking. They were really burned badly. I took him to the hospital in Silverton and they charged me four hundred dollars for the treatment. They asked if I had insurance. I told them I did not. Now I have to pay them.

As he told his story, another couple from the same community approached. They had been listening to our conversation from a slight distance after peeling off from a line of workers returning from harvesting berries in the fields. One of the woman's cheeks was clearly swollen. She was in enough pain that it was difficult for her to talk. Her husband, Isaías, waved me over to look at her. He said,

> My wife Ana María really needs a dentist. As you can see, her tooth is really sore. We don't know where to take her to get it taken out like they do it in Mexico. It doesn't cost a lot there. Here it costs a lot of money. We don't have a lot of money. If we can't find a place to do this cheaply, then we will have to wait until we go back to Mexico.

Following our conversation, I inquired at a local Woodburn clinic that services Mexican immigrants (specifically farmworkers) and others to see how much it would cost to get Ana Maria's tooth pulled. With a 75 percent discount, the cost would be $15 for an appointment and $30 to $40 for the extraction for a total of up to $55. While this is quite cheap by U.S. standards, Isaias and Ana María decided that it was too expensive for them to undertake immediately and that they were going to wait. Besides, they explained, "We have to keep on working right now to earn money for our kids." Thus even with a discounted dental service, the cost of the appointment and the extraction discouraged them.

An additional discouragement was the cost to them of both losing a day's wages. Ana María does not drive, and Isaías would need to borrow a car to take her to the appointment, which, including the drive to and from the clinic, could last for four hours. They would both lose out on a day's wages of $60 each. The actual total cost of having the tooth pulled was thus up to $175 (including lost wages)—a sum too high for them to contemplate. I cite this rather simple example by way of illustrating both the complications of accessing health care and the pressures for both men and women to work whenever they can. Simple survival of the family often depends on two or more minimum wage jobs.

Rearranging the Division of Labor When Both Parents Work

Dolores Alavez describes how she and her husband each worked one to two jobs for many years while raising their four children. When they worked in the fields, they were able to take their children with them, which most women workers did until the mid-1990s, when child labor and pesticide laws were more strictly enforced in Oregon. The children helped their parents to harvest berries. Dolores and her husband also both worked a second job in a local processing plant. Unable to take their children to work there, they used a combination of asking other people who were visiting or living with them to care for the children and taking turns. In this process, Dolores's oldest daughter became an important part of the childcare solution. Nevertheless, her husband also did significant work in caring for the kids while she was working.

DOLORES: I started working in the strawberries in 1987. I got pregnant after I arrived, so I went to the fields pregnant during the first season I worked here. I harvested berries while I was pregnant.

LYNN: How were the working conditions?

DOLORES: The conditions were bad. It was very hard. Harvesting strawberries is the hardest work there is and the worst paid.

LYNN: How much were they paying then?

DOLORES: They were paying eight cents per pound.

LYNN: Were there a lot of women picking berries then?

DOLORES: There were a lot of women. There were also a lot of men and entire families, including children as well. . . .

LYNN: A couple of years later you started to work in the NORPAC plant, in the cannery. What did you do with your kids while you were working in the plant and in the fields? What about the little one who was born in 1998?

DOLORES: Well, in 1999 when we worked in the fields we took the kids with us. I was still nursing my little daughter. I would have to nurse her when I arrived. And then when she cried I would stop working and leave the field to come and feed her. I would sit under a tree where there was some shade and nurse. I left my baby with my daughter, who was six years old then. She looked after the kids for me. My oldest son started to work in the strawberries then. He would carry around little buckets and fill them up. He would also bring empty boxes to fill. He would help me to fill up the boxes with the berries he picked in his little bucket. He was seven years old then.

LYNN: So back then they let children come into the fields?

DOLORES: Yes. All of the rows of berries were full of kids. Whoever wanted to could bring their kids along. If you didn't want to bring them, you left them. I always brought my kids with me until my oldest daughter was big enough to take care of them at home. When she was twelve or thirteen I would leave them with her. . . . During that time when I was working in the strawberries, the season would start and I would work there in the morning and in the afternoon I would go to work in the cannery [processing plant—frozen and canned]. . . . I would start working in the fields at six in the morning and finish up about one or one-thirty. It would depend on how much fruit there was. I would make maybe sixty or seventy dollars, depending on how much I picked. Then I would go to the house, take a shower, get ready, and go to the cannery to work. I would start there at three o'clock in the afternoon and finish up at eleven o'clock at night.

LYNN: So you were working two shifts. Did a lot of people do this?

DOLORES: Yes. The majority of people were working two shifts. My husband did this as well. We would both go to work in the strawberries in the morning and then go to work in the cannery in the afternoon. Later my husband started working with pine trees in the morning, and then he would work in the cannery in the afternoon. When the blueberry season started later in the summer then we would each work the same two shifts—blueberries in the morning, cannery in the afternoon.

LYNN: What did you do with the kids when you worked in the cannery? Could you leave the kids there?

DOLORES: No. You can't bring them there. We had to leave them at home. We would take turns and find other people to help out. A young man from San Agustín who worked in the pine trees in the morning would come to the house in the afternoon to help with the kids. One of my uncles helped out too. Often there would be two or three people from San Agustín staying with us, and they would help us out with the kids. Later, there was a girl from Veracruz who helped us take care of the kids. She came with three sisters, and they didn't find any work. One of them took care of the kids. She didn't have anywhere to live, so we offered her housing. She stayed with us and took care of the kids. She was able to make some money slowly, and then she got her own place to live. But she is still here, and we are still friends. Then after she couldn't take care of the kids anymore, my husband left one of his jobs and we took turns. I took care of the kids in the morning, and he took care of them in the afternoon.

LYNN: Do a lot of families do this?

DOLORES: Yes, the majority. We are still doing this. He works one shift and I work another. Right now he works at night and I work in the afternoon.

> The kids are all bigger now, but I still have to look after the youngest one, who is ten years old. We have four kids. Two of them I brought with me from Mexico and two were born here. Wendy was born in 1988 and Alexis in 1990. My oldest son just got his GED so he can become a citizen.

This exchange illustrates the flexibility in the gendered care of children. Both Dolores and her husband take turns caring for their children while they work, as do visiting male relatives and a live-in guest from Veracruz. The other flexibility illustrated here is the composition of the household itself. Dolores's household serves as a stopping point for relatives passing through and for others, such as the girl from Veracruz, who need a place to live while they get settled. Circulating household members get worked into the domestic division of labor—including care of other people's children—as a part of their responsibilities of household membership, whether permanent or temporary.

In some households in which men are not working, they do more than childcare. Rigoberto Martínez from Juxtlahuaca maintained the household while his wife worked. While Rigoberto wanted to work year-round, his most steady work was seasonal in local fields and orchards. He frequently entertained his younger nephew after school. He stated,

> Pedro, my nephew, used to come over to my house all the time. He came to play Nintendo. I told my sister that he could come any time. I had all the time in the world because I was not working. I cleaned the house, I washed the clothes, and I took my son to school and picked him up. I was at home while my wife worked. That was how we worked it out for that time.

In this case, Rigoberto not only took on responsibility for running his own household and caring for his son, but he also helped his sister out by providing a place for her son to go after school—and a video gaming system.

For single mothers who do not have relatives to care for their children finding childcare can be difficult and expensive. And in some cases men and women just can't arrange to work on opposite shifts. Soledad Cruz Hernández, like Dolores, took her children with her to the strawberry fields when she worked there. She came to the United States from San Agustín Atenango in 1994, following her husband, who first came to Oregon in the mid-1980s. She noted that for women who have to pay for childcare, enforcement of child labor and pesticide laws had a negative consequence.

14. Soledad Cruz
Hernández
and her
granddaughter
in 1999.

Before they used to let you bring your kids. You could sit them in their stroller, and the mothers would go to work. . . . So now, sometimes the women say that they can't go to work. They say, "No, well, if we go to work in the strawberries now, if we don't work really hard to earn some money we won't earn even enough to pay the person who is taking care of our kids." Because of this sometimes they take their kids with them and they try to hide them while they are working in the fields. But a lot of time the growers see, and they tell them they can't bring their kids. But they can't leave their kids alone in the house either. So they have to pay someone to watch their kids. . . . They charge $US1.50 per hour per child.

If women have family members nearby who they can switch with—one sister working in the fields and watching children for another sister one day and vice versa the next—they may be able to keep working. If, however, they do not have a broad family support system and must pay for childcare for more than two children, they can actually lose money by working, especially after paying for a ride to the fields and for lunch and having deductions taken from their hourly wages of $6.50—if they are being paid the minimum.

In their home villages in Oaxaca women spent a significant amount of time close to home and can share childcare with one another. Once they have moved to towns in Oregon like Keizer, Salem, Hubbard, Wood-burn, and other places they are not necessarily living close to relatives and others in their kin network. A car is a requirement, and many women do not drive. Extended kin networks cannot be called upon for daily childcare if, as is often the case, all the members are working—particularly younger couples. Thus the combination of laws that have prevented women from bringing their children to work with them, as they were often accustomed to doing in their gardens and fields in Oaxaca, and the fact that in many families most of the adults are working has cut back on the kind of kin support available to women. In some families this pressure has led to a change in the gendered division of labor, with husbands and wives working split shifts so that one of them can always be at home with the children. This arrangement is not possible, for everyone, however, particularly newcomers who cannot arrange their work schedule to meet their home needs.

Like other low-wage women workers in the United States, Mixtec farmworker women are constantly caught between trying to carry out their mothering roles and working to help support their families. Because they are usually working in minimum wage jobs, they receive no benefits. As pointed out by Grace Chang (2000), immigrant women workers are often viewed in the same way as women on welfare who must participate in workfare programs. Both immigrant women and low-wage U.S. women workers—particularly those who are working to receive public assistance—are seen as disposable workers who don't deserve the same rights as white collar and blue collar mainstream workers. Chang writes,

> The work performed by these groups [citizen welfare workers and non-citizen immigrant workers] and their labor conditions are strikingly similar: invisible, unsafe, unsanitary, hazardous, low-paid stressful work. Their labor is not seen as contract labor, or a service that they provide to society for which they should be compensated. Instead, their labor is constructed as either charity, opportunity, privilege, community service, repayment of a debt to society or as punishment for a crime. In the case of welfare recipients the "crimes" are being poor, homeless, or "unemployed." In the case of immigrants they are criminalized for entering the country (presumed "illegally," of course), and for consuming resources to which they allegedly have no rights. (2000: 159)

While Mixtec farmworker women by no means see themselves as criminals or undeserving of decent working conditions, they do have a high level of awareness of the kind of difficult conditions they work under and the unreasonable demands that may be made of them at work. While working in the berry fields of Oregon, Soledad Cruz Hernández also went to work in several canneries and food processing plants. Soledad and many other women complained of the lack of respect for seniority (i.e., more steady hours were not offered to workers who had been their longer) by supervisors, which also affected their access to benefits offered by the Teamster's union for workers who were viewed as permanent rather than seasonal; they also objected to the way they were continually pushed to work faster and to some of the ridiculous requirements attached to some jobs, including the ability to speak English. In one instance Soledad recalled a job interview she had in a plant. She was applying for a job cutting potatoes for French fries, a position that appeared to offer the chance for more regular, year-round employment that could result in health insurance and other important benefits. "They asked me if I spoke English and I said no. Then they told me that I had to speak English to do the job. Imagine, I needed to speak English to talk to the potatoes. . . . Well, they didn't give me the job because I don't speak English." In this instance she was certain that they used the English requirement to keep Mexican workers out of the more secure jobs. She experienced it as a clear case of discrimination and an effort on the part of the potato plant to keep out undocumented workers by not hiring anyone who couldn't speak English. Through this experience she reflected on the structural position of low-wage women workers like herself and drew clear conclusions about hierarchies of language and race in the labor market.

Transborder Mothering

Although working full-time and managing a family are challenging for migrant women in the United States, the challenge is even greater when the children are in Mexico and their parents are in the United States. In the discussions I have had with dozens of families about their migration histories, a majority have had at least some period of time during which children born in Mexico were separated from their parents, because either one or both parents were in the United States while the children remained in Mexico. Being away from their children for long periods of time is emotionally difficult and trying for women and men alike, especially as the children get older and are no longer emotionally connected to their parents.

There have been many approaches to understanding the gendered implications of transnational families and transnational mothering. Beginning at a structural level, authors such as Rhacel Salazar Parreñas (2001) and Grace Chang (2001) analyze transnational households as ways in which receiving societies can retain low-wage immigrant workers without paying for the costs of social reproduction of workers and their children. When women such as Fidelia are working in the United States, having left their children behind in Mexico to be cared for by relatives, then the costs of social reproduction are assumed by the kin in Mexico who raise the children. At the same time, the wages of workers such as Fidelia can be kept to a minimum. If, in addition to having left their children in Mexico, workers are undocumented, then they are least likely to pressure for higher wages.

Pierrette Hondagneu-Sotelo (1994) suggests that by 1990 the duration of separation of families split between the United States and Mexico had shortened to two years or less, but this situation has changed since the mid-1990s. With the implementation of increased border barriers, patrolling, and sky-rocketing costs for traveling back and forth to the United States for undocumented workers, fewer people return to Mexico. In addition, those who are here may be more reluctant to attempt to bring their children from Mexico to the United States. The anti-immigrant sentiment that has swept the United States since 9/11 has also been a source of discouragement. Nonetheless, people continue to go back and forth. Because men are no longer doing seasonal work in the United States and, following 9/11, are more likely to stay, the number of women and children crossing the border is probably increasing (Shorey 2005). The heaviest toll is on those undocumented immigrants who attempt either to continue visiting Mexico or to bring their children across the border. In 2003, the U.S. Border Patrol captured forty-three thousand children trying to get into the United States, more than six thousand of whom were unaccompanied by adults; all were taken to shelters for children on the border run by the Mexican government (Marizco 2004a). Increasingly, unaccompanied children have become targets of kidnapping, not only by competing smugglers, but by Mexican police as well, who can hold them for ransom (Mariczo 2004a, 2004b).

Salazar offers a strong critique of those who see transnational households as indicating a strong sense of agency on the part of transnational actors. Instead, she sees transnational households as maintaining the inequalities of globalization and promoting separation. Her comments stem from her extended study of Filipina domestic workers in Rome and Los Angeles, who endure separations of at least two years. In some cases Filipina domestic workers have been separated from their children for periods of up to sixteen years, resulting in what Salazar calls second-generation transnational households with the now-adult children of transnational parents forming their own households, sometimes in a different country altogether (2001: 114). Salazar (2001: 108) states of the structural relationships between sending and receiving countries in the context of globalization,

> Transnational households should not be praised as a small-scale symbol of the migrant's agency against the large forces of globalization because their formation marks an enforcement of border control on migrant workers. . . . they result from the successful implementation of border control, which makes families unable to reunite. Border control further aggravates the tensions of transnational family life with the difficult of return migration for undocumented workers.

In deciding whether or not to come to the United States in the first place, women are quite distressed by the thought of leaving their children behind. As pointed out by Hondagneu-Sotelo and Ernestine Alavez in their study of transnational mothering among immigrant Latinas in Los Angeles, "Being a transnational mother means more than being the mother to children raised in another country. It means forsaking deeply felt beliefs that biological mothers should raise their own children and replacing that belief with new definitions of motherhood" (1999: 325). While a variety of mother arrangements exist in both the United States and Mexico, most discussions assume that mothers reside with their children—one mother, one place (Hondagneu-Sotelo and Alavez 1999: 335).

Catalina García (introduced in chapter 4) first contemplated coming to the United States to work in 1989. She was a single mother at the time and still had three children living with her at home. Her oldest daughter was married and economically independent. Her oldest son was living in Tijuana, where he worked as a musician. Her older brother Antonio had returned to Teotitlán to visit and had a car. He had been living in Santa Ana, California, for more than a decade. During a visit in 1989, he offered to drive Catalina to the border, help her cross, and pay for the entire trip. In the passage that follows, Catalina is describing the conversation she had with her brother before going with him to the United States. She describes her initial reluctance to go with him because of her children. She can't imagine leaving them. Later in the conversation, Antonio urges her to go and talk with her mother-in-law to see if she will care for Catalina's children in her absence. Eventually Catalina goes to the States, first for a short period and later for a much more extended period.

> My brother said to me, "I want you to come with me. You can come and see your son for yourself in Tijuana. I am going to drive this car back. You don't have to pay for the trip, you don't have to pay for food. I will take care of everything."
>
> So he told me this and said, "You have to take advantage of this opportunity to go."
>
> I said, "Well, I have other children. Paco isn't my only child. What about the rest of them? Chica, Omar, María, they are all still small. They are all here with me."
>
> He said, "You can leave them with their grandmother."
>
> "No," I said. "I'm not going to leave them with her because I am not going to leave."
>
> He said, "Don't worry. I am just going to take this car there to Santa Ana, and then I am going to come back here. I am only going for a month."
>
> "No," I said. "I don't believe that."
>
> "It's true," he said. "And I already talked to the kids' grandmother about how she will take care of them."
>
> "Well," I said to him, "María is sick and I don't want to leave them."
>
> "Go talk with your mother-in-law," he told me. "We will only go for one month."
>
> So I went to talk with my mother-in-law and then I went with Tonio.

By 1990, Catalina was working as a full-time, live-in nanny for a family in California, as described in chapter 4. For several years she left one of her children, who had a physical handicap, with her mother-in-law in Teotitlán del Valle. Two of her other children were with her in California, although they were living not with her but with her sister's family. She lived with the family whose children she cared for and commuted home on the weekends to visit her two children. Catalina's youngest child remained very attached to her grandmother in Teotitlán and wanted to return to visit her. In the following passage, Catalina describes returning to Mexico with her youngest daughter in the mid-1990s and the tremendous difficulties they had trying to get back into the United States after Clinton's border-enforcement policies of the mid-1990s were instituted. Another consequence of transnational mothering for Catalina was that once she was able to bring her children to the United States with her, they still felt connected to their grandmother, who had raised them for several years while Catalina was working as a nanny. In their study, Hondagneu-Sotelo and Alavez noted mothers' preferences for leaving their children with grandmothers (1999: 329). They speak of the emotional fissure and negotiations women go through with "the other mother" as they communicate with them about the daily care and supervision of their children. An unexplored aspect of this relationship is the feelings of children who are being mothered transnationally. In this case, Catalina's daughter Chica wanted to remain connected to her "other mother" even once she was in the United States. The border control that Salazar writes of is harshly manifested here in terms of the costs of trying to remain connected to family in Oaxaca:

CATALINA: I went back at the end of 1995 and 1996 with my youngest daughter, Chica. She wanted to visit her grandmother and others, so we went back for Christmas, and after Christmas we returned to California. We didn't have papers then, and it was really difficult to get back to the United States. . . . We had to come back through the mountains to California. It was already more difficult then. They put up these big walls, really tall. There were lots of dogs, migra on motorcycles and walking around. They were even on horses. So we had to go through the mountains and from there we had to pass over some big walls by Otai Mesa.

They already put up those big walls so we couldn't pass right on the border. So on this trip we had to go down under a bridge through the drainage system where there was a lot of sewage. We were inside the sewer system walking for three hours. . . . It was really horrible in there. So we got out of the sewer and came out on the side near San Isidro. Then to cross over the border we had to go through a tunnel. We came out on the other side and walked for half a day. And then the migra grabbed us. They put us in jail.

LYNN: Did they put your daughter Chica in jail too?

CATALINA: Yes. And then we came back to Tijuana, and I told her, "No more." I was really worried about her because she was little. Then we did manage to cross over, but in a different place. We went by the beach side of the border with some coyotes. We walked all night long and then the migra got us again. This time they caught us three times while we were trying to cross. I told her on our fourth try, "Chica, if they catch us again we should just go back to Teotitlán. I can't walk any more. I am really tired."

. . . We had paid fifteen hundred dollars for each of us to cross, but you only pay if you get across. The last time we crossed we went with a coyote from Tijuana who passed us over really close to the line. We walked and walked and finally my brother-in-law came to pick us up . . . Thank goodness we made it. All to go home.

Leaving children behind in Mexico also has tremendous emotional costs for women who have migrated to the United States. Many women like Catalina spend periods of time in the United States when they have children on both sides of the border. If women come to join their husbands in the United States they may initially leave children behind and then give birth to others in the United States, who automatically become citizens. In this case, women must worry about children in two distinct contexts. In the United States they hope their children will be able to take advantage of the opportunities they have, particularly in terms of education. They feel additional pressure to send sufficient funds to support their children in Mexico as well as to provide the best lifestyle possible for their children in the United States.

When Fidelia first came to the United States in 1984, she left her two children in Ixpantepec Nieves with her mother-in-law. Pregnant when she arrived, she gave birth to a third child within a few months of settling in Canby, Oregon. She later gave birth to two more children. From 1984 to 1988 she did not see her two oldest children. Her desire to return to Mexico to see them was so great that she preferred returning to Oaxaca to see them over remaining in the United States and obtaining legal residency under the 1986 IRCA provisions. Her husband convinced her to remain. Pleased that she was able to send home enough money for a new house for her mother-in-law and her children who remained behind, Fidelia was nevertheless not entirely happy until all of her children were with her in the United States. Her narrative captures the emotional distress she felt as a result of the separation and the importance she attributed to having all her children with her:

FIDELIA: When I arrived in 1984 with my husband, my dream was that I was going to work. Like the work that you are doing now, writing. I wanted to do something respectable. I thought, let's go to the United States. There is money there and you can have a real life. I saw that my husband sent money to his family, but we didn't have any. So I said, I am going to go and see where I can work.

Well, when I first arrived, I went to work in the strawberry harvest. I was pregnant when I arrived. So I went to work in the strawberry harvest while I was pregnant. I kept working in the berries until one month before my daughter was born. Then I stayed home.

LYNN: How did you feel working the strawberry harvest?

FIDELIA: I felt that my dream was lost because it wasn't like the dream that I had. Instead, I had to go and work in the fields. Then my daughter was born, and I was at home for a little while. Then I returned to work. I was making pretty good money because I had a contract. So I was able to send money home to support my children in Mexico. They were living there with their grandmother.

. . . Then in 1986, about two years after I had been here, you started to hear talk about how we could be able to fix our papers, to legalize. At the time, I really wanted to go and visit my kids in Mexico.

LYNN: This was the amnesty?

FIDELIA: Yes. It was the amnesty. I said, "I am going to go back to Mexico anyway. I don't care about fixing my papers because I have to go and see my children." But my husband said, "You can't go. You have to fix your papers. Why do you want to go back to Mexico?"

So I endured two more years without seeing my children. I was able to pay for a better house for them there in Mexico with the money I earned working. It isn't luxurious, but it's bigger than what we had. The roof is of clay tiles. I built this house for my mother-in-law and for my kids. She was taking care of them in Ixpantepec Nieves.

LYNN: Did you fix your papers in 1986?

FIDELIA: It was in 1987 . . .

LYNN: Were there a lot of women who were fixing their papers then?

FIDELIA: There were, but also a lot of couples. Then after this I saw that a lot of people were bringing their children. After I fixed my papers I could bring my children, and they all stayed here with me. . . . I went back to Oaxaca for my children. Two were born here and three of them were born there. I went back to get the three in Oaxaca, and then all five lived with me here. That was really good. Right now I have a son who is twenty-two years old, another who is sixteen, a girl who is seventeen, another girl who is thirteen, and a boy who is ten. I am really happy because right now my children have everything they need. . . . we are all together now.

Once Fidelia's children were in the United States with her, she could finally relax a little and begin to focus on ways to improve her and her family's life. She learned to drive, found a job outside of the fields, and slowly began to learn English. The emotional security of having her family united in one place was of great importance to her.

Conclusion

Beginning with the bracero program of the 1940s, indigenous women have shown great resilience and resourcefulness in coping with the changes that came, first, with male migration that left them in Mexico alone with small children and then often with their own relocation to the United States. For periods of their lives when they lived in rural Oaxaca, women such as Fidelia and Dolores were able to count on local female kin networks to help them out with childcare, food, and other daily necessities. Once they came to the United States, women and men had to readjust their expectations and understandings of the gendered relations of work and home. Economic survival in the United States for those working minimum wage jobs requires both husbands and wives to work one and often two jobs (see Ehrenreich 2001). Because it is often difficult to bring young children to the United States, children may remain in Mexico. For their parents, fathering and mothering across borders can have high costs. This is no doubt the case for the children as well.

At a structural level, the separation of men and women who are married, of parents from their children, and of family members from one another in the transborder labor and living processes described here represents multiple inequalities: the subordinate economic position of Mexico vis-à-vis the United States; the weak position of Mexican immigrant minimum wage workers in the United States in jobs that do not pay for the social reproduction of the labor force; and the unmet desire on the part of Mexican immigrants to live on a par with people in the United States. Women's experiences and understandings of these inequalities are tied to their own personal and gendered histories within these larger frameworks. Ironically, as they may become somewhat empowered within their own families in the United States once they enter the paid labor force and have husbands who take on a greater share of domestic work, they often lose the support of the female kin with whom they interacted on a daily basis in Mexico. Working two minimum wage jobs is hard for anyone, and the result of a seventy- to eighty-hour workweek plus the labor of raising a family—even with a husband's help—is usually exhaustion. Whether or not women achieve greater gender equality within their marriages and families once they migrate to the United States is difficult to assess. What is most often on their minds initially is simple survival. If they feel a sense of solidarity with and support from their husbands, children, and other extended family, that is an important resource in helping them cope with daily challenges.

CHAPTER 7

Navigating the Borders of Racial

and Ethnic Hierarchies

Within Mexico, indigenous peoples are incorporated into a colonially inherited system of merged racial/ethnic classification in which they are ranked below Mestizos (a constructed category of "mixed race") and White Spaniards, who supposedly have preserved their Spanish heritage over five hundred years (see Stephen 2002: 85–91). While such categories are certainly historically and culturally constructed and not biological, they continue to operate with political and social force in many parts of Mexico as well as among Mexican-origin populations in the United States. Although Mexico is now closer than ever to granting recognition and respect to its living indigenous population, the inability of the Mexican Congress to ratify the San Andrés Accords on Indigenous Rights and Culture, which were signed by the Mexican government and the Ejército Zapatista de Liberación Nacional, or EZLN (Zapatista Army of National Liberation) in 1996, suggests that the granting of equal rights and self-determination to Mexico's indigenous peoples is still elusive. In 2001, the Mexican Congress implemented new legislation on indigenous rights, but it was unacceptable to many.

Following a national bus tour by the EZLN that retraced Emiliano Zapata's entry into Mexico City, an address to the Mexican Congress by Tojola'bal Comandante Esthér, and an outpouring of national support for legislation to enact the San Andrés Accords, the Mexican Congress passed a greatly watered down version of the original accords that left most of the specifics for how indigenous autonomy might be realized to individual state legislatures. While nineteen state legislatures ratified the legislation, nine states (Oaxaca, Chiapas, Guerrero, Estado de Mexico, Hidalgo, San Luis Potosí, Zacatecas, Sinaloa, and Baja California Sur) that together have a large indigenous population rejected the legislation. In Oaxaca, the legislation was rejected by a vote of thirty-eight to four; in Chiapas it was rejected by a vote of thirty-five to five (López Bárcenas et. al 2002: 131). Nevertheless, the necessary majority of states ratified it, and it is now national law. What indigenous rights are and how they should be articulated in law remains a subject of bitter dispute in Mexico.

On the ground, indigenous peoples in Mexico continue to experience discrimination in their everyday interactions. For example, prejudices against indigenous people are often reflected in how they are addressed and treated. For Mixtecos such as Lucia Morales, from San Agustín Atenango, even going to the mostly mestizo district center of Silacayoapan to obtain basic documents such as birth certificates and marriage licenses can be a humiliating experience. A young mother of four, she told me about how she was treated in the municipal offices in Silacayoapan. She waited an entire day to see a clerk to obtain a corrected birth certificate that she needed to get a voting identification card. She commented,

> I waited there for four hours. They waited on other people. Then the señorita who works there tells me, "I am leaving now and you will have to come back on Monday." She saw me sitting there with my two little kids for hours and hours. She just thinks she is better than us. They all do there. Then it started to rain, and I couldn't find a way back because the bus hardly ever comes. I had to carry both my babies through the rain.

Stories of indigenous people being treated poorly by mestizo bureaucrats in places like Silacayoapán and nearby Juxtlahuaca are not uncommon.

Zapotec women from Teotitlán del Valle have described similar experiences when they go to Oaxaca City in order to obtain assistance from official agencies. María Contreras said of her many experiences in government offices, "You walk in and they peg you as Indian from one of the towns—especially if we are speaking Zapotec. Then it is as if you aren't even there. 'They will be right back. Just wait a little bit more,' they tell us. Meanwhile, we have to sit there for hours. We might as well be invisible."

When indigenous families from San Agustín and Teotitlán travel in Mexico, as soon as they identify themselves as coming from Oaxaca they are immediately classified as *chaparritos* (short ones), *Oaxaquitos* (little people from Oaxaca), or *Inditos sucios* (dirty little Indians), and sometimes they're told they can't speak because of their use of their native Mixteco or Zapoteco (see Fox and Rivera-Salgado 2004a: 12). Most are bilingual. These derogatory terms not only follow them throughout Mexico, but are frequently employed in the United States as well by the Mexican-origin population there. Whether in the public schools, local businesses, or surrounding labor camps, the belittling of indigenous peoples that occurs in Mexico is often repeated in Oregon and California. This reality is something that is articulated not only by Mixtec and other indigenous migrants, but also by nonindigenous Mexicans in California and Mexican.

Being Indigenous in Oregon and California

For indigenous migrants who have come to live in Mexican Oregon and Mexican California, the racial/ethnic hierarchy of Mexico continues to be observed but is overlaid with U.S.-based racial categories. Whereas so-called ethnic distinctions are the primary markers of difference in Mexico, particularly in terms of the degree to which people embrace an indigenous identity built on place, language, and ethnic autonomy, once Mexican migrants cross into the United States, what was their national identity, that is, their "Mexicanness," is treated as a racial identity. Scholars of Latino studies are increasingly studying the racialization of cultural and ethnic categories in analyzing the varied experiences of Latinos in the United States (Fox n.d. 2005). As discussed in chapter 5, the construction of all Mexicans historically as "illegals" or "potential illegals" also involves a process of racialization in the nineteenth and twentieth centuries—with regional specificities. As argued by De Genova and Ramos-Zayas, looking at the historical circumstances leading to the production of Latino (and other) racial formations permits one to "situate them within a wider social field framed by the hegemonic polarity of racialized whiteness and blackness in the United States. Thus the 'Latino' (or 'Hispanic') label tends to be always saturated with racialized differences" (2003: 2). The same can be said for the label "Mexican" in the United States. The work of De Genova and Ramos-Zayas also considers how racialized identities and distinctions are negotiated both between Latinos and non-Latinos and among different Latino groups (2003: 10). In particular, they analyze the racialized constructions of "Mexicans" and "Puerto Ricans" in Chicago in relation to the politics of citizenship (2003b).

In the ethnographic examples that follow, my concerns are related to those of De Genova and Ramos-Zayas but focus more on how indigenous migrants in the United States have become and continue to be a racialized category within the Mexican immigrant community and how Mexicano systems of ethnic and racial classification are influenced by and overlap the historically and regionally situated racial hierarchies in southern California and western Oregon. While indigenous migrants can articulate local racial/ethnic hierarchies in places like Woodburn, Oregon, and Oxnard, California, so can nonindigenous Mexican immigrants. In this chapter I address ways in which indigenous migrants themselves have invoked shared experiences of racial oppression as a basis for constructing broader panethnic and panindigenous identities (see Fox 2005: 6).

Sara Lorenzo Vásquez is a twenty-one-year-old woman who lived the first eleven years of her life in Durango, Durango, and then moved to San Diego, California. From there she went with her parents first to Salem, Oregon, and then to Woodburn, where they opened a local bakery, which has since become a successful business. Sara sells a variety of breads, cookies, and treats to many kinds of Mexican-origin residents, and others come in to purchase a snack to eat or baked goods to take home.

Sara has shoulder-length black hair. Her wide face often sports an open smile as she leans on the counter by the cash register of the bakery where she works with her parents. Her arms are well muscled from hoisting trays of bread and pastries as well as from carrying her young daughter. We spoke in September 2003, moving from the counter over to one of the booths in the bakery. The booths open onto the main square of Woodburn and are good people-watching vantage points. A wide range of people come into the bakery, and Sara interacts with them as she keeps a watch on the public square outside the window. In the process she has become something of a local sociologist. Her analysis of local Mexicanos is illustrative of the range of categories that exists throughout the various layers of Mexicans in the community. In addition to documenting the continuation of racial hierarchies present in Mexico, our conversation captures the categories used in the United States—Latino, Hispanic, Chicano—into which people from Mexico are often cast. These are discussed in detail below.

LYNN: Who comes into the bakery to buy stuff?
SARA: The Latinos. Some Americanos come in as well. Maybe once a year a Russian will come in, but they hardly ever come by.

LYNN: How about the rest of the businesses around here downtown? Who shops down here?

SARA: Well, it's mostly Latinos like here. Maybe they need to make the center of town bilingual. Sometimes Americanos go to the businesses, but sometimes they need interpreters. They don't speak Spanish.

LYNN: How do you identify yourself? As Latina, Mexicana, some other name?

SARA: Mexicana [Mexican]. I am Mexicana because I was born there. I feel Mexicana here, too.

LYNN: How would you like your daughter to identify?

SARA: I want her to feel Mexicana, too.

LYNN: How is it different, being Mexicana, from other kinds of people here?

SARA: We feel different, for example, than the Chicanos here. They don't speak Spanish. They don't get along with the Mexicanos. I think that here there is more a feeling of being Mexicano. The majority of people here in Woodburn continue to identify as Mexicanos.

LYNN: Are there differences between Mexicanos? Do people make distinctions among Mexicanos?

SARA: There are people who don't like the Oaxaqueños [Oaxacans]. They say that they are really stubborn, that they are thieves. These are the people who have been here for the least amount of time.

LYNN: Does this mean that there are prejudices among Mexicanos?

SARA: Yes. There are prejudices among the Mexicanos. They divide people into groups. Like they say "the Oaxaquitos" and the rest. They also say that the Chilangos [people from Mexico City] are very egotistical and not very nice. They say that the people from Michoacán are self-important (*presumidos*) and that those from Veracruz and Sinaloa are nonassuming. There are a lot of people from Veracruz here now.

Sara's classification system first mentions Latinos as opposed to Americanos. In this first level of oppositional categories she distinguished between those who speak Spanish, Latinos, and those who do not speak Spanish, Americanos. *Americano* is also a racial reference to Anglos. *Latinos* is not a racial signifier in this context but seems primarily related to language and perhaps to cultural criteria. Then, in choosing a label for herself, she first draws a line around Mexicanos as being different from Chicanos because Chicanos don't speak Spanish and don't get along with Mexicanos. When asked about differences between Mexicans, she focused first on the Oaxaquitos as her first example of distinction, separating the Oaxaquitos from the rest. This is a direct reference to the supposedly short stature of people from Oaxaca, which is related to their indigenous background. The diminutive suffix -itos refers not only to size but also to a state of being childlike, small in other ways. The next distinction she unfolds refers to Mexicans from Mexico City and then people from other states. Interestingly, in her discussion of different groups of Mexicanos the category of "Oaxaquitos" is the only one which makes a physical, racial reference. The others categories are those of character and personality, for example, "egotistical," "self-important," "nonassuming." The Oaxacans are racially marked in this system of difference in ways that groups from other states are not.

Dolores Alavez, a Mixteca from San Agustín Atenango, has frequently been the object of disparaging comments about her Oaxacan origins. The remarks have been made primarily at work and often by other Mexicans. Her discussion of the discriminatory attitudes toward Mixtecos also reveals her feelings about other Mexicanos, particularly those from Michoacán. The divisions and judgments about the several kinds of Mexicanos found in Sara's analysis are somewhat reflected in the words of Dolores as well. Here is part of our discussion on this topic:

LYNN: How do they treat people from Oaxaca around here?
DOLORES: Well, they always talk about us like we are not worth as much as everyone else—especially people from Michoacán and Guanajuato say this. They don't like people from Oaxaca. They always say we are . . . I don't know what. But they always say things about us—there are tensions. With those from Guanajuato, too. . . . For example, they might say to you, "So is it true you are from Oaxaca?" "Yes," I would answer. "Why?" "Because those from Oaxaca are obvious," they would say. . . . They say this because we are short. But I am telling you that there is a little of everything in every state. They are short people, tall people, fat people, and dark people. But I have heard people say, "Those from Oaxaca work really hard, they work harder than anyone else." Like the people from Michoacán. They don't want to kill themselves working. They just want to work at their own speed.

. . . You hear these kinds of comments in the schools as well. There are a lot of fights because the people from Guanajuato and Michoacán don't get along. They start having problems, and then it gets spread to the students in the school. My oldest son says to me sometimes, "I don't think that we Mexicanos should be doing this. If we are here in this country and they see us fighting, then they will think that we are all like that." He thinks we should be more united.

Dolores's response to outright or implied derogatory remarks at work is to fiercely defend her language and culture. Knowing that their coworkers won't understand them, she and her brother recress the insults by speaking Mixteco in the cannery where they work, sometimes in order to criticize those around them without their realizing it. While this makes some of her coworkers uncomfortable, the pressure on Dolores to conform and not speak Mixtec is not nearly as strong as it is for children in public schools.

DOLORES: We have our culture and our customs. We don't just leave them behind. Like me. I have been here for years, but I will never leave my culture. I will never be ashamed to speak Mixteco. Why should I be ashamed to be from Oaxaca? When they ask me, "Where are you from?" I always say with pride, "I am from Oaxaca." Then they will say, "What dialect [indigenous language] do you speak?" "Mixteco," I say. But there are a lot of people who are ashamed, and they don't want to tell people where they are from or that they speak an indigenous language. This shouldn't be. We should be proud of being from there and of speaking our languages. We shouldn't be ashamed of this culture.

LYNN: With whom do you speak Mixteco?

DOLORES: I speak it with my brothers and sisters. I speak it with my brother in the cannery. When there are things we don't want people around us to understand, we speak in Mixteco.

[Dolores laughs] . . . In the cannery they have noticed. One day an older woman said to me, "Dolores, what are you speaking? It isn't Spanish. What is it?"

"It is a *dialecto* [indigenous language,]" I said.

"Which one?" she asked. "No wonder it sounded strange to me. How interesting that you keep on speaking it here."

Racial labeling as Oaxaquitos is also experienced by children in the Woodburn and Salem public schools (and elsewhere). Discussions with children, particularly high school students, suggested that being called a Oaxaquito was fairly standard in school lunchrooms and while on the way to or from school. Parents talk about their children not wanting to speak Mixtec but don't always think about what the consequences of speaking it in public are for their children. Adults like Dolores may have been able to continue speaking Mixteco while working in the cannery, but the pressures on children to assimilate and specifically to leave behind their indigenous language and identity can be very strong.

Mariano González, introduced in chapter 2, first came to the United States in 1979 from San Agustín Atenango and was followed by his wife and six oldest children in 1994. During a conversation with his teenage children, Mariano began talking about the beauty of the Mixtec language. He commented, "It is beautiful to have this language, Mixtec. But there is going to come a time when we are going to lose this language, when we are going to forget it. Our children don't want to speak it. I tell them that it is good that they learn a little bit of Mixtec. It's good for you, I say, but they don't listen to me." His two youngest children are in high school in Salem and speak perfect Oregon English. "We don't want to be called Oaxaquitos. We speak English and Spanish," his thirteen-year-old son Mariano Junior explained to me. While pressure to speak English may not come directly from the larger Mexicano community of the Salem-Woodburn area, it can work as an assimilation strategy among Mexicano students. Speaking Mixtec at school is a sure way of continuing to be called a Oaxaquito.

Even in the farm labor camps surrounding Woodburn's agricultural producing fields, the racial hierarchy of Mexico is spatially articulated through the geography and labeling of cabins. Although labor camps are becoming fewer in number because of growers' concerns about regulations, a sizable number of them still operate in the area under the direction either of growers or of contractors, who are supposed to be licensed but often are not. In a typical camp, cabins accommodate sixteen to twenty workers stacked in bunk beds. In many camps I have visited, the cabins are categorized by the state or the region of Mexico that the workers who live in them are from. In some cases, all the workers in one cabin may be from the same community in Mexico. Often workers from the same town or nearby communities are contracted as a group, and they come directly from Oaxaca, Veracruz, or elsewhere to the Woodburn area. This is especially true of first-time workers.

On a brisk October day in 2000 I was visiting a camp with a friend and collaborator, Lorenzo Alavez (introduced in chapter 5). At the time, Lorenzo was working for PCUN. Inside the labor camp, we found a group of workers in a cabin from Sinaloa. After chatting with them, I asked them to tell me who was in the other cabins. One worker stated, "Well, over there they are from Veracruz. Across from them are people from Michoacán. Toward the back are two cabins where the Oaxaquitos live. They don't even speak Spanish over there. Then next to one of those are some people from Toluca." Lorenzo and I went over to the various

15. Pancho Mendoza
Pérez in 2004.

cabins, and we discovered that what the worker had told us about the states of origin proved to be correct. People from several different places occupied the Oaxaca cabins, and they included Mixteco as well as a few Triqui speakers. While Oaxacan workers may prefer to room together, the cabin system for non-Oaxacans was also a way of reinforcing the separation and assumed inferiority of Oaxacan indigenous migrants for nonindigenous Mexican workers.

Racial/ethnic classification systems among the Mexican-origin population of southern California appear to be similar to those in Oregon. Pancho Mendoza, from Teotitlán del Valle (introduced in chapter 1), lived for two and a half years in Oxnard, California. He spent a great deal of time in the company of other young men and women from Teotitlán. When he played basketball and engaged in other social activities, he regularly spoke Zapotec and publicly identified as Zapotec. Because Pancho is tall, many Mexicanos in California doubted his claim to be from Oaxaca. He was, they said, too tall to be from Oaxaca. In the following narrative, Pancho discusses his understanding of the racial/ethnic system in Oxnard and Moorpark, California. In addition to talking about different categories of migrants and his own identity, he describes a discomforting experience at the hands of some local women whom he labels Chicana. He recounts how they made fun of him and his friends as they were speaking Zapotec on the street. Playing basketball and socializing with friends from Teotitlán who speak Zapotec was an important experience of ethnic validation and pride for him. At the same time, speaking Zapotec in public marked him as Indian in the context of southern California.

PANCHO: I learned about Latinos because I was in the United States and knew some Latinos. I learned that all of the Mexicanos—actually all of those people who come from below the California border—are called Latinos. You can identify more as Mexicano or from such and such a part of Mexico, but there they called everyone Latinos.

LYNN: Did you use that word, *Latino*, to describe yourself?

PANCHO: There? I was a Latino there, why not? All of us who are from that part below the U.S. border are Latinos. But then people always ask you, "Where are you from?" I might say, "Mexico" or "Mexican." Then they say, "But where precisely are you from? [*De donde mero eres?*]"

LYNN: And then? What do you say then?

PANCHO: I say I am from Oaxaca. Because there in Oxnard when you go to apply for a job, they say to you, "Where are you from?" "From Oaxaca?" They say, "People from Oaxaca work." "The people from Michoacán are big, but they don't work. They don't do much work." If you keep saying, "I am from Oaxaca," then they will say, "Well, those from Oaxaca are not afraid of any work. They are not afraid." So you tell them you are from Oaxaca. In Oxnard there are a lot of people from Oaxaca and Guerrero . . .

LYNN: So when you say you are from Oaxaca it was like a recommendation for a hard worker?

PANCHO: Yeah, like that . . . But they didn't identify me as being from Oaxaca. They didn't believe I was from Oaxaca because I am tall. I would say to people, "I am from Oaxaca." They would say, "No, you can't be from Oaxaca, they are all shorter there. You are lying. You are not from Oaxaca." . . . And since I didn't have any identification I could only identify myself by saying, "I am from Oaxaca, from this town." Then they would say again,

"No, you are from Michoacán because you are large. You are lying. You just want to pass yourself off as being from Oaxaca." . . . I would insist, "No. No. I am from Oaxaca. I am Oaxaqueño."

LYNN: So did you identify yourself as being Zapoteco from Teotitlán or indigenous?

PANCHO: Yes, I identified myself as being Zapoteco. When they didn't believe me when I said I was from Oaxaca, I would always continue by saying, "I am from Oaxaca. I am Zapoteco from Teotitlán del Valle. When you like, come and visit Teotitlán. It is a town where a lot of Americans come to visit. They are artisans there. We get a lot of visitors to see the artisans."

LYNN: Did you feel proud when you said this?

PANCHO: Yes, yes yes. I always felt really proud because I am from this land, and I am from the town of Teotitlán.

LYNN: In Oregon, people also talk about people from Oaxaca as being hard workers. But some friends have told me that, for example, in the high schools, kids from Oaxaca get made fun of. They call them *Oaxaquitos, los inditos.* Did this ever happen to you in California?

PANCHO: Nothing exactly like that, but something related, I think. You see, in Oxnard when we meet others from Teotitlán del Valle, we know that they are also Zapotecos. We have the Zapotec language, and we speak to one another in our own language. We walk around with our friends speaking Zapotec. But one time when I was walking with some friends and speaking Zapotec, some people walking in front of us started making fun of us for speaking Zapotec. Because we were speaking Zapotec they thought we were saying something bad about them. But no, we were just speaking our own language. They said, "Hey, look at that bunch of stupid Indians." They thought we were criticizing them. But we were not paying any attention to them. We were talking about our own business, where we live, our own concerns.

LYNN: How did it turn out?

PANCHO: Well, it wasn't a problem for us. We didn't give it much importance.

LYNN: Who made this commentary?

PANCHO: I think they were Chicanas.

LYNN: Did they speak Spanish?

PANCHO: Yes. They spoke Spanish and they were Chicanas. They were some girls, some women. They always think they are very superior by being Chicana. They were speaking English and then in Spanish. That is why I thought they were Chicanas because they could speak Spanish and English. They were not Americanos.

In his discussion, Pancho provides ample evidence of the racial classification system that operates within Mexico and is imported into the United States and operates in places like Oxnard. Being "from Oaxaca" is believed to be associated with short stature and indicative of indigenous ancestry. Because Pancho didn't look like he was from Oaxaca because he was tall, he had to invoke different criteria of indigenousness to convince other Mexicanos that he was from Oaxaca. He then identified himself as Zapoteco from the town of Teotitlán. He explains to people who don't believe he is from Oaxaca that he speaks Zapotec, an Indian language, as a way of proving he is from Oaxaca and therefore indigenous. He makes a place-based and linguistically based claim to being indigenous. For Pancho this is a point of pride, not an insult.

Pancho's discussion of the term *Latino* focuses on what he learned was the basis for the Latino label—everyone who is born below the Mexican border and is from Latin America. In the context of the term *Latino*, he deploys *Mexicano* as a way of being more specific about his identity. From there, he says, when he meets other Mexicanos the process of identity labeling moves to the state and local level. Once he enters the level of identifying himself as being "from Oaxaca," the discussion re-engages with the Mexican racial/ethnic hierarchy focused on an indigenous/nonindigenous dichotomy.

However, when Pancho experiences a taunt from a group of young women who speak both Spanish and English in Oxnard, his discussion joins the racial/ethnic hierarchy of Mexico with a regional southern California racial/ethnic hierarchy that includes the terms *Chicano/a* and *Americano/a*. Chicanos and Chicanas are distinguished from Mexicanos as being from the United States and speaking both Spanish and English. They are differentiated from Americanos/as as being nonwhite and being able to speak Spanish. In his narrative, Pancho integrates the Mexican racial/ethnic hierarchy with a U.S.-based system of labels with a southern California specificity, although his categories overlap significantly with those of Sara Lorenzo Vásquez of Woodburn.[1]

Indigenous Mexican Migrants in the World of U.S. Census Categories

In addition to his experience with the Chicanas, Pancho has had discussions with other individuals who attempt to place him in the larger U.S.

national racial/ethnic system that often follows the evolving categories of the U.S. census in its attempt to classify Mexicans and others now known as Latinos and Hispanics. By the year 2000, the U.S. census had become complex enough so that migrants like Pancho could classify themselves as Native American by race and also designate their ethnicity as Hispanic, specifying Mexican or another national-origin category. But as is true of regional linguistic systems of racial and ethnic classification, the categories available to people like Pancho in 2000 have a significant political and cultural history.

As described by Clara Rodríguez in her study of race categories in the U.S. census, "over time, U.S. decennial census classifications have moved towards a more sharply defined bipolar structure. Basically, two socially constructed polarities have evolved that contain 'whites' at one end and 'other social races' at the other" (2000: 65; de Genova and Ramos-Zayas 2003). Different categories have been featured at different times, and the meaning of categories has shifted through time. Many people think of the simplified version of this statement as "The racial system of the United States is based on a black-white polarity." While black and white have been consistent categories, their meanings have shifted. For example, in the 1800s, a white person was anyone who was less than one-quarter Negro. By 1924, however, fixation on preventing miscegenation through marriage resulted in the prohibition of any one with "a single drop of Negro blood" from marrying a white person (Rodríguez 2000: 41).

Mexican

The category of "Mexican" is an excellent example of the shifting meaning of color within the construction of racial categories in the United States in the twentieth century. In the 1930 census, the category "Mexican" appeared for the first and the last time—primarily to allow census enumerators to describe Mexican laborers. After that, Mexicans were often classified as "White." The motivation for creating a separate "Mexican" census category in 1930 may have been to cover the majority of people emigrating from Mexico who were not perceived as "White" or "Indian." Instructions to census enumerators stated, "Practically all Mexican laborers are of a racial mixture difficult to classify, though usually well recognized in the localities where they are found. In order to obtain separate figures for this racial group, it has been decided that all persons born in Mexico, or having parents born in Mexico who are not definitely white, Negro, Indian, Chinese or Japanese, should be returned as Mexican ('Mex')" (Hayes Bautista 2004: 29).

Whites Who Are "Persons with Spanish as a Mother Tongue,"
"Persons with a Spanish Surname"

The Mexican census category was short-lived. In the 1940 census it disappeared, and the Bureau of the Census recategorized those registered in 1930 as "Mexican" as "White." Instructions stated that "persons of Mexican birth or ancestry who were not definitely Indian or of other Nonwhite races were returned as White" (U.S. Bureau of the Census 1942: 3, cited in Rodríguez 2000: 212). From 1940 until 1980, the Census Bureau counted Mexicans and other Latin Americans as "White."[2] The topic of "Indian" ancestry among Mexicans in the United States was largely absent from view until 2000, but popular culture as well as antimiscegenation and other laws suggest the continued importance of color in identifying Mexicans in the United States. Ironically, during the period when Mexicans were officially classified in the U.S. census as "White," they became recategorized in popular culture as "illegal aliens," a term with racial allusions to teeming dark hordes waiting to cross the U.S.-Mexican border. Beginning in the 1950s with Operation Wetback and the rise of a culture in the United States that was explicitly anti–Mexican immigration (see chapter 3), Mexicans were portrayed as anything but white in the press and in films.

In 1948, one of the plaintiffs in *Perez vs. Lippold*, a California Supreme Court case that resulted in California's antimiscegenation law being declared unconstitutional, was Andrea Perez, who was of Mexican descent. The California civil code stated, "All marriages of white persons with Negros, Mongolians, and members of the Malay race or mulattoes are illegal and void" (Supreme Court of California 1948: 1). Petitioner Perez stated in her application for a marriage license that she was "White" and that petitioner Sylvester Davis was a "Negro." While the marriage would still have involved "crossing" of racial lines if Perez had been given a racial designation other than "White," the fact that she was clearly marked and known to be of Mexican descent may have contributed to some thinking that the marriage was not truly "interracial" since it involved two "nonwhites." One of the justices in the case noted the ambiguity of the category "Mexican" as a race:

Civil Code sections 60 [referring to California state law] like most miscegenation statutes . . . prohibits marriages only between "white persons"
and members of certain other so-called races. Although section 60 is more
inclusive than most miscegenation statutes, it does not include "Indians" or
"Hindus" . . . nor does it set up "Mexicans" as a separate category, although
some authorities consider Mexico to be populated at least in part by persons
who are a mixture of "white" and "Indian." . . . Thus, "white persons" may
marry persons who would be considered other than white by respondent's
authorities, and all other "races" may intermarry freely. (Supreme Court of
California 1948: 6)

A key question for the period from 1930 until 1980 has been how to
document the presence of people of Mexican, Latin American, and Caribbean descent in the United States if they were primarily recorded as
being "White." From 1940 to 1980, however, cultural criteria were used in
the census. The 1940 census used a linguistic definition to determine
"persons of Spanish mother tongue." In the 1950 and 1960 censuses,
"persons of Spanish surname" were reported. In the 1970 census, a sub-
group of what was perceived to be the Hispanic community was asked to
choose among several Hispanic origins listed on the questionnaire, such
as "Mexican" or "Puerto Rican." As summarized by Rodríguez, "Between
1940 and 1970, Hispanics were counted according to three different cultural criteria, linguistic (1940), surname (1950 and 1960), and origin
(1970)" (2000: 102).

"Hispanic" and Race

In 1980, the category of "Hispanic" appears on the census for the first
time, and respondents are asked to indicate their race and also whether
or not they are of Hispanic or Spanish origin. The two questions appear
as follows:

4. Is this person _____? Fill in one circle.
White Asian Indian
Black or Negro Hawaiian
Japanese Guamanian
Chinese Samoan
Filipino Eskimo
Korean Aleut

Vietnamese Other—specify _____
Indian (Amer.) Print Tribe _____ . . .
7. Is this person of Spanish/Hispanic origin or descent? Fill in one circle
No, not Spanish/Hispanic.
Yes, Mexican, Mexican-American, Chicano.
Yes, Puerto Rican.
Yes, Cuban.
Yes, other Spanish/Hispanic.

Beginning with the 1980 census, the term *Hispanic* became a specially designated term that included four subcategories: Mexican, Mexican American, or Chicano; Puerto Rican; Cuban; Other Spanish/Hispanic. Yet because the term lumped together groups with very disparate histories, sociodemographic characteristics, language capabilities and knowledge of Spanish, political interests, and treatment upon immigration to the United States, many activists and community members found the term *Hispanic* problematic. The term is a catchall that lumps together the categories of language, ethnicity, nationality, and the socially constructed notion of race. Finally, *Hispanic*" refers directly to Spanish descent, leaving out the significant populations of Latin America and the Caribbean that have rich indigenous and African histories. The Spanish *Hispano* was not new in 1980, but in fact had been used since the nineteenth century by Spanish-origin populations in the West and the East, particularly in New Mexico by people of Mexican origin (see Dávila 2001: 15).

Chicano

The category "Chicano" also appears on the 1980 U.S. census, reflecting the importance of the Brown Pride movement that began in the 1960s and was fueled by movements such as those of César Chávez and the United Farm Workers and Corky Gonzalez and the Crusade for Justice as well as by the land grant movement in New Mexico, the creation of United Mexican American Students (UMAS) in Los Angeles, activist community newspapers such as *La Raza* in Los Angeles, Movimiento Estudiantil Chicano de Aztlán (MEChA), the creation of Chicano studies, and the Brown Berets' occupation of Catalina Island. Corky González was one of the first prominent activists to reclaim the name Chicano (Haney López 2004: 150; R.Gutiérrez 1993). While the origin of the term is unclear, prior to the 1960s *Chicano* was used as a racial slur by non–

Mexican Americans to describe all Mexican American people in urban, Spanish-speaking neighborhoods. In the hands of González and others, it became a term of ethnic pride. Drawing on the notion of "Black is Beautiful," the terms *Chicano* and *Brown Power* were used as ways of inverting terms of insult and turning them into prideful ones. *Chicano* was a celebration of nonwhite identity—working explicitly against the idea of "Whites with Spanish Surnames" and "Mexican-American," terms that some felt expressed assimilation. *Chicano* was a rejection of two kinds of whiteness: that of the Anglo community and that within the Mexican community (Haney López 2004: 206).[3]

Ultimately, Chicano identity became tightly linked to the original homeland of Aztlán, the northern homeland referred to in Aztec self-histories held to have been located in pre-1848 northwest Mexico. Thus Aztlán is also understood by Chicano activists as referring to Mexican national territory ceded to the United States by the Treaty of Guadalupe Hidalgo in 1848. In "El Plan Espiritual de Aztlán/The Spiritual Plan of Aztlán," a document written in March 1969 at the Chicano Youth Liberation Conference in Denver, Aztlán is described as Chicano national territory. In this document, Chicanos are linked directly to the indigenous peoples of the Americas, who are conceived of as a bronze people but also as a mestizo nation. The Plan de Aztlán makes historical reference both to the Mexica or Aztec indigenous inhabitants of Mexico as well as asserting that Aztlán is a "mestizo nation." Chicanos are racially distinguished through ancestry and territory from foreign Europeans, or "Gabachos" and "Gringos.

While the framers of the Plan Espiritual de Aztlán clearly did not interpret *mestizaje* as drawing on white superiority in the mixing of the races, the Chicano understanding of mestizaje and subsequent popular cultural manifestations of Chicanismo that draw on symbols of Aztec indigenous culture come from a profoundly different understanding and experience of "being indigenous" than that of many Mixtec and Zapotec migrants. The category of "Chicano" is a significant field of interaction for indigenous migrants as are the categories of "Hispanic" and "Latino." These are census categories as well as social constructions of race which have strongly influenced popular American culture and the kinds of social fields migrants live and work in.

Race, "Hispanics," and "Latinos"

With regard to the categories of "Latino" and "Hispanic" and "Chicano" and their further elaborations in the 1990 and 2000 censuses, conflation of race and ethnicity has always been at the heart of the matter. Popular cultural understandings of race in the United States are built on four colors that roughly correspond to geographic areas: black (Africa), white (Europe), red (Native North America), and yellow (Asia). As Rodríguez (2000), Sanjeck (1994), and others have pointed out, these four color groups continue to have corresponding categories on census forms, despite a slew of critiques that show there is no basis for them. The 1980 and 1990 census forms used the four-color scheme in the race question, but the specifics varied. In 1980 and 1990, people were requested to "fill in one" racial category. This was followed by the question "Is this person of Spanish/Hispanic Origin," followed by primarily national identity designations, "Mexican/Mexican American/Chicano, Puerto Rican, Cuban," and "Other Spanish/Hispanic." In the 1980 and the 1990 census forms, the person filling out the form was asked to specify what "Other" means. In 1990, specific examples were provided, "Print one group, for example, Argentinean, Colombian, Dominican, Nicaraguan, Salvadoran, Spaniard, and so on" (1990 U.S. Census).

One of the most interesting results that emerged from analysis of the 1980 and 1990 censuses was that more than 40 percent of Hispanics choose the "some other race" category—i.e., not self-identifying as "White," "Black or Negro," "Indian," or "Asian or Pacific Islander." In addition, many who chose the "some other race" box wrote in the "name of their 'home' Latino country or group to 'explain' their race–or 'otherness'" (Rodríguez 2000: 7). The referents put in the "some other race" box were often cultural or national-origin terms such as *Dominican*, *Honduran*, or *Boricua* (Puerto Rican). Rodríguez suggests that this indicates "the fact that many Latinos viewed the question of race as a question of culture, national origin, and socialization, rather than simply biological or genetic ancestry or color" (2000: 7). By the year 2000, the percentage of Hispanics who chose the "some other race" category was 51 percent (Huizar Murillo and Cerda 2004: 280). As pointed out by Fox, in choosing to answer the race question with "Other," Latinos are creating their own de facto racial category (2006: 45).

The 2000 census contained two other interesting changes. First, the term *Latino* was added to the question's wording and response options "Spanish/Hispanic/Latino." As discussed above, the term *Hispanic* was included for the first time in the 1980s census and was disparaged by many as an inaccurate, government-created category. The term *Latino* refers to people in the United States of Latin American or Caribbean origin and is a term born of social struggles and activism, much like Chicano. As explained by Arlene Dávila,

> By the 1960s and 1970s, however, the terms "Hispano" and "Hispanic" were seen to be contrary to the cultural nationalism that accompanied larger struggles for civil empowerment by both Chicanos and Puerto Ricans and thus a denial of their identity and a rejection of their indigenous and colonized roots. Ironically, it was shortly after these cultural struggles that the United States government coined the offical designation of "Hispanic" to designate anyone of Spanish background in the United States. This explains why Latino activists generally regard "Hispanic" as more politically "sanitized" terminology than "Latino/a" even though both terms are equally guilty of erasing differences while encompassing highly heterogeneous populations that can be equally appropriated for a range of politics. (2001: 15)

Other scholars, including Susana Oberlar, have made similar points. Oberlar has suggested that the creation of the label *Hispanic* not only conflated differences between Chicanos and Puerto Ricans as they were engaged in nationalist movements that were increasingly militant, but also disproportionately empowered Cuban exiles (1995: 81–84). De Genova and Ramos-Zaya make a similar point (2003a: 4).

The other significant change in the 2000 census was to put the "Spanish/Hispanic/Latino" question first. Then the form asks what the person's's race is, providing fifteen printed options, along with "Some Other Race"; it also allows people to mark one or more races. These are noted as Questions 7 and 8, as seen below in the 2000 U.S. Census form.

"Hispanic American Indians"

The 2000 census was also the first to allow indigenous Mexicans to make their presence known through two distinct census categories. A campaign mounted by the Front of Binational Indigenous Organizations

United States
U.S. Department of Commerce • Bureau of the Census

This is the official form for all the people at this address. It is quick and easy, and your answers are protected by law. Complete the Census and help your community get what it needs — today and in the future!

Start Here / Please use a black or blue pen.

1. How many people were living or staying in this house, apartment, or mobile home on April 1, 2000?

[ ] Number of people

INCLUDE in this number:
- foster children, roomers, or housemates
- people staying here on April 1, 2000 who have no other permanent place to stay
- people living here most of the time while working, even if they have another place to live

DO NOT INCLUDE in this number:
- college students living away while attending college
- people in a correctional facility, nursing home, or mental hospital on April 1, 2000
- Armed Forces personnel living somewhere else
- people who live or stay at another place most of the time

2. Is this house, apartment, or mobile home — *Mark ☒ ONE box.*
- [ ] Owned by you or someone in this household with a mortgage or loan?
- [ ] Owned by you or someone in this household free and clear (without a mortgage or loan)?
- [ ] Rented for cash rent?
- [ ] Occupied without payment of cash rent?

3. Please answer the following questions for each person living in this house, apartment, or mobile home. Start with the name of one of the people living here who owns, is buying, or rents this house, apartment, or mobile home. If there is no such person, start with any adult living or staying here. We will refer to this person as Person 1.

What is this person's name? *Print name below.*

Last Name

First Name   MI

OMB No. 0607-0856: Approval Expires 12/31/2000

Form **D-61A**

4. What is Person 1's telephone number? *We may call this person if we don't understand an answer.*

Area Code + Number

[ ][ ][ ] - [ ][ ][ ] - [ ][ ][ ][ ]

5. What is Person 1's sex? *Mark ☒ ONE box.*
- [ ] Male
- [ ] Female

6. What is Person 1's age and what is Person 1's date of birth?

Age on April 1, 2000

Print numbers in boxes.

Month   Day   Year of birth

➔ **NOTE: Please answer BOTH Questions 7 and 8.**

7. Is Person 1 Spanish/Hispanic/Latino? *Mark ☒ the "No" box if **not** Spanish/Hispanic/Latino.*
- [ ] No, not Spanish/Hispanic/Latino
- [ ] Yes, Mexican, Mexican Am., Chicano
- [ ] Yes, other Spanish/Hispanic/Latino — *Print group.*
- [ ] Yes, Puerto Rican
- [ ] Yes, Cuban

8. What is Person 1's race? *Mark ☒ one or more races to indicate what this person considers himself/herself to be.*
- [ ] White
- [ ] Black, African Am., or Negro
- [ ] American Indian or Alaska Native — *Print name of enrolled or principal tribe.*

- [ ] Asian Indian
- [ ] Chinese
- [ ] Filipino
- [ ] Other Asian — *Print race.*
- [ ] Japanese
- [ ] Korean
- [ ] Vietnamese
- [ ] Native Hawaiian
- [ ] Guamanian or Chamorro
- [ ] Samoan
- [ ] Other Pacific Islander — *Print race.*

- [ ] Some other race — *Print race.*

➔ **If more people live here, continue with Person 2.**

16. First page of U.S. 2000 Census Form.

(FIOB) encouraged indigenous immigrants to register their presence in the census, particularly in California (Huizar Murillo and Cerdas 2004). Here is how this occurred.

One of the racial options, "American Indian or Alaska Native," left a space to indicate a specific "Tribe."[4] According to the Census Bureau, "American Indian or Alaska Native" refers to "people having origins in any of the original peoples of North and South America (including Central America), and who maintain tribal affiliation or community attachment. It includes people who indicated their race or races by marking this category or writing in their principal enrolled tribe such as Rosebud Sioux, Chipewa, or Navajo" (U.S. Census Bureau 2001: 2). The 2000 census showed a significant growth in the number of people who self-identified as "American Indian" *but also* in the number of people who identified themselves as both Hispanic and American Indian. In other words, self-identified Latin American indigenous migrants could "identify both ethnically as Latinos and racially as American Indians" (Fox 2006: 45). In the 2000 census, 407,073 people reported themselves as both "Spanish/Hispanic/Latino" *and* "American Indian or Alaska Native." This was 1.2 percent of the total Hispanic population (U.S. Census 2001: 10, table 10). This significant growth resulted in headlines such as "California Overtakes Oklahoma as State with Most American Indians" in the *San Jose Mercury News*, signaling not only the growth in indigenous migrants primarily from Mexico and Central America, but also the beginning of self-designation on the census (Huizar Murillo and Cerda 2004: 279). Most did not write in the name of a tribe, as this is a U.S.-based concept that makes no sense in the Mexican and Central American context, where until the 1980s and 1990s panethnic identities such as "Mixtec," "Maya," and others were not commonly used (see Kearney 1988, 1995a, 2000; Nagengast and Kearney 1989; Warren 1998).

As pointed out by analysts of these data, it should be "taken as suggestive rather than definitive, that is[,] the numbers should be understood as minimum estimates rather than absolute counts" (Huizar Murillo and Cerda 2004: 283). The data reported under the category of "Hispanic American Indians" show that California is home to the largest population of such people, with 154,362 reported. The greatest concentration of Hispanic American Indians in California was reported in Los Angeles County, with 51,379; Orange County, with 11,492; San Bernardino, with 10,111; and San Diego, with 9,084 (Huizar Murillo and Cerda 2004: 288–89). Oregon reported 5,081 Hispanic American Indians (Huizar Murillo and Cerda 2004: 283–84). The researchers Edward Kissam and Ilene Jacobs concluded after a detailed analysis of the 2000 census in five rural communities in California with higher-than-average concentrations of Mexican immigrants of indigenous origin that the data on "Hispanic American Indians" represent a serious undercount (2004: 325). Because many of the langauges spoken by indigenous migrants are not listed and are usually coded as "Other" or "Spanish," indigenous ethnicity often does not register in the census forms for houses that are completed. Kissam and Jacobs also suggest many ways in which indigenous residents are undercounted in marginal neighborhoods, in rural labor camps, and in other areas where people don't receive mail or are reluctant or unable to report on everyone. Thus while the census data give the official number of "Hispanic American Indians" in Oregon as 5,081, it is quite likely that the number is higher (see Davis 2002). This is also likely for California as well.

Mixtec migrants have continued to be based in their historically marginalized lands in the state of Oaxaca and face an ongoing struggle for their rights as indigenous peoples and immigrant workers and as socially valued citizens of Mexico and residents of the United States.[5] Culturally, Mixtecos and Zapotecos and other indigenous migrants of Latin American origin are still not seen—literally—as part of the state's indigenous population and continue to struggle against the racism imported from Mexico which labels them as inferior to other Mexicans. This may begin to change, however, as new organizations such as the Organización de Comunidades Indígenas Migrantes Oaxaqueños (OCIMO, described in the next chapter), formed in 2004, begin to develop a presence in the state. OCIMO secretary Valentín Sánchez, who is from San Juan Cahuayaxi, explained, "In OCIMO, we promote indigenous cultural events in order to decrease the discrimination toward indigenous people among Hispanics. We think that one of the reasons why discrimination exists is that many Hispanics don't know about the cultural wealth of the indigenous people of Oaxaca." Indigenous migrant organizations play a central role in helping migrants cross racial and ethnic borders more successfully even as they try to change them.

CHAPTER 8

Grassroots Organizing in Transborder Lives

Introduction

Antonia Zárate Reyes is sitting in a circle of women nursing her month-old son. She cradles the back of his head in her hand as she pulls him off of one breast and adjusts him in front of the other. After he has latched onto her breast, she uses her free hand to run her fingers through the wisps of her hair that have escaped from the elastic holding it at the back of her neck. She pushes the hair off her forehead. Antonia centers herself in her seat and turns to listen to another woman speak. Her purple sweatshirt is slightly stained by breast milk. Gustavo, Antonia's three-year-old son is sitting on the floor next to her playing with several small Match-Box cars. Periodically Antonia turns her face toward him, smiles gently, and asks, "Estás bien, Gustavo? [Are you okay?]" He seems engrossed in his play. The cars are engaged in a series of dramatic crashes.

Next to Antonia sits Soledad Cruz Hernández. Her black, wavy hair is streaked with gray and moves with her head when she nods in agreement with what another person has said. Soledad has pulled a green sweater over her shoulders and crossed arms as she tries to stay warm. The room is chilly. Next to Soledad is her granddaughter, Ana. Ana is sitting on a low chair and using a higher chair as a table. She is intently coloring the dress of a fairy princess bright orange.

Outside of the circle of chairs on the other side of the room are four long tables lined up end to end. They are piled high with pine tree trimmings. One table has several spools of red velveteen ribbon, scissors, and wire on it. A few red bows are scattered at one end. This is the wreath-making station where the women will work once their meeting is finished. The group assembles and sells the Christmas wreaths every fall as a fundraising project they run cooperatively. Antonia and Soledad are members of

17. Women of the Mujeres Luchadoras Progresistas (MLP) assembling wreaths in 1999.

Mujeres Luchadoras Progresistas (MLP), formed in the mid-1990s in association with PCUN. Begun as a woman's income-producing project, the group also provides farmworker women with an opportunity to foster pride and mutual solidarity and to learn new skills in public speaking, leadership, accounting, and public education.

As the meeting breaks up, Antonia, Soledad, and I sit down to talk about the two women's experiences in the group as well as their personal histories. Our initial conversation takes place in November 1999. Antonia begins talking

ANTONIA: My husband came here to Oregon before I did. He suffered a lot when he first arrived. First he went to California and all he did was to pick strawberries. Then he worked in lettuce and broccoli. When he first got here with some other people from our town, they had no place to stay. They slept outdoors in the brush. They spent the whole night like that, outside. They didn't have anything to eat either. They arrived with no money and all they could do was to eat broccoli. Then they went to work for a *patrón* who sold them their lunch, but it was cold and he charged them lots of money for it. When they got their paychecks he deducted money for their lunch. Yes, he suffered a lot then.

He came here to Oregon in 1985. They always had to hide from the *migra* as well. They used to hide in the bins where they stored the vegetables in the fields. There were a lot of immigration raids then. . . . .

LYNN: And you still wanted to come?

ANTONIA: Well, by the time I came he knew how to get around better. Where I was born, in San Mateo Tenuchi in Oaxaca, everyone was poor. There was nothing there, so coming here didn't look so bad.

LYNN: Did your family plant corn there?

ANTONIA: Well, my father had some communal land that we planted with corn and beans, but often we couldn't harvest anything there. It's not like it is here. There is no water. You can't have orchards there. Everything is very expensive there as well. We tried planting vegetables there to have a small business, but we couldn't sell them. No one has money to buy anything.

LYNN: Were you able to go to school there?

ANTONIA: Yes. I went to school a little bit. I finished primary school. I didn't keep studying in secondary school, though, because there wasn't enough money for me to keep on studying. My father wasn't able to give me money so that I could keep on going to school . . . We are twelve brothers and sisters. So I stopped going to school at the age of twelve. Even when I did go to school, the teachers barely taught us anything. . . . I got to know my husband when I was nineteen years old. After we were married, I stayed with my father in San Mateo Tenuchi, and my husband came to the United States.

While I stayed with my father, I worked with him in the countryside. We went to plow with oxen. I helped him out a lot with this. I really enjoyed this work. When we were lucky enough to harvest we would walk out to the field and harvest our corn and our beans. This work is a little bit heavy, but when we planted we would have corn, sometimes lots of corn. But it was barely worth selling because the price of corn got so cheap. You work really hard and then when you sell the corn you get practically nothing for it. It wasn't working out for us there. I couldn't support my kids on what we got selling our corn. As the kids grew, I could see it was going to be really hard to get them what they needed.

LYNN: So was this when you decided to leave San Mateo, even knowing how your husband had suffered in the United States?

ANTONIA: Well, by that time he had already been back and forth to the United States various times. This time I am telling you about was when he got his green card, his Social Security card, what was it called?

LYNN: Amnesty?

ANTONIA: Yes, he got his amnesty. Then he got a green card. Then he got residency. I came here in 1991 or 1992. We went to California. It wasn't so hard then because he had his green card. As soon as I got here we started to work in the strawberries. I had to be really careful, though, because unlike him I didn't have any papers at that time. I couldn't really go out. Then I got pregnant and I couldn't work. After a while he put in my application for residency. I think that was in 1994. We had to wait until 1998 when I finally got my green card. It took four years . . .

LYNN: Why do you think it was important for you to come to the group [Mujeres Luchadoras Progresistas]?

ANTONIA: Well, this group really gives me a lot of pleasure. I didn't know about things before. I was really shy and I had some problems. I felt like I was all alone. . . .

LYNN: Do you have any family members here?

ANTONIA: I do, but we don't live close together. We are all spread out.

LYNN: So does it feel different here with the group?

ANTONIA: Yes. I do feel different. I like being here with everyone. . . . I started coming here a year ago. That's when I started to realize how the group worked and how it can help us. There are women living here who don't have jobs. So here we can help each other out with a little bit of work. And it's

18. Participants at the PCUN 2001 annual convention.

better to come here than to be alone in the house. There we can feel bored. Sometimes there are problems there as well. It can really get to you when you are just shut up alone in your house. But we come here and get together, and we share our problems and help to resolve them. Here we feel comfortable talking, and we are helping each other with our problems. We tell each other what is going on and give each other advice.

Two and a half years later, I watched as Antonia was elected to the board of directors at PCUN's annual convention in 2001. She has become a charismatic public speaker and a leader within PCUN, now comfortable asserting her ideas in a wide range of arenas. She has also participated across Oregon and nationally in labor and immigrants' rights events. MLP was an important part of her personal development as a leader in the arenas of labor rights, immigrant rights, and the rights of migrant women at home and in the larger mixed organizations they participate in.

Conceptualizing Politics, Rights, and Citizenships in Local and Transborder Organizing

As indigenous migrants such as Antonia increasingly come to settle in the United States, we must come to see them not as temporary residents whose loyalties and concerns are primarily tied to their natal communities. Instead, we must look for ways to conceptualize a simultaneous presence in multiple sites and ways of understanding political participation that incorporate a broad understanding of rights, citizenships, and binational as well as non-national and national contexts of political action. In this chapter, I discuss five organizations that indigenous migrants (primarily Mixtec) are participating in to illustrate the interlinked forms of grassroots organizing that cut across the class, ethnic, and gendered dimensions of transborder migration and settlement. By showing the relationships among these organizations as well as their meaning for those who participate, I hope to illustrate how the concept of interlinked networks or meshworks is useful in understanding the complex web of relationships that are reshaping notions of territory and politics. The grassroots organizations highlighted here include (1) Pineros y Campesinos Unidos del Noroeste (PCUN); (2) Mujeres Luchadoras Progresistas (MLP); (3) the San Agustín Transborder Public Works Committee (Comité Pro Obras de San Agustín); (4) the Oregon Law Center's Indigenous Farmworker Project; and (5) Organización de Comunidades Indígenas Migrantes Oaxaqueños, or OCIMO (Organization of Oaxacan Indigenous Migrant Communities). These types of grassroots organizations are vehicles through which transborder migrants can claim and then strive to obtain a variety of rights that may routinely be denied to them formally through the law (as in the lack of the right of farmworkers in many states in the United States to collective bargaining) or rights that can be legally claimed but are often not respected because of forms of intimidation (for example, undocumented mothers not claiming the rights of their citizen children to Medicaid and Temporary Aid to Needy Families (TANF) out of fear of being reported to the INS). In addition, the claiming of existing rights not granted and new rights can result in the creation of the structural conditions and interpersonal and organizational relationships necessary for the integration of indigenous migrants into more formal political systems.

Major cities like Los Angeles and other places in which many transborder migrants are concentrated emerge, according to Saskia Sassen, not only as strategic sites for globalized economic processes and the concentration of capital, but also for new types of potential actors. While Sassen concentrates her analysis on global cities such as Los Angeles, New York, Tokyo, Paris, London, Brasilia, Mexico City, and others, some of the characteristics she attributes to global cities—denationalized platforms for global capital and sites for the coming together of increasingly diverse mixes of people to produce a strategic cross-border geography that partly bypasses national states—can also be found to some degree outside of global cities (Sassen 2004: 649). Woodburn, Oregon, is such a place. By the year 2000, Woodburn was 50 percent Latino, and 44.5 percent of the population was of Mexican origin (see chapter 3).

In these cross-border geographies, Sassen suggests, it is important to capture the difference between powerlessness and "the condition of being an actor even though one is initially lacking in political power" (2002: 22). She uses the term "presence" to name this condition. She suggests that in the context of the strategic space of the global city people like transborder indigenous Mexican migrants can "acquire a presence in the broader political process that escapes the boundaries of the formal polity. Their presence signals the possibility of a politics" (2002: 22). The specific context will determine what kind of politics. In Los Angeles, for example, a wide range of nonformal political participation has emerged from the Mexican immigrant presence, from federated hometown associations and transborder organizations that negotiate directly with U.S. and Mexican public officials (see Fox and Rivera 2004a) to major participation in unions like UNITE-HERE (see Milkman 2005). Participation in these forms of nonparty politics has also allowed some groups, for example, UNITE-HERE, to exert influence in mayoral races in Los Angeles. The immigrant rights marches of February, March, April, and May 2006 left no doubt about the "political presence" of Mexican immigrants in many parts of the United States.

The processes and conditions that Sassen suggests hold for global cities can also be found outside of global cities and increasingly even in smaller cities. The ever-increasing numbers of Mexican immigrants and most recently of indigenous migrants in the western United States (and elsewhere) can have similar results: These actors can develop a "presence" that can exist as a precursor to more organized political participation. In the case of the examples of political organizing discussed here, the notion of presence is important in two senses. First, a significant concentration of people who are connected through preexisting kin, community, and other networks is necessary in order to build critical mass for any kind of consistent organizing from an internal perspective. Second, presence is important as projected into the larger community within which any organizing effort exists. As stated by Sassen in terms of global cities,

Current conditions in global cities are creating not only new saturations of power, but also operational and rhetorical openings for new types of political actors which may have been submerged, invisible or without a voice. A key element of the argument here is that the localization of strategic components of globalization in these cities means that the disadvantaged can engage the new forms of globalized corporate power, and secondly that the growing numbers and diversity of the disadvantaged in these cities under these conditions assumes a distinctive "presence." This entails a distinction between powerlessness and invisibility or impotence. (2002:21)

Even in smaller cities such as Woodburn (population 20,000) and Salem, Oregon (population 142,940), "the localization of strategic components of globalization" such as the integration of commercial agricultural and food processing at a global level localized in food processing plants that work with fruits and vegetables from around the world, cross-border labor contracting, widespread availability of the Internet, e-mail, phone cards, and cell phones, and consular outreach programs that target immigrant populations outside their home country have provided conditions for new kinds of political presence and organizing. A larger context of ongoing political activism has also been a vital part of the context out of which these organizations have grown in their Oregon sites. In addition, the presence of several generations of Mexican immigrants who settled permanently in the Willamette Valley region beginning in the 1950s has also been central in some cases in supporting the organizations in my five case studies (see Kissam 2005a on the role of Tejanos/Tejanas in rural California civic life).

Two of my case studies pertain to organizations that operate primarily within a limited geographical area—Marion County in the cases of PCUN and MJP. The San Agustín Public Works Committee and OCIMO represent political processes that cut across nation-states and operate within and between state boundaries. This is also the case for the Frente Indígena Oaxaqueño Binacionl (FIOB), which has served as an important model and articulating organization for the San Agustín committee and OCIMO.

Part of the reason for discussing such organizing efforts is to encourage us to arrive at different understandings of citizenship, both in relation to transborder organizations and in relation to forms of political organizing which engage people who are not legal citizens in local and regional forms of politics. Current conversations in the literature on transnationalism have focused on the topic of transnational citizenship and its relationship to a wide range of political processes. We are all aware of current processes in which groups of people are claiming rights across borders and constructing what we could call transnational political communities. People such as Bauböck have pointed out the necessity of going beyond a narrow state-centered approach by "considering political communities and systems of rights that emerge at levels of governance above or below those of independent states or those that cut across international borders" (2003: 704). Jonathan Fox suggests that we think about what we truly mean by transnational citizenship. He suggests that we explore the distinction between claiming rights and gaining rights. He writes, "Influence is not the same as rights, and all rights are not citizenship rights. For example, human rights are not equivalent to citizenship rights" (2005: 174). This raises the question of whether or not there are different kinds of citizenships. If the core criteria of formal rights and membership mean that citizenship is a relational concept between citizens and a state and/or a political community, then what happens when the state is not the central polity or political community that people relate to (see Fox 2005: 175; Coll 2004)?

For some time, the concept of cultural citizenship has been debated in the social sciences and humanities. While some have hailed cultural citizenship as an important concept for understanding the ways in which political cultures change and new rights are first asserted, claimed, and then integrated into formal political systems, others have dismissed the concept as irrelevant because it does not deal with traditional definitions of citizenship as a vertical relationship between the individual and the state. My perspective in this discussion is that if we want to understand processes of political participation and incorporation, we have to look at cultural and economic processes as part of the political. I understand democracy as the broadening of rights and responsibilities to the greatest extent possible to extend equality to the diversity of people who participate in a community or association and are subject to its decisions (see Bauböck 1994: viii). To understand processes of democratization through time and across space we have to explore how people move from claiming rights to gaining rights and what we might understand as more formal citizenship. The concept of cultural citizenship can be a tool in this process. First formulated by Renato Rosaldo in the late 1980s, the concept of cultural citizenship suggests an idea of culture "whereby different cultures are equally constitutive of society and expressive of humanity" (Yúdice 2003: 22). Rosaldo underlines how legal concepts of citizenship that underscore universal, formal political rights for all members of a nation mask real inequalities that can be observed.

Rosaldo suggests that by looking at how different people struggle to overcome multiple exclusions from a variety of political arenas, we help to illuminate processes of what he calls "full democratic participation." Cultural citizenship involves everyday activities through which marginalized social groups can claim recognition, public space, and eventually specific rights (see Flores and Benmayor 1997). Recognition of cultural citizenship allows us to illuminate important processes which are part and parcel of changing formal political systems and the specific rights extended to legal citizens. Indigenous peoples in Mexico and in the United States have been involved in an ongoing struggle to first establish legitimate forms of cultural citizenship and then to move some parts of their cultural citizenship into the arena of legal citizenship as formal rights defined in the constitutions and legal codes of specific nations and international governing bodies. Cultural citizenship is one of many senses of citizenship that must be explored if one is to understand the unique set of rights that transborder indigenous migrants are seeking to achieve in the multisited and multiple arenas of their lives.

Cultural citizenship offers anthropologists a model for understanding how Mexican migrants in the United States can be recognized as legitimate political subjects claiming rights for themselves and their children based on their economic and cultural contributions regardless of their official legal status (see Coll 2004). In other words, the kinds of civil rights, respect, and recognition granted to legal U.S. citizens can be extended to all residents in the United States who are contributing to U.S. society through their labor, their creation and nourishment of communities, and their cultural contributions. The notion of cultural citizenship is an alternative concept to legal citizenship, which labels many migrants (the undocumented) in the United States as illegal aliens; it is also a way of reaffirming the contributions of indigenous migrants outside the framework of U.S. immigration law and within the framework of border-crossing transnational communities. Offering an alternative to legal definitions of citizenship also works against the racialization of all Mexican immigrants as illegals (see De Genova and Ramos-Zayas 2003c: 21–22). As such, cultural citizenship can be a model for understanding certain kinds of transnational citizenships as well.

The positive proposition of cultural citizenship provides an opening for Mexican immigrant workers to belong as citizens in the communities they live in. It also positively affirms recognition, respect, and celebration of cultural differences associated with processes of border crossing and migration. While some recent work (see Appadurai 1996; Hardt and Negri 2000) suggests that global capitalist processes, universal neoliberal economic principles and policies, and the hegemony of North American popular culture forms may increase cultural and economic homogenization on a global scale, the idea of cultural citizenship suggests that place-based and trans-place forms of cultural difference and local and regional social movements are also a part of global transformations (see Dirlik 2000; Harcourt and Escobar 2002; Sahlins 1999). The reification of cultural difference has emerged in conjunction with the questioning of cultural and national borders in processes of globalization and migration. Thus cultural citizenship suggests both recognition of cultural differences maintained through processes of migration and the opening up of the term *citizen* so that it embraces the contributions of all who live in local towns and communities.

PCUN *and Indigenous Farmworkers*

For a period from the late 1980s to the mid-1990s, the indigenous (primarily Mixtec, but also Triqui, Zapotec, and Mayan) farmworker population changed significantly in two ways in Oregon. First, many of the men who became legal permanent residents sent for their wives and children. Second, once their families arrived, they settled more permanently and in communities like Salem came to form significant clusters of people from the same community; often these clusters were built around sibling groups who came to bring their nuclear families with them from Oaxaca and San Quintín or from places like Madera and Fresno, California. For example, in Salem most of the twenty or so nuclear families that make up a cluster from San Agustín and that now have their own branch of a transborder public works committee arrived in the late 1980s and early 1990s. Most of these families were established by 1994 or so and have children, both undocumented and U.S. citizens, who are working their way through the public school system and in some cases have moved on to junior college and beyond. They are typical of what some a call mixed-status household. Researchers from the Urban Institute estimated in 1999 that about one-quarter of all California families lived in mixed-status households (Fix and Zimmerman 1999).

While many families continue to have some undocumented members, all of them have some type of documents and are working. As Eric Schlosser writes, "Counterfeit green cards, Social Security cards, driver's licenses, SAW work histories—the documents necessary to obtain employment as a farmworker—can be easily obtained in rural California for $50.00. The process usually takes about an hour" (2003: 100). This continues to be the case in Oregon as well.

While undocumented relatives of established Mixtec families continue to come to Oregon, during the past four to five years a new wave of young men has come to occupy an important niche in the seasonal berry and other harvests in the state. The trend of family settlement and female migration has slowed considerably, and increasingly seasonal workers are again lone men, often young (see McConahay 2001). They are found primarily in labor camps and are brought by labor contractors who work them through a circuit encompassing California, Oregon, and Washington. Some of them are Mixtec, but recruiters are reaching into Triqui communities and into the state of Veracruz as well. Kissman, Intili, and García (2001) note this trend and place particular emphasis on teenagers being recruited as farmworkers:

> In 2000, we find that indigenous ethnic minorities within a Latino farm labor force are making up a greater and greater proportion of the local farm labor force throughout the country.... Along the entire length of the Eastern Seaboard, there are increasing numbers of Guatemalan and Mexican Maya, Zapotec workers from central Oaxaca state and smaller numbers of Mixtec and Triqui migrants from western Oaxaca state and the eastern areas of the state of Guerrero, which adjoins the leading sending regions of Juxtlahuaca and Silacayoapan. Along the Pacific Seaboard, there is an equally dramatic increase in the numbers of indigenous farmworkers but dominant networks are the Mixtec and Triqui ones; interestingly the ethnic composition of the labor force of working teenagers in California and Oregon is now very similar to that of Baja California in the late 1980s. (2001: 6)

Increasingly, as Mixtec families have settled in the state, they have moved out of the seasonal farm labor sector and into other kinds of agricultural work, primarily nurseries. Some continue to work in food processing and freezing plants, but as they age they prefer to stay out of the fields. Children of Mixtec migrants who settled in Oregon between 1988 and 1994 are employed primarily in the service sector in jobs at places like K-Mart, gas stations, and KFC. The berries and other crops in the fields are increasingly being picked again by recent young, male, indigenous recruits. During the past three decades in Oregon, PCUN has had contact with many of the indigenous farmworkers who have passed through the state or settled there.

PCUN has its origins in the 1970s. At that time, several organizers inspired by the work of César Chávez began to plan how they could build a social movement of Mexican immigrants and farmworkers in Oregon. Their initial organizing strategies were influenced by the climate of harassment and fear faced by Mexican immigrant farmworkers in the Willamette Valley. In May 1977, the Willamette Valley Immigration Project (WVIP) opened its doors to provide legal representation for undocumented workers, first in Portland. In 1978, WVIP moved permanently to Woodburn. The staff and organizers of WVIP went on to facilitate the creation of PCUN in 1985. The initial goal of PCUN was to change working conditions for tree planters and farmworkers. The eight-year track record of WVIP was crucial to building trust in the farmworker and tree planter community so that open discussion of a union for farmworkers could begin. During the 1990s, the union engaged in a series of actions aimed at opening up political and cultural space for immigrant Mexican farmworkers and raising farmworker wages. it achieved its first contracts with small organic growers. During the summer of 2002 the union was finalizing negotiations with NORPAC, a cooperative of 240 growers that had been the focus of a ten-year boycott. (See Stephen 2001b for a general history of PCUN.)

Securing Amnesty for Oregon Farmworkers

Many Mixtec farmworkers and tree planters first came into contact with the PCUN in the mid-1980s. Some of them were living in labor camps targeted by the union for organizing. The vast majority, however, came to know the union through help they received in processing their amnesty cases in 1986 and 1987. Within days of IRCA's enactment in November 1986, PCUN held a number of large forums attended by more than eight hundred people in Woodburn, Salem, Independence, and other locations in Oregon.

The first meetings focused on informing people about how undocumented people could apply for U.S. residency under the 1986 law. PCUN staff also warned people about potential discrimination against Latino workers because of the employer sanctions included in the IRCA legislation. During 1987, PCUN and the Centro de Servicios Para Campesinos (CSC; Service Center for Farmworkers) staff devoted most of their time to working with those seeking amnesty through the IRCA and SAW programs. By the summer of 1987, PCUN and the CSC had a combined staff of ten. With this small staff, they managed to process thirteen hundred legalization cases from June 1987 to June 1988, representing at that point more than 10 percent of the total cases in the state. Their work in this area also significantly increased their membership: In the period from October 1986 to June 1988, PCUN signed up nearly two thousand new members. Probably up to a third of these new members were Mixtec men and a few women. Later, when the men brought their wives and children, some of them returned to the CSC to receive assistance in petitioning for their residency. Since 1986, the immigration services offered by the union are a key reason why Mixtec workers have continued to relate to PCUN in an ongoing way. Mixtecs workers also became deeply involved in negotiating the first contracts PCUN won more than a decade later, were recruited as labor organizers, and came to occupy key spots on the union's governing board and in MLP.

For indigenous farmworkers, PCUN offered legal assistance at a crucial time (in 1987 following the IRCA and SAW legislation). By demonstrating that they had the resources and skills to help people gain legal residency in the United States, staff from PCUN won their confidence and began to talk to them about the conditions they labored under as low-wage workers in the fields. As the 1990s progressed, some of the Mixtec membership of PCUN settled permanently in Oregon and began to move into other sectors of work, particularly nurseries, canneries, and food processing.

Improving Conditions for Indigenous Farmworkers and Others

For indigenous farmworkers who had been laboring in Oregon for up to six years without documentation, the assistance PCUN offered in securing their legal residence was and is greatly appreciated. After PCUN's membership grew dramatically in 1987, the union began to concentrate on the struggle to achieve collective bargaining. During the 1990s, the union engaged in a series of actions aimed at opening up political and cultural space for immigrant Mexican farmworkers. Some of these actions concerned labor law violations. Because such actions involved the defense of Mexican immigrant farmworkers, they need to be understood

19. Ramón Ramírez, PCUN president since 1995.

not only as labor actions but also as ethnic and cultural actions. Workers who benefit from such actions feel a sense of validation not only as workers, but also as Mexican immigrants. For some growers and others who may question the need for workers to assert their rights, such actions upset the cultural order of local power arrangements and begin to remake the place of "the illegals" in communities such as Woodburn. I highlight a few of these actions below with comments from organizers and participants to illustrate their meaning in terms of creating a new sense of belonging and local, cultural citizenship for indigenous Mexican immigrant workers and others.

During the summer of 1990, PCUN activists conducted a "red card" wage campaign to help workers keep track of their earnings. Workers were given red cards to fill in with their daily earnings. Totals were kept and compared to pay stubs. PCUN organizers distributed over 10,000 time cards and were able to document 250 cases in which workers received less than the minimum wage. PCUN filed wage claims with the Oregon Bureau of Labor and Industry for 40 workers, and collectively they received more than $3,000 in illegally withheld pay. PCUN was also able to force a labor contractor to pay back $9,000 he had illegally withheld from farmworker paychecks through inflated charges for housing, food, and transportation. The president of PCUN, Ramón Ramírez, (not a pseudonym) recalls:

> We targeted five farmers . . . and Kraemer was the top one. All the workers would complain. . . . They came here all the way from Mount Angel, you know, just to complain about the Kraemers. I remember we talked to him that year. We said, "What's the deal man?." . . . The Kraemers had this labor contractor. . . . He would bring workers up here; most of the workers he brought were Mixteco. He would charge them for rides, for food. . . . He would feed them stuff like *tacos de arroz* [rice tacos]. And he would charge them forty dollars per week for food, for tacos de arroz. . . . The Kraemers would give him a check and so what he was doing is that he would have a list of how much money you owe, then you'd sign your check and give it to him. He'd cash it for you and maybe give you back the difference of what you owe. . . . So that year, you know, we submitted over one hundred wage claims to Kraemer. Then we won nine thousand dollars. And we were able to develop this good relationship with probably about three or four crews of farmworkers.

These concrete gains made a positive impression on farmworkers and were important in creating a climate in which growers felt obligated to pay their workers minimum wage and contractors who supplied workers to growers were held accountable for their treatment of workers.

PCUN was responsible for the first union-organized strike in the history of Oregon farm labor in 1991, and in 1992 widened the pressure on key growers by beginning a boycott of NORPAC, a grower cooperative that included some of the growers that workers had most complained about. In 1995, PCUN began a massive organizing campaign to honor their tenth anniversary and to raise wages for work in strawberry fields.

During the anniversary campaign, PCUN used trilingual radio spots in Spanish, Mixtec, and Triqui. PCUN sent organizers to Madera, California, to alert workers headed to Oregon about the campaign. Madera has been a stopping point for many Mixtec and Triqui migrants who come seasonally to Oregon to work. In this campaign, the union self-consciously acknowledged the indigenous ethnicity of a significant part of the workers they sought to represent and defend. In 1995 and to this day, there are Mixtec and Triqui workers who speak little or no Spanish who are completely under the thumb of labor contractors. In order to communicate with them, the union has used multilingual organizers and radio broadcasts and announcements to reach workers who are not literate.

Filemón Gutiérrez is one of the indigenous farmworkers PCUN reached. He, like many farmworkers in Oregon, began working in California. Filemón is a compact, muscular man who sits easily in his chair. His dark brown eyes are framed with long eyelashes that give him a boyish look despite his twenty-seven years. Born in 1973 in the small community of Santa Cruz Río Venado in the municipality of Constancia del Rosario in the Mixteca region of southwestern Oaxaca, Filemón has spent many years as an agricultural worker in Mexico and in the United States. Married to a Mixtec woman, he now has two children. Filemón was one of the first farmworkers in Oregon to work under a union contract with PCUN. He arrived in Madera, California, in 1989 and later went to Oregon with a relative who was a *coyote* connected to a labor contractor. In February 2000, he discussed his life in Oaxaca and his experiences as an agricultural worker in the United States. The interview was conducted with Kristina Tiedje, who was then a graduate student in anthropology working with me at the University of Oregon. Here Filemón focuses on his experiences in Oaxaca before coming to the United States and on his time in Madera before coming to Oregon.

FILEMÓN: The town I grew up in is called Santa Cruz Río Venado. It is near Putla, in the municipio of Constancia del Rosario. There we live from the cultivation of coffee and bananas. We have seven or eight different kinds of bananas, each with a different name. We also have oranges, guayabas, and mamays. We live from growing and selling this fruit and coffee . . .

. . . But you know, we barely make any money. They pay us very little for our bananas and other crops. . . . What we got for our bananas wasn't even enough for us to buy a pair of pants or even a pair of shoes . . .

. . . Sometimes the prices for bananas are so low that we don't even bother to harvest them. We just let them rot. And speaking of bananas, you know the same bananas that we sometimes let rot on the trees there in my hometown, they sell for up to a dollar here. I have been in stores here in the United States where they want up to a dollar for a banana that is almost rotten.

So why did I come here? Well, when some of my *paisanos* came back from working in the United States, they had new clothing and shoes . . . I remember when I was a kid I used to like to play and my clothes would rip. So my mother would sew my clothes back together again and again. I only had one pair of pants, you understand? My mother had to keep fixing the same pants over and over. So when I used to see people come back from *el Norte* and they were well dressed and had money, well I paid attention. It was clear that I wasn't going to be able to keep on studying. So I said to myself, well if I can't keep going to school, I may as well be able to have something like that. It was maybe having clothing or something like that which motivated me to come to the United States . . .

There is another thing you should know about me. I speak another language. I speak Triqui. I don't even know how to speak Spanish very well. There are many people who don't speak Spanish. My grandfather didn't know how to speak Spanish or my grandmother. They only speak Triqui. When I came here to the United States I learned how to speak some Spanish in California. Then I married a woman who speaks Mixteco. I speak Triqui, so now we speak in Spanish so we can understand one another . . .

KRISTINA: When did you come here for the first time?

FILEMÓN: I arrived in California in 1989 with my brother-in-law. He got me over the border. We arrived in California in a group of six or eight. We arrived at a really small house, and we were there for three or four days while he looked for a larger place for us to live. I was still a boy when I arrived. I was only sixteen years old.

There in Madera, California, we had to get up at four thirty in the morning in order to go to work. It took us an hour to an hour and a half just to get to work. The *raiteros* [those who provide transport from labor camps to the fields] would go from house to house to take people to work. It was hard there. We had to pay for everything—for a ride, for a place to live, for food. And then you have debts to pay off to the coyote from your trip up here. My first year I really didn't know about how all of this worked.

There and when I first arrived here in Oregon, those *mayordomos* would hire you to work on a contract. They don't pay you by the hour; they pay you by the box. . . . Now, my situation is better, thanks to PCUN. Now we get paid by the hour which is much better. PCUN helped to push the growers to pay us by the hour. It is a better system.

Lorenzo Alavez, introduced in chapter 5, began working with the PCUN as an organizer during 1997 and continued until April 2002. He was representative of the union's efforts to reach out to and organize Mixtec workers. During the winters of 2000, 2001, and 2002, he spent several months in Mexico working for the union and visiting workers in their home communities in Oaxaca, Guerrero, and Veracruz. During these visits he would warn potential workers about the kinds of "come-ons" contractors would use and tried to tell them about the real working conditions and about the union. For two years he was able to track some workers from labor camps in Oregon back to their home communities. Visiting workers in these three Mexican states was a central part of the union's strategy to build workers' confidence and support of the union on one farm in particular, where some of the same workers returned several years in a row.

The late 1990s brought PCUN a historic victory when Oregon's first collective bargaining agreement for farmworkers was signed. It was with Nature's Fountains Farms. Later, three others were signed. The agreements provided for more than a dozen rights and protections for farm-workers not afforded by law, including seniority, grievance procedures, overtime, paid breaks, and union recognition. Dolores Alavez, a Mixtec immigrant worker introduced in chapter 5, was the leader of one of the negotiating teams that worked on the first PCUN contracts. For her, the contracts were an important step in achieving better treatment and working conditions. In the fall of 2000 we discussed how the contracts came about and what they meant to her.

DOLORES: I think the grower contacted PCUN to tell them that they needed workers. PCUN called a meeting with me and my brother to go and see the ranch. We went to see the fields and spoke with the grower. He spoke in a way that we hadn't heard from the other growers. He said he wanted to change everything and he wanted to treat us with respect. We saw that he had really good intentions in terms of treating us differently than the other growers had. We went to look at the rows of berries, and they asked us what we thought. We said we thought that they were good and that they would produce well. So we agreed to work with him. . . . There were fourteen of us working there.

LYNN: How were the working conditions with the contract? Was it like the other places you worked?

DOLORES: No. Because we had a bathroom, we had fresh water, and we each had a glass with our name on it. We were able to take our break and our lunch. Normally you didn't get to take a break and lunch. In the other places the bathrooms were filthy, and they gave us warm water to drink. And we didn't even take the time to drink the water because if we did then we wouldn't be able to pick the amount of fruit we wanted to in order to earn money. The fields were sometimes already picked when we arrived because there were so many people waiting to pick. If you didn't work really fast then you didn't earn money for your food. He paid us by the hour for the contract . . . a little more than the minimum wage. . . . he also guaranteed us eight hours of work per day. That was unique.

Filemón Gutierrez also came to work on a PCUN contract in blueberries. He talked about his experiences working in Oregon before his contract with PCUN and the difference it made to him to be paid by the hour at a decent wage.

FILEMÓN: I came to Oregon with the same brother-in-law who brought me to California. He was the coyote. He knew a labor contractor who brought us here. At first he brought us to work for a man who lives close to here in Monitor. He wore glasses and he never bathed. He had a house, and we stayed there. It wasn't so good. But little by little you find out about the work.

KRISTINA: Did you work for him for a year?

FILEMÓN: [smiling] No. Just for a few days. You know when you get to a farm you start asking people about how the work is. So we left there and went to another ranch that belonged to the Kraemers. We worked that year in the strawberry harvest, in the raspberry and blackberry harvest. Then I started working with PCUN and learning about my rights.

Then later in 1998 I worked on a PCUN contract in the blueberry harvest. It was much better than the way I worked before because everyone makes money. We all earn the same wage. No one says to you, "You have to pick so many boxes in order to earn any money." I liked this a lot better. They paid me $ 7.20 per hour last year [1999, when the minimum wage was $6.50 per hour]. Working with PCUN, I didn't have to get paid by the pound. I got paid by the hour. With their contract we all received the same wage.

In 2002, PCUN reached agreement on a framework for collective bargaining with members of NORPAC. The ten-year boycott was suspended. Negotiations are ongoing as PCUN organizers and NORPAC representatives work to hammer out specific guidelines for election processes to be used by farmworkers as they consider union representation on twenty-one farms. This process brought the union, Mexican farmworkers, Anglo growers, and the Woodburn area national attention. In 2005, the agricultural lobby introduced HB 3258 in the Oregon state legislature, a bill that would have placed farmworker collective bargaining under the Employment Relations Board (ERB), a state agency handling public em-

20. PCUN members at an immigrant rights rally in Salem, Oregon, in 2003.

ployee unionization. The proposal did not include key provisions articulated by PCUN and supported by Oregon's governor Ted Kulongoski, including mandatory binding arbitration of first contracts. In floor debate, Rep. Brad Witt (D-Clatskanie) characterized HB 3258 as "the perfect mechanism by which the avoidance of collective bargaining agreements can be institutionalized." The bill was defeated in August 2005 in part because of the hard work of PCUN (PCUN 2005).

The 1990s saw indigenous Mexican PCUN members become involved in more targeted cultural struggles as well. During 1997, local PCUN members, staff, and allied organizations in Woodburn rallied residents in support of naming one of two new public schools for César Chávez. The Woodburn school board's refusal to do so (they named the schools Heritage and Valor) prompted local residents to form the citizen's group Voz Hispana (Hispanic Voice). During the summer of 1997, Voz Hispana rallied more than eighty Latino residents to attend three consecutive school board meetings. Some of the key participants in these meetings were fifty farmworker families who reside at the Nuevo Amanecer housing project built by PCUN's sister organization, Farmworker Housing Development Corporation. This group included many Mixtec families living in the housing project. In these meetings, Voz Hispana pressured the school board to name the library at Valor Middle School for Chávez, to erect a permanent display about Chávez and his work, to declare his birthday on March 31 César Chávez Day in all Woodburn schools, and to demand that special schoolwide and classroom activities be organized in celebration of that day. The school board accepted all of these points. Since then, special curricula and assemblies have been organized around César Chávez to promote a sense of pride in the farmworker movement as well as to provide a broader range of people with an education about the work and beliefs of this national hero. Voz Hispana continues to take an interest in local politics and has also developed an interest in Latino voting and election participation in Woodburn. While these efforts did not specifically recognize Mixtec or other indigenous ethnicities, they did help to validate indigenous famrworkers' sense of belonging in Woodburn. Several years later, a specifically indigenous-identified organization, OCIMO, emerged in Woodburn, building on some of these local political experiences.

This abbreviated history of PCUN provides an overview of the multiple ways in which cultural citizenship has been extended to indigenous Mexican farmworkers who are among its members. Membership is defined as those who pay quarterly dues of twenty-seven dollars. Benefits include an insurance policy that pays three thousand dollars in case of the death of a member, representation in immigration affairs, access to English and citizenship classes, and other resources. Beginning with issues of immigration abuses, detentions, and deportations, PCUN's work challenged the established racial, cultural, and political order in Woodburn and elsewhere in Marion County where Mexican farmworkers were seen as "illegal" outsiders who did not have a voice at work, in the schools, or in the communities where they lived. For indigenous farmworkers, who were even further marginalized within local Latino and Mexican contexts, the work of the union functioned at an additional level, defending them as equals to other Mexican immigrants.

The union and its predecessor, WVIP, have done crucial work over the past twenty-five years in securing labor rights, winning small contracts, changing the terms of debate about conditions of employment in agriculture, defending the rights and needs of indigenous Mexican farmworkers and others, and achieving recognition for Mexican immigrant farmworkers as legitimate members of the communities they live in. The tools they have used to accomplish this have included grassroots organizing, leadership training, cultural events, radio broadcasts, and the creation of spin-off organizations such as MLP, described in more detail below.

The concept of cultural citizenship offers a way of validating the contributions of Mexican indigenous farmworkers such as Filemón and Dolores. Cultural citizenship in a wider Latino society in the United States allows "immigrants who might not be citizens in the legal sense or who might not even be in the country legally, but who labor and contribute to the economic and cultural wealth of the country" to be "recognized as legitimate political subjects claiming rights for themselves and their children," and in that sense to be citizens (Flores and Benmayor 1997: 11). Thus citizenship—particularly locally—becomes predicated not on the possession of certain immigration documents, but on concrete contributions to the community one lives in and the right to basic protections and respect. PCUN provided an important route by which indigenous farmworkers gained a presence in the region in the sense described above by Sassen; in addition, it enabled them, despite their marginalized condition as undocumented and indigenous workers, to claim specific rights such as guaranteed minimum hourly wages for harvesting and the right to a union contract and improved working conditions. In its work, PCUN is very much in line with what have come to be called community unions, which focus on a combination of service, advocacy, and organizing with specific emphasis on issues of work and wages (Fine 2005: 153).

Mujeres Luchadoras Progresistas (MLP)

Increasing numbers of indigenous women migrated from Mexico to Oregon in the late 1980s and early 1990s, often following their farmworker husbands who had been legalized through the 1986 amnesty program, IRCA. These women's needs were different from those of male farmworkers and demanded a different kind of organizational space. PCUN participants and staff took notice and began discussions of what kind of organization could be useful to women farmworkers outside of the union. Women who were arriving in Oregon from Oaxaca or from Baja California may have had some limited exposure to grassroots organizing, but many came from communities in which women's political participation has been limited in some regard.

As explained in chapter 2, a majority of Oaxaca's municipal governments are run according to what are called *usos y costumbres*, under which local assemblies following customary law elect local officials and participants in the formal system of governance. A study of the 418 Oaxaca municipalities that follow customary law (such as that described for Teotitlán del Valle in chapter 2) found that "in 10 percent of them women do not exercise their right to vote in internal elections, and their public participation is low or null; in 9 percent they do not vote but do hold community positions; in 21 percent they vote but their public participation is low or null; and finally, in 60 percent they vote, hold positions, and participate in the public life of the community" (Velázquez 2004: 488). Women in rural Oaxacan communities did not "receive" the right to vote at any specific point in time. In many cases, women have begun to formally vote and participate in community decision making as a part of local organizing efforts linked to indigenous rights or other kinds of social movements, or when political parties permeate their communities (see Stephen 2005b: 286–87).

The numbers of women in formal positions of political leadership are also low. Velasquez's study showed that for the 1998–2001 period, 32 town counselors were named (including 5 female municipal presidents) in 27 municipalities; for the 2002–04 period, 54 town counselors were elected, corresponding to 41 municipalities (including 6 female municipal presidents) (2004: 488). These figures work out to the following conclusion: an average of 8.5 percent of the municipalities run by usos y costumbres have women in local government positions. Rates of participation of women in the remaining 152 municipalities in which elections are run through political parties are not clear. There, women must participate in political parties in order to hold posts. My experience as an electoral observer in several Oaxacan elections suggests that parties can be quite effective in turning women out to vote and that their rate of voting is probably significant in most communities where local elections are run through political parties. Female voter turnout, however, gives little indication of more extended civic participation.

Women in Oaxaca have had significantly higher rates of participation and are exercising political leadership in the area of productive projects. The women's cooperatives in Teotitlán del Valle (discussed in chapter 9) are one such example (see Stephen 2005a). In the Mixtec region of Oaxaca, FIOB has successfully organized women into rotating credit associations and in small productive projects such as mushroom and chicken production. Operating in approximately ten communities, these projects are run by women and involve the generation of small loans and income. While such experiences are important, they are not widespread, and many Mixtec and other indigenous women who arrive in Oregon have not participated in organizing projects of any kind. Their social world is centered on their extended family and their daily routines.

The need for a women's leadership development project crystallized in 1992, when PCUN's service center staff noticed a marked increase in women members who were reporting spousal abuse, sexual harassment in the workplace, and other problems. In 1995, supported by a three-year grant from A Territorial Resource, a precursor organization to MJP called the Farmworker Women's Leadership Project was begun by PCUN. In the early days of the group, women were polled by PCUN staff about what kinds of classes or services would be most helpful with them. Many stated that they wanted to learn to drive. In the absence of the ability to drive, women's mobility was often very limited, particularly if they were living in labor camps, in worker housing on farms, or on the outskirts of Woodburn or other surrounding towns. Some initial driving classes were offered but were difficult to maintain owing to resistance from some men and other factors. Two economic projects were tried before efforts finally settled on the production of Christmas wreaths. In 1995 and 1996, the Women's Project produced crocheted items and piñatas and sold them through a bazaar. Although both of these products sold success-fully, they were very labor intensive and the financial returns were low. With the Christmas wreath project in 1997, however, the group hit its stride. The wreaths, made from pine branches gathered in the na-tional forests, are assembled in the union hall on long tables and deco-rated with red velvet ribbons and pine cones. In 1997 the group took the name Mujeres Luchadoras Progresistas. Fidelia Domínguez of Ixpan-tepec Nieves, Oaxaca (introduced in chapter 7), discussed the early days of the women's group:

> The first year of the group, they had a project to make piñatas to sell. But when I came into the group we tried to think about something where we could make money more quickly over a short period of time. They made all these piñatas but it wasn't so easy to sell them. They had to wait a long time to sell the piñatas and it took a long time to make them. So we decided to make Christmas wreaths. It was my idea. We made 125 wreaths the first year in 1997. The second year we made 500, and this year we made 900. But our dream is to have a bigger business.

In 2002, MLP sold twelve hundred Christmas wreaths and by 2004 had worked its way up to fifteen hundred. This cooperative business venture has permitted the women involved to learn how to balance a checkbook, give financial reports, and plan projects. In addition to providing a small source of income and financial management experience, MLP gives farmworker women an opportunity to foster a sense of satisfaction, pride, and mutual support and to learn new skills in public speaking and leadership. The group offers a refuge for women, and they describe the meetings as having a "family feeling." Organizational spaces in which women are the sole participants have proven to be important throughout Latin America in fostering basic confidence and skills among women (see Stephen 1997).

Fidelia Domínguez first came to the Service Center at PCUN in 1997 in order to straighten out an auto insurance claim. She joined the Women's Project and eventually was elected president. She recalled how much the group means to many newly arrived women, who are socially isolated, lonely, and miss their extended families in Mexico. The kind of space created by a group of women provides many who arrive with a special haven in which they can share their feelings and work with others to resolve common issues. Having a women-only space also gives women the confidence to speak up. Once they have gained self-confidence within the women's group and are comfortable taking positions and speaking up in public, they can translate these skills to other arenas, including union leadership, participation in local political forums such as PTA meetings and City Council meetings, and the renegotiating of domestic roles. Fidelia explained to me how she became a member of the group, how women grow in the group, and why it is important that the group be composed of women only:

FIDELIA: I learned how to drive in 1989, and in 1997 I had an accident. They sent me some papers from the insurance, but I didn't know how to read English. That was when I remembered about PCUN. They helped me to get a lawyer. I had to go to court. I didn't know what my insurance covered . . .

. . . One day I said to one of the women who works at PCUN in their Service Center, "What am I going to do? I am going crazy because nothing like this has ever happened to me before. I don't have any work now and I don't know what I am going to do. Please help me." She said to me, "Why don't you come to the women's group we have? You can come. Come and talk with us about your ideas." So I went to the women's group and I got to be very close with them. . . .

LYNN: How do women find out about the group?

FIDELIA: Most of them come because they are poor and don't know what to do. There are also families where they don't have work. Or the husband may be working, but he doesn't earn enough money so that kids can be maintained. There are women who can't pay the rent and single mothers who also come. They are all women who feel there is no one to help them. They come to the group and we all try to help. We have small projects that allow people to make a little bit of extra money . . . for example, with our wreath project.

LYNN: What do people learn in the group?

FIDELIA: The first thing that happens is that it helps women to cope with all they have been through. When someone comes to meet with us they start to talk. It is like family if you don't have a family. Women start to feel confident, and then they can talk. They have a good time and start to forget all of their problems. For example, if I feel alone and I have four children and I never get out of the house, I can come to the group to talk about how I feel. I can come to talk with other women about how I am worried about my son in junior high school. In the group people feel like they have a lot to share because we are a group of women and we always respect one another.

LYNN: Are there many women from Oaxaca in the group?

FIDELIA: There are. There are also some from Michoacán and from Guatemala as well.

LYNN: What did you learn from the group specifically?

FIDELIA: I learned so much. I learned how to speak. Not that I literally couldn't speak before, but I learned how to speak up. I lost my fear. I learned how to speak in front of a lot of other people in public. I am not afraid to do that anymore. Before, I was a very fearful person. I used to tremble if I had to speak in front of people. But now I have the courage to speak . . . In Oaxaca a lot of women are afraid to speak in front of people. I can't explain it. We get very nervous and we don't have the courage to speak in public. Only men do that. Here, I was lucky and learned how to do that. . .

. . . Right now my dream is to keep on making the fresh Christmas wreaths, but we want to find a project that will give us work throughout the year. There are a lot of women who don't have work and who don't have papers to work. They can't just go out and get a job. We want to help them so that they can earn money to support their children. I don't want their kids to suffer. This is my idea, but we have to discuss it with the entire group.

Fidelia talks about the importance of "learning how to speak." She explains that she means speaking in public and feeling like one has the right to hold an opinion and voice it. She notes how in Oaxaca women are very afraid to speak in front of anyone, particularly in front of men. Over its ten-year history, perhaps one of the most important functions of MLP has been to serve as a training ground for upcoming women leaders in PCUN, in the community of Woodburn and elsewhere. While the Christmas wreath project has continued to be a financial success and an important underpinning of the group, the development of self-confidence and female leadership has been a major outcome of the group.

In 2002, MLP became independent of PCUN and is now a self-standing nonprofit organization. Union activists and the women in the group both viewed this as a success, as an indication of the capacity of the women to be self-supporting and to run their own organization. That year they received a grant from the Peace Development Fund to "develop an organized and collective response to the racism, sexism, and economic oppression faced by Latina farmworkers" (Peace Development Fund 2002).

In February 2005, the board of directors of MLP announced an initiative to improve their management and business skills by integrating technology into their work. In cooperation with the Cipriano Ferrell Education Center (named for the first president of PCUN and located in the Nuevo Amanecer farmworker housing development), members of MLP enrolled in computer classes using the computer lab in the Ferrell Education Center. They hope to be able to directly market their Christmas wreaths online and to communicate by e-mail with their customers throughout the state. Being able to use the Internet and e-mail is an extension of learning to speak. As discussed in the next chapter, digital technology is an important component of the grassroots organizing efforts indigenous migrants are engaged in.

San Agustín Transborder Public Works Committee

It's really nice having this language, Mixtec . . . For my generation, speaking Mixtec makes me think about my youth and the kids I knew growing up. We used to speak Mixtec in school. There, we had a teacher who told us that we shouldn't speak Mixtec, that we should speak Spanish among ourselves.

That is what he said. But we didn't know how to speak Spanish. Our parents spoke pure Mixtec. My mother and father didn't know how to speak Spanish. That is why I couldn't speak Spanish growing up. Now speaking Mixtec reminds me of where I am from. When I get together with other men here on the public works committee and talk in Mixtec, I feel different. (Mariano González)

Mariano González, introduced in chapter 2, has been a major mover in the transborder public works committee of San Agustín, whose first project was the purchase of land to expand the town's cemetery. Though now resident in the United States, he remains actively connected to San Agustín Atenango through his leadership in the transborder public works committee. Mariano explained the origin of the public works committee in the fall of 2001 when he and others were requested to organize and raise funds to purchase a piece of land to expand the cemetery:

On October 19 of 2001, we received an official letter from our town authority, telling us that there was a piece of land for sale. The piece of land was called Inocencia. The letter said that this person was willing to sell this land to the community for our cemetery. After we got the letter, we called up all of the people from our town living here. We had a big meeting in a large park near here to see who was interested. Whole families came to the meeting. We asked if they wanted to help out in purchasing the land. They said yes. They agreed. So they named some of us to a committee. It had a president, secretary, treasurer, and two *vocales*. Everyone nominated us. And they voted. We were named to the committee. I am the president.

While we were talking, Mariano asked a friend of his (also in the leadership of the committee) to bring out the list of names. His friend Lorenzo (introduced above) returned with a computerized list of names in tiny six-point type. He and Lorenzo counted the names and announced that there are eighty people total, including children. There are even single mothers on the list. Mariano looked up and continued describing the committee:

The work we do is really important. Because it is about the needs of the town we really worked hard on this. Every person gave $200, and we raised $7,899 right here in Salem. We were in touch with all of the other committees, and we had a big meeting in Santa Maria. We rented a hall and we had a meal. Then we began to report on our money.

Lorenzo becomes animated as Mariano is talking and begins chiming in with details about the get-together in Santa María, California, the phone calls to other committees, and their ideas for new projects. The committee has met together locally on a regular basis. In addition, representatives from approximately ten locations in the United States where the committee has members have had periodic meetings. Committees are located in Vista and Santa María, California; Portland and Salem, Oregon; Chicago; Flagstaff and Grand Canyon, Arizona; Reno and Las Vegas, Nevada.

In a separate conversation, Alejandro Mendoza explained that the transborder public works committee replicates the structure of all municipal committees. It is viewed as a form of public service to the community—a form in which those who live outside of San Agustín can engage:

> It works just like all of the committees that we have coming out of the *municipio*. It's structure is the same and each position on the committee also has a *suplente*, or substitute. . . . In the same way we are also elected by an assembly here, like the cargos in our community are that are not elected by political party—like the *alcaldes* [judges]. If you are elected to take on one of these positions you can't object—either here or there in San Agustín.

Although people from San Agustín who, like Lorenzo, Alejandro, and Mariano, are living more or less permanently in the United States and are serving on the transborder public works committee are viewed as performing some level of service as a part of their citizenship obligations in San Agustín, this does not seem to completely get them off the hook. All three have returned at least once for a two-year period in order to serve a local cargo, and they expect to do so again in the future. Lorenzo had to return when he was elected as an alcalde in 2001, and in 2004, when he was elected as treasurer of the communal land commission; Alejandro was a *regidor*, or city counselor, from 1981 to 1983; and Mariano was *comisariado ejidal* in 1981–85. All three men have probably been able to delay their return to serve in other cargos in their community through their service through the transborder public works committee, but this will not prevent their being called again to serve. It is quite likely they will return to San Agustín again to serve another cargo—with all the attendant difficulties explained in chapter 2.

By the fall of 2002 more than sixty thousand dollars had been raised from all branches of the San Agustín Atenango Transborder Public Works Committee. The ten federated committees came together to meet in Santa María, California. After that, representatives from the federated committee took the money to San Agustín. When the original parcel of land became unavailable, a different one was purchased. Daniel Cruz Pérez, introduced in chapter 2, explained to me how the land transaction had worked. Daniel worked with the committee from San Agustín:

> Well, you have to know that around here people plant corn, squash, and beans. All of the land is *bienes comunales* [communal land[. We don't have any official private property, but in fact people have been selling their communal land rights to one another since the 1960s, when larger numbers of people began to leave. Now only about 10 percent of the community is here and actually farming. So the first piece of land that we thought we were going to buy, called Inocencia, the person who had the rights to it, the communal land rights, wanted too much money. So the public works committee stopped trying to buy this piece of land and approached several people with adjoining land and compensated them.

In August 2004, Daniel and I walked out to see what progress had been made on the new cemetery. We walked along the hillsides, which were somewhat green. Their terraced edges indicated that they had been farmed in the past, but now hosted cattle and goats where corn had once been planted. Below us was richer, flatter bottom land that was sometimes planted with an hectare of corn. We walked down to level bottom land, where the new cemetery was being built. It was partially walled, and a new road had almost been completed out to where it lay. A large cross marked the place where the ground had been sanctified by a priest brought in from neighboring Tonalá. Several small metal crosses marked new graves. The new cemetery was already being used, even as construction on the wall and road was being finished. Daniel explained,

> Yes. It is already being used. The priest came to bless the ground. It is a total of 7½ hectares of communal land that was purchased. Well, actually, it wasn't the land itself that was purchased. We paid the owners to terminate their communal rights. We compensate each person. There were four different people. . . . In total we spent $495,000 pesos [roughly $50,000] paying people to give up their rights to the land. They turned over their communal land rights documents to the communal land committee [*comisariado de bienes comunales*], and the land is now here for the cemetery. No one else has the right to use it. And since it is the cemetery it is for everyone who wants to return home to be buried or who already lives here.

From 2002 to 2006, those living in the community contributed volunteer labor, or *tequio*, to build a wall around the new cemetery and to build a new road that runs between the community and the land. The new cemetery project is a focal point for residents of San Agustín, who live in many locations. The cemetery project ties people in disparate locations to their common system of governance through tequio, contributions, and public service and produces a new common good that everyone in good standing in the community has access too. The right to burial in the local cemetery is one of the basic rights that community members have if they have fulfilled their service responsibilities (see Stephen 2005b). By August 2006, the new cemetery was completed and held dozens of graves.

This is a concrete example of a form of political organizing that has harnessed economic remittances from agricultural workers and others in the United States directly to a collective development project in rural Mexico. Recent studies have focused on the role of remittances from the United States in productive investment in Mexico. While a majority of remittances are spent on current consumption needs, some parts of remittances are spent on investments in human capital, agricultural inputs, and small businesses (Massey and Parrado 1994; Taylor 1999). Even when remittances are spent on consumption goods, the fact that they give people more disposable income can help to expand local markets (Durand, Parrado, and Massey 1996; Cohen 2001). A recent study of the impact of community organization on the role of remittances in four Zapotec communities in Oaxaca suggests the importance of looking beyond individual remittances and household uses of them. Leah Van-Wey, Catherine Tucker, and Eileen Diaz-McConnell (2005) found that forms of community organization—particularly the continuation of assemblies of *comuneros*, civil and religious cargo systems at least partially permeated by usos y costumbres, as described in chapter 2, and the regular use of tequio for community development and public works—could strongly influence the mobilization of migrant remittances for maintaining communal resources and local infrastructure. Further, their study suggests that in two communities where important aspects of usos y costumbres continue to be followed and migrants are penalized for lack of participation in community institutions and responsibilities, local forms of government also reinforced a continued sense of community membership among transborder migrants and were an "important context to reinforce ethnic and community identity, and reconfirm the advantages of collective action" (2005: 100). This latter conclusion supports the findings of earlier studies that explored how strong forms of local governance that involved collective responsibilities and rights could facilitate the creation of transnational political organizations and effective hometown associations (Nagengast and Kearney 1990; Rivera Salgado 1999). In a study of twelve rural communities in the central valleys of Oaxaca, Jeffrey Cohen and Leila Rodríguez found that remittances from migrant households tended to contribute equally with nonmigrant households to communal projects. They further suggest that "migrant and non-migrant household[s] also contribute time and effort in equal parts to community management, serving in village offices and contributing to local project[s] in cash and kind" (2005: 60). Felipe López, Luis Escala-Rabadan, and Raúl Hinojosa-Ojeda (2001) have pointed out how hometown associations can provide collective remittances that are used to build shared community infrastructure and collectively engage migrants in efforts to develop their communities. The Oaxacan case studies are important in pointing out a line of research largely overlooked in dozens of studies of remittances: the role of community organization and local culture in capturing remittances for communitywide development projects that can benefit all.

Another important aspect of transborder organizing is the way in which such projects function as cultural spaces that can reinforce a sense of community-based and pan-Mixtec ethnic identity among their participants. For Manuel, Lorenzo, Alejandro, and others who have participated in the Comité Pro Obras de San Agustín in Salem, the experience has been rejuvenating, and they have found it exciting to have ongoing contact with other committees from their community. Another man who served on the committee described it as follows: "The committee is like a community." Men involved in the committee have clearly found it to be an important cultural and social space. They reported that most meetings are conducted in Spanish "because the young people don't speak *dialecto* [Mixtec]," but when the leadership of the committee gets together to plan for larger meetings they will often break into Mixtec. This, they stated, reminded them of how community assemblies were run at home in Oaxaca. "There, we have to speak in Spanish and Mixtec," reported Alejandro. "There are old people there who don't speak Spanish and now young people who don't speak much Mixtec. So we really need both languages."

Although women attend meetings and vote, none were named to the leadership positions on the committee. This mirrors the dynamics of community assemblies in San Agustín, where women can now attend meetings but have been named to very limited positions in the local cargo system. In Salem, women are present at meetings of the public works committee but are not particularly vocal or central to its activities beyond paying their dues, attending meetings, providing food for meetings, and discussing projects. The committee does not appear to be a mechanism for expanding women's political participation and leadership. It may sometimes serve to preserve and strengthen male-dominated political culture in the United States (see Goldring 1996 for a discussion of male domination in hometown associations). Women from San Agustín who have participated in MLP are much more likely to find room for growth and development as leaders there than in the public works committee. Four or five women from San Agustín who live in the Woodburn area have participated in both organizations.

For the men from San Agustín (particularly for those ages thirty–sixty)—many of whom also belong to PCUN—the hometown association committee seems to have opened up an important cultural space where they can reconnect with the Mixtec language, with the governance structure of their community, and with their childhood memories and experiences. The emergence of the public works committee has also further connected them with other clusters of paisanos from home and increased their feeling of connectedness to them in the United States. Community is thus reconstituted not only in specific locales, but also through interlinked networks in the United States and Mexico (Kearney 1995a: 232). For Mixtecos in Salem, the public works committee has provided an ethnically based mode of organization.

Panindigenous Organizing of Oaxacan Migrants in Oregon

The ever-increasing presence of Mexican indigenous workers in the state of Oregon has resulted in two new forms of panindigenous organizing at the statewide level. Both build on the work of PCUN with indigenous farmworkers as well as on networks between local hometown associations, such as the Public Works Committee of San Agustín Atenango.

The Oregon Law Center's Indigenous Farmworker Project[1] provides community education to Oregon's indigenous farmworkers by visiting labor camps, by presenting information at workshops and through radio announcements (in Spanish, Mixteco Alto, Mixteco Bajo, and Triqui) and call-in shows, and by distributing information about farmworkers' legal rights in employment via cassettes in Spanish, Mixteco Alto, Mixteco Bajo, Triqui, and Zapoteco. Begun in 2002, by 2005 the project had three Mixteco community outreach workers (Valentín Sánchez, Santiago Ventura, and Marcelina Martínez), a coordinator of the Sexual Harassment Project (Laura Mahr), a coordinator of the Indigenous Farmworker Project, and an attorney (Julie Samples). Staff have spoken with almost ten thousand indigenous farmworkers in Oregon over the past three years, and the Woodburn office, where it is based, serves as a community center of sorts, a place where indigenous workers call to ask for community referrals as well as stop by to pick up the latest edition of *El Oaxaqueño*, a newspaper published in California.

The project has also engaged in pathbreaking work to break the communication barrier that so many indigenous farmworkers come up against in their interactions with institutions they have regular contact with, such as schools, hospitals, doctors' and dentists' offices, social service agencies, and courts. Staff from the Indigenous Farmworker Project and from the Oregon Judicial Department have collaborated to provide interpreter training to indigenous speakers. So far, they have trained over thirty people who speak Akateco, Kanjobal, Q'uiche, and Mam (Maya languages spoken by Guatemalan indigenous farmworkers) as well as indigenous languages of Mexico, including Mixteco Alto, Mixteco Bajo, Nahuatl, Poqochi, Purepecha, Triqui, and Zapoteco. Over one-third have served as interpreters in Oregon's courts, and in 2006 training for medical translation began. Indigenous Farmworker Project staff also offer cultural competency training to service providers (including medical clinics, social service and governmental agencies, coalitions, and other nonprofit groups) so that these groups can deliver more effective services to indigenous populations. To reach providers at every level, staff of the Indigenous Farmworker Project have conducted over eighty presentations and training sessions in the past three years in Oregon and Washington and at national conferences in California, Wisconsin, and Washington, D.C.

In 2004, the Indigenous Farmworker Project partnered with PCUN and SALUD (SALUD Medical Center in Woodburn) (additional partners include Portland State University, Farmworker Justice Fund, Inc., and Dr. Linda McCauley) to develop a project to address the occupational safety and health needs of indigenous farmworkers in Oregon. The goal of this four-year program is to develop innovative and greatly needed methods of improving the capacity of indigenous migrant farmworkers to understand the hazards associated with agricultural work and increase their access to economic, health, and social services. During the first year of the project, partners conducted eight focus groups (four with indigenous and nonindigenous farmworkers [both male and female], two with female indigenous and nonindigenous farmworkers, and two with medical providers) and also carried out a pilot survey of twenty farmworkers (indigenous and nonindigenous) to ascertain their needs and and learn about their experiences. Several of these focus groups were conducted in indigenous languages. The approach has been unique in the experience of indigenous farmworkers, who comment that they are surprised they are finally being asked what it is they need: After one of the focus groups, an indigenous participant thanked the Indigenous Farmworker Project "for taking us [indigenous people] into account" (Samples 2005).

To address a challenging issue that has been long neglected in Oregon and in many other states, the Indigenous Farmworker Project received a grant to to address sexual harassment and assault in the workplace. The Sexual Harassment Program (El Proyecto en Contra del Acoso Sexual en el Campo), begun in June 2005, addresses the issues of sexual harassment and sexual assault farmworkers face in order to obtain employment, retain employment, and receive a better wage in agricultural work. The program focuses on both indigenous and nonindigenous farmworkers and includes informal know-your-rights sessions in homes, at labor camps, and at community events. In addition, this program collaborates with health-care providers and social service agencies to address barriers to providing care to victims of sexual harassment or sexual assault.

Organización de Comunidades Indígenas Migrantes Oaxaqueños (OCIMO)

In 2004, the basis for ethnically based organizing of indigenous Mexican migrants in Oregon was broadened with the formation of Organización de Comunidades Indígenas Migrantes Oaxaqueños (OCIMO, Organization of Oaxacan Indigenous Migrant Communities). OCIMO identifies itself as a coalition of organizations and individuals from the state of Oaxaca that focuses on the problems encountered by indigenous migrants in Oregon. In June 2004, the group of people that came to make up OCIMO invited a candidate for the governorship of Oaxaca to visit Woodburn. In September 2004, OCIMO participated in a hunger strike with PCUN, UNETE (a volunteer political and social service organization for farmworkers and other immigrants in Medford), and other Oregon immigrants' rights organizations in support of the DREAM Act. The DREAM Act is a bipartisan piece of legislation pending in Congress to clear up the immigration status issues and address barriers to education and work confronted by U.S.-raised children of undocumented immigrants. In September 2004, OCIMO opened an office in Salem in a ceremony attended by more than 150 people from a wide range of organizations. PCUN has been supportive of OCIMO and maintains a close relationship with its board of directors. The leadership of OCIMO includes two Mixtec women, one of whom works with PCUN. As of 2005, OCIMO's program was focused primarily on indigenous rights and promoting indigenous women's participation at cultural events. Its active volunteer base included thirty to forty men and women from primarily Mixtec communities like Santa Maria Tindú, San Juan Cahuayaxi, Tlaxiaco, Santa Rosa, and San Juan Mixtepec.

Whether in the public schools, local businesses, or the surrounding labor camps, the belittling of indigenous peoples that occurs in Mexico is often repeated in Oregon. Because of this discrimination (see chapter 7), OCIMO has made the promotion of indigenous cultural events and activities a priority. The secretary of OCIMO, Valentín Sánchez, who was born in San Juan Cahuayaxi but grew up in the United States, explained in October 2005:

What I have seen here among people from my own community of Cahuayaxi is that most of them have an average age of twenty-five to thirty years. A lot of them don't even know about their own culture, and in some cases they even deny its existence. This contributes to the discrimination that exists among mestizos toward indigenous peoples.

I think the only way to decrease discrimination among ourselves is to learn who we are and disseminate this information to the mestizos and the larger community. I will give you an example. Here in Woodburn, there are a lot of indigenous people. We know there is an annual fiesta Mexicana, and we all go to the fiesta. The only things we see are mariachis, which are supposed to be a representation of all of Mexico in general. There are no other examples of what else exists in Mexico. I think we can do that work.

In the fall of 2005, OCIMO organized a workshop on Mixtec codices that featured two linguistic anthropologists, Nancy Troike and Martin Johnson. The workshop brought together local Mixtec residents, students of Oregon State University and Portland State University, and OCIMO membership. The effort reflects the comment made by Valentín about the importance of Mixtec migrants and immigrants educating themselves about their own history and culture and disseminating this information to the larger Mexicano, Latino, and Anglo communities. Santiago Ventura, introduced in the preface, joined our discussion at a local bakery in Woodburn. He focused on the kind of knowledge contained in the codices not only as something Mixtecos should know about, but also as information that should be acknowledged in public education in Mexico as well as in the United States. He stated,

> Let's take the example of the codex workshop. Discussion of the codices is confined to the academic world. But if we don't listen to this information, if we don't comment on what is in the codices, and if we don't learn about them ourselves, then the academics will continue to produce book after book. But if we take part in this discussion I think we have a lot to contribute and at the same time the academics can learn from what we know from our people . . .
>
>   . . . In Mexico, the Ministry of Public Education doesn't even recognize things like the codices. They are never mentioned in school. I didn't even know about their existence until I read a book by Alfonzo Caso [the Mexican anthropologist]. Then I said, "What is going on that they are talking about the Mixtec people in this book? How come I didn't know about this?" So what we have to do is educate our own people so that they have enough pride to say here in the United States, "Hey, you know what, I have a history just like people in the United States who came here and encountered indigenous groups and started Thanksgiving. But my history goes much further than that. It goes back for thousands of years, and we can show it by the existence of written codices, figurines that were made to be worn as necklaces and bracelets of gold, and much more. . . .
>
>   . . . What we want is for our young people who are interested in our history to go to the university and participate in the interpretation of our own history, maybe have a career in anthropology. For the rest, we want people to say, "I am Mixteco and I want to tell you my history." We want to

promote the idea of people in our community learning their own history and sharing it.

OCIMO is not only functioning as a cultural space for indigenous migrants in Oregon, but also hopes to make a difference in lowering levels of discrimination against indigenous migrant workers. In the future it may serve an important role in articulating the other organizations discussed here. In the meantime, it is the first instance in Oregon of a panindigenous organization that is run entirely by indigenous immigrants and is setting its own agenda.

Conclusions

The organizations described in this chapter—PCUN, MLP, the San Agustín Transborder Public Works Committee, the Oregon Law Center's Indigenous Farmworker Project, and the newly formed OCIMO—are examples of the kinds of grassroots organizing efforts that Mixtec transborder migrants in Oregon have participated in. In fact, a number of them have participated in two or more of these organizations at once. The concentration of increasing numbers of Mixtecos and other indigenous Mexican migrants in the Salem, Woodburn, and Portland area is indicative of the kind of presence of national and ethnic diversity that Sassen attributes primarily to global cities, but which can be encountered in other sites as well, including smaller and more rural locations (see Kissam 2005a, 2005b). Through their presence in organized entities such as PCUN, MLP, and OCIMO, indigenous Mexican migrants are participating in broader political processes that escape the boundaries of the formal political system linked to electoral politics, yet are also increasingly able to participate in that system as well—albeit often indirectly. Cultural and economic processes that operate outside of formal political systems can and do influence such systems. For that reason I have suggested that the term *cultural citizenship* is useful for conceptualizing how marginalized social groups move from claiming recognition, public space, and eventually specific rights to changing formal political systems. The exercise of cultural citizenship can also mobilize people to pressure formal political structures in ways that defend existing rights—such as the acceptance of the validity of Mexican consular identification cards (*ma-*

trícula consular) as a document in obtaining driver's licenses and open-ing a bank account and for receiving electric, gas, and water services.

The breadth of organizational venues that Mixteco migrants are par-ticipating in just in the localized region of Salem, Keizer, and Woodburn, Oregon, suggests that the concerns of transborder indigenous migrants remain focused on a wide range of issues. These include the relations of production and reproduction, the politics of immigration and immi-grant rights, culturally based issues such as language and local cultural expression and maintenance, sexism in the workplace and at home, collective memory and connection to communities of origin, and the creation of community across borders and through networks. This list of concerns certainly suggests that Mixtec migrants are not assimilating into so-called mainstream U.S. culture and continue to cultivate ethnic distinctiveness in relation to both people of Mexican descent in the United States and Native Americans.

PCUN originally captivated people's attention and enthusiasm through both their legal services center, which played a pivotal role in helping undocumented workers receive amnesty in the mid-1980s, and their campaigns to raise strawberry picking and other wages. Since that time, Mixtec workers have played key roles in negotiating contracts and pro-viding leadership in field organizing efforts. Because the purpose of the union is primarily focused on labor relations, immigration, and a broad defense of Latino immigrants' rights, Mixtecs have valued the union's assistance and commitment in these areas and its recognition of their validation as an important part of the Mexican transborder farmworker population.

The work that PCUN and the previously existing service center have carried out over the past twenty-five years is representative of a growing sector of organizations known as community unions. Janice Fine sug-gests that such organizations seek improvements in workers' home lives as well as in their work lives through the following means:

> Service delivery: including legal representation to recover unpaid wages and
> deal with immigration, English classes, worker rights education, access to
> health clinics, bank accounts and loans.
> Advocacy: including researching and releasing exposés about conditions
> in low-wage industries and lobbying for new and better laws to improve
> working conditions; bringing suits against employers
> Organizing: building organization and leadership development among

workers to take action on their own behalves for economic and political change. (2005: 155)

Fine notes that such forms of identity as gender, ethnicity, and race stand in for craft or industry as the principal means of recruitment and the building of bonds between workers (2005: 155). In the case of PCUN, because agricultural labor is so heavily concentrated in Mexican migrant laborers—and increasingly indigenous—nationality, race, ethnicity, and "craft" have congealed into a significantly overlapping set of identities. In a national study of immigrant worker centers (a subset of community unions), Fine identified close to 133 worker centers in more than 80 communities. In 1992 there were fewer than 5 centers nationwide, suggesting that PCUN, whose service delivery and advocacy work began in 1978 and its organizing in 1985, was a pioneer in such work.

The timing of the development of community unions such as PCUN and their increasing identification with an undocumented and ethnically diverse immigrant population makes sense in relation to the demographics of immigration—particularly from Mexico. From the standpoint of indigenous migrants such as Filemón, Dolores, Alejandro, Fidelia, and others, participation in PCUN has also been important in integrating them into other forms of political participation.

PCUN has been active in the creation and support of Latino voter groups such as Voz Hispana. Voz has been involved in key state and national electoral and referendum campaigns. As part of the larger immigrants' rights coalition of CAUSA, which extends throughout Oregon, Voz and PCUN have been important participants in defeating ongoing anti-immigrant legislation.

In 2005, House Bill 3195 would have prohibited school districts from offering instruction in more than one language to students whose native language is not English, effectively eliminating ESL funding. Due to public pressure, the bill died in the House Education Committee. Whether or not people are citizens and registered voters, such anti-immigrant measures affect them. Through their participation in PCUN, MLP, and OCIMO, indigenous migrants have become involved in working against such anti-immigration bills and in exercising their political presence and cultural citizenship in the process.

Apart from their participation in PCUN and MLP, Mixtec transborder migrants have participated in organizational forms like the Comité Pro Obras de San Agustín that provide a cultural and organizational space for expressions of ethnic identity—specific local, ethnic identities reaching across the U.S.-Mexican border through a series of networked committees that draw their unity from links to one community in Oaxaca. In addition to providing a ground for community development based on collective remittances (for example, through projects such as the cemetery expansion), organizational spaces such as the public works committee act as an extension of Oaxaca-based forms of local government and collective participation that link transborder community members to one another in multiple sites and provide a means for reinforcing collective rights and responsibilities in transborder San Agustín.

Cross-border organizations like the San Agustín Public Works Committee, which has participated with broader federated transborder organizations like FIOB, have been important in exerting political pressure in Mexico as well as in the United States. The public works committee, FIOB, and OCIMO have attracted the attention of Mexican consulates in the United States, of Mexican political figures campaigning in the United States, and of people working to legislate the right of Mexicans living abroad to vote—a right won in 2005. The public works committee and OCIMO have been involved in translocal organizing efforts that are deeply tied to more formal political processes and the expansion of democratic institutions.

In relation to conceptualizing how transmigrants are linked, Escobar's notion of meshworks may be useful in terms of thinking about how people from communities like San Agustín are connected to one another through multiple networks and ties and also how these networks are linked to other networks, some of which span the United States and Mexico and some of which are particular to each country. These linked networks and the discourses emanating from them are also brought back to the physical community of San Agustín by individuals who return to live there, whether for long or short periods of time. Thus even people who have never left San Agustín enter the orbit of a wide range of discourses that are based far from where they live.

While the Comité Pro Obras includes women in its membership and meetings, its organizational structure is dominated by men; further, the national and international networking aspects of the committee appear to be carried out primarily by men (see Goldring 1996). Mixtec women like Fidelia and Antonia have found a more welcoming space in MLP, where both the gendered and ethnic dimensions of their experiences are validated. MLP numbers many indigenous women from Mexico and Guatemala, and although ethnicity is not the only focus of the group, it has discussed members' experiences of ethnic discrimination. In addition, the perception of "not being able to speak" articulated by Fidelia is an experience many indigenous women have in common relating to the exclusionary aspects of usos y costumbres in community governance. Thus while transborder community organizations such as the San Agustín Public Works Committee can reinforce some of the positive aspects of usos y costumbres community governance, their gendered exclusions in naming a primarily male leadership reinforce some of the alienation indigenous women may feel from public political processes in their home communities. Through their participation in MLP as a women-only space (which facilitates trust and expression), participants are able to learn a variety of leadership, management, and organizing skills that permit them to participate actively in other organizational forms jointly with men.

CHAPTER 9

Transborder Ethnic Identity

Construction in Life and on the Net

E-MAIL AND WEB PAGE CONSTRUCTION

AND USE

It is midday on a Sunday in Teotitlán del Valle in August 2004. In the center of town in the artisans' market, people are sitting in their booths waiting for tourists to show up. So far it has been a slow day. One of the booths is staffed by the family of Federico Chávez, who works with one of Teotitlán's thirteen weaving cooperatives. The group is called Ben Ruinchi Laadti (People Who Weave). Two years earlier, Federico's son Eric created a website for his family. He also has an e-mail account which serves as a contact for the weaving cooperative they participate in. Their hope is to direct American tourists to do business with them, bypassing some of the large merchants in the community that have a strong hold on the U.S. market for Teotiteco textiles.

Federico is a handsome man with streaks of gray in his black hair. He is dressed neatly in a white cotton shirt tucked into gray chino pants. He leans against the side of the booth. Below him, Eric is sitting on a low stool. Eric has on jeans and a T-shirt with a Coca-Cola logo on it. Eric calls out to me in perfect English.

ERIC: "Hey, Lynn, how are you today? Come over here and visit with us for a while. It's Sunday, time to relax."
LYNN: Thanks. I will. Any more room in the shade?
ERIC: Sure. We have more room. Come sit down. We can talk about the website I was telling you about.

LYNN: [changing to Spanish] Why did you make the website?

FEDERICO: Well, we wanted to be active participants in modernity. We thought that having a website was important for the future. We saw it as a long-term project.

LYNN: Can people buy their textiles directly on the Internet with a credit card?

ERIC: No. We prefer that they come and buy with us. The idea is that they see the website and come to see us here. They can buy with us here. They can write to us through our e-mail account as well. We use it to keep in touch with some of our family too.

LYNN: Where do you get your e-mail?

ERIC: We get it at the house. I have my computer hooked up to the telephone. Teotitlán has been wired for the Internet for two years now. I have been getting e-mails at home for two years now.

LYNN: How many e-mails do you get?

ERIC: I get about two per week and a lot of junk, promotions as well.

LYNN: I noticed that your website is in English. Where did you learn such good English?

ERIC: I learned from a teacher here. My sister studied with her as well. We get to practice with people who come here to buy. We had to make the website in English because most of the people we want to sell to are English speakers. . . . I have something to ask you. There is this woman who says she is writing a book about what she calls Southwest designs. She contacted me through my e-mail and has asked for permission to reproduce the whole Website in her book. The website I made tells all about how textiles are made—the dyes, the looms, everything. She wants to put it all in her book. Do you think this is a good idea? We have some of our designs up there.

LYNN: Well, if you post things on the Internet then they are already public. What do you think? Some people want to try to protect their designs. There has been a lot of controversy about Zapotec weavers producing "Navajo" designs.

FEDERICO: Well, what they don't know is that some of what are called Navajo designs came from Mexico. Those designs are mixed with those from Mexico. We know about this.

ERIC: All kinds of designs are on the Internet. On our site we ask people not to reproduce any images without our permission. At least the person making the book e-mailed me to ask.

Federico and Eric continue to discuss the hazards and advantages of posting their designs on the web.

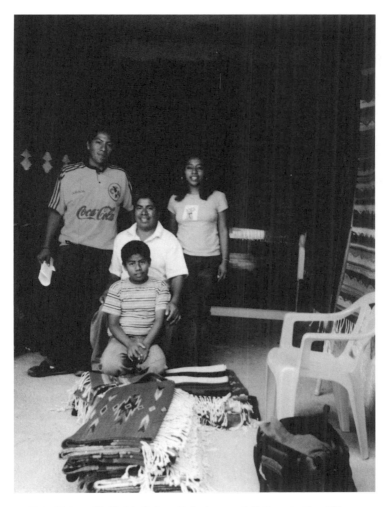

21. Eric Chávez (*left*), his father, Federico, and siblings in Teotitlán del Valle textile market.

They are not alone in this discussion. Other Teotitecos in weaving cooperatives are also putting together websites and carefully considering what to put in them. Weaving cooperatives began to emerge in the mid- to late-1980s in Teotitlán del Valle in an effort to compete with local merchants who, in conjunction with U.S. importers, control a significant part of the market for Teotiteco wool textiles (Wood 2000a, 2000b). The thirteen cooperatives, which involve between 10 and 15 percent of the local population (about 450–500 people out of 4,000) pool their textiles to sell collectively at local and national exhibitions, sometimes purchase materials together, and frequently participate in workshops for weaving and dying techniques as well as for marketing. In addition, they function as social solidarity groups that offer material and emotional support to members during hard times. Many of the cooperatives have also been active in local and state politics. Most important, in the words of cooperative members, they remove weavers from the position of being *mano de obra*, or wage labor working for a local merchant (see Stephen 2005a, 2005b). Migrants from Teotitlán to other parts of Mexico and to the United States have been some of the key movers and shakers behind the cooperative movement found there. They are currently looking at digital technology—specifically websites and e-mail—as tools for directly accessing the U.S. market and tourists who come to Oaxaca. The local community museum in Teotitlán is also using its website as a multilingual and multicultural space both to attract visitors to the community and to stake public claims about the uniqueness of Teotiteco history and culture and their links to a larger indigenous population and movement in Mexico.

Twenty-four kilometers west of Teotitlán in Oaxaca City, Emiliana Cruz Pérez is standing in front of an ATM machine in a Farmacias del Ahorro. She has come to Oaxaca City from San Agustín Atenango to purchase school uniforms for her children. School starts in a few weeks. She is hoping to find better prices than in San Agustín. She will pay for the school uniforms with pesos from a bank account in the United States based in Salem, Oregon. Her husband, Rigoberto, has been working in the United States for five years now, and on a trip back to San Agustín last year he gave her an ATM card with which to draw on the U.S. account. This way, explains Emiliana, "we don't have to pay the fees to the money transfer companies. I can just use this card when I need it. I always come into Oaxaca to get cash and to buy the uniforms for my children." Emiliana and her children are one of the 1.6 million families in Mexico being supported by economic remittances sent home by Mexican immigrants living in the United States. In 2004, remittances from the United States totaled US$17 billion (Diego Cevallos 2005) and in 2005 were over US$20 billion. Worldwide, migrant remittance payments from more than 150 million international migrants in 2003 were estimated to be $140 billion (Zarate-Hoyes and Anderson 2005). In the state of Oaxaca remittances represent 100 percent more than the federal budget for the state (Zarate-Hoyes and Anderson 2005). In a town like San Agustín, about one-third of whose population work in the United States, remittances are crucial parts of household budgets. Electronic technology is a part of these important cross-border financial networks. In addition, e-mail and cell phone connections have been important in keeping the ten subcommittees of the transborder Comité Pro Obras described in chapter 8 connected to each other in the United States and to municipal officials in San Agustín.

Farther west in the town of Santiago Juxtlahuaca in the office of the Frente Indígena Oaxaqueño Binacional (FIOB, changed to the Frente Indígena de Organizaciones Binacionales in 2005), Rosa Anabel (Rosy) Méndez Moreno is sitting behind a computer on a rolling desk chair. Her two young daughters have come to work with her that day and are busy spinning each other around on the other desk chair. The woman who normally takes care of them has taken the day off to go to Ixpantepec Nieves to sell things to pilgrims who have come to celebrate the fiesta there honoring the Virgen de Las Nieves. Rosy is answering e-mails, sending out the latest FIOB communiqué concerning the contested Oaxacan elections, and talking to Mixtec men and women arriving at the office. While she is sitting there, Gerardo Vásquez Colmenares comes in, sits down, and begins to help her, moving the conversation from halting Spanish to Mixteco. Gerardo is a high school student from Tinuma de Zaragoza who is studying in Santiago Juxtlahuaca. He is a volunteer in the FIOB office.

A young man from the municipio of San Juan Mixtepec is about to leave for the United States to work. He has come to the FIOB office to receive an official FIOB ID card. Rosy explains this to me:

> A lot of people come into the FIOB office here before they go to the United States to get a FIOB ID. They want to have some form of ID before they leave to go to the United States We make them a FIOB ID before they leave. These are people who don't have voter identification cards or other forms of

identification. If *the migra* grabs them in the United States, then they can show this to them so that they will return them to Mexico. Sometimes the migra picks up people from Guatemala as well, and they want to send Mixtecos from Oaxaca back to Guatemala. With this, they can see they are Mexican.

... Also, if people have a problem in the United States then they can go to one of our offices there. We have an office in Fresno, in Santa Maria, and in Los Angeles, California. They can go there. Then someone in the office there can communicate with us here, send an e-mail so we know what the problem is. We can be in touch with the families here. A lot of our current members of FIOB who are working with us locally now in the Juxtlahuaca area are the wives of men who are migrating. They stay behind and work with the organization.

Later Gerardo explains this further to me. He is typing information onto a form to produce ID cards to which pictures will be added before being laminated. He states,

Like Rosy said, a lot of people are leaving and they have no identification. I am from Tinuma de Zaragoza, which is in the municipio of Juxtlahuaca. In my town about fifty families have stayed behind and about one hundred families are gone to the United States. I would say that about one-third to two-thirds of the town are gone now. Some of them went and didn't return. We have some people who go to work in the strawberries in Oregon as well as living in California. We are here communicating with people in many places at once.

Digital border crossing is often an important dimension of transborder communities. While much has been made of the role of the Internet in building solidarity for the Zapatista movement in Chiapas (see Cleaver 1998; Stephen 2002), outside of electronic money transfers and the use of ATMs little attention has been paid to how digital communication is becoming a factor in many aspects of the lives of transborder migrants: in maintaining family relationships, in cross-border political organizing, in fostering solidarity, in articulating human rights defense, and in constructing ethnic identities. Digital technology has become increasingly important for transborder migrants in both the United States and Mexico. The Mexican Internet Association has stated that about twelve million Mexicans used the Internet in 2003. According to a survey they conducted that year, male Internet users outnumber female by 2 to 1, about 23 percent of Internet users are age eighteen to twenty-four, 42 percent are age twenty-five to thirty-four, 20 percent are age thirty-five to forty-four, and 12 percent are age forty-five and over (Lloyd Mexican Economic Report 2004). In the United States e-mail and cell phones are used by immigrants to keep in touch with those at home. Some community of origin clubs have set up their own websites or pressured municipal governments in their hometowns to set up websites that are monitored from the United States to follow local elections, to keep up on the progress of public works projects being funded by remittances from the United States, and to organize political pressure in both Mexico and the United States (Smith 2002). The Mexican government offers online resources to Mexican migrants in the United States through its virtual consulates (La Embajada de Mexico en Los Estados Unidos), websites dedicated to helping migrants, such as the web-based Guia del Migrante Mexicano (Guide for Mexican Migrants), published online by the Secretaría de Relaciones Exteriores of Mexico (2005) (the site generated much protest by anti-immigrant groups in the United States), and programs that facilitate electronic bank transfers for migrants.

Immigrant uses of digital technologies across borders have been described in some recent conversations as "virtual diasporas." Michel S. Laguerre (2002) defines *virtual diaspora* as follows:

> The use of cyberspace by immigrants or descendants of an immigrant group for the purpose of participating or engaging in online interactional transactions. Such virtual interaction can be with members of the diasporic group living in the same foreign country or in other countries, with individuals or entities in the homeland, or with non-members of the group in the hostland and elsewhere. By extension, virtual diaspora is the cyberexpansion of real diaspora. No virtual diaspora can be sustained without real life diasporas and in this sense, it is not a separate entity, but rather a pole of a continuum.

For my purposes here in understanding transborder migrants' use of digital technology, the most useful aspect of this definition is its insistence in seeing the "virtual diaspora" as an extension of a "real diaspora." In my conceptual discussion of transborder migration I have avoided using dichotomizing terms such as *foreign country* versus *homeland* or *homeland* versus *hostland* in order to emphasize the multisited reality of transborder communities and organizations. If we return to the models of integrated social fields and meshworks I have adopted for understanding and visualizing how transborder communities and organizations function and are experienced, we need to modify this definition of virtual diasporas. Instead we can use the term *virtual transborder communities* defined as follows:

> The use of cyberspace by immigrants or descendants of an immigrant group for the purpose of participating or engaging in online interactional transactions, wherever their actual physical location. Virtual transborder communities are extensions of real transborder communities. No virtual transborder community can be sustained without real life transborder crossing and in this sense, it is not a separate entity, but rather a pole of a continuum. (adapted from Laguerre 2002)

Here, I will focus on two primary examples of the use of digital technology by transborder communities and organizations. The first explores how women and men from more than thirteen cooperatives and a community museum committee in Teotitlán del Valle have worked out their ethnic identity as they create messages and images for web pages that are aimed not only at others in their transborder community, but also at Mexican and American Net surfers in general. The second example is FIOB's use of e-mail and its website to build a public presence in Mexican and U.S. cyberspace. The FIOB has also used the Internet as an organizing tool to exert political pressure in both the United States and Mexico. Both the weavers of Teotitlán and FIOB activists have used digital technology as part of a process that Jonathan Fox calls the "scaling up" of collective identity from home community, to shared region of origin, to shared panethnic indigenous identity (Fox 2006: 47). In fact, both groups have taken a similar approach to how they publicly construct their ethnic identities—simultaneously linking local, regional, national, and transborder or binational dimensions of indigenous identity with a multisited understanding of location. This comparison makes it evident that there are processes internal to Mexico as well as related to the experience of migration and exploitation that can facilitate the integration of ethnic indigenous identity from the local to the regional level (and beyond), as first advanced by Carol Nagengast and Michael Kearney in their study of Mixtec identity and pan-Oaxacan organizing in northwest Mexico and California (1990).

The Production of Cultural Distinctiveness

While we often think of processes of cultural globalization as being tied to corporate ad campaigns promoting such products as Nike, Coke, and the Gap (Klein 2002), other productive processes involve the self-conscious creation of cultural messages of distinctiveness with the goal of consolidating ethnic identities and rewriting the way a particular group's history has been told from the outside. Website creation is a form of digital border crossing that involves a dialogue—usually at multiple levels—around cultural memory and contested ideas about shared heritage and tradition. What I am calling here cultural messages of distinctiveness found in websites such as those I will discuss can also be understood as what Linda Tuhiwa Smith calls "indigenous research projects." She says of indigenous research projects:

> The implications for indigenous research which have been derived from the imperatives inside the struggles of the 1970s seem to be clear and straightforward: The survival of peoples, cultures, and languages; the struggle to become self-determining, the need to take back control of our destinies. These imperatives have demanded more than rhetoric and acts of defiance. The acts of reclaiming, reformulating, and reconstructing indigenous cultures and languages have required the mounting of an ambitious research programme, one that is very strategic in its purpose and activities and relentless in its pursuit of social justice. (1999: 142)

The kinds of projects Smith outlines include "Claiming, Testimonies, Story Telling, Celebrating Survival, Remembering, Indigenizing, Intervening, Revitalizing, Connecting, Reading, Representing, Gendering, Envisioning, Reframing, Restoring, Returning, Democratizing, Networking, Naming, Protecting, Creating, Negotiating, Discovering, and Sharing" (1999: 141–61). Many of these projects are reflected in the material analyzed below from Teotitlán del Valle and the FIOB and should be included in our understanding of the goals of virtual indigenous transborder communities and organizing efforts.

While unraveling the mechanics of cultural memory production might be viewed by some as an invitation to debunk essentialized versions of indigenous identities attached to a romantic past, the reality is much more complex. As many theorists have emphasized, the memories that people draw upon to create their recollections are based not just on personal experience, but on a wide range of public images, mass media, and other forms of representation. As discussed by Phillip Scher, such processes can be called "reproductive imagination," which he defines according to the *Oxford English Dictionary* as "that faculty of the mind by which are formed images or concepts of external objects not present to the senses and of their relations (to each other or to the subject): hence frequently including memory" (OED 1989: 1377, Scher 2003: 16).

Website Creation and Ethnic Identity Construction in Greater Teotitlán del Valle

In the process of creating messages that are projected to local, national, and international audiences, Teotitecos have selectively turned to the work of historians, anthropologists, and archaeologists to buttress their claims of originality and uniqueness. Cultural memory in these processes is a hybrid of selective extracts taken from texts written by outsiders, images from a variety of sources, consultation with elders, group discussion about what key points and symbols are, and finally the generating of text and visual images that project an agreed-upon message. My analysis of the community museum exhibit and a web page created by six cooperatives highlights three key elements:

1. Being first. Groups from Teotitlán create materials that emphasize their identity as the "first" Zapotec settlement in Oaxaca. Here, geographic space and place become an important part of cultural memory and claims of uniqueness.

2. Consistent cultural links to a precolonial past. Cultural messages emphasize key elements of historical continuity between the current period and the precolonial period, particularly through language, place, and textile dying and processing techniques.

3. Being Zapotec and part of a larger indigenous community Teotitecos emphasize their regional identity as both Zapotec in terms of language and culture as well as being a native people. Here, the local dimensions of ethnic identity are simultaneously linked to regional and panindigenous levels.

Being First

In a wide range of materials created by Teotitecos (often in consultation with anthropologists and archaeologists) they consistently emphasize their identity as the first major Zapotec settlement in Oaxaca. INAH (Instituto Nacional de Antropología e Historia) archaeologists who worked with community committees in 1992 to assist in setting up a new community museum were instrumental in establishing date ranges which are now used by many groups in the community to establish Teotitlán's claim as a key first Zapotec population site in the Valleys of Oaxaca. In the community museum, a piece of pottery is used to date the first settlement of Teotitecos. A display states "La cerámica más antigua hasta ahora encontrada en Teotítlán pertenece a la Epoca Monte Albán 1 (450 BC–100 DC). [The oldest piece of pottery found so far in Teotitlán is dated to Monte Albán I (450 BC to 100 AD)]." The pottery is displayed along with later pieces dated to Monte Albán II (roughly 100–200 AD in the museum timeline). A timeline chart, "Tiempos de la historia de los Zapotecos en Teotitlán y de los Valles de Oaxaca/Times in the history of the Zapotecs in Teotitlán and in the Valleys of Oaxaca," displayed at the museum situates the first settlements of Teotitecos and inserts them into a larger timeline of archaeological time periods. The timelines begin fifteen hundred years before the arrival of the Spaniards and ends in 1521, the date Hernán Cortés arrived in the Valleys of Oaxaca.

The timeline shows that Teotitlán had an early principal occupation of about 150 people during the time period of Monte Albán I (800–400 BC) and became "one of the most important centers in the Valleys of Oaxaca" that occupied parts of neighboring towns during the period of Monte Albán V (800–1500 AD). The timeline and archaeological artifacts establish Teotitlán as a seminal place in Oaxaca and Teotitecos as people who can claim a long, place-based history in the state and the nation. "Being first" and being tied to a specific piece of geography have become fundamental aspects of the cultural memory that is deployed within the museum as well as by others who create messages about local history (see El Museo de Teotitlán del Valle 2006 for the timeline, and Stephen 2005b: 194–99 for a history of the museum).

The information codified in the museum and verifying the longevity of Teotitlán as a Zapotec population site has been incorporated into other materials that groups like the cooperatives use to publicize their projects on the web and elsewhere. A text prepared by six cooperative groups which came together to work on a web page with the Secretaría de Asuntos Indígenas del Estado de Oaxaca (Ministry of Indigenous Affairs of the State of Oaxaca) also emphasizes that Teotitlán was the first Zapotec population. The Ministry of Indigenous Affairs was approached in 2002 because of personal ties between cooperative members and this office. Cooperative members also thought the preparation of the text was precisely the kind of project the ministry should be supporting.

In 2003 the director changed, and website materials were gathered and turned in to the new office staff. By August 2004, most of the materials were digitized, and the site was mounted and available online until the end of September 2005. The website was accessible through the portal of the Secretaría de Asuntos Indígenas de Oaxaca (SAI) http://www.oaxaca .gob./sai/. In January 2005, a new governor Ulises Ruiz, took office in Oaxaca and appointed a new director of the secretaría. The entire website for the Oaxacan state government was reorganized, and the Teotitlán cooperative webpage was no longer assessible through the portal of the SAI.

I was recruited by cooperative leaders in 2002 to assist in the preparation of a website. The webpage offers a general history and images of Teotitlán del Valle and then goes on to discuss the formation of the cooperatives and to highlight each of the six that are represented on the webpage. The general introduction of the webpage, which I was asked to translate from Spanish to English during the summer of 2004, reads as follows:

> Teotitlán del Valle is a town of Zapotec origin located in the eastern part of the state, 40 kilometers outside of the state capital of Oaxaca City. The town was founded pre-Hispanically, with the first population dating to 2000 years ago. The original inhabitants of Teotitlán called the town XaGuia or Xaquia, which means "Below the Rock" in the Zapotec language.[1] According to the *Geographic Relations of Burgoa*, Teotitlán is the site of the first Zapotec population. The town is said to have been founded by Petela, a priest and military chief. The first Zapotec ceremonial center was created in Teotitlán to honor the supreme being of the universe.

In this introduction to the community written by several women cooperative leaders, "being first" is tied to a specific piece of the geographic landscape, a large rock formation that towers above the community. The formation, which is called *Xiabets*, or brother rock, in Zapotec, is the rock referred to in the Zapotec name for Teotitlán, XaGuia (below the rock). This formation can be seen in early colonial maps, such as one of neighboring Macuilxóchitl that accompanies the *Relaciones Geográficas del siglo xvi, Antequera* (Acuña 1984). The women who wrote the introduction for the cooperative webpage cited above draw on the ethnohistorical source of the *Geographic Relations* first published in 1674 to further document Teotitlán as "the first population."

In preparation for the cooperative website, I was employed by Josefina Jiménez and Aurora Bazan, longtime community leaders of women's cooperatives and other organizing efforts, to take photographs for the website. Josefina has been an activist in the women's cooperatives in Teotitlán for many years. Aurora served as a Federal Indigenous Representative (Diputada Federal Indígena) from the state of Oaxaca in 1997–2000, representing the Partido Verde Ecologista de México (Ecological Green Party of Mexico). She was also the first indigenous woman to serve on the Comisión de Concordia y Pacificación (National Commission of Concord and Pacification, COCOPA), an intermediary organization in resolving the conflict between the Zapatista Army of National Liberation (EZLN) and the Mexican government. She was deeply involved in trying to get the Mexican government to legislate the San Andrés Accords on Indigenous Rights and Culture, which were signed under President Ernesto Zedillo with the EZLN in February 1996. In addition, Aurora has attended many forums on indigenous rights in Mexico and elsewhere around the world. She is currently active with the National Plural Indigenous Assembly for Autonomy (ANIPA), a national network of indigenous organizations and communities in Mexico that has been working for indigenous self-determination. In addition, she participated in the International Commission of Art of Indigenous Peoples of the United Nations during 2004 and 2005.

Through these experiences, Aurora has been a key participant in a panindigenous movement for rights of self-determination within Mexico. She carries this perspective over into her work on the website and in the cooperative she works with. With her long, wavy black hair that she wears gathered at the nape of her neck, Aurora has a youthful smile that gleams in her eyes as she talks about the importance of indigenous rights. Insistent, patient, and passionate, she moves seamlessly between local, grassroots projects such as weaving cooperatives and a composting project she began in Teotitlán del Valle and state and national discussions about indigenous rights.

During the summer of 2004, she campaigned for Ulises Ruiz Ortiz, who was the PRI candidate for governor of Oaxaca and took office after a highly contested election. Her rationale was to pressure from inside the campaign to get as much as she could for indigenous peoples in the state. Ruiz Ortiz served with Aurora as a state representative in the Mexican Congress from 1997 to 2000, and because of her personal connection to him she felt she could work effectively in pressuring him to support indigenous rights. In a speech directed toward the indigenous voters of Oaxaca, she clearly articulated a vision of a panindigenous Oaxacan electorate that could unite around a common identity. Her speech in part stated,

> We realize the enormous differences between the quality of life in our world, of indigenous peoples, and of the mestizo world. Just two basic figures can illustrate this: while the average life span of the Mestizo population is 73.7 years, ours is 69.5 years. The people in primarily indigenous *municipios* suffer from very high levels of poverty. . . . Even worse than this is the constant and steady loss of our identities, our cultures, and our consciousness as peoples and nations with a future. It's enough to point out the loss of indigenous languages as an example of what I tam talking about.
>
> The original peoples in Oaxaca, we indigerous people who are statistically a majority in Oaxaca, we deserve a better destiny [than we have had], Mr. Future Governor because with the indigenous vote, you are taking care of the destiny of the richest culture in all of Mexico. (Bazán López 2004)

By the summer of 2006, a widespread social movement was calling for the removal of Ruiz Ortiz as governor. Many indigenous communities, including Teotitlán, were not pleased with his record.

Aurora and Josefina carefully considered the kinds of images and texts they wanted to put into the collective website representing their own and other people's cooperatives.

On the appointed day, I picked Josefina up at her house on the edge of town, and we went to get Aurora. They had a list of specific sites they wanted me to photograph. The first was Xiabets. The second was the Catholic church from the sixteenth century, then the archaeological zone behind the church, and finally the food market. These were the four visual images they and other cooperative members had agreed were most important to represent Teotitlán on the website. Of all the pictures we worked to capture, the most discussion went into what would be the best angle to capture Xiabets. We drove up alongside it and snapped a photograph. They then directed me to go out a road to a large dam which presents a sweeping view of Xiabets and the town below. There we took about eight photographs. As I was focusing and shooting, Aurora and Josefina were busy naming other significant pieces of the landscape in Zapotec and discussing their significance. They spoke about their relationship to one another:

(above) 22. X́iabetz, or "brother rock," in Teotitlán del Valle.
23. Sixteenth-century church in Teotitlán del Valle.

24. Archaeological site behind church in Teotitlán.

"There is *Xia Jyu* [*cabeza de tierra*/head of the land] and *Xia Les* [*cabeza de la piedra*/head of the rock]—they say that is where the first people lived. People have found a lot of *ídolos* [idols] up there," commented Josefina.

"Back there behind that tree if you keep going is a sacred stream that we used to walk to when I was a child," answered Aurora. "We should go there. My mother used to take us there to collect leaves for a special tea."

The conversation based on the landscape and its importance continued, expanding to include medicinal plants, animals that lived behind the dam in the mountains, and a wide range of topics associated with the land. The discussion that accompanied our photographing of Xiabets reveals how place-based and literally "in the land" cultural memory is for people like Aurora and Josefina when they are creating representations of their own history. The integration of archaeological, ethnohistorical, and local knowledges reveals the hybridity of ongoing knowledge construction and the ways in which the different networks that Josefina and Aurora are connected with come together in the creation of textual and visual representations of their community and ethnic identity. Both have been involved with the establishment of the museum at different phases of its development, including helping to contribute to exhibits, mobilizing the museum committee to take a stand on a road-building project that would have bulldozed a newly found archaeological site, and in bringing attention to the role of women in community history. In the process of their work with cooperatives and the museum as well as in statewide and national indigenous politics, they have come to know archaeologists, anthropologists, and policy makers. In putting together materials about the groups they are involved in, they draw on these actors and the information they have received from them. Their personal, family connections to the landscape and to the flora and fauna they have come to know in the landscape are also a part of their memory. Thus like the archaeological information they deploy, their cultural memory is deeply based in place.

Strong Links to the Precolonial Past

A second element of the cultural messages that Teotitecos have created about themselves through the museum and the cooperative websites emphasizes key aspects of historical continuity in their role as weavers before the colonial era and in the continuation of precolonial dying techniques. As is documented in the community museum and in several ethnohistorical documents and codices, the people of Teotitlán were weavers who paid tribute in lengths of cotton cloth. The women of the community were well known as weavers who used backstrap looms. A wide variety of natural dyes were used by weavers as well, many of which continue to be used today. The exhibit dedicated to explaining the history of weaving in the community states,

> La elaboración de textiles tiene una larga historia en Teotitlán del Valle. A fines del siglo XV el señorío de Teotitlán pertenecía a la provincia de Coyolapan que tributaba al reino de Moctezuma. Mandaban cada tres meses 400 cargas de mantas bordadas y 800 cargas de mantas grandes a Tenochtítlán. Las mujeres tejían las mantas de algodón en el telar de cintura, así contribuían para que se cumplieran las obligaciones que los Mexicas impusieron a su pueblo.

> The production of textiles has a long history in Teotitlán del Valle. At the end of the 15th century, the nobility of Teotitlán belonged to the province of Coyolapan that paid tribute to the kingdom of Moctezuma. They send 400 *cargas* (bundles) of embroidered textiles and 800 loads of large textiles to Tenochitlán every three months. The women wove cotton cloth on backstrap looms and thus were able to contribute to the obligations that the Mexica placed on their town. (Comité del Museo 1991–2001)

The Spaniards introduced wool and stand-up treadle looms to the community about 1535. Thus for more than four centuries Teotitecos have been producing wool textiles that have incorporated a wide range of shapes, designs, textures, and dying techniques. The emphasis on continuity with precolonial forms of production as a part of cultural memory production is a continuation of the strategy of firstness. It is simultaneously a subtle strategy for documenting colonization and survival through colonization when looked at in the context of larger portrayals of weaving techniques and knowledges. In the realm of folk art, Teotiteco textile production is considered representative of an authentic expression of indigenous Mexicanness. It is that, but it is also representative of the conditions of colonialism under which Zapotec weavers and other artisans lived after 1519.

Colonialism enters the museum website discussion on weaving:

> A partir del año 1521, la región de los Valles Centrales se quedó bajo el dominio español. Poco después empezaron los frailes dominicos con la evangelización de Teotítlan. Se cuenta que el primer obispo de Oaxaca, López de Zárate, trajo borregos de Europa entre 1535 y 1555 a Teotitlán. También introdujo el telar de píe y enseñó nuevas formas para tejer. Desde entonces nuestros antepasados adoptaron esa técnica, la combinaron con diseños propios dando inicio a una expresión artística única.

> After 1521, the region of the Central Valleys came under the control of the Spanish. A short time afterwards, Dominican Friars began to evangelize in Teotitlán. The first Bishop of Oaxaca, López de Zárate, brought European sheep to Teotitlán between 1535 and 1555. He also introduced the treadle loom and new forms of weaving. Since that time our ancestors have adopted that technique and combined it with our own designs to develop a unique form of artistic expression. (Comité del Museo 1999–2001)

On the website created by the cooperatives, colonial rule comes into focus more sharply. Aurora, Josefina, and other writers emphasize the ways in which their ancestors were used for their labor. The website text states,

> Under Spanish rule in the 16th century, indigenous towns continued to pay tribute under the system of *encomienda*. Indigenous peoples continued to produce cotton cloth and clothing that was sent to Spain. During the colonial period they also produced cochineal dye that became one of the most prosperous industries in New Spain.

The Spanish took advantage of indigenous skills in producing cloth and dyes and set up vast textile-producing workshops in some parts of Mexico. In Teotitlán, the Spaniards introduced the shuttle loom and wool and Teotitecos began to produce woolen products.

In describing their textiles today, cooperative members have made clear connections with their precolonial past both in how they describe their textiles and in visual representations showing traditional dye techniques. One cooperative that takes its name from the historical land mark Xiabets describes its work on the website as follows: "We are combining the modern with the traditional without losing the originality of the original pieces (and their designs) that have endured for more than five centuries in Teotitlán del Valle." This text is accompanied by a photograph of the group posed in front of a wide range of textiles hung in the background with traditional dye substances in the foreground. One group member is grinding cochineal dye on a *metate*, or mortar and pestle grinding stone. Metates are still used in the community to prepare traditional foods and to prepare dyes. Complementing the text, the photograph is a visual representation of continuity with the precolonial past.

Another group, Dgunna Ruinchi Laadti (Women Who Weave), which is linked to the first women's cooperative founded in 1986, describes one of the group's goals as "retaking elements of pre-Hispanic origin in the production of our *sarapes* and tapestries such as washing the wool using *amole* [a traditionally used plant that yields a soaplike substance] in place of detergent and using natural dyes such as cochineal, huizache and pomegranate."

The creation of web pages and other materials about themselves is a way for Teotiteco artisans to project the meaning of their arts for themselves wherever they are and to move beyond the market demands of capitalism. Cultural memory of place, physical elements of the landscape such as plants used for dyes, and the changing technology of the loom from backstrap to treadle-loom along with a change in material from cotton to wool are intimately linked to colonialism and their ability to survive and thrive as artisans over a long period of time.

Being Zapotec and Indigenous

A third element of the production of cultural memory reflected in these websites is an emphasis on being Zapotec and indigenous. A key element for defining *Zapotec* is not only the specific place-based elements discussed above, but also continued and even increased deployment of spoken and written Zapotec. This trend is all the more interesting given the fact that the use of Spanish has increased considerably over the past twenty years. By 2004, the linguistic norm in Teotitlán was bilingualism in Spanish and Zapotec, with a significant sprinkling of English learned while living and working in the United States or locally in order to communicate with American and European tourists. Since the mid-1980s (precisely when the number of Spanish speakers increased), the use of written Zapotec has significantly increased. Many of the signs in Teotitlán are now in Zapotec and Spanish and often in English as well—particularly for textile stores and businesses. The museum website has some texts in Zapotec, and all but one of the cooperatives that have emerged since the mid-1980s have adopted Zapotec names that they include on their collective website.

The emergence of a pan-Zapotec identification process began in the 1980s and 1990s as part of a larger articulation of indigenous rights movements that grew by leaps and bounds in the political opening created by the emergence of the EZLN and its initiation of peace accords focused in many ways on indigenous rights (see Stephen 2002; Mattiace 2003; Rus, Hernández, and Mattiace 2003). The heightened national discourse in the 1990s on what it means to be indigenous in Mexico has certainly affected the ways in which Teotitecos construct their ethnic and cultural identity in websites as well as in daily life interactions (for example, see chapter 7, where Pancho describes being Zapoteco in Oxnard, California).

Encouragement not only for panethnic identity construction but also for membership in "indigenous Mexico" has been expressed in contradictory ways in Mexican policy, politics, and popular culture. The rewriting of the Mexican Constitution in 1992 to recognize Mexico as a multicultural nation is consistently cited by cooperative leaders. They also often mention the San Andrés Accords on Indigenous Rights and Culture signed by the EZLN and the Mexican government in February 1996 but never implemented. National discussions about "the indigenous question" are still ongoing and occupy significant political space at local, state, and national levels. A wide range of networks, face-to-face interactions, and web materials are accessible to cooperative members and others in the community of Teotitlán focused on indigenous rights. The ever-widening network of people involved in creating a sense of

Zapotecness as well as of "being Indian" inside of Mexico and outside has added complexity to processes of cultural memory and ethnic identity production as manifested in messages of cultural distinctiveness reflected in digital arenas such as the Teotitlán websites.

The Frente Indígena de Organizaciones Binacionales: Transborder Digital Organizing in Mexico and the United States

The ability to simultaneously incorporate indigenous ethnic identities at local, regional, national, and even binational levels for specific political purposes and goals (see Fox 2006; Blackwell 2006) is aptly illustrated by the Frente Indígena de Organizaciones Binacionales (FIOB). The integration of different levels of ethnic identity and strategies of political organizing in the FIOB is closely linked to the personal histories of some of its key leaders. For example, Rufino Domínguez Santos began working on a local issue in his community, went on to work with a regional indigenous peasant organization in the Isthmus of Tehuantepec, and then began organizing indigenous migrants in Baja California and later California—all before helping to found the Frente Mixteco-Zapoteco Binacional (FM-ZB, Mixtec-Zapotec Binational Front), which later became the FIOB.

Rufino was born in 1965 in the Mixtec community of San Miguel Cuevas. He has a youthful face and wavy black hair that matches his dark eyes. He is an intense listener who simultaneously exudes energy and patience. Having more than two decades of political organizing experience under his belt, he is a charismatic speaker who is not afraid to push back hard at politicians and establishment figures, whether the president of Mexico, the governor of Oaxaca, or the governor of California. Rufino's political organizing trajectory has been influenced by his experiences in both Mexico and in the United States. In 2001, Rufino was given the Outstanding Community Leadership award by the Ford Foundation, the Advocacy Institute, and the Robert F. Wagner Graduate School of Public Service of New York University. Since December 2001, Rufino has served as general coordinator of the FIOB. He was elected to a second term in March 2005. I quote extensively below from his writing about his political formation and the origins of the FIOB as an illustration of how his individual experiences, the particular time period they occurred in, and the places they occurred in contribute to the complex vision of ethnicity brought by him and others to the FIOB. A multilevel model of ethnicity is also apparent on the virtual representations and texts of the FIOB on the Internet. He writes,

> Throughout my childhood, I worked in the fields with my father, tending livestock or carrying firewood on my back, carrying water, grinding corn. I also went to the primary school in my village. In 1979, I began attending secondary school in Juxtlahuaca. It was a long way from home, so I boarded with the Hermanos Maristas,[2] a group of Catholic monks who offered me housing, food, and financial help towards my studies. There were thirty of us in my cohort, youngsters from the Mixteco and Triqui ethnic groups.
>
> The monks taught us many things, from household chores to how to live a responsible life. We studied the Bible everyday with a sense of social awareness, attempting to understand the injustices our communities were suffering. The Maristas also taught us liberation theology. . . . What I am today I owe in large part to them and to my father, because that is how I began to organize people in my village to fight for change.
>
> In 1980, Deputy for Communal Property Gregorio Platón Gil began to abuse his power. He imposed fines on migrants who did not live in the village, and if they refused to pay they were incarcerated, expelled from the village, even threatened with death. He ordered the rape of women and burned down the houses of his opponents. I had to organize people so that we could change this.
>
> On October 30, 1983, after a year of organizing efforts, we decided to peacefully take over the municipio office and force Platón Gil to resign. Unfortunately, he was armed. Along with several of his supporters, he managed to force me and two of my companions into the municipio building, where we were detained and tortured for almost four hours. I thought I was going to be killed. Then my father arrived, accompanied by virtually the entire village—men and women alike—to rescue me. (Domínguez Santos 2004: 69–70)

In 1983, after he was tortured, Rufino left his town and went to study in Tehuantepec, Oaxaca. There he participated in protests organized by the Coalition of Workers, Peasants, and Students of the Isthmus (COCEI, Coalición de Obreros, Campesinos e Estudiantes del Istmo) (Stanley 2001).

> This is when the idea arose to create a Village General Assembly to depose this cacique; the assembly came into being in February 1983. In April 1984, I fled to Sinaloa state after receiving death threats. In Sinaloa we founded the Organization of Exploited and Oppressed People (OPEO) with the counsel

of Benito García Sánchez, leader of the Independent Central of Agricultural Workers and Peasants (CIOAC). I then traveled to Valle de San Quintín, Baja California. Although my original intention had been to cross the border into the United States, I stayed in San Quintín and participated in major mobilizations and strikes alongside CIOAC. I finally reached Madera, California, in November 1984, and since then I have been organizing migrant communities . . .

. . . In the mid-1980s, organizations of Oaxacans began to emerge in California spurred by a number of factors: the human rights violations indigenous migrants suffer, both in our own county and in the United States; discrimination; racism; unjust wages; our inability to communicate in languages other than our indigenous tongue; and our general lack of information regarding available social resources and our legal rights. Over time, one of the biggest challenges proved to be how to unite these organizations into a single organization that could best assist indigenous Oaxacan migrants. To this end, the central leaders from different organizations— Zapotecs César Sánchez Liébana and Rodrigo Ruiz, and Mixtecs Filemón López, Juan Lita, and myself—met in Los Angeles in October 1991 and founded the first coalition organization, the Mixteco-Zapoteco Binational Front (FM-BZ). . . .

. . . The FM-ZB soon began to grow and extend to other indigenous villages, including those of Triqui and Mixe, who called for a change in the organization's name. A Binational Assembly was convened in Tijuana in September 1995, which was attended by a hundred delegates from the states of Oaxaca, Baja California, México, and California. The assembly participants agreed to call the new organization the Oaxaca Indigenous Binational Front (FIOB) with no reference to any specific indigenous organizations . . .

. . . FIOB's organizational structure has several levels. The highest authority is the Binational General Assembly (AGB), which convenes every three years. The AGB elects the Central Binational Council (CCB), composed of ten members from Oaxaca, Baja California, and California; the CCB also has a group of advisors. The State Assembly is made up of members of the State Council and meets before the Binational General Assembly in each of the states. . . . The Regional Assembly in each state elects regional and district councils within that state. At the local level, local committees elect a Community assembly. We currently have three offices in Oaxaca, two in Baja California, and two in California, all with modern communications technologies (email, fax, telephone, and Internet) to support coordination of our binational activities. (Domínguez Santos 2004: 70–72)

As can be seen in Rufino's autobiographical narrative, his early experience with Marist priests combined an education in social justice with an interethnic experience as he went to school with both Trique and Mixtec students. His first political organizing was in his own community followed closely by an intense experience in 1983 with the COCEI. Formed in the 1970s, the COCEI is one of the earliest examples in Oaxaca of a regional, indigenous, peasant organization with a pan-Zapotec identity that succeeded in defending claims to land, credit, wages, benefits, and municipal services as well as using Zapotec ethnic identity as a strategic organizational focus (see Rubin 1997; Campbell 1993, 1994). In 1981, the COCEI won municipal elections and was allowed to govern for two and a half years until it was impeached by the Oaxaca state legislature and forcibly removed from office by army and police forces in 1983. Rufino took part in intense demonstrations by COCEI supporters at the time and observed what could happen to a regional organization that promoted cultural programs around Zapotec language and identity, reclaimed land, and developed public works projects benefiting the poor.

From Tehuantepec he returned to his own community to help organize a community assembly to rid San Miguel Cuevas of a local cacique and to democratize local government. From there he went to Sinaloa to work among agricultural workers with CIOAC and then to Baja California. In joining other indigenous leaders in 1991 to found what would become the FIOB, he brought his Oaxacan, Sinaloan, and Baja California experiences with him. By the early 1990s—both within Mexico and in the United States—panethnic indigenous organizing in relation to specific indigenous ethnicities (that is, Zapotec, Mixtec, etc.) had already consolidated (see Kearney 1988, 1995a; Nagengast and Kearney 1990) The formation of the FM-ZB occurred at a time when both panethnic and panindigenous organizing and conversations among indigenous Mexicans were on the rise within Mexico as well as in the United States.

When Mexico led the way in Latin America to the recognition of indigenous rights by being the first to ratify Convention 169 of the International Labor Organization (ILO) in 1989, a strong impetus for interethnic indigenous dialogue and organizing was generated. After changing Article Four of its constitution in 1990 to recognize Mexico as a nation having a pluricultural composition and the conferring of cultural rights on indigenous peoples, the state opened further ground for political debate and opposition when it conducted several fly-by-night "consultations" with indigenous peoples that left out most organizations and communities. Such tactics led to autonomous regional meetings that often protested the lack of input by indigenous peoples into the legislation process for implementing Article Four of the Constitution; the meetings also erected a platform for furthering indigenous discussions on the meaning of autonomy at a national level. For example, in Oaxaca, on September 6, 1993, a National Forum of Civil Society titled "The Poor Construct Their Own Social Policy" brought together indigenous representatives from Guerrero, Oaxaca, Chiapas, and Hidalgo who together developed a critique of the government's plan for implementing Article Four. Other similar meetings took place throughout Mexico. In 1992 many indigenous organizations participated in a wide range of activities protesting five hundred years of colonialism. This spurred the formation of the FM-ZB, according to Domínguez Santos: "FM-ZB was intended to coordinate with other indigenous organizations in opposition to official celebrations marking the Quincentenary of Christopher Columbus's arrival in the Americas" (2004: 71).

During this period in the early 1990s, technology was evolving, particularly the use of e-mail and faxes. The FM-ZB was not unusual in quickly turning to such electronic aids to coordinate political activities on both sides of the border. By 1992, the FM-ZB had communicated a list of needs to the governor of Oaxaca, Diodoro Carrasco Altamirano. It included specific demands for public works and community services in places such as Santa Cruz Mixtepec, Juxtlahuaca; Tlacolula, Oaxaca; San Fransisco Higos, Silacayoapan; and in Los Angeles and San Diego, California; the document also included demands from the Valley of San Quintín, Baja California. The communiqué that went out via e-mail, fax, and the newspaper of the FM-ZB/FIOB, *El Tequio*, read in part,

C. Lic. Diódoro Carrasco Altamirano
Constitutional Governor of the State of Oaxaca, City Hall
Oaxaca, Oaxaca

The representatives of the organizations that form the Zapotec-Mixtec Binational Front in California, USA, are addressing ourselves to the government of the state that you represent to demand your intervention and immediate resolution of the following:

Resolve the demands already set out by the government of the community of Santa Cruz Mixtepec, Juxtlahuaca, Oaxaca that consist of:

—Construction of a dam and a network of distribution canals
—Financial support to finish the municipal auditorium
—Installation of a national telegraph office
—Installation of a national telephone line. . . .

. . . Tlacolula, Oaxaca Demands

—Cancellation of the past municipal elections and convocation and realization of a popular referendum that will clean up and make transparent the recent results of municpal elections
—Financial and technical support for the potable water supply in order to meet the needs of the population of Tlacolula . . .

. . . San Fransisco Higos, Silacayoapan, Oaxaca demands:
—that you find a peaceful and negotiated solution to the conflict of agrarian boundaries that it has with the community of San Mateo Tunuchi, Tecomaxtlahuaca, Oaxaca. . . .

. . . The organizations of the Mixtec-Zapotec Binational Front, but particularly the Committee for Mixteco Social Unification (csum), demands the following for the Mixtecs in the Valley of San Quintín in Baja California Norte:

Respect for the rights of the labor union of Oaxacan agricultural workers and effective support on the part of state governments (Oaxaca and Baja California) and the federal government for the improvement of their material conditions of life.

In the 13 de Mayo (Colonia Vicente Guerrero) they need potable water and an elementary school.

In the Colonia "Nueva Era" (San Quintín) they need electricity, potable water, and an elementary school. . . .

. . . We demand financial support for the formation of the Casa de la Cultura Oaxaqueña in Los Angeles, California, under the direction and responsibility of the Oaxacan organizations in this area.

We demand that the government of the state give financial support for the purchase of instruments for the Mixtec philharmonic band that the Popular Mixtec Civic Committee is forming in the north county of San Diego.

We demand financial support for an annual basketball tournament "Benito Juárez" in the Los Angeles area . . .

. . . We demand the formation of a permanent bipartisan commission (Oaxacan state government and fm-zb) to deal with the problems of immigrant Oaxacan workers including: human rights, labor rights, rights to housing and that this commission take place in a venue on the northern border (Tijuana–San Diego).

Los Angeles, California. December 7, 1992
"For the Respect of the Rights of Indigenous Peoples."
(Frente Mixteco-Zapoteco Binacional 1992)

In this single document sent out to a wide range of e-mail lists and faxed to state government offices in Oaxaca and Baja California, the FM-ZB pulled together a set of demands from multiple locations in two states in Mexico and one in the United States. They used the communiqué as a way to set out a wide-ranging agenda that included public works, education, culture, and sports; the writing spoke to the very specific needs of particular communities but also articulated a demand for common cultural institutions such as a Casa de la Cultura Oaxaqueña (Oaxacan Cultural Center) in Los Angeles that would serve a panindigenous Oaxacan population. The document cites nine specific communities in Oaxaca, two specific neighborhoods, or *colonias*, in San Quintín, two cities in California, and a series of broad demands related to indigenous Oaxacan workers in Baja California and in the state of California—simultaneously articulating the local, the regional, and the binational with both very specific and far-reaching demands. The integration of these three levels of ethnic identity and an organizing model of strategically interlacing the three levels of action has continued to characterize the organization as well as its representation of itself on the Internet through its website and through archived editions of *El Tequio*, which is available online (archived issues date to 1992) (http://www.lan eta.apc.org/fiob/teqanteriores.html). The first edition of *El Tequio* was published in 1991.

In 1993, the FM-ZB held its first binational congress in Los Angeles, at which it set up an organizational structure and began to move forward with its first big project, creating a staff position for a person who would explain labor rights to Mixtec farmworkers in conjunction with California Rural Legal Assistance. This position was filled by Rufino Domínguez Santos. At the same time, the Frente also began to organize in Oaxaca with small productive projects growing pomegranates, cactuses, and strawberries to provide income for the family members of migrants to the United States who remained behind (Bacon 2002).

In 1993, the FM-ZB continued its efforts to network with other indigenous organizations in Mexico, in the United States, and around the world. In October 1993, Domínguez participated in a forum in Tlahuitolpec, Mixe, Oaxaca, titled the "Indo–Latin American Symposium: Fundamental Rights of Indigenous Peoples." International indigenous representatives from all over Latin America attended. Discussion centered on the concepts of culture, *pueblos* (peoples/communities),[3] territory, self-determination, and indigenous rights. The symposium was organized by Servicios del Pueblo Mixe, A.C., a regional Mixe organization that has close ties to FM-ZB/FIOB (*El Tequio* 1993).

That same month, two representatives went to the Ceremonial Center of the Otomi People ñatho ñahñu in Temoaya, México, where they participated in the Second Continental Encounter of Indigenous Peoples, Nations, and Organizations.[4] A major theme of this meeting was indigenous self-determination and coordination of indigenous rights at a continental level (the Americas). Arturo Pimentel, general coordinator of the FM-ZB at the time, also attended an international seminar in Santa Cruz, Bolivia, in October 1993 that focused on "strategies of development, systems of cooperation and investment in indigenous communities," bringing together representatives from Mexico and Bolivia. Then in November 1993, two FM-ZB activists participated in a forum in San Pablo Guelatao, Oaxaca, the "Third Assembly of the Zapotec Pueblos of the Sierra Juárez," at which a series of human rights violations were denounced and the protection of natural resources was discussed. The FM-ZB supported the demands of the meeting and publicized them through their networks (*El Tequio* 1993).

These kinds of regional and international meetings were crucial in helping the FM-ZB develop its networks. The exchange of information and construction of e-mail lists used to apply pressure in specific political campaigns were valuable resources generated at these meetings and others. The early 1990s were a historically strategic time for the thickening of networks of contacts, what I have here called meshworks after Escobar (2003). The importance of these networks in Latin America in addition to the connections forged in the early 1990s among Mexican, U.S., Latin American, and European networks of activists became quickly evident with the public appearance of the EZLN on January 1, 1994. As a binational indigenous organization already networked throughout Latin America and the United States, the FM-ZB became one of many support links for the EZLN in the campaign to stop the Mexican government from going to war in early 1994 and in subsequent solidarity and organizing efforts.

Following the Zapatista rebellion in 1994, FM-ZB mounted actions to pressure the Mexican government to not use military force and joined in hunger strikes and demonstrations in front of the offices of Mexican consulates and other government offices in California (Bacon 2002). The use of e-mail lists and faxes was crucial in these efforts, both in the United States and in Mexico. In September 1994, the FM-ZB held its second binational assembly in Tijuana, Baja California, where the principal objective was to change the name of the organization. That objective was met when the assembly renamed the organization the Frente Indígena Oaxaqueño Binacional (FIOB, Oaxacan Indigenous Binational Front), reflecting the integration of a wide range of Oaxacan indigenous ethnic groups into the organization. It also officially marked the articulation of a pan-Oaxacan indigenous identity category.

The effectiveness of the FIOB in putting the rights of indigenous workers in front of both the U.S. and Mexican governments was recognized by the EZLN in October 1995, when FIOB general coordinator Arturo Pimentel was named as an advisor to the EZLN for a large forum they convened entitled "Indigenous Rights and Culture" in San Cristóbal de las Casas in January 1996. Prior to the meeting in San Cristóbal, regional preparatory forums were held throughout Mexico and in the United States. The FIOB participated in a regional forum in Oaxaca and organized one in the city of Madera, California, sending out a joint call for participation with the EZLN (*El Tequio* 1996). That same year the FIOB opened up an office in Juxtlahuaca and organized the "First Conference on Indigenous Women in California." After the conference, a women's committee was set up to begin organizing women's productive projects on both sides of the border as well as to increase communication between indigenous women who did not attend the conference and FIOB.

An August 1996 binational action targeting the government of Oaxaca demonstrates the continued transborder nature of the FIOB's organizing and the use of Internet lists to mobilize participants. On August 6, a detailed e-mail was sent out to at least four Chiapas solidarity lists containing thousands of names as well as to a wide range of lists in Mexico and the United States (including Native net). The e-mail described a two-day binational action meant to coincide with the visit of Oaxacan governor Altamirano to Los Angeles on August 10. The action called for people from at least twenty-nine Mixtec communities in Oaxaca (including San Agustín Atenango) to block the highway running between Huajuapan de León, Juxtlahuaca, and Pinotepa Nacional. At the same time, the FIOB was organizing a peaceful occupation of the Mexican consulate in Los Angeles and holding a demonstration in Tijuana in the Plaza of Santa Cecilia (Rivera Salgado 1996). The list of demands directed to the governor included potable water, roads, a solution to land conflicts between communities in Oaxaca, ending the militarization of the Mixtec region, and respect for the FIOB. Like the 1992 communiqué cited above, many demands were very local and very specific. For example, demand number fifteen called for the installation of long distance telephone service, financial support for housing improvements for two hundred people, and support for a community credit association in San Agustín Atenango. After naming twenty-two specific communities in Oaxaca with similar demands, the 1996 communiqué voiced support for migrant housing in Baja California and for a basketball tournament and demanded that Mexican consuls in the United States recognize indigenous rights and set aside resources to attend to indigenous migrants (Rivera-Salgado 1996). The list of demands was sent, presumably by fax and e-mail, to the president of Mexico, to Mexican consular offices in California (Fresno, Los Angeles, and San Diego), and to the governor of Oaxaca.

In 1997, the FIOB inaugurated its own webpage. It was put together in Mexico City with the support of several organizations, including LaNeta, Oxfam America, and El Consejo de la Raza. While FIOB had previously been dependent on extensive use of e-mail lists, faxes, radio, and word of mouth to publicize their events, demands, and political actions, having a webpage added another dimension to their ability to reach a wider public. In an explanation of why the webpage is important, the FIOB states, "This technological advance of globalization is a very important instrument of struggle that can be very effective for an organization like ours because we can be seen and read about from any part of our Mother Earth" (Centro Binacional para el Desarollo Indígena Oaxaqueño).

The FIOB website has proven to be important in generating pressure from the United States and Mexico when FIOB activists have been threatened, detained, and jailed. In August 1998, Romualdo Juan Gutiérrez Cortés—a joint FIOB–PRD candidate for local congressional representative for the twenty-first district of Juxtlahuaca/Silacayoapan in the Mixteca region—defeated the ruling party (that is, the PRI) candidate, the first time that had ever happened in the district. After his victory was certified, FIOB leaders came under harassment in the Mixteca region of Oaxaca. Letters demanding that the harassment stop were sent to the

Oaxaca state government from the United States, Canada, Europe, and Asia, and they are credited by the FIOB with helping to protect leaders (Centro Binacional para el Desarollo Indígena Oaxaqueño). In 2002, upon completion of his term as state representative, Gutiérrez Cortés was arrested and jailed in Oaxaca on charges of armed robbery. The reason for his arrest apparently lay in a political struggle. An internal split in the FIOB in 2001 had resulted in the disavowal of former FIOB general coordinator Arturo Pimentel Salas when he refused to step down from his coordinator position after becoming a candidate for state representative. The FIOB's statutes stipulate that anyone holding an official FIOB position must resign if he or she becomes a formal political candidate with a political party (Domínguez Santos 2004:75). Refusing to resign, Pimentel sought revenge, and the arrest of Gutiérrez Cortés was part of this pattern of revenge. A wildfire e-mail campaign run from the FIOB webpage as well as through a broad range of lists resulted in the liberation of Gutiérrez Cortés and dismissal of all charges (*El Tequio* 2002).

The FIOB organizers also used Internet communication to organize a campaign in 2000 in the state of California to get indigenous migrants to register in the U.S. census as both indigenous and Hispanic (see chapter 7 for a discussion of Hispanic American Indians). A crucial facet of the campaign was offering assistance in the necessary languages (Zapotec, Mixtec, Mixe, Triqui, and others) to people in filling out their census forms in order to count not only as Latino, but also as indigenous. By building up a presence of indigenous Mexicans through the official forum of the census FIOB organizers hoped to be able to use the numbers to exert pressure for public resources. As stated in the FIOB newsletter,

> It is important to write or mark "Indigenous" or "Mixtec" or "Zapotec "or "Triqui" on the census form. Having a government statistic of the number of indigenous peoples who are living in this country [the United States] is important and will benefit us all in allowing us to solicit government services to meet the specific needs we have as indigenous peoples. (Vásquez 1999)

With this campaign, FIOB was taking panethnic identity to another level by seeking to establish a public and official profile for Oaxacan indigenous migrants within the broader racial/ethnic category of Latino. The mechanics of making this happen, however, involve the mobilization of specific ethnicities through language. Some Mixtec speakers could fill out their census forms to register as "Hispanic American Indians" only if they had Mixtec-specific translation that helped them to fill out the form in Spanish.

During the past ten years, FIOB has realized many of the projects that appeared as demands in the communiqués cited above from 1992 and 1996. The projects are grounded in local communities and neighborhoods in the three principal states the FIOB works in, California, Baja California del Norte, and Oaxaca, yet focus on cross-border issues and organizing strategies that function in the United States and Mexico alike. Funding sources in Mexico have included the National Indigenous Institute (INI), the National Commission for the Development of Indigenous Peoples, and the Oaxacan state government, among others. U.S. sources of project funding have included the Welfare Foundation, the MacArthur Foundation, the Ford Foundation, the Vanguard Foundation, the Rockefeller Foundation, the Inter-American Foundation, the National Endowment for Democracy, the California Endowment, and the Wellness Foundation (see Domínguez Santos 2004: 72–75; Cano 2005). In March 2005, the general coordinator announced that the FIOB would be dispersing $628,955 in its binational projects (Cano 2005).

The "Education and Training on Human Rights, Organizational Work, and Law Project" has trained ten men and women to work in migrant communities of origin and of settlement in Oaxaca and California. One of the most successful programs has been the "Project of Indigenous Interpreters," which has trained several groups of people in five indigenous languages of Oaxaca, including Chatino, Zapoteco, Triqui, Mixteca Bajo, and Mixteco Alto. This project also aided a sister organization in setting up a similar project with Mayan language interpreters. The FIOB-trained interpreters have worked in government offices, social services, and courts, not only in California, but also in Oregon, Washington, Arizona, Florida, and New York. Frequently, requests for FIOB-trained translators come through e-mail. The "Health Project for Indigenous Migrants" focuses on organizing workshops on health issues affecting indigenous communities and on promoting the diagnosis of diabetes, tuberculosis, HIV, and other diseases. The project functions in California's Central Valley and in Los Angeles (Domínguez Santos 2004: 72). In another project, twenty-five people have been trained in Madera and Fresno counties to raise awareness about how collective action can facilitate social change in migrant communities. Cultural activities such as the annual Guelaguetza celebrations of Oaxacan culture through music, song, and dance have been cosponsored by the FIOB, as have the annual Benito

Juárez basketball tournaments that now include participation by more than thirty teams of Oaxacan migrants (Centro Binacional Para el Desarollo Indígena Oaxaqueño).

In March 2005, at its fifth binational assembly in Oaxaca, 120 voting delegates from California, Baja California del Norte, and Oaxaca voted to change the name of the FIOB to reflect a wider panethnic vision. Keeping its acronym but dropping the "Oaxacan" part of its name, the FIOB changed its name to Frente Indígena de Organizaciones Binacionales. The leadership now has Purepecha representation from Michoacán. In a press release following the March assembly, FIOB articulated its broader indigenous membership:

> The Frente Indígena Oaxaqueño Binacional (Oaxacan Indigenous Binational Front or FIOB), founded fourteen years ago, has undergone changes in its membership in the past two years. The organization has expanded with the addition of new indigenous members, mainly migrants living in Baja California (Mexico) and California (United States), who come from the states of Guerrero, Hidalgo, and Michoacán, among others. These people have recognized our founding documents, our mission, our vision and our strategies for struggle to ensure a better future for our migrant and non-migrant communities on both sides of the border. (FIOB 2005)

The FIOB's more than twenty thousand members also ratified a new mission statement as follows: "To contribute to the development and self-determination of the migrant and non-migrant indigenous communities, as well as struggle for the defense of human rights with justice and gender equity at the binational level" (Cano 2005). With this statement and the name change, FIOB solidified its organizational definition of ethnic identity at a binational or transborder level to "migrant and non-migrant indigenous peoples/communities," which includes Mexico as an implicit part of the ethnic label. Declarations from the Fifth FIOB Binational Assembly in 2005 were transborder in scope and aimed at state and federal governments in both the United States and Mexico. They included calls for the Oaxacan governor, Ulises Ruiz Ortiz, to halt violence against municipal leaders waging social struggle and to open a dialogue with Oaxacan social organizations in the context of respect and plurality; rejection of HR 418, the Real ID Act, which prohibits states from issuing driver's licenses to undocumented immigrants (approved by the U.S. Senate and House in April 2005); rejection of George W. Bush's guest-worker initiative, which called for three-year renewable contracts for guest workers; support for finalizing Mexican legislation that would permit Mexicans living abroad to vote in national elections; a call to the Mexican senate to find an immediate solution to the demands by former braceros that their tax contributions to the U.S. government be returned to them; a call to support labor rights in Baja California; and finally a call linked to more specific demands to address the needs of indigenous peoples living in Baja California (FIOB 2005). The new mission statement and demands were posted immediately on the FIOB website.

Conclusions

The FIOB has consistently and successfully combined a transborder approach to organizing with the recognition of indigenous ethnic identity as being simultaneously rooted in communities, in specific ethnic/languages groups, in the state of Oaxaca, and now throughout Mexico. The virtual transborder organizing of the FIOB has matched this profile, first, through e-mail and fax campaigns and, second, through its website and print and web-based newsletter, *El Tequio*. Both FIOB and the weavers of Teotitlán through their museum and cooperative website have insisted on the importance of being able to scale ethnic identity up or down and have insisted, in fact, on the importance of projecting indigenous ethnic identity simultaneously across multiple levels and borders. Through their digital productions invoking both the rootedness of place and place-based histories and transborder and transhistorical presences, the indigenous activists in FIOB and from Teotitlán del Valle have constituted their own theories of contemporary indigenous Mexican ethnicity. If we closely examine the ways in which the two groups have constructed their identities in digital form, we can learn much about indigenous models of ethnicity.

While social scientists have been busy debating whether or not indigenous ethnicities have moved from the local level to the regional level to the transnational level, indigenous intellectuals such as Josefina Jiménez and Aurora Bázan López from Teotitlán del Valle and Rufino Domínguez Santos from FIOB have set out in practice their own definitions. Rather than labeling their efforts as either essentialist or constructionist, I suggest that we embrace their examples of geographical, spatial, and historical multisitedness and simultaneity and let them speak for themselves.

The digital materials and networks constructed by FIOB activists and

Teotiteco weavers are a tangible part of transborder lives that both embrace and challenge dominant models of globalization. Place- and geography-specific elements of Teotiteco and FIOB ethnic identities insist on a particular location as one part of the cultural memory of ethnic identity production. For the Teotitecos who made the museum and cooperative websites, it is their emphasis on firstness in terms of being an original Zapotec population site in Oaxaca, and that is the center of their rootedness in place. For the FIOB, it is their continued presence in and representation of demands from specific local communities in Oaxaca where migrants are from as well as specific communities in Baja California and California where they have settled. Such community-local specificity works against the cultural homogenization that is inherent in the branding phenomenon of globalization—loyalty to a brand, not to a specific product at a global level. At the same time, Teotiteco and FIOB activists have incorporated panethnically specific levels of ethnicity— that is, "Zapotec" and "Mixtec"—and panindigenous levels of ethnicity —"indigenous peoples"—into their political and cultural strategies. Panethnic and panindigenous levels of identity suggest a certain level of shared understandings, values, and goals with others who are not from the same community, the same region, or even the same state of Mexico, but who are struggling around shared issues in the United States and in Mexico.

Just as indigenous migrants such as the Zapotec and Mixtec documented here crossed many borders that they did not invent (racial, ethnic, class, state, national, legal, gender), their multilayered approach to ethnic identity deployment suggests the possibility of retaking these boundaries and using them effectively for concrete political, cultural, and economic objectives as well as resituating themselves in histories.

If we return to Linda Tuhiwa Smith's call for indigenous research projects, the digital materials created by FIOB and Teotiteco weavers offer ready examples of "survival of peoples, cultures, and languages; the struggle to become self-determining, the need to take back control of our destinies" in a transborder and globalized context (Smith 1999: 142).

Stuck: A Cross-Border Telephone Conversation

Natalia Gómez Bautista from Teotitlán del Valle (introduced in chapter 6) had her son Rodolfo call me and leave a message to be in touch with her. I have known Natalia and Rodolfo for twenty-three years. Such messages come when she is truly worried about something. Having not had a telephone in her life until ten years ago, she is not accustomed to calling just to say hello. My oldest son took the message, which, he reported, had been left in English. Rodolfo speaks very good English, learned during the years he worked in a nursery in Santa Ana, California. I call back to talk with Rodolfo and Natalia.

After ten rings, Natalia answers the phone. I imagine her slowly walking from the yard into the small storefront where the Telmex telephone is located. Natalia opened a small store in the front room of her house many years ago to help with her family's cash flow. The phone was installed some ten years ago. It is in constant use. There is often a line of people waiting to talk with relatives in Tijuana and in the United States. The phone is accessed by buying a phone card that has credit on it for a specific amount—twenty pesos, fifty pesos, one hundred pesos. This phone is used by families in the surrounding block who don't have a telephone line of their own. Probably 80 percent of the conversations are between Teotitlán and Santa Ana, usually in a mixture of Zapotec and Spanish. We also speak in Spanish with some Zapotec.

NATALIA: Hello?

LYNN: Hello, Natalia, How are you?

NATALIA: I am doing okay. I was making lunch. It takes me a long time to walk across the yard to the phone. You know, my knees are still bothering me. One day they are okay, the next day they are not. Up and down. I was also really sick in March and April. My daughter Martina came back from

California and was here for six weeks taking care of me. It's hard for her to leave her job and come. So now she wants me to move to Los Angeles to live with her. She says if I am close by she can take care of me.

LYNN: Do you want to go?

NATALIA: Well, what would I do there? When I went to Tijuana I didn't even like the food there. I can't imagine what it's like on the other side. What will I do when she goes to work? Who will I talk to?

LYNN: Well, can you stay there in Teotitlán?

NATALIA: My son says he wants to go back to the United States to make some money. Things are really difficult here. The two clients who buy our *serapes* have stopped coming. We don't have any money right now. My son says he wants to go to work in California. He says I should go with him. But I told him I can stay here while he is gone.

LYNN: Will you stay alone? Can you walk to the market to buy food?

NATALIA: No, I can't really walk very far.

LYNN: What do you think about someone coming to live with you?

NATALIA: Well, maybe. I don't know who it would be. All my children and grandchildren are in the United States in Santa Ana . . . I could go, but . . . I can't really walk over the border either.

LYNN: And will your son leave you alone?

NATALIA: No. He says he won't do that. So we are kind of stuck. Stuck in a bad situation. My children are all there and can't really leave, and I can't leave here. This is my home.

Natalia and I have had this conversation many times over the past ten years as she has gotten older and her health has declined. All of her children except for her youngest son are in the Los Angeles area of California. Her youngest son has remained in the house with her and struggled with some help from his siblings to support his aging parents. Natalia's husband died several years ago of long-term diabetes. While most of her children have firmly built a life in the United States, she has never wanted to go, clinging strongly to her home, friends, and the cultural traditions of Teotitlán del Valle. Like many transborder families, hers is stuck in the political, cultural, and economic integration of the United States and Mexico—both sobered by the limitations and challenged by the possibilities.

The Rule of Juxtaposition

In my search for a metaphor to describe the "stuck" position articulated by Natalia about her transborder extended family, what Homi Bhabha calls "the rule of juxtaposition" or "the unsolvable dialectic" seems most apt (n.d.). In a close reading of William Edward Burghardt Du Bois's novel *The Dark Princess: A Romance*, Bhabha explores how Du Bois juxtaposes irresolvable contrasts such as the Jim Crow color line of the South and the beauty of a sunset in Montego Bay. In part, Bhabha suggests that the novel explores links between Indian nationalism and black nationalists in the United States at a time when international discussions of racial equality were on the rise. In the novel, Bhabha argues, the search for solidarity reveals the contradictions of difference as characters encounter the "color line within the color line" in a discourse of international racial solidarity. Using the metaphor of "the rule of juxtaposition" and "the unresolvable dialectic of Hegelian thinking cross time and cultures," Bhabha suggests a strategy for reading interlinked contradictions. Here I find his metaphor useful for understanding the juxtaposition of the limits and possibilities generated by the globalization of capital, culture, migration, and politics.

The rule of juxtaposition can be seen here as the simultaneous coexistence of (1) the integration of the U.S. and Mexican political economies through trade, immigration, and other state- and corporate-driven policies resulting in increased stratification in both countries and increased poverty at the lower levels of society with (2) the increased movement of people across borders and their increasing political and cultural presence as manifested through social movements, cultural production, declaration of different kinds of citizenships, and the sharpening of multileveled ethnic differences situated in a transborder context. The rule of juxtaposition allows us to avoid the dilemma of either declaring transborder migrants as the new force of change in the Americas or predicting that the power relations of capital will generate a doomsday finale of neverending exploitation and immobility for transborder communities. Instead, I have chosen to mesh the structural constraints imposed by global relations of economic and political power with the possibilities generated by the increased movement of peoples within and across borders and the recomposition of local, regional, national, and transborder and binational spaces that results.

Construction of the Global through Partial Denationalization:
Trade and Immigration Policy

In her continuing theorization of globalization, Saskia Sassen has pointed out how the global and the national significantly overlap and interact in the late twentieth and early twenty-first centuries. For example, she argues that "the global economy" is not something that can just be taken as a given. On the contrary, the global economy has to be produced and secured, often through national structures (2001: 262). She elaborates:

> Global processes are often strategically located/constituted in national spaces, where they are implemented usually with the help of legal measures taken by state institutions. The material and legal infrastructure that makes possible the global circulation of financial capital, for example, is often produced as "national" infrastructure—even through increasingly shaped by global agendas. This insertion into the national of global projects, originating both domestically and externally, begins a partial unbundling of national space. It is only partial, as the geography of economic globalization is strategic, rather than diffuse. (2001: 264)

Ultimately, Sassen suggests that these insertions of the global into the national result in a partial denationalization that can change the properties of the national (2005: 265).

Here, I want to use Sassen's suggestion of how the global is constituted in part through the national by looking specifically at how this process has occurred through trade and immigration policies linking the United States and Mexico. I see the process of U.S.-Mexican integration as part of what Sassen is describing as globalization built in part through a partial denationalization. Like Sassen, I feel that transborder migrants are one of the subjects that are capable of illuminating this process.

One of the important dimensions of globalization through the national has to do with the ways in which labor and consumer markets are globally integrated and mediated through trade and immigration policy at national and binational and, increasingly, multinational levels. In the case of U.S.-led trade and immigration policies, such processes of globalization must also be linked to what some have called "the new imperialism" (Harvey 2003). Multilateral trade agreements such as the North American Free Trade Agreement (NAFTA) and the Central American Free Trade Agreement (CAFTA) take uneven national economic playing fields and place them in competition with one another. The result is often a small gain in jobs in service, assembly, or technical sectors for a few at the expense of the loss of many more jobs in small manufacturing, agriculture, and other sectors. NAFTA is a textbook example of this and a sound predictor of what is likely to happen with CAFTA.

While we have often thought of global trade agreements as facilitating the movement of capital and goods, they are also de facto labor and immigration policies. The coupling of labor policy with immigration policy has a long precedent in the United States, particularly with regard to its relationship to Mexico. A key contradiction of the past five decades of U.S.-driven trade and immigration policy toward Mexico is that trade agreements that were supposed to stimulate job growth in Mexico and immigration policies that were supposed to limit and slow down Mexican immigration to the United States have had the opposite effect. They have worked together to encourage and indirectly facilitate Mexican immigration to the United States—particularly undocumented immigration (see Massey, Durand, and Malone 2002).

One result of this increased Mexican migration to the United States— particularly over the past two decades—has been the thickening and enrichment of what I call transborder communities. While many scholars write of contemporary transborder communities as "deterritorialized" and "reterritorialized," my research suggests that this process is not new—just accelerated and intensified. In fact, one early colonial historical source documents Zapotec migration to what is now Chiapas and Guatemala before 1520. In the *Relación de Iztepexig* (referring to the Zapotec sierra town of Ixtepeji), it is noted that in order to pay tribute to Moctezuma and to the Mixtecos who were their regional rulers, the people of Ixtepeji "went to Tehuantepec to look for the gold and feathers that they had to provide and to the provinces of Soconusco [modern-day Chiapas] and Guatemala, renting themselves out as cargo carriers to the merchants and also in cultivation of lands in those provinces where they remained from six to seven months to a year" (my translation) (Acuña 1984: 255).[1] In other words, the indigenous peoples of Oaxaca—at least the Zapotec and probably others as well—have been engaging in border-crossing migration for more than five centuries.

I deliberately use the term *transborder communities* instead of *transnational* because migration has a long history, going back even before the twentieth century in many places, and the boundaries being crossed entail much more than the U.S.-Mexican border. The local and regional specificities of migration histories are central factors in just how transborder communities have come to be constituted in the twenty-first century. In other words, U.S. trade and immigration policy have been crucial structural influences, but particular local histories, cultures, and understandings of migration are also important. In some places, such histories and circumstances have yielded instances of transborder organizations and networks that can defy the object of empire—promoting corporate capitalism and privatizing resources, space, and all imaginable forms of intellectual property.

During the past several decades of U.S.-Mexican relations embedded in the global economy the following concrete outcomes of economic and immigration policy have had profound implications for patterns of migration to the United States from Mexico:

—the loss of price supports for subsistence farmers in Mexico;
—the loss of corn and other basic crop markets for small farmers due to flooding of Mexican market with U.S. corn and other crops;
—lower average wages for rural and urban workers in Mexico;
—a net loss of jobs in Mexico;
—the development of service sector jobs and continuation of farm labor jobs in the United States, often dependent on undocumented workers;
—a lack of enforcement of employer sanctions in the United States for hiring undocumented workers;
—a combination of granting of legal residency to amnestied workers and steady reenforcement of the U.S. border, which has reduced return visits to Mexico and encouraged family members to come to the United States and remain;
—increased numbers of undocumented migrants from Mexico, particularly from 1990 to the present;
—an increase in the presence of indigenous migrants, further diversifying the migrant pool;
—since the 1940s, several waves of Mexican migration (often linked to U.S. policies such as the bracero program, IRCA, and IIRIRA), each creating sets of networks running from communities in Mexico to the United States and to different sites within the United States and Mexico.

This list of outcomes suggests the ways in which U.S. economic and immigration policy designed to support processes of globalization—particularly the circulation of capital and goods—have also resulted in the circulation of people and the creation of communities, networks, institutions, social movements, and forms of cultural production and communication which work across the national in ways that can be seen as one aspect of the partial denationalization processes described by Sassen. An important addition to Sassen's ideas of partial denationalization is the model of simultaneity of location, space, and levels of identity that indigenous transborder migrants have constructed through their individual and collective experiences as documented here.

Concepts for Understanding Transborder Lives

A key criterion for building on transborder activists' insights into how to conceptualize their lives is to avoid dichotomies. I have relied here on a set of integrative concepts to facilitate transborder understandings of legality and citizenship, labor, gender and family relations, ethnicity, and grassroots organizing. The idea of interlinked networks or meshworks (Escobar 2003) can help us to conceptualize how people in communities like San Agustín Atenango and Teotitlán del Valle are connected to one another through ties of kinship, *compadrazgo*, and transborder forms of association such as hometown associations or transborder public works committees; it can also show how each of these nodes in a network is linked to other kinds of organizations and networks in the United States and Mexico. As a transborder or binational organization, the FIOB is also a part of a widely articulated set of networks linked to many transborder communities in Oaxaca, to indigenous rights networks worldwide, to immigrant rights networks, and more.

The concept of "social field" (Glick Schiller 2003; Levitt and Glick Schiller 2004) enables us to visualize the simultaneity of connections that transborder migrants have in more than one physical location at once and how the social, economic, political, and religious activities of one community stretch across space and borders. Multiple sets of laws, institutions, values, and social conventions can work at once within one social field, as seen, for example, in the case of male farmworkers who learn the rules of undocumented farm labor in labor camps, participate in U.S. churches and immigrant rights organizations, and return home to take on a cargo as part of their community citizenship requirements in Oaxaca.

The rapidly changing composition of many parts of the United States to include ever-growing numbers of Latino, primarily Mexican, immigrants who are multiracial and multiethnic in their collective composition has resulted in a growing sector of Mexican migrants who are developing a "presence" that is somewhere between powerlessness and the condition of "being an actor even though one is initially lacking in political power" (Sassen 2002: 22). As the presence of Mexican indigenous migrants grows in the West, South, and elsewhere, their incorporation into ongoing political processes and their initiation of their own political processes can result in the declaration of alternative kinds of citizenships that are distinguished from legal citizenship in the United States and Mexico.

In a review of literature on transnational citizenship, Jonathan Fox suggests that there are two domains for citizenship. The first domain is rights as "enforceable claims on public authorities (national or international)." The second domain is understood in terms of "membership in society-based political communities (i.e., those defined by ethnonational identities or transformative ideologies, which in turn could be civic or religious)" (2005: 193). By opening up two possible domains for citizenship, Fox's model enables us to talk about citizenship in relationship to states, on the one hand (the United States and Mexico in this case), and in relationship to what Renato Rosaldo, William Flores, and Rina Benmayor have called cultural citizenship, on the other—the everyday activities through which marginalized social groups can claim recognition, public space, and eventually specific rights (Flores and Benmayor 1997: 15). Indigenous peoples in Mexico and the United States have been involved in an ongoing struggle, first, to establish legitimate forms of cultural citizenship and, second, to move some parts of their cultural citizenship into the arena of legal citizenship as formal rights defined in the constitutions and legal codes of specific nations and international governing bodies. Transborder indigenous migrants have been involved in similar processes, often working within two national contexts to expand their rights.

In terms of transnational citizenship, Fox suggests three forms. The first is parallel transnational participation that "refers to individuals who are active in more than one political community, but whose organized communities do not themselves come together." As an example, he points to Mixtec indigenous farmworkers in Oregon (discussed here in chapter 8) who participate simultaneously in PCUN and in the San Agustín Transborder Public Works Committee. The two organizations have not yet come together. Interestingly enough, however, the two organizations and specific individuals in them have been linked through the

FIOB, an association Fox characterizes as engaging in "simultaneous binational participation" (2005: 189). The simultaneous multisited actions of the FIOB in Tijuana, Los Angeles, and on the highway linking many towns in the Mixteca region of Oaxaca in 1996 would be one such example. In contrast to the parallel participation of people from San Agustín in PCUN and in the Transborder Public Works Committee, through FIOB, "migrants use the same membership organization to fight for human rights vis-à-vis local, state, and national governments" (Fox 2005: 188). Integrated transnational participation, Fox writes, involves "multiple levels and arenas, as in the FIOB's trajectory, or the application of the concept of multilevel citizenship to describe membership in local, regional, national, and transnational polities in Europe" (2005: 189). While Fox seems to grant participants in the FIOB and in PCUN and the San Agustín Transborder Public Works Committee legitimate transnational citizenship according to his criteria of domains and intensity of activity of membership, shared political ideals, mutual affinity, shared targets, and joint action, he ultimately suggests that "the terms *dual* or *multiple* citizenships are preferable to the more open-ended concept of transnational citizenship. Multi-layered citizenship is evocative and captures meaningful new trends, but there is nothing necessarily cross-border about it." (2005: 195).

While some members of the two transborder communities focused on here would meet Fox's criteria for transnational citizenship, others would not. And some would meet the criteria at one point in their lives and not at another. Posing strict criteria for conceptualizing transnational citizenship can be useful from a formal analytical perspective but may not prove as useful as the more loosely defined concepts of cultural citizenship or multiple citizenships to capture the evolving sense of participation in political communities either simultaneously in different places or in political communities that in and of themselves operate across borders. What is surely evident is that the concept of citizenship must be expanded to take account of the multiple ways in which transborder migrants are building political presence on many dimensions and participating in a wide range of political spaces and movements as a part of their transborder lives.

A final conceptual lesson gained through analysis of the cultural production of transborder indigenous migrants included here is an understanding of ethnicity as simultaneously incorporating community, place-based definitions with panethnic and panindigenous models of identity usually linked to national identity. The FIOB model of simultaneously projecting demands for one particular Mixtec community in Oaxaca of Baja California with demands for Oaxacan indigenous migrants as well as all Mexican indigenous migrants is an example of this. The same kind of logic is found in Teotitecos' projection of themselves as the "original" indigenous settlement in Oaxaca, as Zapotec, and as a part of indigenous Mexico—both in the United States and in Mexico. A similar conceptualization of ethnicity can be found among Zapatista communities living in rebellion in Chiapas (see Fox 2006: 48; Stephen 2002). The fact that similar understandings of indigenous ethnic identity have evolved in different parts of Mexico and among Mexicans suggests that a multileveled concept of ethnicity should become the norm and not the exception in social science analysis. This idea builds on Gupta's and Ferguson's suggestion that what have often been thought of as "marginal zones" or borderlands (not necessarily literal, but symbolic or transborder in the sense understood here) are a more adequate conceptualization of the "normal" locale of the postmodern subject (1992: 18).

Policy and Programs

Consideration of the contradictions inherent in processes of globalization in relation to U.S. trade policy toward Mexico permits us to visualize the ways in which policies intended only to promote the movement of capital and goods have been deeply intertwined with the movement of people and have interacted with immigration policy. The long-term results of U.S. trade and immigration policy have been to dramatically increase the number of undocumented Mexican migrants to the United States, to encourage them to stay longer, and to facilitate the thickness and richness of transborder communities and networks over time. While specific state-based policies such as the bracero program implemented by the U.S. and Mexican governments in 1942 and NAFTA, implemented by the same two states in 1994, have significantly affected directly and indirectly where, when, and how people have migrated within Mexico and also to the United States, the power of these policies in the lives of indigenous migrants is also deflected, refracted, and refocused through the changing larger contexts that transborder communities develop and change in. As migrant networks developed and thickened with time in specific locations within Mexico and later in the United States, these networks and the people and resources attached to them have come to be able to compete with and in many cases outsmart state-controlled legal systems, labor markets, political systems, and border-patrolling institutions and technologies. These communities are both beyond and within the control of nation-states. Anthropology and particularly ethnography can serve as an important tool for helping to conceptualize the ways in which transborder communities are negotiating the contradictions of empire. Ideas such as meshworks, social fields, transborder, transnational, and cultural citizenship offer ways of understanding the significant social, economic, cultural, and political relations that migrants are building in the age of neoliberal globalization and the new imperialism.

Beyond generating useful conceptual tools for understanding transborder lives we might also ask what kind of immigration policy would make sense to decrease the risks for those living in such communities. As of the writing of these conclusions a variety of proposed acts are on the table in Congress. Rather than address each one specifically I want to suggest a philosophy that calls for recognizing and adjusting the status of large numbers of people who are already here and contributing economically, socially, culturally, and politically to both the United States and to Mexico. In addition, we need to radically rethink current strategies for militarizing and patrolling the border. Much higher levels of cooperation and teamwork are necessary with the justice system and various police and armed forces of Mexico and the United States. The primary routes for crossing from Mexico into the United States are not controlled by the U.S. Border Patrol, but by interlinked groups of drug and people smugglers based on both sides of the border, groups who clearly pay protection money to armed forces and the police. Until very high levels of corruption within the Mexican justice system and armed and police forces are addressed on a binational basis with similar standards on the U.S. side of the border, the high levels of danger currently associated with crossing will not decrease.

Of the deaths of migrants on the border, many are from the states of Mexico, Guanajuato, Veracruz, and the heavily indigenous states of Oaxaca and Chiapas (Marosi 2005). In addition are the *desaparecidos*—the disappeared who died but were never found. Their fate remains an open wound in the hearts of their family members and transborder communities.

Notes on Collaborative Research

The eight years of research reflected in this book have been informed by what I call collaborative activist ethnographic research, a term I would like to reflect on a bit. What do the words "collaborative activist ethnographic research" mean, individually and collectively?

TO COLLABORATE: To work or cooperate with others, to participate or take part in or have a share with others, as in an activity or quality;

ACTIVIST: To take specific action in support of a particular sociopolitical process with which one is aligned and to which one feels accountable (see Hale 1997: 836; Falla 1997);

ETHNOGRAPHY: Sherry Ortner defines ethnography as "the attempt to understand another life world using the self—as much of it as possible—as the instrument of knowing" (Ortner 1995: 173). In this same description Ortner emphasizes Geertz's commitment to thickness as one of the key parts of ethnography: "producing understanding through richness, texture, and detail rather than parsimony, refinement, and (in the sense used by mathematicians) elegance" (1995: 173);

RESEARCH: systematic study or investigation in a particular field, usually as a basis for arriving at new facts and interpretations.[1]

As we see from these definitions, there are some aspects of what I am calling collaborative activist ethnographic research that are on a collision course. Collaboration implies cooperation, having a share or a part in a process. Being an activist suggests that one is aligned and committed to a particular sociopolitical process. Ethnography invokes the self and rich description as a means to knowing, while research suggests uncovering facts, information, and interpretations. The notion of research leaves uninterrogated whether or not such information, facts, and interpretations are the result of particular processes and locations or simply exist in the world waiting to be committed to paper. Obviously, collaborative activist research—whether of an ethnographic nature or not—suggests close attention to the process of research as well as to the agenda behind it and the impact of the research on those who participate. Collaborative activist ethnography thus suggests that major attention be paid to what have been called by some the politics of location. By invoking this term, I follow the lead of Interpal Grewal and Caren Kaplan (1994), who propose that we acknowledge the differences between ourselves as researchers and those we may collaborate with, and that we situate what we are doing in the transnational political economy and take responsibility for the ways that difference is coded in national and transnational structures of capital, power, and culture.

Collaborative activist ethnography requires a deep questioning of many of the issues of the politics of location, which implies not only an interrogation of the location of the anthropologist, but also of collaborating institutions and actors. There are internal hierarchies in communities, organizations, and families which form an important part of most collaborative contexts. At the same time, we have to go beyond self-flagellation about the imperialism and neocolonialism of all anthropological endeavors and attempt to honestly and critically assess what Charlie Hale has called "analysis that is politically positioned and accountable without subordinating analytical rigor to conclusions driven by a pre-established political agenda" (Hale 1997: 837). This is a notable challenge in collaborative research, where a presumed common political agenda is often the unspoken reason why anthropologists work with particular organizations and actors and vice versa. In what I have called activist research, the presumed underlying commitment by all to the same sociopolitical process or cause may be a major pitfall; it may impede collaborations from actually functioning and producing results that can be held accountable to some kind of analytical rigor and not be measured just in terms of political correctness.

The following dimensions and questions about collaborative activist ethnography have been brought to my attention and I would like to share them with readers:

1. The locations of collaborating participants (class, race, gender, sexuality, region, language, ethnicity) and global connections. How are the participants linked to each other through global, national, and regional structure of power, capital, and culture?

2. Internal hierarchies found within collaborating groups. Are there internal hierarchies of power in organizations that affect the outcome of projects? Leaders and staff versus membership in an organization as well as gender, ethnic, age, and class variation can translate into power differences within an organization.

3. The political frames assumed by the differing participants. Is the topic politically meaningful in one way for one group of participants and meaningful in another way for another group of participants?

4. Analytical orientations of participants. What is considered analysis? What is considered useful analysis? Is there equal interest in all aspects of the project by all participants? If the primary emphasis is on one category of analysis, does that squeeze out other categories?

5. The audience—who is a particular "product" created for? This can determine the form that it takes (book, video, brochure, mural, etc.) and the language and perspective used.

6. The access to resources that all participants have. What kinds of resources do different participants have? How does that impact power relations in the collaborative project?

7. The stakes for participants in the outcomes of research—political and otherwise. How have all participants experienced and been affected by the topic of the study? How are they aligned in relation to the political forces present? To whom are they accountable? What expectations are there for the research? (See Hale 1997: 836.)

8. Censorship and decision making. How are disagreements settled? How are different "truths" documented? Should all participants sign a letter of agreement or contract?

I have found that collaborative research entails a commitment to the integration of the self, of individual stories and perspectives, as key ingredients in the way that information is conveyed—in the spirit of an ethnographic approach. Both point first and foremost to the importance of the politics of location, in which the power relations that permeate the group or groups of people involved in one project are central to the way the project is planned, what kind of information is gathered, how it is gathered, what is released, and how it is packaged. Both internal hierarchies of power along lines of class, ethnicity, race, gender, and other dimensions as well as the global, national, and local links that tie people together through the structures of power, capital, and culture become major sources of tension in collaborative activist ethnographic research.

If significant differences in power, in access to resources, and in the stakes in the outcomes of the research are not addressed, then egalitarian decision-making processes—however well intentioned—cannot function. One of the key lessons I have learned is to acknowledge differences in power, access to resources, and the stakes of the outcome of the research among participants and to set up mechanisms in decision-making processes to attempt to compensate for these differences.

Flexibility is another key ingredient in decision-making processes in collaborative research. It is highly likely that those within an organization who have positions of authority and who have been participating for long periods of time in an organization will have more influence in what kind of information is collected from whom and in what form the final analysis takes. If the process for debating disagreements allows for different points of view and takes into account views that emerge in the process of research, then we have a better chance of producing results that have some degree of rigor in their content and analysis and are not just crafted to meet preconceived notions of what is "the correct story."

Conducting collaborative activist research in situations where there are high levels of conflict requires intense scrutiny about the impact of research on those who participate. If the project involves people who live inside a particular set of political forces and others who live outside, then this has to be considered very seriously in setting up decision-making processes related to the release of information. Those most directly influenced by the outcome of the research should have the greatest say in what information is released to whom, in what form, and when. These are questions that need to be thought about in short-term information gathering as well as in longer-term projects where there may be a significant lag time between the time information is collected and when it is released. One of the major problems for many organizations in collaborating with traditional ethnographic work is that if the product is going to be an ethnography, it will take years before the information is published. One possible solution is to think of different types of "products" from the collaborative research such as webpages and e-mail list postings that address the immediate needs of collaborating organizations and can also provide material for richly researched ethnographies.

In sum, collaborative activist ethnographic research is a complex model for conducting anthropology. It is infinitely more time-consuming and fragile than the solo anthropologist collecting data and publishing those data when he or she is ready to do so. Collaborative research, however, is rapidly becoming the norm in many situations in which anthropologists work. Communities and organizations around the world are increasingly educated and part of larger movements for civil, human, and labor rights that have as their bottom line the right of people to control information about themselves and even their own biological material. Anthropology has a golden opportunity to reform many of the older models of fieldwork to match this current reality. Rather than delegate collaborative research to the realm of "applied anthropology" and believe that it is not analytically rigorous, why not follow a model for collaborative research that allows both for useful outcomes for collaborating organizations and individuals as well as theoretically interesting and well-written ethnography (see Singer 2000)? If anthropologists cannot rise to the challenge of producing results that are useful to those they work with as well as interesting to an audience of anthropologists and students, our ability to influence policy and public opinion will continue to decline. Let's rise to the occasion.

Preface

1 Civil and religious *cargos* are part of a local system of governance based on more than 250 unpaid jobs. Jobs range from mayor, judges, and police officers, to service on school and irrigation committees. They also include firefighters, service on committees regulating the use of communal land, and jobs caring for the local Catholic Church. The communal land system also involves a series of volunteer jobs or cargos that include commissioner, secretary, treasurer, representatives, and service on a vigilance committee to secure the boundaries of the community's titled communal land.

2 Among Mixtecs in Oregon, I conducted thirty life-history interviews of two to four hours each; in-depth interviews with growers, contractors, union staff, social service providers, and others who work closely with Mixtec migrants; extensive participant observation in homes, in the fields, in labor camps, in food processing facilities, at cultural events, rallies, and at political events where Mixtec migrants participate; many hours of conversation with Mixtec farmworkers; archival research on the history of farmworkers, their organizations, and Mexican and Mixtec cultural organizations. I also collected data on Mixtec migrants as part of a larger random sample household survey on migration histories and experiences of 120 households conducted in Woodburn, Oregon, in September 2003 as part of a U.S. Department of Agriculture (USDA) project titled "Towards a New Pluralism: Strategies for Rural Communities Impacted by Immigration." This project also involved in-depth life histories.

3 In the course of conducting this new research in Teotitlán del Valle and with Teotitecos who live elsewhere in Mexico and in the United States (particularly California), I worked closely with the cooperatives, providing interview transcripts and photographs to everyone and helping to design and produce brochures and a collective webpage (see chapter 10). The research over five summers in Teotitlán, partially documented here, involved more than sixty in-depth interviews with leaders and participants in cooperatives (many of whom had migrated at one point in time to other parts of Mexico or

to the United States), community members not connected to the cooperatives, a wide range of return migrants and their family members, and community members living permanently in California and other parts of Mexico. Participant observation was carried out in community assemblies, meetings of cooperatives, at rituals and cultural events, and in homes. Data have been collected in both Spanish and Zapotec.

4 This is a pseudonym. From this point on, all names are pseudonyms unless otherwise indicated. I have used pseudonyms to protect the identities of those who either are or have at one time been undocumented in the United States and to protect family privacy.

Chapter 1. Approaches to Transborder Lives

1 *Guelaguetza* refers to reciprocal goods exchanges in which one party gives an animal or quantity of grain, bread, or other necessary ritual food item to a receiving party. The recipient and giver note the amount in notebooks each keeps. When the giver is going to sponsor a ritual event, she will "call in" her good—in this case a turkey—as needed.

2 Sixteen households in San Agustín participate in the government-subsidized milk program, and 391 women are enrolled in Oportunidades. In Teotitlán del Valle, 184 households participate in the government-subsidized milk program, and 389 women are enrolled in Oportunidades (Secretaría de Desarrollo Social 2002).

3 The Oregon reporter Gabriela Rico, of the Salem-based newspaper *The Statesman Journal*, noted that dozens of readers had written to her about private citizens patrolling the U.S.-Mexico border. The story netted dozens of responses on the paper's website. "The majority of those who replied said that they support the efforts of the Minuteman Project, which is mobilizing people to the Arizona desert" (Rico 2005). What follows is only one expressive example:

Jason Piter, Salem:
YES, without a doubt! Our government is more concerned about violating the so-called "rights" of illegal aliens, rather than protecting our own citizens against this horde of invaders. I say if the government won't protect our borders from invasion, than we the people should do whatever it takes to keep our country protected from illegal aliens. (*Statesman Journal* 2005).

Chapter 2. Transborder Communities in Context

1 In October 1947, the land was measured and officially accepted by the community (Departamento Agrario 1947).

2 A *cofradía* refers to a religious brotherhood which is responsible for financing and carrying out the cult activities celebrated for the saints represented in the local church religious brotherhoods.

Chapter 3. Mexicans in California and Oregon

1 In this chapter I develop brief histories of Mexicans in California and Mexicans in Oregon. While there has been a bonanza of scholarship on the history of Mexicans in California and on Mexican immigrants in that state, there is relatively little on the state of Oregon. The pioneering work of the historian Erasmo Gamboa on Mexican agricultural workers in the Northwest during the early and mid-twentieth century is an exception and is drawn on heavily here. I hope that students reading this chapter will be inspired to continue the important work of documenting the histories of Mexicans in Oregon.

2 The New Pluralism Project explored the evolution of rural U.S. communities where the primary migration flows are from rural areas of Mexico to rural agricultural areas in the United States. The project was carried out by Aguirre International and funded by USDA-CSREES Grant# 2001–36201–11286. Members of the Woodburn research team that administered a 126-household random-sample questionnaire and conducted in-depth interviews included myself, Ed Kissam, Anna García, Jessica Cole, Rachel Hansen, Tami Hill, Gabriela Romero, Danielle Robinson, and Edwin Vega. I am grateful to all of them and to Ed Kissam for the chance to work with them on this project.

Chapter 4. Transborder Labor Lives

1 José Luis is referring to a lawsuit, *Señorino Ramírez Cruz et al. vs. United States, et al.*, filed on March 2, 2001. The Cruz plaintiffs filed the suit in the U.S. District Court for the Northern District of California. The named defendants are Mexico, Banco de Mexico, Banco Nacional de Crédito Rural, S.N.C. (successor to the Banco de Crédito Agrícola, S.A.), the United States, and the Wells Fargo Bank. Bracero workers in the 1940s were forced to transfer 10 percent of their wages to banks in Mexico to be used for creation of savings accounts that they were supposed to be able to claim upon return to Mexico. Approximately thirty-five million dollars were never repaid to braceros. On August 23, 2002,

Charles R. Breyer, U.S. District Court Judge, granted the United States motion to dismiss the breach of fiduciary duty claim filed by the plaintiffs as well as motions filed by the Mexican defendants and Wells Fargo with respect to the claim to the breach of fiduciary (Breyer 2002).

In 2005, the Mexican government announced that former braceros would receive a onetime payment of 38,000 pesos or about US$3,500. As of August 2006, José Luis was still waiting for his check.

Chapter 5. Surveillance and Invisibility

1 In April 2001, the deadline for applying for the LIFE act was extended by the Bush administration.

2 While *illegal alien* is the technical, legal term used by U.S. Customs and Border Protection (formerly the INS), many people consider the term inappropriate and offensive. More neutral terms such as *undocumented worker* are preferable. I use the term *undocumented* throughout this book.

3 Ironically, the employer sanction provision of the IRCA legislation has been very weakly enforced since 1986. Officials often argued that they spend most of their enforcement budget going after "big criminals" like drug smugglers and do not have the resources to enforce the employer sanctions. The alternative view is that it is widely understood that growers are dependent on undocumented labor and that enforcing the employer sanctions is a politically unpopular action to take and one that could affect the budget of U.S. Customs and Border Protection in Washington, because the agricultural lobby would be upset by any real enforcement of these sanctions.

4 *Latino* refers to persons who live in the United States and trace their ancestry to Latin America or, in some cases, to the Caribbean or Spain. The 2001 U.S. Census identified 35.8 million people as "Spanish/Hispanic/Latino." The term *Latino* appeared for the first time in the 2000 census. In that census, people of Spanish/Hispanic/Latino origin could identify as Mexican, Puerto Rican, Cuban or "other Spanish/Hispanic/Latino." The Mexican American population, sometimes also referred to as Chicano (a more politicized term for people of Mexican origin linked to activist movements of Mexican Americans in the 1960s and 1970s), reached 20.6 million, or 7.3 percent, of the total U.S. population of 281.4 million (Guzmán 2001: 1–2).

5 The number of farmworkers varies according to the source cited. PCUN organizers state that there are approximately 100,000 farmworkers; the 1997 Census of Agriculture puts the number at 124,000; and the Oregon Employment Department puts the numbers between 40,100 and 86,400 in 1999, depending on the month. Many farmworkers who stay in the state for long periods of time work not only in the fields from June to September, but also in

canneries, frozen food plants, restaurants, childcare, and construction at times of the year when they are not in the fields (see League of Women Voters of Oregon 2000). An estimate from 2002 that includes agricultural workers and workers in nurseries, greenhouses, and food-processing plants is 103,453 (Larson 2002). This number seems the most valid.

6 These headlines are (in order), "Wheat Saved by Mexicans," *The Oregonian*, October 11, 1944; "Mexicans Aid Flax Industry," *The Oregonian*, October 14, 1944; "Mexican Harvesters Doing a Great Job in Fields and Orchards, Say Growers and Farmers Who Have Seen Them Work," *The Oregonian*, October 3, 1943.

7 This headline is from *The Oregonian*, May 15, 1953.

Chapter 6. Women's Transborder Lives

1 In his book *The Meanings of Macho: Being a Man in Mexico City*, Matt Gutmann discusses at length the involvement of working-class men in Mexico City in childcare, shopping, clothes washing, and other domestic chores. In almost all cases, these men's wives or partners are working in the paid labor force. In the case of migrant couples and families discussed here, most women were not in the paid labor force while they were living in Oaxaca. Once these women migrated to the United States, all entered the paid labor force and most remained there. The situation Gutmann describes of urban working-class couples in the 1990s closely resembles that of the migrant families I discuss here once they are living in the United States.

Chapter 7. Navigating Racial and Ethnic Hierarchies

1 It is notable that neither Sara nor Pancho makes reference to African Americans in their discussion of racial and ethnic categories in their lives. This does not mean that the category doesn't exist or isn't meaningful in the context they live in, but that it wasn't deployed by them in our conversations.

2 After World War II, the number of Cubans and Puerto Ricans who emigrated to the United States increased. By the 1960s and 1970s more Dominicans and Central Americans as well as South Americans were migrating to the United States.

3 The legal and police discrimination and violence that Chicano activists faced in Los Angeles and elsewhere also help to fashion Mexican racial identity and Chicanoness. Many activists, including those involved in a key trial known as the East L.A. Thirteen, argued in court that because Mexicans were nonwhite they suffered discrimination. As the analyst Ian Haney López writes,

"Another conclusion also seems apt: because Mexicans suffered legal discrimination, they came to see themselves as brown" (2004: 175). He says of the East L.A. Thirteen trial and its relationship to the establishment of Mexicans as a distinct group, "These common sense connections, accentuated by the black struggle for equality, provided Mexicans in East Los Angeles with a framework of ideas and relationship for understanding not just their social situation, but themselves. For the defendants, East L.A. Thirteen became a forum for proving that they were a minority race. More than the testimony of experts, however, the prosecution itself served for many as the most compelling evidence that they were not white" (Haney López 2004: 177).

4 In October 1997, the Office of Management and Budget (OMB) announced the revised standards for federal data on race and ethnicity. The minimum categories for race are now American Indian or Alaska Native; Asian; Black or African American; Native Hawaiian or Other Pacific Islander; and White. Instead of allowing a multiracial category, as originally suggested in public and congressional hearings, the OMB adopted the Interagency Committee's recommendation to allow respondents to select one or more races when they self-identify. With the OMB's approval, the Census 2000 questionnaires also included a sixth racial category: Some Other Race. There are also two minimum categories for ethnicity: Hispanic or Latino and Not Hispanic or Latino. Hispanics and Latinos may be of any race (U.S. Census Bureau 2000).

5 Ironically, the Kalapuyan peoples of Oregon, including the Grand Ronde Tribe, also worked as agricultural workers in hop harvests and other crops in Oregon and elsewhere in the Northwest in the nineteenth and twentieth centuries (see Raibmon 2005). The history of Native agricultural workers in Oregon now spans two centuries.

Chapter 8. Grassroots Organizing in Transborder Lives

1 The section on the Oregon Law Center's Indigenous Project and spin-off projects was written by Julie Samples and edited by me. I thank her for this important contribution to this chapter.

Chapter 9. Identity Construction on the Net

1 The name Teotitlán is Nahuatl and means Lugar de Dios o Dioses in Spanish or Place of the God(s) in English.
2 The Marists are an order of monks who have been very active in the liberation theology movement. Liberation theology emphasizes a preferential

option for the poor and teaches that the church should be involved in struggles for economic, political, and social justice.

3 The word *pueblos* in Spanish has multiple meanings, signifying indigenous nations, indigenous peoples, or specific indigenous communities. In this discourse it is used to mean indigenous peoples (see Fox, Stephen, and Rivera 1999).

4 This meeting was a continuation of The First Encounter held in Quito, Ecuador, in 1990.

Conclusions

1 I thank Alejandro de Avila for pointing out this source to me.

Epilogue

1 This definition is from *Macmillan Contemporary Dictionary* (New York: Macmillan, 1979), 847.

Acuña, Rene, ed. 1984. *Relaciones geográficas del siglo XVI, Antequera*. Vol. I. Mexico City: Universidad Nacional Autónoma de México, Instituto de Investigaciones Antropológicas.

Alba, Richard. "Language Assimilation Today: Bilingualism Persists More Than in the Past, But English Still Dominates." San Diego: Center for Comparative Immigration Studies, University of California, San Diego. November 2004. http://www.ccis-ucsd.org/PUBLICATIONS/wrkg111.pdf. Accessed November 21, 2005.

Alba, Richard, and Victor Nee. 2003. *Remaking the American Mainstream: Assimilation and Contemporary Immigration*. Cambridge: Harvard University Press.

Aldama, Arturo. 2001. *Disrupting Savagism; Intersecting Chicana/o, Mexican Immigrant, and Native American Struggles for Self-Representation*. Durham and London: Duke University Press.

Almaguer, Tomás. 1994. *Racial Fault Lines: The Historical Origins of White Supremacy in California*. Berkeley and Los Angeles: University of California Press.

Almond, Andrea. 2004. "Activists Want Better Migrant Death Counts Near U.S.–Mexico Border." Associated Press, November 6, 2004. San Diego.

Anzaldua, Gloria. 1987. *Borderlands/La Frontera: The New Mestiza*. San Francisco: Spinsters/Aunt Lute.

———. 1999. *Borderlands/La Frontera*. San Francisco: Aunt Lute.

Appadurai, Arjun. 1996. *Modernity at Large: Cultural Dimensions of Globalization*. Minneapolis: University of Minnesota Press.

areaConnect. "Hispanic or Latino and Race. Woodburn Oregon Population and Demographics Resources." http://woodburnor.areaconnect.com/statistics.htm. Accessed June 20, 2005.

Bacon, David. "Binational Oaxacan Indigenous Migrant Organizers Face New Century." Americas Program. August 21, 2002. International Relations Program. Silver City, New Mexico. http://americas.irc-online.org/articles/2002/02080axaca.html. Accessed June 7, 2005.

———. 2003. "Transnational Working Communities: A Photo Documentary

Project by David Bacon." Martin Luther King Jr. Labor Center/Bread and Roses Cultural Project, New York City. November 2003. Website: http://translocal-flows.ssrc.org/english/bacon/. Accessed October 17, 2005.

——. 2004. "NAFTA's Legacy—Profits and Poverty." *San Francisco Chronicle*, January 14, 2004. Available at http://www.commondreams.org/views04/0114-04.htm. Accessed Dec. 15, 2004.

——. 2005. "Communities Without Borders." *The Nation*. October 24, 2005. http://www.thenation.com/doc/20051024/bacon. Accessed October 12, 2005.

Bade, Bonnie. 2004. "Alive and Well: Generating Alternatives to Biomedical Health Care by Mixtec Migrant Families in California." In *Indigenous Mexican Migrants in the United States*, ed. Jonathan Fox and Gaspar Rivera-Salgado, 205–48. Center for U.S.-Mexican Studies and Center for Comparative Immigration Studies. University of California, San Diego.

——. 2000. "Is There a Doctor in the Field? Underlying Conditions Affecting Access to Health Care for California Farmworkers and Their Families." Sacramento: California Program on Access to Care, California Policy Research Center.

——. 1994. "Sweatbaths, Sacrifice, and Surgery: The Practice of Transmedical Health Care by Mixtec Migrant Families in California." Ph.D. diss., University of California, Riverside.

Baker, Al. 2001. "Security: City Tried to Become Safer in Ways Large and Small." *New York Times*, October 5, 2001, B10.

Bauböck, Rainer. 1994. *Transnational Citizenship: Membership and Rights in International Migration*. Aldershot: Edward Elgar.

——. 2003. "Towards a Political Theory of Migrant Transnationalism." *International Migration Review* 37(3): 700–23.

Bazán López, Aurora. 2004. "Speech to Ulises Ruiz Ortiz, voters in Teotitlán del Valle." August 2004.

Berenstein, Leslie. 2005. "This Year Likely to be Worst in Migrant Deaths. *San Diego Union Tribune*, August 10, 2005. http://www.signonsandiego.com/uniontrib/20050810/news_1n10deaths.html. Accessed September 12, 2005.

Besserer, José Federico. 2002. "Contesting Community: Cultural Struggles of a Mixtec Transnational Community." Ph.D. diss., Stanford University.

——. 2004. *Topografías transnacionales: Hacía una geográfica de la vida transnacional*. Mexico, D.F.: Universidad Autónoma Metropolitana, Unidad Ixtapalapa, Divisón de Ciencias Sociales y Humanidades.

Bhabha, Homi. n.d. "Scrambled Eggs and a Dish of Rice: W. E. B. Du Bois's 'Dark Princess.'" In *A Global Measure*. Cambridge: Harvard University Press, forthcoming.

Blackwell, Maylei. 2006. "Weaving in the Spaces: Transnational Indigenous Women's Organizing and the Politics of Scale." In *Dissident Women: Gender and Cultural Politics in Chiapas*, ed. Shannon Speed, Aída Hernández Castillo, and Lynn Stephen, 115–54. Austin: University of Texas Press.

Breyer, Charles R. 2002. "United States District Court for the Northern District of California, *Senorino Ramírez Cruz et al. v. U.S. A., et al., Defendents.*" No 01-00892 CRB Memorandum and Order. August 2, 2002. http://apmp .berkeley.edu/images/stories/bracero.nodis.2aug02.pdf#search=%22Charl es%20R.%20Breyer%202002%20Senorino%20California%22. Accessed August 31, 2006.

Bures, Frank. 2002. "A New Accent on Diversity." *Christian Science Monitor*, November 6, 2002, 11–15.

Burns, Melinda. 2004a. "Flight of the Cloud People." Santa Barbara: Newspress. November 23, 2004. http://www.sbcoast.com/mixtec/plight112804 .html. Accessed December 13, 2004.

———. 2004b. "Teens Replacing Adults in Santa Maria's Fields: Juvenile Judge Seeing More Teen Migrants." Santa Barbara: Newspress. May 23, 2004. http://www.sbcoast.com/mixtec/052304kids.html. Accessed December 13, 2004.

———. 2004c. "The Price of Corn." Santa Barbara, Calif.: Newspress. http:// www.sbcoast.com/mixtec/priceofcorn100304.html. Accessed December 13, 2004.

California-Mexico Health Initiative. 2005. "Mexican Origin Population in California: Health Fact Sheet." California Policy Research Center. University of California, Office of the President. Berkeley. http://www.ucop.edu/ cprc/cmhimopfs.pdf. Accessed March 17, 2005.

Camarota, Steven A. 2000. "Zogby Poll on Immigration and Terrorism: Americans Think Lax Immigration Enforcement Helped the Terrorists." Center for Immigration Studies, Washington, D.C.

Campbell, Howard. 1993. "Class Struggle, Ethnopolitics and Cultural Revivalism in Juchitán." In *Zapotec Struggles: Histories, Politics and Representations from Juchitán, Oaxaca*, ed. Howard Campbell, and Leigh Binford et al., 213–44. Washington, D.C.: Smithsonian Institution Press.

———. 1994. *Zapotec Renaissance: Ethnic Politics and Cultural Revivalism in Southern Mexico*. Albuquerque: University of New Mexico Press.

Cano, Arturo. "El camino del FIOB y su apuesta por el desarrollo: Los indios sin fronteras." *Masoiare, La Jornada*. April 3, 2005. http://www.jornada .unam.mx/2005/abro5/050403/mas-cano.html. Accessed June 8, 2005.

Carrasco, Gilbert Paul. 1997. "Latinos in the United States: Invitation and Exile." In *Immigrants Out! The New Nativism and the Anti-Immigrant Impulse in the United States*, ed. Juan F. Perea, 190–204. New York: New York University Press.

Carroll, Susan, and Yvonne Wingett. 2004. "Prop. 200 Now Law in Arizona: Tucson Judge Clears It; Foes Plan to Appeal." *The Arizona Republic*. Dec. 23,

2004. http://www.azcentral.com/arizonarepublic/news/articles/1223prop
200hearing23.html. Accessed August 31, 2006.

Castañeda, Alejandra. 2006. *The Politics of Citizenship of Mexican Migrants.*
New York: LFB Scholarly Publishing.

Castañeda, Xóchitl, and Patricia Zavella. 2003. "Changing Constructions of
Sexuality and Risk: Migrant Mexican Women Farmworkers in California."
Journal of Latin American Anthropology 8(2): 126–50, 2003.

Centro Binacional para el Desarrollo Indígena Oaxaqueño. n.d. "El FIOB en el
Telaraña Mundial." http://www.fiob.org/proyectos/telarana.html. Accessed
June 8, 2005.

Cevallos, Diego. 2005. "New Restrictions Draw Angry Response from Mexico." May 12, 2005. Interpress News Service. http://ipsnews.net/interna
.asp?idnews=28654. Accessed June 2, 2005.

Chance, John. 1990. "Changes in Twentieth-Century Mesoamerican Cargo
Systems." In *Class, Politics, and Popular Religion: Religious Change in Mexico
and Central America*, ed. Lynn Stephen and James Dow, 27–42. Washington, D.C.: American Anthropological Association.

Chang, Grace. 2000. *Disposable Domestics: Immigrant Women Workers in the
Global Economy.* Boston: South End Press.

Chavez, Leo. 2001. *Covering Immigration: Popular Images and the Politics of the
Nation.* Los Angeles and Berkeley: University of California Press.

Cleaver, Harry. 1998. "The Zapatistas and the Electronic Fabric of Struggle." In
Zapatista! Reinventing Revolution in Mexico, ed. John Holloway and Eloina
Peláez, 81–103. Sterling: Pluto Press.

Cockcroft, James. 1998. *Mexico's Hope: An Encounter with Politics and History.*
New York: Monthly Review Press.

Cohen, Jeffrey. 2001. "Transnational Migration in Rural Oaxaca, Mexico: Dependency, Development, and the Household." *American Anthropologist*
10(4): 954–67.

——. 2004. *The Culture of Migration in Southern Mexico.* Austin: University of
Texas Press.

Cohen, Jeffrey, and Leila Rodríguez. 2005. "Remittance Outcomes in Rural
Oaxaca, Mexico: Challenges, Options, and Opportunities for Migrant
Households." *Population, Space, and Place* 11: 49–63.

Coll, Kathleen. 2004. "Necesidades y Problemas: Immigrant Latina Vernacu-
lars of Belonging, Coalition, and Citizenship in San Francisco, California."
Latino Studies 2(2): 186–209.

Comaroff, John, and Jean Comaroff. 1992. *Ethnography and the Historical
Imagination.* Boulder: Westview Press.

Comité del Museo. 1999–2001. Sala dos, numero 26a. El Museo de Teotitlán
del Valle. Web page. http://www.oaxaca-arket.com/Teotitlanmuseo/texitiles
_historia.htm. Accessed September 30, 2005. Removed 2006.

Confederated Tribes of the Grand Ronde. n.d. "Home Page. Our History Page." http://www.grandronde.org/index.html. Accessed June 20, 2005.

Cook, Roberta. 1990. "Evolving Vegetable Trading Relationships." *Journal of Food Distribution Research* 21(1): 31–46.

———. 1991. "Implications of the North American Free Trade Agreement (NAFTA) for the U.S. Horticulture Sector." Paper presented at the Agribusiness Conference on the Impacts of the Free Trade Agreement with Mexico in the California Fruit and Vegetable Industry, Institute of Agribusiness. Santa Clara, California.

———. 2002. "The U.S. Fresh Produce Industry: An Industry in Transition." In *Postharvest Technology of Horticultural Crops*, ed. Adel A. Kader, 5–30. Davis: University of California Davis, Agricultural and Natural Resources, Publication 3311.

Cornelius, Wayne. 1989. "Mexican Migration to the United States: An Introduction." In *Mexican Migration to the United States: Origins, Consequences, and Policy Options*, ed. Wayne Cornelius and Jorge Bustamente, 1–24. San Diego: Center for U.S.-Mexican Studies, University of California, San Diego.

———. 2005. "Controlling 'Unwanted' Immigration: Lessons from the United States, 1993–2004." *Journal of Ethnic and Migration Studies* 31(4): 775–94.

Dávila, Arlene. 2001 *Latinos, Inc. The Marketing and Making of a People*. Berkeley: University of California Press.

Davis, Alex. 2002. "Indigenous Farmworkers Get Legal Aid." *Statesman Journal*, October 23, 2002. http://news.statesmanjournal.com/article.cfm?i=50401. Accessed November 11, 2004.

De Genova, Nicholas. 1998. "Race, Space, and the Reinvention of Latin America in Mexican Chicago." *Latin American Perspectives* 25(5): 87–116.

———. 2005. *Working the Boundaries: Race, Space, and "Illegality" in Mexican Chicago*. Durham: Duke University Press.

De Genova, Nicholas, and Ana Y. Ramos-Zayas. 2003a. "Latino Racial Formations in the United States: An Introduction." *Journal of Latin American Anthropology* 8(2) 2–17.

———. 2003b. *Latino Crossings: Mexicans, Puerto Ricans, and the Politics of Race and Citizenship*. New York: Routledge

———. 2003c. "Latino Rehearsals: Racialization and the Politics of Citizenship between Mexicans and Puerto Ricans in Chicago." *Journal of Latin American Anthropology* 8(2): 18–57.

De Ita Rubio, Ana. 2003. "Los Impactos Socioeconómicos y Ambientales de la Liberalización de los Granos Básicos en el Contexto del TLCAN: El Caso de Sinaloa." Paper presented at the Second North American Symposium on Assessing the Environmental Effects of Trade. Mexico City, Mexico. March 25–26, 2003. http://www.cec.org/files/PDF/ECONOMY/DeIta_es.pdf. Accessed December 12, 2005.

De la Peña, Moisés T. 1950. "Problemas Sociales y Económicos de Las Mixtecas." *Memorias del Instituto Nacional Indigenista* 2(1). Mexico, D.F.: Ediciones del Instituto Nacional Indigenista.

Departamento Agrario. 1947. "Acta de Posesión y Deslinde Relativa a la Confirmación de Terrenos Comunales al Poblado de San Agustín Atenango, Mpio. Mismo Nombre, Estado de Oaxaca. [Act of Possession and Boundary Marking Relative to the Confirmation of Comunal Lands of the Population of San Agustín Atenango, County of the same name, state of Oaxaca]." Expediente 276.1/104, Tomo 1, fojas 53- 59. Archivo Agrario del Registro Agrario Nacional, Oaxaca, Oaxaca.

Dirección General de Estadística. 1906. *Censo general de la República Mexicana verificado el 29 de octubre de 1900*. Mexico City: Secretaría de Fomento.

Dirlik, Arif. 2000. "Place-Based Imagination: Globalism and the Politics of Place." In *Places and Politics in an Age of Globalization*, ed. Roxann Praznick and Arif Dirlik, 15–51. Lanham, Md.: Rowan and Littlefield.

Domínguez Santos, Rufino. 2004. "The FIOB Experience: Internal Crisis and Future Challenges." In *Indigenous Mexican Migrants in the United States*, ed. Jonathan Fox and Gaspar Rivera-Salgado, 69–80. La Jolla: Center for U.S.-Mexican Studies, Center for Comparative Immigration Studies, University of California, San Diego.

Durand, Jorge, Emilio A. Parredo, and Douglas S. Massey. 1996. "Migradollars and Development: A Reconsideration of the Mexican Case." *International Migration Review* 12: 485–501.

Eades, Jeremy. 1987. "Anthropologists and Migrants: Changing Models and Realities." In *Migrants, Workers, and the Social Order*, ed. J. Eades, 1–16. London: Tavistock.

Ehrenreich, Barbara. 2002. *Nickel and Dimed: On (Not) Getting by in America*. New York: Metropolitan Books.

Ellingwood, Ken. 2005. *Hard Line: Life and Death on the U.S.-Mexico Border*. New York: Vintage Books.

El Museo de Teotitlán del Valle. 2006. Webpage. "Tiempos y Eventos en la Historía de los Zapotecos en Teotitlán y en los Valles de Oaxaca/Times and Events in the history of the Zapotecs in Teotitlán and in the Valleys of Oaxaca." http://www.oaxaca-market.com/Teotitlanmuseo/Teo_Tiempos .htm. Accessed April 14, 2006. Removed August 2006 for unknown reasons.

El Tequio. 1993. "El Frente Mixteco-Zapoteco Binacional Participa en Foros Internacionales." *El Tequio*, December 1993. http://www.laneta.apc.org/ fiob/dic93/indice.htm. Accessed June 8, 2005.

———. 1996. "Convocatoria al Foro Indígena Nacional." *El Tequio*. http://www .fiob.org/eltequio/teq96/indice.htm. Accessed June 8, 2005.

———. 2002. "Exijimos Libertad al Profesor Romualdo Gutiérrez Cortés." *El Tequio*, September, October, 2002. http://www.fiob.org/eltequio/teqsept02/ indicesept02.html. Accessed June 8, 2005.

Escobar, Arturo. 2003. "Actors, Networks, and New Knowledge Producers: Social Movements and the Paradigmatic Transition in the Sciences." In *Conhecimento Prudente para Uma Vida Decente*, ed. Boaventura de Sousa Santos, 605–30. Porto: Afrontamento. (In Portuguese.)

Fair, Ray C., and Diane Macunovich. 1995. "Explaining the Labor Force Participation of Women 20–24." Cowles Foundation, Yale University. Cowles Foundation Discussion Papers 1116. http://ideas.repec.org/p/cwl/cwldpp/1116.html. Accessed August 31, 2006.

Falla, Ricardo. 1997. "Comment: Response to 'Consciousness, Violence, and the Politics of Memory in Guatemala' by Charles Hale." *Current Anthropology* 38(5): 826–30.

Fanjul, Gonzalo, and Arabella Fraser. 2003. "Dumping Without Borders: How U.S. Agricultural Policies Are Destroying the Livelihoods of Mexican Corn Farmers." Oxfam Briefing Paper 50. Washington, D.C.: Oxfam International. http://www.oxfam.org/eng/pdfs/pp030827_corn_dumping.pdf. Accessed April 3, 2004.

Fine, Janice. 2005. "Community Unions and the Revival of the American Labor Movement." *Politics and Society* 33(1): 153–99.

FIOB. 2005 "Public Statement of Changes to the FIOB." http://www.fiob.org/urgentaction/vassemblyresolution.html. Accessed June 8, 2005.

Fix, Michael, and Wendy Zimmerman. 1999. *All under One Roof: Mixed-Status Families in the Era of Reform*. Washington, D.C.: Urban Institute. http://www.urban.org/Template.cfm?Section=ByAuthor&NavMenuID=63&template=/TaggedContent/ViewPublication.cfm&PublicationID=6599. Accessed May 16, 2005.

Flores, William V. 1997. "Immigrants and Latino Cultural Citizenship." In *Latino Cultural Citizenship: Claiming Identity, Space, and Rights*, ed. William V. Flores and Rina Benmayor, 255–77. Boston: Beacon Press.

Flores, William V., and Rina Benmayor. 1997. "Introduction: Constructing Cultural Citizenship." In *Latino Cultural Citizenship: Claiming Identity, Space, and Rights*, ed. William V. Flores and Rina Benmayor, 1–23. Boston: Beacon Press.

Foley, Neil. 1997. *The White Scourge: Mexicans, Blacks and Poor Whites in Texas Cotton Culture*. Berkeley: University of California Press.

Fox, Jonathan. 2006. "Reframing Mexican Migration as a Multi-Ethnic Process." *Latino Studies* 4: 39–61.

———. 2005a. "Unpacking Transnational Citizenship." *Annual Reviews in Political Science* 8: 171–201.

———. 2005b. "Mapping Mexican Migrant Civil Society." Paper presented at the Conference titled, "Mexican Migrant Civic and Political Participation," at the Mexico Institute and Division of United States Studies, Woodrow Wilson International Center for Scholars. Cosponsored by the Latin American and Latino Studies Department, University of California, Santa Cruz. November 4–5, 2005.

———. 1992. *The Politics of Food in Mexico: State Power and Social Mobilization.* Ithaca: Cornell University Press.

Fox, Jonathan, and Gaspar Rivera Salgado. 2004a. "Building Civil Society among Indigenous Migrants." In *Indigenous Mexican Migrants in the United States,* ed. Jonathan Fox and Gaspar Rivera-Salgado, 1–68. La Jolla: Center for U.S.-Mexican Studies, Center for Comparative Immigration Studies. University of California, San Diego.

———. 2004b. *Indigenous Mexican Migrants in the United States.* La Jolla: Center for U.S.-Mexican Studies, Center for Comparative Immigration Studies, University of California, San Diego.

Fox, Jonathan, Lynn Stephen, and Gaspar Rivera Salgado. 1999. "Indigenous Rights and Self-Determination in Mexico." *Cultural Survival Quarterly* 23(1), April. http://www.culturalsurvival.org/publications/csq/csq_arti cle.cfm?id=34B19312–834F-4372-A5E2–70121DBC43A3&region_id=4&sub region_id=170&issue_id=7. Accessed June 9, 2005.

Frente Mixteco–Zapoteco Binacional. 1992. "Pliego General de Demandas Que Presentan al Gobierno del Estado de Oaxaca Las Organizaciones del Frente Mixteco–Zapoteco Binacional." December 7, 1992. Published in *El Tequio,* 1992. http://www.fiob.org/eltequio/teq92/pliego.htm. Accessed June 7, 2005.

Fullerton, Howard N., Jr. 1999. "Labor Force Participation: 75 Years of Change, 1950–98 and 1998–2025." *Monthly Labor Review* 3–12, December.

Galarza, Ernesto. 1964. *Merchants of Labor: The Mexican Bracero Story.* Santa Barbara: McNally and Loften.

Gamboa, Erasmo. 1990. *Mexican Labor and World War II: Braceros in the Pacific Northwest, 1942–1947.* Austin: University of Texas Press.

———. 1991. "Mexican Mule Packers and Oregon's Second Regiment Mounted Volunteers, 1855–1856." *Oregon Historical Quarterly* 92: 41–59.

———. 1995. "The Bracero Program." In *Nosotros: The Hispanic People of Oregon,* ed. Erasmo Gamboa and Carolyn Buan, 41–46. Portland: Oregon Council for the Humanities.

Ganz, Marshall. 2000. "Five Smooth Stones: Strategic Capacity in the Unionization of California Agriculture." Ph.D. diss., Harvard University.

Garcia, Matt. 2001. *A World of Its Own: Race, Labor and Citrus in the Making of Greater Los Angeles, 1900–1970.* Chapel Hill: University of North Carolina Press.

García Arellano, Fredi. 2000. "Los viajeros Mixtecos de la comunidad de Independencia." Tesis de licenciatura, Departamento de Antropología, Universidad Autónoma Metropolitana, Unidad Iztapalapa.

García Canclini, Néstor. 1995. *Hybrid Cultures: Strategies for Entering and Leaving Modernity.* Minneapolis: University of Minnesota Press.

Glenn, Evelyn Nakano. 1992. "From Servitude to Service Work: The Historical Continuities of Women's Paid and Unpaid Reproductive Labor." *Signs* 18(1): 1–44.

Glick Schiller, Nina. 1995. "Editor's Foreword: The Dialectics of Race and Culture." *Identities* 1(4): iii-iv.

——. 2003. "The Centrality of Ethnography in the Study of Transnational Migration: Seeing the Wetland Instead of the Swamp." In *American Arrivals: Anthropology Engages the New Immigration*, ed. Nancy Foner, 99–128. Santa Fe: School of American Research Press.

Glick Schiller, Nina, and Georges Eugene Fouron. 2001. *Georges Woke Up Laughing: Long Distance Nationalism and the Search for Home*. Durham: Duke University Press.

Goldfrank, Walter. 1994. "Fresh Demand: The Consumption of Chilean Produce in the United States." In *Commodity Chains and Global Capitalism*, ed. Gary Gereffi and Michael Korzeniewicz, 267–79. Westport, Conn.: Greenwood Press.

Goldin, Claudia. 2000. "Labor Markets in the Twentieth Century." In *Cambridge Economic History of the United States*, ed. Stanley Engerman and Robert Gallman, 572–79. New York: Cambridge University Press.

——. 2002. "Gender Gap." The Concise Encyclopedia of Economics: Library of Economics and Liberty. http://www.econlib.org/library/Enc/ Gender Gap.html. Accessed December 21, 2004.

Goldman, Adam. 2005. "Founder of Minuteman Project Speaks to Anti-illegal Immigration Supporters in Vegas." *North County Times*, May 29, 2005. http://www.nctimes.com/articles/2005/05/30/news/state/52905200938.txt. Accessed September 15, 2005.

Goldring, Luin. 1996. "Gendered Memory: Reconstructions of Rurality Among Mexican Transnational Migrants." In *Creating the Countryside: The Politics of Rural and Environmental Discourse*, ed. Melanie DuPuis and Peter Vandergest, 303–29. Philadelphia: Temple University Press.

González, Nancie L. Solien. 1998. *Sojourners of the Caribbean: Ethnogenesis and Ethnohistory of the Garifuna*. Urbana: University of Illinois Press.

González-Lopez, Gloria. 2003. "*De madres a hijas*: Gendered Lessons on Virginity across Generations of Mexican Immigrant Women." In *Gender and U.S. Immigration: Contemporary Trends*, ed. Pierrette Hondagneu-Sotelo, 217–40. Los Angeles and Berkeley: University of California Press.

Grewal, Interpal, and Caren Kaplan. 1994. *Scattered Hegemonies. Postmodernity and Transnational Feminist Practices*. Minneapolis: University of Minnesota Press.

Gupta, Akhil, and James Ferguson. 1992. "Beyond 'Culture': Space, Identity, and the Politics of Difference." *Cultural Anthropology* 7(1): 6–23.

Gutiérrez, David. 1995. *Walls and Mirrors: Mexican Americans, Mexican Immigrants, and the Politics of Ethnicity*. Berkeley: University of California Press.

Gutiérrez, Ramón. 1993. "Community, Patriarchy, and Individualism: The Politics of Chicano History and the Dream of Equality." *American Quarterly* 45(1): 44–72.

Gutmann, Matthew. 1995. *The Meanings of Macho: Being a Man in Mexico City*. Berkeley: University of California Press.

Guzmán, Betsy. 2001. "The Hispanic Population: Census 2000 Brief." Washington, D.C.: U.S. Census Bureau.

Hale, Charles. 1997. "Consciousness, Violence, and the Politics of Memory in Guatemala." *Current Anthropology* 38(5): 817–24.

Hall, Stuart. 1988. "New Ethnicities." In ICA *Document* 7, 27–31. London: Institute for Community Arts (ICA).

Haney López, Ian F. 2004. *Racism on Trial: The Chicano Fight for Justice*. Cambridge: Harvard University Press.

Harcourt, Wendy, and Arturo Escobar. 2002. "Women and the Politics of Place." *Development* 45(1): 7–13.

Hardt, Michael, and Antonio Negri. 2002. *Empire*. Cambridge: Harvard University Press.

Harvey, David. 2003. *The New Imperialism*. Oxford: Oxford University Press.

Hayes-Bautista, David. 2004. *La Nueva California: Latinos in the Golden State*. Berkeley: University of California Press.

Health, Education, and Human Services Division. 1997. "Agricultural Guestworker Program: Changes Could Improve Services to Employers and Better Protect Workers." Washington, D.C.: General Accounting Office.

Hirsch, Jennifer. 2003. *A Courtship after Marriage: Sexuality and Love in Mexican Transnational Families*. Berkeley: University of California Press.

Hondagneu-Sotelo, Pierrette. 2003. *Doméstica: Immigrant Workers Cleaning and Caring in the Shadows of Affluence*. Berkeley: University of California Press.

———. 1994. *Gendered Transitions: Mexican Experiences of Migration*. Berkeley: University of California Press.

Hondagneu-Sotelo, Pierrette, and Ernestine Alavez. 1999. " 'I'm Here, but I'm There': The Meanings of Latina Transnational Motherhood." In *Gender and U.S. Immigration: Contemporary Trends*, ed. Pierrette Hondagneu-Sotelo, 317–40. Berkeley: University of California Press.

Huizar Murillo, Javier, and Isidro Cerda. 2004. "Indigenous Mexican Migrants in the 2000 U.S. Census: 'Hispanic American Indians.' " In *Indigenous Mexican Migrants in the United States*, ed. Jonathan Fox and Gaspar Rivera-Salgado, 279–303. La Jolla: Center for U.S.-Mexican Studies, Center for Comparative Immigration Studies, University of California, San Diego.

Hulshof, Marije. 1991. "Zapotec Moves: Networks and Remittances of U.S.-Bound Migrants from Oaxaca, Mexico." Amsterdam: Koninklijk Nederlands Aardrijkskundig Genootschap. Instituut Voor Sociale Geografie, Faculteit Ruimtejlijke Wetenschappen, Universiteit van Amsterdam.

Huntington, Samuel P. 2004. *Who We Are? The Challenges to America's National Identity*. New York: Simon and Schuster.

Instituto Nacional de Estadística, Geografía e Informática (INEGI). 1984. *Décimo censo general de población y vivienda, 1980*. Estado de Oaxaca. 2 vols. Mexico City: Dirección General de Integración y Análisis de la Información.

———. 2000. "XII Censo General de Población y Vivienda 2000, Oaxaca." http:// www.inego.bog.mx/difusioin/espanol/poblacior./definitivos/oaxa/indice .htm. Accessed May 11, 2003.

Inter-University Program for Latino Research. 2000. "Census 2000, Latino Population Counts: Population Change for Mexican by State." http://www .n.d.edu/iuplr/cic/origins_html/3.html. Accessed February 22, 2005.

Iszavich, Abraham. 1988. "Migración Campesina del Valle de Oaxaca." In *Migración en el Occidente de México*, ed. G. López-Castro, 187–99. Zamora, Michoacán: Colegio de Michoacán.

Jacobs, Stevenson. 2001. "Fox Touts Immigration to U.S. as Opportunity." *The News*, December 19, 2001. Mexico City.

Jehl, Douglas. 2005. "Intelligence Officials Cite Wide Terror Threats." *New York Times*, February 17, 2005. http://www.nytimes.com/2005/02/17/inter national/americas/17intel.html?th/. Accessed February 17, 2005.

Johnston, Paul. 2001. "The Emergence of Transnational Citizenship among Mexican Immigrants in California." In *Citizenship Today: Global Perspectives and Practices*, ed. T. Alexander Aleinkoff and Douglass Klusmeyer, 253–77. Washington, D.C.: Carnegie Endowment for International Peace.

Kada, Naokoo, and Richard Kly. 2004. "Blurred Borders: Trans-Boundary Impacts and Solutions in the San Diego-Tijuana Border Region." International Community Foundation. http://www.icfdn.org/aboutus/publications/blurrborders/40definitions.htm. Accessed December 15, 2004.

Kearney, Michael. 1988. "Mixtec Political Consciousness: From Passive to Active Resistance." In *Rural Revolt in Mexico and U.S. Intervention*, ed. Daniel Nugent, 113–24. La Jolla: Center for U.S.-Mexican Studies, University of California, San Diego.

———. 1991. "Borders and Boundaries of State and Self at the End of Empire." *Journal of Historical Sociology* 4(1): 52–74.

———. 1995a. "The Effects of Transnational Culture, Economy, and Migration on Mixtec Identity in Oaxacalifornia." In *The Bubbling Cauldron: Race, Ethnicity, and the Urban Crisis*, ed. Michael Peter Smith and Joe R. Feagin, 226–43. Minneapolis: University of Minnesota Press.

———. 1995b. "The Local and the Global: The Anthropology of Globalization and Transnationalism." *Annual Review of Anthropology* 24: 547–65.

———. 1998. "Transnationalism in California and Mexico at the End of Empire."

In *Border Identities: Nation and State at International Frontiers*, ed. Thomas W. Wilson and Hastings Connan, 117–41. Cambridge: Cambridge University Press.

——. 2000. "Transnational Oaxaca Indigenous Identity: The Case of Mixtecs and Zapotecs." *Identities* 7(2): 173–95.

Kearney, Michael, and Federico Besserer. 2004. "Oaxacan Municipal Governance in Transnational Context." In *Indigenous Mexican Migrants in the United States*, ed. Jonathan Fox and Gaspar Rivera Salgado, 449–67. La Jolla: Center for U.S.-Mexican Studies, Center for Comparative Immigration Studies, University of California, San Diego.

"Key Moments in the Hispanic History of California." 2005. Scholastic. http://teacher.scholarstic.com/activities/hispanic/calhistory.htm. Accessed February 18, 2005.

Kissam, Edward. 2005a. "Diversity within Central Valley Mexican Immigrant Communities." Draft.

——. 2005b. "Transnational Migration Networks and the Evolution of a New Pluralism in Rural U.S. Communities," September 8, 2005, draft.

——. 2005c. Woodburn Monograph. July 20, 2005, draft.

Kissam, Edward, and Ilene J. Jacobs. 2004. "Practical Research Strategies for Mexican Indigenous Communities in California Seeking to Assert Their Own Identity." In *Indigenous Mexican Migrants in the United States*, ed. Jonathan Fox and Gaspar Rivera-Salgado, 303–42. La Jolla: Center for U.S.-Mexican Studies, Center for Comparative Immigration Studies, University of California, San Diego.

Kissam, Edward, Jo Ann Intili, and Anna García. 2001. "The Emergence of a Binational Mexico–US Workforce: Implications for Farm Labor Workforce Security." Paper prepared for America's Workforce Network Research Conference, U.S. Department of Labor, June 26–27, 2001.

Klein, Naomi. 2002. *No Logo: No Space, No Choice, No Jobs*. New York: Picador.

Kramer, Andrew. 2002. "Russian Roots Alive in Oregon Village." *Chicago Tribune*, January 4, 2002. http://www.cdi.org/russia/johnson/6005–9.cfm. Accessed September 20, 2005.

Kraul, Chris. 2000. "Mexican Immigrants Sending More Money Home." *New York Times*, September 24, 2001.

Krauze, Enrique. 2004. "Identity Fanaticism: In Defense of Mexican Americans." *New Republic*, June 21, 2004, 28–32.

KVOA. 2005. "Anti-illegal Immigration Conference Opens in Nevada Amid Protests." KVOA, Tucson, Arizona, May 29, 2005. http://www.kvoa.com/Global/story.asp?S=3405917. Accessed September 15, 2005.

Laguerre, Michel. 2002. "Virtual Diasporas: A New Frontier of National Security." Prepared for workshop sponsored by Virtual Diasporas in Global

Problem Solving Project. April 25, 2002. Nautilus Institute, Berkeley, Calif. http://www.nautilus.org/archives/virtual-diasporas/paper/Laguerre.html. Accessed June 2, 2005.

LaLande, Jeff. 2005. "High Desert History: Southeastern Oregon." Portland: Oregon Historical Society. http://www.ohs.org/education/oregonhistory/narratives/subtopic.cfm?subtopic_ID=460. Accessed September 19, 2005.

Larson, Alice. 2002. "Migrant and Seasonal Farmworker Enumeration Profiles Study: Oregon." http://www.ohcs.oregon.gov/OHCS/ISD/PPR/docs/FWICEnumerationstudy.pdf. Accessed March 29, 2005.

League of Women Voters of Oregon. 2000. *Farmworkers in Oregon*. Report. Salem: League of Women Voters of Oregon Education Fund.

Levitt, Peggy. 2001. *Transnational Villagers*. Berkeley: University of California Press.

Levitt, Peggy, and Nina Glick Schiller. 2004. "Conceptualizing Simultaneity: A Transnational Social Field Perspective on Society." *International Migration Review*, Fall. http://www.findarticles.com/p/articles/mi_qa3668/is_200410/ai_n9471690. Accessed June 15, 2005.

Lloyd Mexican Economic Report. 2004. "Profile of Mexican Cybernauts." March 2004. http://www.mexconnect.com/MEX/lloyds/llydeco0304.html. Accessed June 2, 2005.

López, Felipe, and David Runsten. 2004. "Mixtecs and Zapotecs Working in California: Rural and Urban Experiences." In *Indigenous Mexican Migrants in the United States*, ed. Jonathan Fox and Gaspar Rivera-Salgado, 249–78. La Jolla: Center for U.S.-Mexican Studies, Center for Comparative Immigration Studies. University of California, San Diego.

López, Felipe H., Luis Escala-Rabadan, and Raúl Hinojosa-Ojeda. 2001. "Migrant Association, Remittances, and Regional Development Between Los Angeles and Oaxaca, Mexico." Research Report Series No. 10. Los Angeles: North American Integration and Development Center, School of Public Policy and Social Research, UCLA. http://naid.sppsr.ucla.edu.

López Bárcenas, Francisco, Guadalupe Espinoza Sauceda, Yuri Escalante Betancourt, Ximeno Gallegos Toussaint, Abigail Zúñiga Balderas. 2002. *Los derechos indígenas y la reforma constitutcional en México*. 2d ed. Mexico, D.F.: Centro de Orientación y Asesoría a Pueblos Indígenas, A.C., Ediciones Casa Vieja, Ce-Acatl, Redes.

Lugo, Alejandro. 2000. "Theorizing Border Inspections." *Cultural Dynamics* 12(3): 353–74.

Mahler, Sarah. 1995a. *American Dreaming: Immigrant Life on the Margins*. Princeton: Princeton University Press.

——. 1995b. *Salvadorans in Suburbia : Symbiosis and Conflict*. Boston: Allyn and Bacon.

Manzano, Phil, and Michael Walden. 1981a. "Immigration Raid Nabs 92 in

Salem: Mushroom Plant Roundup Biggest in Recent History." *Statesman Journal*, August 14, 1981, 1A.

——. 1981b. "Effects Ripple Outwards from INS Raid." *Statesman Journal*, August 14, 1981, 1A.

Marizco, Michael. 2004a. "Smuggling Children, Part I: Young Immigrants Become Human Cargo." *Arizona Daily Star*, November 21, 2004. http://www.azstarnet.org/dailystar/relatedarticles/49066.php. Accessed September 7, 2005.

——. 2004b. "Smuggling Children, Part II: Three Tries, $2,300 Later, Mom, Son Reunited." *Arizona Daily Star*, November 22, 2004. http://www.azstar net.com/sn/border/49178. Accessed September 26, 2005.

Marosi, Richard. 2005. "Border Crossing Deaths Set a 12-Month Record." *Los Angeles Times*. October 1, 2005. http://www.latimes.com/news/local/la-me-deaths1oct01,0,1913222.story?coll=la-story-footer&track=morenews. Accessed October 2, 2005.

Martin, Philip. 2003a. *Promise Unfulfilled: Unions, Immigration, and the Farm Workers*. Ithaca: Cornell University Press.

——. 2003b. "Mexico–U.S. Migration." Institute for International Economics, Washington, D.C. http://www.iie.com/publications/papers/nafta-migration.pdf. Accessed February 22, 2005.

Martínez, Konane M. 2005. "Health Across Borders; Mixtec Transnational Communities and Health Care Systems." Ph.D. diss., University of California, Riverside.

Massey, Douglas. 1997. "March of Folly: U.S. Immigration Policy after NAFTA." *American Prospect* 37: 1–16, March–April.

Massey, Douglas, and Emilio Parrado. 1994. "Migradollars: The Remittances and Savings of Mexican Migrants to the United States." *Population Research and Policy Review* 13: 3–30.

Massey, Douglas, Jorge Durand, and Nolan J. Malone. 2002. *Beyond Smoke and Mirrors: Mexican Immigration in an Era of Economic Integration*. New York: Russell Sage Foundation.

Mattiace, Shannan. 2003. *To See with Two Eyes: Peasant Activism and Indian Autonomy in Chiapas, Mexico*. Albuquerque: University of New Mexico Press.

McConahay, Mary Jo. 2001. "The New Face of Farm Labor: Indian Teens from Mexico, Guatemala." *Pacific News Service*, August 27, 2001. http://www.pacific news.org/content/pns/2001/aug/0287farmlabor.html.

McWilliams, Carey. (1935) 2000. *Factories in the Field: The Story of Migratory Labor in California*. Berkeley: University of California Press.

Medina, Laurie Kroshus. 1996. "Defining Difference, Forging Unity: The Co-Construction of Race, Ethnicity, and Nation in Belize." *Ethnic and Racial Studies* 20(4): 757–80.

Meeks, Brook. 2005. "Minutemen End Border Watch, Plan to Expand: Gov. Schwarzenegger Praises Group Heading to California." MSNBC, May 4, 2005. http://www.msnbc.msn.com/id/7725470/. Accessed Sept. 15, 2005.

Menchaca, Martha. 1995. *The Mexican Outsiders; A Community History of Marginalization and Discrimination in California*. Austin: University of Texas Press.

———. 2001. *Recovering History, Constructing Race: The Indian, Black and White Roots of Mexican Americans*. Austin: University of Texas Press.

Milbank, Dana, and Mary Beth Sheridan. 2001. "Fox Presses for Immigration Agreement: Mexican Leader Seeks Pact with U.S. by Year's End." *Washington Post*, September 6, 2001, A01.

Milkman, Ruth. 2005. "Latino Immigrant Mobilization and Organized Labor: California's Transformation in the 1990s." Paper presented at conference titled "Immigrant Political Incorporation." Educational programs, Radcliffe Institute for Advanced Study, Harvard University. Cambridge, Mass., April 22–23, 2005.

Minuteman Project. 2005. Minuteman Poster. http://www.minutemanproject .com/pdf/poster3.pdf. Accessed April 7, 2005.

Mora Vásquez, Teresa. 1982. *La Mixteca Baja, Su Migración: Nieves Ixpantepec y San Nicolás Hidalgo, Oaxaca*. Mexico: DEAS-INAH.

Nagengast, Carole, and Michael Kearney. 1989. "Mixtec Ethnicity: Social Identity, Political Consciousness and Political Activism." *Latin American Research Review* 25(2): 61–91.

Narita, Tetsuro. 2006. "Remittances to Latin America: Moving towards More Precise Data Collection." Hitotsubashi Research Center for Statistical Analysis in Social Sciences. March 2006. Tokyo: Institute of Economic Research, Hitotsubashi University. http://hi-stat.ier.hit-u.ac.jp/research/discussion/ 2005/pdf/D05–154.pdf. Accessed August 29, 2006.

National Center for Farmworker Health. n.d. "Migrant and Seasonal Farmworker Analysis, Oregon." Available through Oregon Department of Health and Human Services, Migrant Health Office. http://www.oregon.gov/DHS/ ph/hsp/migrant/migrant.shtml. Accessed September 26, 2005.

Nevins, Joseph. 2006. "Collateral Damage on the Border." *New American Media*. Commentary. http://news.ncmonline.com/news/view_article.htm l?article_id=cf028b3100b578bf3b7355410b1c17b9. Accessed August 28, 2006.

Newsmax. 2005. "Schwarzenegger Praises Minutemen." Newsmax, April 29, 2005. http://www.newsmax.com/archives/ic/2005/4/29/91814.shtml. Accessed September 15, 2005.

Ngai, Mae. 2004. *Impossible Subjects: Illegal Aliens and the Making of Modern America*. Princeton: Princeton University Press.

Nusz, Nancy, and Gabriella Ricciardi. 2003. "Our Ways: History and Culture of Mexicans in Oregon." *Oregon Historical Quarterly* 104: 110–23, Spring.

Oakland Museum of California. 2003. "Picture This: California's Perspectives on American History." World War II/ Post-World War II Era 1940s–1950s/ Braceros. http://www.museumca.org/picturethis/4_3.html. Accessed February 19, 2005.

Oboler, Suzanne. 1995. *Ethnic Labels, Latino Lives: Identity and the Politics of (Re)Presentation in the United States*. Minneapolis: University of Minnesota Press.

Oregon Historical Society. 2004. "Our Ways: History and Culture of Mexicans in Oregon." Oregon Historical Society. Portland. http://www.ohs.org/edu cation/Our-Ways-Exhibit-2.cfm. Accessed March 17, 2005.

Ortner, Sherry. 1995. "Resistance and the Problem of Ethnographic Refusal." *Comparative Study of Society and History* 37: 173–93.

Passel, Jeffrey. 2005a. "Estimates of the Size and Characteristics of the Undocumented Population." Washington, D.C.: Pew Hispanic Center. http://pewhis panic.org/files/reports/44.pdf. Accessed March 29, 2005.

——. 2005b. "Unauthorized Migrants: Numbers and Characteristics." Washington, D.C.: Pew Hispanic Center. http://pewhispanic.org/files/reports/ 46.pdf. Accessed June 15, 2005.

Passel, Jeffrey, Randy Capps, and Michael Fix. 2004. "Documented Immigrants: Facts and Figures." Washington, D.C.: Urban Institute. http://www .urban.org/UploadedPDF/1000587_undoc_immigrants_facts.pdf. Accessed March 29, 2005.

PBS (Public Broadcasting System). "The Border: Interactive Timeline. 1953: Operation Wetback. The U.S. Immigration Service deports more than 3.89 million people of Mexican heritage." http://www.pbs.org/kpbs/theborder/ history/index.html. Accessed February 21, 2005.

PCUN (Pineros y Campesinos Unidos del Noroeste). 2005. "Campaigns. Legislative Attacks on Farmworkers and Immigrants Defeated." PCUN website. Woodburn, Oregon. http://www.pcun.org/. Accessed December 14, 2005.

——. 2003. "Construction Begins on Cipriano Ferrel Education Center." PCUN Update #46, p. 4. February, 2003. Woodburn, Oregon; PCUN headquarters. http://www.pcun.org/updates/update46.pdf. Accessed November 21, 2005.

Peace Development Fund. 2002. Grantees. http://www.peacefund.org/what/ wtgrlist_02.htm. Accessed November 21, 2005.

Periodico Oficial. 1947. Resolución Presidencial dictada para resolver en definitiva el expediente de conflicto de límites de bienes comunales del poblado de San Agustín Atenango, Municipio del mismo nombre, Estado de Oaxaca. Periodico Oficial, Tomo XXIX, Num. 51: 422–25.

Pew Hispanic Center. 2006. "Estimates of the Unauthorized Migrant Population for States Based on March 2005 CPS. Fact Sheet." April 26, 2006. Washington, D.C.: Pew Hispanic Center. http://pewhispanic.org/files/fac tsheets/17.pdf. Accessed August 29, 2006.

Pew Research Center. 2003. "Remittance Senders and Receivers: Tracking the Transnational Channels." Washington, D.C.: Pew Hispanic Center.

Pitti, José, Antonia Castañeda and Carlos Cortes. 2004. "Mexican Americans in California." Washington, D.C.: National Park Service. Online book. http://www.cr.nps.gov/history/online_books/5views/5views5b.htm. Accessed February 18, 2005.

Population and Demographic Resources. 2005a. "Oxnard California Population and Demographics Resources 2005." http://oxnard.areaconnect.com/statistics.htm. Accessed February 21, 2005.

——. 2005b. "Los Angeles California Population and Demographics Resources 2005." http://losangeles.areaconnect.com/statistics.htm. Accessed February 21, 2005.

——. 2005c. "San Bernardino California Population and Demographics Resources 2005." http://sanbernardino.areaconnect.com/statistics.htm. Accessed February 21, 2005.

——. 2005d. "Santa Ana California Population and Demographics Resources 2005." http://santaana.areaconnect.com/statistics.htm. Accessed February 21, 2005.

Public Citizen. 2001. "Down on the Farm: NAFTA's Seven-Years War on Farmers and Ranchers in the U.S., Canada, and Mexico." Washington, D.C.: Public Citizen Global Trade Watch. http://www/citizen.org/pctrade/nafta/reports/naftaAG/NAFTAAGREPORT.htm. Accessed February 18. 2002.

Raibmon, Paige. 2005. *Authentic Indians: Episodes of Encounter from the Late-Nineteenth-Century Northwest Coast.* Durham: Duke University Press.

Reider, Robert. 1942. "School Children Mobilized and Trained in Farm Work." *Extension Service Review* 13(10): 146–47.

Reyes, Belinda. 2004. "U.S. Immigration Policy and the Duration of Undocumented Trips" In *Crossing the Border: Research from the Mexican Migration Project*, ed. Jorge Durand and Douglas S. Massey, 299–320. New York: Russell Sage Foundation.

Reyes, Belinda, Hans P. Johnson, and Richard Van Swearingen. 2002. "Holding the Line? The Effects of the Recent Border Build-up on Unauthorized Immigration." San Francisco: Public Policy Institute of California. http://www.ppic.org/content/pubs/R_702BRR.pdf. Accessed March 29, 2005.

Rhodes, Cathy. 1999. "Focusing on Interpreting." *Access to Justice Journal* 1(1): 1–2. Salem, Ore.: Access to Justice for All Committee.

Richards, Leverette. 1953. "Agents Sweep Rising Tide of Mexican Illegals South to the Border." *The Oregonian*, May 1, 1953, 4M.

Rico, Gabriela. 2005a. "Readers Give Support to Vigilante Patrols." *Statesman Journal*, March 8, 2005. http://159.54.226.83/apps/pbcs.dll/article?AID=/20050308/NEWS/503080333 Accessed March 8, 2005.

——. 2005b. "Oaxaca Connection." *Statesman Journal*, November 12, 2005, 1G.

——. 2005c. "Money Sent from U.S. Can Be a Boon or a Bane." *Statesman Journal*, November 12, 2005, 10G.

Ritthichai, Chaleampon. 2003. "Immigrant Soldiers." *Gotham Gazette*, May 2003. http://www.gothamgazette.com/article/immigrants/20030501/11/ 368. Accessed October 17, 2005.

Rivera Salgado, Gaspar. 1996. "Jornada de Resistencia Civil de FIOB." E-mail circulated to Chiapas solidarity lists, Native net, others. http://www.native-net.org/archive/nl/9608/0013.html. Accessed June 8, 2005.

——. 1999a. "Migration and Political Activism: Mexican Transnational Indigenous Communities in Comparative Perspective." Ph.D. diss., University of California, Santa Cruz.

——. 1999b. "Mixtec Activism in Oaxacalifornia: Transborder Grassroots Political Strategies." *American Behavioral Scientists* 47(2): 1439–58.

——. 1999c. "Welcome to Oaxacalifornia." *Cultural Survival Quarterly* 23(1): 59–61.

Rodríguez, Clara E. 2000. *Changing Race: Latinos, the Census, and the History of Ethnicity in the United States*. New York: New York University Press.

Rosaldo, Renato. 1997. "Cultural Citizenship, Inequality, and Multiculturalism." In *Latino Cultural Citizenship: Claiming Identity, Space, and Rights*, ed. William V. Flores and Rina Benmayor, 27–38. Boston: Beacon Press.

Rothenberg, Daniel. 2000. *With These Hands: The Hidden World of Migrant Farmworkers Today*. Berkeley and Los Angeles: University of California Press.

Rothman, Barbara Katz. 2002. *Recreating Motherhood: Ideology and Technology in a Patriarchal Society*. New York: W. W. Norton.

Rothstein, Arthur H. 2006. "Death of Illegal Immigrants Takes Toll on Border Coroners." Associated Press. *The New Mexican*. August 13, 2006. http:// www.freenewmexican.com/news/47832.html. Accessed August 28, 2006.

Rouse, Roger. 1992. "Making Sense of Settlement: Class Transformation, Cultural Struggle, and Transnationalism among Mexican Migrants in the United States." In *Towards a Transnational Perspective on Migration*, ed. Nina Glick Schiller, 25–52. Annals of the New York Academy of Sciences 645.

——. 1995. "Thinking Through Transnationalism: Notes on the Cultural Politics of Class Relations in Contemporary United States." *Public Culture* 7(2): 353–402.

Rubin, Jeffrey W. 1996. *Decentering the Regime: Ethnicity, Radicalism, and Democracy in Juchitán, Mexico*. Durham: Duke University Press.

Runsten, David, and Michael Kearney. 1994. *A Survey of Oaxacan Village Networks in California Agriculture*. Davis: California Institute for Rural Studies.

Rus, Jan, Rosalva Aída Hernández Castillo, and Shannan Mattiace. 2003.

Mayan Lives, Mayan Utopies: The Indigenous Peoples of Chiapas and the Zapatista Rebellion. Lanham, Md.: Rowan and Littlefield.

Rus, Jan, and Robert Wasserstrom. 1980. "Civil-Religious Hierarchies in Central Chiapas: A Critical Perspective." *American Ethnologist* 7(3): 466–78.

Sahlins, Marshall. 1999. "Enlightenment? Some Lessons from the Twentieth Century." *Annual Reviews in Anthropology* 28: i–xxiii.

Salazar Parreñas, Rhacel. 2001. *Servants of Globalization: Women, Migration, and Domestic Work.* Stanford: Stanford University Press.

Samples, Julie. 2005. "'Taking us into account': Female Indigenous Farmworkers in Oregon." Paper presented at the Institute for Women's Policy Research Conference, June 2, 2005, Washington D.C.

———. 2003. Personal communication.

Sánchez, George. 1993. *Becoming Mexican American: Ethnicity, Cultural and Identity in Chicano Los Angeles, 1900–1945.* New York: Oxford University Press.

Sanjek, Roger. 1994. "The Enduring Inequalities of Race." In *Race*, ed. Stephen Gregory and Roger Sanjek, 1–17. New Brunswick: Rutgers University Press.

Sassen, Saskia. 1991. *The Global City: New York, London, Tokyo.* Princeton: Princeton University Press.

———. 2001. "Spatialities and Temporalities of the Global: Elements for a Theorization." In *Globalization* ed. Arjun Appadurai, 260–78. Durham: Duke University Press.

———. 2002. "The Repositioning of Citizenship: Emergent Subjects and Spaces for Politics." *Berkeley Journal of Sociology* 46: 4–25.

———. 2004. "Local Actors in Global Politics." *Current Sociology* 52(4): 649–70.

Sasuly, Richard. 1942. "Camps Guide Farm Labor." *Agricultural Situation* 26(2): 20–21.

Scher, Phillip. 2003. *Carnival and the Formation of a Caribbean Transnation.* Gainesville: University of Florida Press.

Schlosser, Eric. 2003. *Reefer Madness: Sex, Drugs, and Cheap Labor in the American Black Market.* Boston: Houghton Mifflin.

Secretaría de Desarrollo Social (SEDESOL). 2002. "Municipios con presencia de la SEDESOL en al menos un programa social." Oaxaca. December 31, 2003. http://www.sedesol.gob.mx/subsecretarias/prospectiva/cgp/inf_dic 2002/indic_nivel_mun_si_20.pdf. Accessed March 10, 2005.

Secretaría de Relaciones Exteriores de México. 2004. "Guía del Migrante Mexicano." http://www.sre.gob.mx/tramites/consulares/guiamigrante/default .html. Accessed June 5, 2005.

Seeper, Jerry. 2005. "Mexico Seeks Protection for Illegals." *Washington Times*, March 8, 2005. http://washingtontimes.com/national/20050308–121241– 8430r.htm. Accessed March 3, 2005.

Shorey, Ananda. 2005. "Migrant Smugglers Getting Creative." Associated

Press, April 4, 2005. http://wireservice.wired.com/wired/story.asp?section =Breaking&storyId=1013627&tw=wn_wire_story. Accessed April 5, 2005.

Singer, Merle. 2000. "Why I Am Not a Public Anthropologist." *Anthropology News* 41(6): 6–7, September.

Smith, Linda Tuhiwai. 1999. *Decolonizing Methodologies: Research and Indigenous Peoples*. London: Zed Books.

Smith, Robert. 2004. "Actual and Possible Uses of Cyberspace By and Among States, Diasporas, and Migrants." Paper presented at Virtual Diasporas and Global Problem Solving Project. Nautilus Institute, Berkeley, Calif. June 10, 2002. http://www.nautilus.org/gps/virtual-diasporas/paper/SmithPaper .html. Accessed June 5, 2005.

———. 2005. *Mexican New York: Transnational Lives of New Immigrants*. Berkeley and Los Angeles: University of California Press.

Sneider, Daniel. 2003. "The U.S. Isn't Only One Losing Jobs to Other Nations." *San Jose Mercury News*, August 14, 2003. Available at http://www.spokesman review.com/breaking-news-story.asp?submitdate=2003815112059. Accessed December 14, 2004.

Stanley, Eduardo. 2001. "De los Campos de Oaxaca a Líder Binacional: Rufino Domínguez, Premio de Liderazgo 2001." *La Jornada*, December 30, 2001. http://www.jornada.unam.mx/2001/dico1/011230/mas-lider.html. Accessed June 7, 2005.

———. 2005. "Fortalece Organización Indígena." *Pacific News Service*. March 17, 2005. eduardostanleymcast.net.

Statesman Journal, The. 2005. "Poll Responses of the Idea of Private Citizens Patrolling the U.S.–Mexico Border." *Statesman Journal*, March 5, 2005. http://www.statesmanjournal.com/apps/pbcs.dll/article?AID=/20050305/ NEWS/503050348&SearchID=73201444135303. Accessed March 9, 2005.

Stephen, Lynn. 1991. *Zapotec Women*. Austin: University of Texas Press.

———. 1997. *Women and Social Movements in Latin America: Power from Below*. Austin: University of Texas Press.

———. 2001a. "Globalization, the State, and the Creation of Flexible Indigenous Workers: Mixtec Farmworkers in Oregon." *Urban Anthropology and Studies of Cultural Systems and World Economic Development* 30(2–3): 189–214.

———. 2001b. *The Story of PCUN and the Farmworkers' Movement in Oregon*. Eugene: University of Oregon, University Publications.

———. 2002. *Zapata Lives!: Histories and Political Cultures in Southern Mexico*. Berkeley: University of California Press.

———. 2004. "Mixtec Farmworkers in Oregon: Linking Labor and Ethnicity through Farmworkers' Unions and Hometown Associations." In *Indigenous Mexican Migrants in the United States*, ed. Jonathan Fox and Gaspar Rivera-Salgado, 179–204. La Jolla: Center for U.S.-Mexican Studies, Center for Comparative Immigration Studies. University of California, San Diego.

———. 2005a. "Women's Weaving Cooperatives in Oaxaca: An Indigenous Response to Neoliberalism." *Critique of Anthropology* 25(3): 253–78.

———. 2005b. *Zapotec Women: Gender, Class, and Ethnicity in Globalized Oaxaca*. Rev. ed. Durham: Duke University Press.

———. 2005c. "Negotiating Global, National, and Local 'Rights' in a Zapotec Community." *Political and Legal Anthropology Review* 28(1): 133–50.

Stephen, Lynn, Patricia Zavella, Matt Gutmann, and Felix Matos Rodríguez. 2003. "Introduction." In *The Américas Reader: Culture, History, and Representation*, ed. Lynn Stephen, Matt Gutmann, Felix Matos Rodríguez, and Patricia Zavella, pp. 1–30. Malden, Mass.: Blackwell Publishers.

Supreme Court of California. 1948. http://www.brownat50.org/brownCases/ PreBorwnCases/PerezvLippoldCa111948.tlml. Accessed October 23, 2004.

Suro, Roberto. 2004. "Remittances, Senders and Receivers: Tracking the Transnational Channels." Washington, D.C.: Pew Hispanic Center. http://pew hispanic.org/reports/report.php?ReportID=23. Accessed March 29, 2005.

Taylor, Edward J. 1999. "The New Economics of Labour Migration and Returns to Households in Rural Mexico." *International Migration* 37 (1): 63–88.

Taylor, Edward J., Antonio Yuñez-Naude, Fernando Barceinas Paredes, and George Dyer. 2005. "Transition Policy and the Structure of Agriculture in Mexico." In *North American Agrifood Market Integration: Situation and Perspectives*, ed. Karen Huff, Karl D. Meilke, Ronald D. Knutson, Rene F. Ochoa, James Rude, and Antonio Yuñez-Naude, 86–118. Texas A&M University, University of Guelph, El Colego de México.

Taylor, Paul. 1931. "Increases of Mexican Labor in Certain Industries in the United States." *Monthly Labor Review* 32(1): 83–89.

———. 1937. "Migratory Farm Labor in the United States." *Monthly Labor Review* 44(3): 537–47.

The Economist. 2005. "The Grapes of Wrath, Again: The Miserable State of California's Farm Workers." *The Economist*, September 10, 2005, 46.

Turner, Eugene. 1998. "SSRIC Teaching Resources Depository. Exploring the US Census." Chapter 5. Population Growth. Online resource. http://www .csub.edu/ssric-trd/modules/cens/censch5.htm. Accessed February 22, 2005.

Urrea, Luis Alberto. 2004. *The Devil's Highway: A True Story*. New York: Little, Brown.

U.S. Census Bureau. 1942. *16th Census of the United States, 1940: Population, First Series, Number of Inhabitants, California*. Washington, D.C.: Government Printing Office.

———. 1990. U.S. Census Form. Facsimiles of Respondent Instructions and Questionnaire. http://www.census.gov/prod/1/90dec/cph4/appdxe.pdf. Accessed April 8, 2005.

———. 2000a. "Racial and Ethnic Classifications Used in Census 2000 and Beyond." http://www.census.gov/population/www/socdemo/race/race factcb.html. Accessed April 7, 2005.

———. 2000b. "Race and Hispanic or Latino: 2000, Census 2000 Redistricting Data" (Public Law 94–171), Geographic Area: Oregon—County. http://factfinder.census.gov/servlet/GCTTable?_bm=n&_lang=en&mt_name=DEC_2000_PL_U_GCTPL_ST2&format=ST-2&_box_head_nbr=GCT-PL&ds_name=DEC_2000_PL_U&geo_id=04000US41. Accessed June 20, 2005.

———. 2001. "Overview of Race and Hispanic Origin." Census 2000 Brief. http://www.census.gov/prod/2001pubs/cenbr01–1.pdf. Accessed April 7, 2005.

———. 2003a. "The Foreign-Born Population: 2000."

———. 2003b. "U.S. Armed Forces and Veterans. Facts and Features." April 10. 2003. http://www.census.gov/Press-Release/www/2003/cb03-ff04se.html. Accessed October 17, 2005.

———. 2005. "Oregon Quick Facts." http://quickfacts.census.gov/qfd/states/41/41047.html. Accessed June 20, 2005.

VanWey, Leah K., Catherine M. Tucker, and Eileen Días McConnell. 2005. "Community Organization and Remittances in Oaxaca." *Latin American Research Review* 40(1): 83–107.

Vásquez, Leoncio. 1999. "La Comunidad Indígena y el Censo 2000." *El Tequio*, June–September 1999. http://www.laneta.apc.org/fiob/teqjunio99/indice3.html. Accessed June 8, 2005.

Velasco, Laura. 1986. "Los motives de la mujer migrante de la Mixteca de Oaxaca." Tesis de licenciatura, Facultad de Psicología, Universidad Autónoma de México.

———. 1995. "Migración femenina y estrategias de sobrevivencia de la unidad doméstica: Un caso de estudio de mujeres Mixtecas en Tijuana." In *Mujeres, migración y maquila en la frontera norte*, ed. Soledad González Montes, Olivia Ruiz, Laura Velasco, and Ofelia Woo, 37–64. Mexico City: Programa Interdisciplinario de Estudios de la Mujer, El Colegio de México/El Colegio de la Frontera Norte.

———. 2002. *El regreso de la comunidad: Migración indígena y agentes étnicos: Los Mixtecos en la frontera México-Estados Unidos.* Mexico City: El Colegio de México/El Colegio de la Frontera Norte.

Velásquez, Cristina. 2004. "Migrant Communities, Gender, and Political Power in Oaxaca." In *Indigenous Mexican Migrants in the United States*, ed. Jonathan Fox and Gaspar Rivera-Salgado, 483–94. La Jolla: Center for U.S.-Mexican Studies, Center for Comparative Immigration Studies. University of California, San Diego.

Villarejo, Don, David Lighthall, Daniel Williams, Anne Souter, Richard Mines, Bonnie Bade, Steven Samuels, and Stephen McCurdy. 2000. *Suffer-*

ing in Silence: A Report on the Health of California's Agricultural Workers.
Davis: California Institute for Rural Studies.

Warren, Kay. 1998. *Indigenous Movements and Their Critics: Pan-Maya Activism in Guatemala.* Princeton: Princeton University Press.

White, Marceline, Carlos Salas, and Sarah Gammage. 2003. *Trade Impact Review: Mexico Case Study. NAFTA and the FTAA: A Gender Analysis of Employment and Poverty Impacts in Agriculture.* Washington, D.C.: Women's Edge Coalition.

Wides, Laura. 2004. "Film Explores a Day in the Life of California Without Latinos." *North Country Times,* May 12, 2004. http://www.nctimes.com/articles/2004/05/18/entertainment/movies/5_12_0413_20_11.prt. Accessed December 21, 2004.

Wood, William Warner. 2000a. "Flexible Production, Households, and Fieldwork: Multisited Zapotec Weavers in the Era of Late Capitalism." *Ethnology* 39(2): 133–48.

———. 2000b. "Stories from the Field: Handicraft Production and Mexican National Patrimony: A Lesson in Translocality from B. Traven." *Ethnology* 39(3): 183–203.

Woodall, Patrick, Lori Wallach, Jessica Prach, and Darshana Patel. 2001. "Down on the Farm: NAFTA's Seven-Years War on Farmers and Ranchers in the U.S., Canada and Mexico." Washington, D.C.: Public Citizen's Global Trade Watch.

Yúdice, George. 2003. *The Expediency of Culture: Uses of Culture in the Global Era.* Durham: Duke University Press.

Zabin, Carol. 1997. "U.S.-Mexico Economic Integration: Labor Relations and the Organization of Work in California and Baja California Agriculture." *Economic Geography* 73(3): 337–55.

Zabin, Carol, Michael Kearney, David Runsten, and Ana García. 1993. "A New Cycle of Poverty: Mixtec Migrants in California Agriculture." Davis: California Institute for Rural Studies.

Zabin, Carol, and Sallie Hughes. 1994. "Economic Integration and Labor Flows: Stage Migration in Farm Labor Markets in Mexico and the United States." *International Migration Review* 29(2): 395–422.

Zahniser, Steven, and William Coyle. 2004. *U.S.-Mexico Corn Trade during the NAFTA Era: New Twists to an Old Story.* U.S. Department of Agriculture. Outlook Report (FDS04D01), May 2004. http://www.ers.usda.gov/publications/FDS/may04/fds04D01/. Accessed August 31, 2006.

Zárate-Hoyes, German, and Scott Anderson. 2005. "GIS Tracks Earnings Sent Home by Mexican Migrants." *ESRI GIS and Mapping Software. ArcUser Online,* January–March 2005. http://www.esri.com/news/arcuser/0205/remittance1of2.html. Accessed June 2, 2005.

Zavella, Patricia. 2003. "Talkin' Sex: Chicanas and Mexicanas Theorize about

Silences and Sexual Pleasures." In *Chicana Feminisms: A Critical Reader*, ed. Gabriela Arredondo, Aída Hurtado, Norma Klahn, Olga Nájera Ramírez, and Patricia Zavella, 228–53. Durham: Duke University Press.

——. 2000. "Engendering Transnationalism in Food Processing: Peripheral Vision on Both Sides of the U.S.-Mexico Border." In *Las nuevas fronteras del Siglo XXI: Dimensiones culturales, políticas y socioeconómicas de las relaciones México–Estados Unidos*, ed. Norma Klahn, Pedro Castillo, Alejandro Alvarez, Federico Manchón, 397–424. Mexico, D.F.: La Jornada Ediciones: Centro de Investigaciones Colección: La Democracia en Mexico.

——. 1997. " 'Playing with Fire': The Gendered Construction of Chicana/Mexicana Sexuality." In *The Gender/Sexuality Reader: Culture, History, Political Economy*, ed. Roger N. Lancaster and Micaela di Leonardo, 402–18. New York: Routledge.

Arizmendi, Yareli, 139
Asian immigration, 68–69
Atenango. *See* San Agustín Atenango

baby sitting. *See* domestic service
  work
Bacon, David, 65
Bade, Bonnie, 193
Baja California, 119
Bauböch, Rainer, 239
Bautista, Mariano, 95, 116–20, 160–61,
  163–64
Bazan, Aurora, 286–89, 291–92
Benmayor, Rina, 316
Besserer, Federico, 22, 40, 113–14, 122,
  133–34
Bhabha, Homi, 311
bodies of migrants as illegal, 26
border concepts, 6, 23, 34; dynamics of
  surveillance and invisibility, 143–45,
  155–64; hybridity of borders, 23–27;
  linguistic borders, 18; moveable and
  flexible borders, 144; national borders, 6, 18, 23, 27; racialized fears of
  aliens, 28–31, 143–44, 148–50, 153–
  54, 175–77, 201. *See also* transborder
  concepts
border crossings, xiii–xvi, 9–19; anti-
  immigrant militias and, 25, 29–31;
  Clinton administration policies
  and, xiv, 204; *coyote* fees for, 157,
  162, 166–70, 205; dangers and
  traumas of, xvi, 25, 157–64; death
  rates for, xiv, 25, 319; *desaparecidos*
  and, xiii–xv, 319; economic incen-
  tives for, 160–63; fears of terrorism
  at, 143–44, 148–50; legal, 33; returns
  to Mexico and, 149, 161; surveillance
  experiences of, 155–64; by women
  and children, 201–4
border patrol. *See* U.S. Border Patrol
bracero program, 12, 26–27, 48, 145,
318; in California, 57, 70, 72–73;
Cruz vs. U.S. and, 111, 329–30n1;
divided families in, 180–82; migration networks for, *105*, 106, *112*; in
Oregon, 81–84; in San Agustín
Atenango, 108–11, *112*; in Teotitlán
del Valle, 96–97, *105*, 106; wages for,
72–73, 307
Burns, Melinda, 120–21, 123
Bush, George W., administration,
149–50, 306–7

California, 32; agricultural workers in,
68–77; Anglo-American workers in,
71–72; antimiscegenation law in,
222–23; bracero program in, 57, 70,
72–73; domestic service workers in,
134–42; gold rush in, 67–68; grape
boycott in, 74; health care in, 192–
93; Hispanic American Indians in,
229; history of, 66–77; human rights
in, 66–67; immigration to urban
centers in, 77; labor laws in, 74; labor
organizing in, 73, 74–75; land own-
ership in, 67–68, *77*; Mexican population in, 75, 76–77; Operation Wetback in, 73; Proposition 187 in, 28–
29; racial experiences of migrants in,
217–20; re-creations of Mexico in,
63–77; research methods and, 327–
28n3; temporary worker program
in, 70–72; undocumented workers
in, 72–76; UNITE-HERE in, 237
California Agricultural Labor Relations Act (ALRA), 74
California Alien Land Law of 1913, 69
California Homestead Act of 1862, 67
California Land Act of 1851, 67
camperos, 166
canneries. *See* food economies
cargo systems. *See* civil cargos; religious cargos

Caso, Alfonzo, 268

Castañeda, Alejandra, 65

Castañeda, Xóchitl, 54–55

Catholicism: liberation theology 295, 332–33n2; on women's sexual practices, 53–54

CAUSA coalition, 271

Central American Free Trade Agreement (CAFTA), 312–13

Centro de Servicios Para Campesinos (CSC), 244

Chang, Grace, 199, 201

Chávez, César, 74, 89–90, 224, 263

Chávez, Eric, 274–75, 276

Chávez, Federico, 274–75, 276

Chavez, Leo, 151–52

Chemeketa Community College 90

Chicanos label, 224–25, 331–32n5

childcare. See domestic service work

Chinese Exclusion Acts, 69

Chinese workers, 68–69

Cholos, 37

Cipriano Ferrell Education Center, 89

civil cargos, ix–x, 32, 40–43, 260 327n1; ayuntamiento (government branch) and, 56; governance of communal lands and, 42, 46–47; impact of migration and politics on, 48–49, 56, 57, 59–61; knowledge of local customs and, 44–45, 57–58; role of transborder organizations on, 262–63; women's responsibilities for, 55–58. See also local governance

civil governance. See local governance

class borders, 6, 18, 34

Clinton, Bill, administration, xiv, 204

Coalición de Obreros, Campesinos e Estundiantes del Istmo (COCEI), 295–97

cochineal dye, 291–92

cofradías, 48–49, 329n2 (chap. 2)

Cohen, Jeffrey, 104, 106–7, 121, 263

collaborative activist ethnography, 321–25

colonial borders, 6, 23, 34

Comaroff, Jean, 152

Comaroff, John, 152

Comisariado de Bienes Comunales, ix–x

Comité Pro Obras de San Agustín, 236; constructions of local identities by, 258–64, 271–72; multisited areas of operation of, xii, 9, 20, 238; transnational citizenship, 316–17

Communal Lands Commission, ix–x

community unions, 270–71

compadrazgo relationships, 57

Compañia Nacional de Subsistencia Popular (CONASUPO), 123–27

comunidades agrarias, 125

construction of cultural identity. See productions of cultural identities

construction work, 107

Coordinación Estatal de Atención al Migrante Oaxaqueño, 120–21

Cornelius, Wayne, 146

court interpreters, x

Courtship after Marriage, A (Hirsch), 191–92

coyotes, 157, 162, 166–70, 205

Crusade for Justice, 224

Cruz, Patricia, 153–54

Cruz Hernández, Soledad, 197–98, 200, 231–33

Cruz Pérez, Daniel, 35–40, 163, 191, 261

Cruz Pérez, Emiliana, 277–78

Cuevas. See San Miguel Cuevas

cultural borders, 6, 23, 34

cultural citizenship, 239–41, 252–53, 269–73, 316–18, 319

cultural identities. See productions of cultural identities

cultures of migration, 121

events of, 267–69; in global cities, 236–38, 269; hometown associations, 262–63, 280; for indigenous farmworkers, 241–53, 265–66; Internet communication and organizing by, 278–79, 281; legal rights projects of, 265–66; legislative activities of, 267; meshworks and, 19–20, 33–34, 280–81, 301; occupational health and safety projects of, 266; panindigenous organizations, 264–69, 297–98; political organizing of, 294–307; anti–sexual harassment projects of, 265; transborder organizations, xii, 9, 20, 23–24, 33–34, 238, 258–64, 271–72, 278–79; transnational citizenship and, 238–39; UNITE-HERE, 237; women's groups, 231–35, 253–58, 272–73; women's participation in, 264; in Woodburn, 88–90. *See also* Internet; names of specific organizations

migrant vs. immigrant status, 148

migration networks, xv–xvi, 19–20, 26–27, 314; internal migrations, 103–4, 109–16, *115*, 182; meshworks, 19–20, 33–34, 280–81, 301; from San Agustín Atenango, 8–9, 108–22, *115*; from Teotitlán del Valle, 95–108, 157–59; in Woodburn, 86–88, 170. *See also* bracero program; border crossings; labor contractors and recruiters; labor markets

Minuteman Project, 25, 29–31, 328n3

mixed-status households, 146–47, 241

Mixtec migrants: agricultural work of, 118–22, 178; decline of peasant agriculture and, 122–31; divided families amongst, 182–85; female migration patterns of, 178–79, 187; gendered divisions of labor of, 195–99; internal migrations of, 111–18, 187; lan-

guage use of, 45, 215–16; migration networks of, 112–22; out-migration of, 120–22; political experiences of, 255; racial discrimination experiences of, 214–17, 230; role of labor contractors and, 108–22, 166–69; seasonal migrations of, 112–13, 242–43; transborder organizations of, xii, 9, 20, 23–24, 33–34, 238, 258–64. *See also* San Agustín Atenango

Mixteco-Zapoteco Binational Front (FM-ZB), 294, 296–302. *See also* Frente Indígena de Organizaciones Binacionales

Morales, Lucia, 210

Mora Vásquez, Teresa, 112–13

Movimiento Estudiantil Chicano de Astlán (MEChA), xi–xii, 224

Mujeres Luchadoras Progresistas (MLP), 182, 231–36, 253–58, 272–73; Christmas wreath project of, 255–56, 258; geographical area of operation of, 238; origins of, 253; skills and leadership development projects of, 255–58; use of Internet by, 256

multilayered models of citizenship, 34, 316–18. *See also* cultural citizenship

multilocational models, 65

multisited experience, 9

municipal governance. *See* local governance

NAFTA (North American Free Trade Agreement), 26–27, 312–13, 318–19; impact of, on Mexican agriculture, 124–31; impact of, on Mexican immigration, 145; *maquiladora* sector, 124, 130–31; service-based economy and, 141

Nagengast, Carol, 281

nannies. *See* domestic service work

Migrant Communities (OCIMO).
See Organización de Comunidades
Indígenas Migrantes Oaxaqueños
organizing. See migrant organizations
Ortner, Sherry, 321

panindigenous identification and
identities, 264–69, 293–94, 297, 306,
308, 317–18
parallel transnational participation,
316–17
partial denationalization, 34
Partico de Acción Nacional (PAN), 60
Partido de la Revolución Democrática
(PRD), 35–40, 60
Partido Revolucionario Institucional
(PRI), 37–39, 60
pateros, 166
Perez, Andrea, 222–23
Pérez, Emiliana, 12–14, 17–19
Perez vs. Lippold, 222–23
Pimentel Salas, Arturo, 301–2, 304
Pineros y Campesinos Unidos del
Noroeste (PCUN), xi–xii, 34, 88–
89, 236, 241–53, 270–72, 316–17;
amnesty work by, 243–44; anniversary campaign of, 246–47; collective
bargaining agreements of, 249–51;
community unions of, 270–71; cultural struggles of, 251–53; focus on
working conditions by, 244–51; geographical area of operation of, 238,
243; legal services center of, 243–44,
270; membership dues and benefits
of, 252; origins of, 243; outreach of,
to indigenous workers, 246–49;
"red card" wage accountability
campaign of, 243–44; strikes and
boycotts of, 246, 250, 267; women's
organizing in, 233, 235, 255–58
"Plan Espiritual de Aztlán El"/"The
Spiritual Plan of Aztlán," 225

political organizing. See migrant
organizations
political parties, 39–40, 49, 60
polleros, 166
Porros, Clemente, 151
postnational concept, 27–28
principales, 49
PROCAMPO program, 127–28
productions of cultural identities: by
community museums, 283–85; cultural citizenship and, 239–41, 252–
53, 269–73, 316–18; emphasis on indigenous identity in, 292–94; indigenous research projects and, 282;
on Internet websites, 281–83, 307–8;
links to precolonial past in, 289–92;
panindigenous identification of,
264–69, 293–94, 297–98, 308, 317–
18; re-creations of Mexico, 63–66;
reproductive imagination of, 283;
role of local landmarks in, 285–89
Program of Direct Supports for Marketing and Development of
Regional Markets, 128
Projecto en Contra del Acoso Sexual
en el Campo, El, 265
Proposition 200 (Arizona), 29, 192
Proposition 187 (California), 28–29
Public Law 45, 72
pueblos, 301, 333n3

quinceañeras, 59

racial and ethnic borders, 6, 18, 23, 32–
34, 209–30; among Mexicans in
the United States, 211–20; anti-
immigrant Anglo-nationalism and,
28–31; antimiscegenation laws and,
222–23; bodies of migrants as illegal, 26; in California in 1849, 66–67;
Chicano brown pride movement
and, 224–25, 331–32n3; conflation of
race and ethnicity in the United

tances to home in, 277–78; role of labor contractors in, 108–22; seasonal work in, 109–21; subsistence agriculture in, 126; woven palm products of, 47–48. *See also* Mixtec migrants

San Agustín Atenango Transborder Public Works Committee, 236; constructions of local identities by, 258–64, 271–72; multisited areas of operation of, xii, 9, 20, 238; transnational citizenship, 316–17

San Andrés Accords on Indigenous Rights and Culture, 209–10, 293–94

Sánchez, Felipe, 58–61

Sánchez, Valentin, 230, 267–68

Sánchez Liébana, César, 296

Sánchez Martínez, Marcos, 44–45

Sanjek, Roger, 226

San Mateo de Libres, 47

San Miguel Cuevas, ix–x

Santa Ana, California, 96, 157–59

Santa María, California, 120–21

San Vicente de Palmar, 47

Sassen, Saskia: on global cities, 134–35, 236–38, 253, 269; on partial denationalization, 312–15

Scher, Phillip, 283

Schlosser, Eric, 242

Schwarzenneger, Arnold, 31

Seasonal Agricultural Workers Program (SAW), 76, 86–88, 145–48, 165, 244

Second Continental Encounter of Indigenous Peoples, Nations, and Organizations, 301, 333n4

Secretaría de Asuntos Indígenas del Estado de Oaxaca, 284–85

Secretaría de Relaciones Exteriores de Mexico website, 280

Señorino Ramirez Cruz et al. vs. United States et al., 111, 329–30n1

September 11, 2001, attacks: availability of work after, xvi, 13–14; immigration policies after, 18, 28–29, 149–50; racialized fears of immigrants and terrorism after, 28–31, 153–54, 175–77, 201; tourism in Teotitlán after, 60

service work, 106–7, 242–43, 314. *See also* domestic service work

Servicios del Pueblo Mixe, A.C., 301

Sexual Harassment Program, 265

sexuality, 32; cohabitation and, 55; serial monogamy practices and, 53–55; sexual harassment projects and, 265; single parenthood and, 51–52, 53; standards of acceptable behavior of, 53–55; Zavella's "peripheral vision" and, 54–55

simultaneous binational participation, 316–17

single parenthood, 51–52, 53

Sistema Nacional para el Desarollo Integral de la Familia (DIF), 56

Smith, Linda Tuhiwa, 282, 308

social fields, 20–22, 315, 319

social remittances, 18–19

Social Security Administration, 148

St. Luke's Catholic Church, 89

state borders, 6, 23

State Center for Assistance to Oaxacan Migrants, 120–21

surveillance and invisibility of immigrants: agricultural workers and, 164–72; at border crossings, 143–48, 155–64; of farm camps, 143–44; fears of terrorism and, 143–44, 148–50, 175–77; of food processing industry workers, 171–75; labor contractors and, 165–69; legal constructions of illegal aliens and, 144–54, 330n2, 331nn6–7; life in a cave and, 163–64; *mayordomos* and, 169–75; power hierarchies and, 176; racialized aspects of, 152–54

LYNN STEPHEN

is Distinguished Professor of Anthropology at the University
of Oregon. She is the author of *Zapotec Women: Gender,
Class, and Ethnicity in Globalized Oaxaca*, rev. ed. (Duke
University Press, 2005); *Zapata Lives!: Histories and Cultural
Politics in Southern Mexico* (2002); and *Women and Social
Movements in Latin America: Power from Below* (1997). She is
editor of *Hear My Testimony: Maria Teresa Tula, Human
Rights Activist of El Salvador* (1994) and coeditor (with Matthew Gutmann, Felix Matos Rodriguez, and Patricia Zavella)
of *Perspectives on Las Américas: A Reader in Culture, History
and Representation* (2003); (with James Dow) of *Class, Politics, and Popular Religion in Mexico and Central America*
(1990); and (with Shannon Speed and Aída Hernández Castillo) of *Dissident Women: Gender and Cultural Politics in
Chiapas* (2006).

Library of Congress Cataloging-in-Publication Data
Stephen, Lynn.
Transborder lives : indigenous Oaxacans in Mexico,
California, and Oregon / Lynn Stephen.
p. cm.
Includes bibliographical references and index.
ISBN 978-0-8223-3972-4 (cloth : alk. paper)
ISBN 978-0-8223-3990-8 (pbk. : alk. paper)
1. Indians of Mexico—Mexico—Oaxaca (State)—Migrations
2. Indians of Mexico—Relocation—West (U.S.)
3. Indians of Mexico—Employment—West (U.S.)
4. Frontier workers—Mexico—Oaxaca (State)
5. Migrant labor—Mexico—Oaxaca (State)
6. Oaxaca (Mexico : State)—Emigration and immigration.
7. West (U.S.)—Emigration and immigration. I. Title.
F1210.1.O11S74 2007
304.8089'91411—dc22   2006038001